Cases of the Reincarnation Type

VOLUME I

Ten Cases in India

Cases of
the Reincarnation Type

Volume I

Ten Cases in India

Ian Stevenson, M.D.

University Press of Virginia

Charlottesville

The University Press of Virginia
Copyright © 1975 by Ian Stevenson

First published 1975

Library of Congress Cataloging in Publication Data

Stevenson, Ian.
  Cases of the reincarnation type.

  Includes index.
  CONTENTS: v. 1. Ten cases in India.
  1. Reincarnation—Case studies. I. Title
  [DNLM: 1. Parapsychology—Case studies. BL518 S847c]
  BL515.S746   133.9′013   74-28263   ISBN 0-8139-0602-4 (v. 1)

Printed in the United States of America

For Dorris Carlson

Contents

Preface

IN THE course of studying some cases of the reincarnation type I began the investigation of many others. I have thus in various stages of preparation a large number of case reports. Because this originally manageable group has become intractably large, it has proved expedient, for convenience of publication, to issue the case reports in a series of volumes.

Most volumes in this series will contain cases of particular geographical (or cultural) areas. Some will contain cases grouped together or placed in a particular volume because they have special features in common, for example, birthmarks. This volume, the first in the series, contains reports of ten cases in India; the second volume will include ten cases of Sri Lanka; the third will be mainly devoted to fifteen cases of Thailand, Lebanon, and Turkey.

In the present volume I have included a lengthy General Introduction that provides an updated description of my methods of investigation and an analysis of the ineradicable—but, I trust, not fatal—sources of error they retain. At the end of the third volume in the series I shall include a chapter of General Discussion that will bring up to the present my own views about the interpretation of the cases to the extent that those included in these first three volumes (together with other case reports I have previously published) seem to support the interpretations I favor. If readers will obligingly consider these chapters on methods and interpretations as applying *in general* to the later volumes of this series, I shall need to provide for them only much shorter corresponding chapters. I shall then concern myself in such chapters of the later volumes exclusively with whatever modifications the cases of these later volumes or my own improved understanding and altered opinions should require.

I.S.

Division of Parapsychology
Department of Psychiatry
University of Virginia
Charlottesville, Virginia 22901
January 1975

Acknowledgments

MY DEBTS to the many persons who have assisted me in these investigations exceed by far my ability to repay them. I hope that my gratitude here publicly expressed may serve to reduce the obligation a little.

To the following persons in particular I wish to extend thanks.

Dr. Jamuna Prasad, Director, Bureau of Psychology, Allahabad, assisted in arranging most of the field trips I have made to India since 1964. On many of these he himself acted as principal interpreter. At other times he arranged for one of his colleagues to accompany me, and on still other occasions he has gone himself to make preliminary or more detailed study of particular cases.

Dr. L. P. Mehrotra, Lecturer in Education, Ishwar Saran Degree College, Allahabad, affiliated with Kanpur University, Kanpur, and formerly of the Bureau of Psychology, Allahabad, has accompanied me as an interpreter on every field trip within India since 1969 and has also at other times journeyed to various parts of India to investigate cases on my behalf. Dr. Mehrotra has also been helpful in the suggestions he has given me after reading many of the case reports in earlier drafts.

Mr. K. S. Rawat, Mr. P. Dayal, Mr. Vishwanath, Mr. S. K. Singh, and Mr. V. K. Sharma, all of the Bureau of Psychology, Allahabad, assisted as interpreters and in other aspects of the collection of data.

Prof. P. Pal of Chinsurah, West Bengal, assisted in the study of numerous cases of eastern India. In addition to acting as an interpreter for me in West Bengal, Professor Pal also independently investigated a number of cases, including (in this volume) those of Kumkum Verma, Dolon Champa Mitra, and Sunil Dutt Saxena. He afterward made his extensive notes of these studies available to me.

Swami Krishnanand of Bhadran, Gujarat, acted as interpreter for the investigation of the case of Rajul Shah and has assisted in many ways in the study of other cases of Gujarat. Prof. C. T. K. Chari drew my attention to some correspondence pertinent to the case of Rajul Shah, and Prof. V. V. Akolkar then arranged for me to have copies of this correspondence for use in my report of the case.

Mr. Jagdish Chandra of Bareilly gave me permission to quote from the pamphlet published by his late father, K. K. N. Sahay, which reported his investigations (in the 1920s) of several cases, including that of Jagdish Chandra himself and of Bishen Chand Kapoor.

Dr. A. B. Chawdhury, Director of the Hospital of the Calcutta School of Tropical Medicine, furnished me with a summary of the admission to that hospital of Nishith De, the identified previous personality in the case of Dolon Champa Mitra. Mr. B. C. Chatterjee facilitated the arrangements in Burdwan for some of the interviews connected with this case.

Muni Mahendra Kumarji ("Diviteeya") and Mr. B. M. Shamsukha of New Delhi added to my understanding of the concepts of reincarnation in Jainism by discussions I had with them and by their guidance to other sources of information.

I wish to thank the Director of the Widener Library, Harvard University, for enabling me to have photocopies of certain pages from Dr. Joseph Elder's unpublished dissertation concerning the belief in reincarnation in a village of Uttar Pradesh. I am grateful also to the staff of the Alderman Library of the University of Virginia for many services in furnishing me with books and xerographic copies of books.

Dr. Erlendur Haraldsson, of the Department of Psychology, University of Iceland, Reykjavik, conducted (with Dr. L. P. Mehrotra) one interview in connection with the case of Ramoo and Rajoo Sharma.

Dr. Seshagiri Rao, Department of Religious Studies, University of Virginia, read a draft of my introductory chapter for the cases of India, and from his helpful suggestions I was able to improve it considerably. Dr. Rao also reviewed the Glossary for accuracy.

Many other colleagues have contributed to the improvement of this work, but I particularly sense my obligations to Dr. J. G. Pratt, of the Division of Parapsychology, University of Virginia School of Medicine, and Mrs. L. A. Dale, Editor, American Society for Psychical Research, New York. Dr. Pratt read major portions of the typescript, and Mrs. Dale read the entire book, parts of it more than once. Both have elevated its quality by their many comments.

Mr. Champe Ransom, Mr. David Williams, and Miss Manjula Kamal, my able research assistants at various times, have earned my thanks by their competent work in the library and in detecting many slips and inconsistencies that might otherwise have remained. Mr. Ransom in particular, with the benefits of a legal training added to a natural skepticism, made important contributions to the investigation of the cases and the reports of them.

I contemplate with mingled shame and satisfaction the length of time it has taken to finish this book. If contentment be allowable, it can only derive from the numerous revisions I have made in preparing the text. These have come sometimes after later visits to the sites of the cases for rechecking old information, seeking out new witnesses, and observing the further development of the subjects. But I have also revised in the hope of improving the clarity of my presentation. All this has involved an extraordinary amount of retyping, and yet one could find no expression of complaint on the faces of my amiable secretaries: Mrs. Carole Harwell, Mrs. Cynthia Henderson, and Mrs. Bernardine Stento.

I have previously published reports of the cases of Bishen Chand Kapoor and Rajul Shah in the *Journal of the American Society for Psychical Research*. I am grateful to the Editor and Trustees of the A.S.P.R. for permission to make use of the material published. In preparing the accounts of these previously published cases for the present volume, I have revised the earlier reports according to any subsequently available information.

For financial assistance as well as much personal encouragement I wish to thank the Parapsychology Foundation, the John E. Fetzer Foundation, the McDonnell Foundation, and an anonymous donor who has been particularly generous with friendship as well as money.

In works of this kind the author commonly concludes his acknowledgments by exculpating all the named persons from anything defective that remains in the book despite their efforts to save the author from his mistakes. I am perfectly willing, and indeed eager, to issue such a plenary indulgence to all my interpreters, colleagues, research assistants, and others. About the informants on the cases, however, I wish to say something special. In the first place, they, no less than the persons already mentioned, deserve my gratitude. But they have it in larger measure: they gave their time and exposed their private lives, and they did so, with rare exceptions, in the most liberal manner imaginable. Some of them added an extraordinary hospitality, and I only occasionally wondered if they thought that serving a meal to me offered their sole hope of terminating an interview that had already gone on far longer than anything of the kind they had ever experienced before. Such lengthy interviews, which often brought the interpreters to glance at their watches and obliged me to ignore these signals as long as I could decently do so, were conducted so that the information received would be as precise as possible. Thus it is my intention not to absolve the informants of responsibility for this book (and its companions in this series) but, on the contrary, to place much of the responsibility on them.

I should like readers to share my confidence that I have reported faithfully what the witnesses for the cases told me. To a degree I have made myself a mere scribe of what I listened to. One interpreter has sometimes reproached me for being stooped over my notepad when the subject or another informant fleetingly showed some particularly evidential sign of emotion or told with a gesture what he could not find words to describe. I admit my inability to attend to two things at once, but I thought it particularly important eventually to be able to say, as I now can, that each statement in the tables of the subjects' statements and recognitions derives from a relevant section of my field notes or from the notes or letters of associated fieldworkers such as the interpreters.

Several informants have taken unusual trouble in patiently answering questions about small details by correspondence after or between my visits. It would be unfair perhaps to single out any of these persons for special mention, but they will understand my appreciation nevertheless.

Cases of the Reincarnation Type

VOLUME I

Ten Cases in India

General Introduction

The Present Scope of Research on Cases of the Reincarnation Type

SINCE the publication in 1966 of my first reporting cases of the reincarnation type (Stevenson, 1974a) I have continued to investigate cases in many different parts of the world. The files in the Division of Parapsychology at the University of Virginia now contain data on almost 1,300 cases. Of this number about four-fifths have received some investigation by myself or my colleagues. The remainder I have admitted to our collection for the purposes of analyses of patterns in large numbers of cases. I have included them as probably authentic because my information about them derives from published reports that seem worthy of confidence or because fieldworkers known through personal acquaintance as competent to obtain the testimony sent reports of them to me.

The cases in the collection, which have more than doubled in number since 1966, continue to have about the same distribution among the countries where I have studied them. This pattern for the origin of the cases mainly derives from the fact that I have concentrated my efforts in a limited area. In Asia I have worked mostly in the countries represented by cases in this and the next two volumes: India, Sri Lanka, Thailand, Lebanon, and Turkey. I have also continued investigations in Alaska among the Tlingit Indians and have made some modest extensions to neighboring groups of natives such as the Eskimos, Haidas, and Tsimsyans. In recent years I have begun investigations in Burma.

From previous experience I knew the cases to be abundant in the places mentioned. I was fortunate also in having well-qualified assistants in most of them. And as I became gradually more familiar with these various cultures and better able to assess the details of individual cases against their backgrounds, it seemed unwise to sacrifice such advantages in order to explore for cases in other parts of the world. However, I have received increasing information leading me to believe that cases occur just as frequently in some other countries where I have not yet investigated them. I think that we shall find many more cases of this type as soon as resources and qualified persons become available for expanding the investigations.[1]

[1] This preliminary information leads me to expect that we should find many cases of the reincarnation type in Japan; Nigeria and other countries of West Africa, especially Senegal;

In one respect the distribution of cases known to me has varied from that which I described in 1966. In my first book of case reports I stated that I had few from the United States (other than Alaska) and also relatively few from Europe. It remains true that in relative numbers we have far fewer cases from the United States (apart from Alaska) and Europe than we have from Asia. However, the number of cases reported to me from the United States has increased markedly since 1966, and more reports have also come from Europe. Of the American and European cases, suffice it to say here that on the whole they resemble in their characteristics the cases from Asia, although the children subjects of these Western cases rarely claim to remember as much detail about the previous lives they talk about as do their Asian counterparts. As of 1974 I have investigated in the United States (apart from Alaska) more than forty cases of the type in which the subjects began to talk about the previous lives they seemed to remember at the same young age when most Asian subjects also first express their memories. The number of fairly recently reported cases in both Europe and the United States has justified reserving two separate volumes of this series to deal with them.

I have stated before, but will emphasize again, that the number of cases known to me (or my associates in the various countries where I have applied my main efforts) bears only the loosest relationship to the actual incidence of cases of this type in these countries. We still depend far too much on newspaper reports for first information about the cases. And journalists tend to publish the more dramatic cases, or ones that occur where they happen to live and that they therefore cannot overlook. I am certain that the real incidence of cases in all the countries represented in these volumes far exceeds the incidence known to me. How much greater it is I cannot say. A certain number of cases are withdrawn from investigation after we have received some preliminary information about them. This happens when the persons concerned, often because of religious conflicts, will not permit study of a case which, from secondhand reports, seemed promising and worthy of careful research. On the other hand, we are also now learning about more of what I call "private cases," those that have been quietly noticed within a family or a small circle of friends and have never been made known to newspapers or the public at large. Perhaps because I have become better known in the areas where I have worked, informants have tended in recent years to open up more of these cases for investigation. The opportunity to study such unpublicized cases in India has caused me to revise some of the impressions I had developed earlier about the characteristics of the typical case in India. My previous conjectures depended too much on cases learned about from newspaper reports.

Vietnam; northern Israel (among Druses there); Nepal; and southern India. (Nearly all presently known Indian cases are from northern India.)

I am certain also that if investigators would spend some time in the villages of the countries having cases or likely to have them, they would soon discover many more cases than are now known. My own experiences have already shown this, especially in Turkey but also in other countries. I have sometimes gone to a new village to interview an informant about a known case and there found other persons who have told me about one or more new cases for which I could at that time only register the names of the informants and express the hope of returning to study the cases later.

The importance of mere numbers of cases should not be exaggerated. All the cases have some weaknesses. Indeed, if they all had the same ones, which I do not believe is so, adding to their numbers by however many would not increase their importance much. On the other hand, the large number of cases should carry some weight. No skeptic should think, for example, that if he could, because of some flaw or other, dispose of all the reported cases, he would have forever dealt with all the available evidence of reincarnation. For new cases would arise, and he would have to renew his efforts at criticism with these cases.

We have heard much about the need for a repeatable experiment in parapsychology. I share the earnest wish of my colleagues that we may soon be able to provide such a demonstration. In the meantime, I respectfully draw attention to the repeatable case. The hope of the repeatable experiment is that of being able to invite someone to a laboratory and to promise him that on the date he chooses he will witness a convincing demonstration of some paranormal phenomenon under controlled conditions. I do not know of any parapsychologist today willing and able to make such a proposal for a laboratory demonstration of extrasensory perception. There is much more assurance of being able to provide on demand a case of the reincarnation type. I can put my finger on several countries on a map and positively guarantee that if an investigator goes to the place indicated he will find cases similar to those described in this book within 50 kilometers, or even within 10, of the place I point out.

The large number of cases now "registered" with us and under investigation also furnish data for the extensive analyses, which I have already begun, of characteristics of the different cases from many parts of the world. Provided we test our cases carefully for authenticity, the larger the number of them in any single culture, the more confident we can be that conclusions about their patterns in that culture will be correct, and the more useful the study of their similarities and differences will be when compared with those of other cultures. I have published three reports of analyses of characteristics of the cases in different cultures: namely, cases among the Tlingits of Alaska (Stevenson, 1966), Turkey (Stevenson, 1970), and Sri Lanka (Stevenson, 1973). The article analyzing the Turkish cases includes a comparison of the characteristics of the cases of that country with those of the cases of Sri Lanka and Alaska. Further analyses of cases in other cultures are planned.

The more important data of all the cases are being transferred to checklists in preparation for a computerized analysis.

The Selection of Cases for the Present Volume

I have chosen cases to include in this and the next two volumes mainly on the basis of thoroughness and completeness of investigation.[2] I do not mean that I consider any case closed. I always hope to obtain additional information about the cases, and I have in recent years made extra efforts to follow up on many of the children subjects as they reached adolescence and passed into adulthood. But I consider that for the cases included here there are adequate data for analysis and for making judgments about their authenticity and other important features.[3]

The cases selected for inclusion here do not provide material for any argument about their interpretation not discussed in my first book of case reports (Stevenson, 1974a). I shall make a stronger claim for other books, now in preparation, that will be devoted exclusively to cases with birthmarks, deformities, or other medical aspects. Cases whose subjects have birthmarks, deformities, or physical illnesses corresponding to similar lesions or diseases in the related previous personalities seem to me to have great importance both for the correct interpretation of many other cases of the reincarnation type and for some further understanding of important questions in biology and medicine. In my first book of case reports I included some examples of subjects with birthmarks and one with a deformity. Since the writing of that book, however, I have greatly extended the investigation of cases of this type and have studied many more of them. In this and the next two volumes a few of the subjects had birthmarks, to which I shall refer in appropriate places. In general, however, the birthmarks of these cases have quite subsidiary importance.

Particular Features of Cases Included in This Book

Since the cases here presented permit the marshaling of no fresh arguments bearing on choices among the various interpretations for them, it may be

[2] The reader should understand that the remarks of this section pertain to the cases in this volume as well as those from Sri Lanka, Thailand, Turkey, and Lebanon that will be included in the next two volumes of this series.

[3] A later volume of this series will include reports of some cases that have been studied less extensively than those in this and the next two volumes. We sometimes can find no previous personality whose life corresponded to the subject's statements; obviously, we can study only one side of such a case. This later volume will also include some other variant cases with details that make them less typical of the average Asian case than those of the first two books in the series.

asked whether they provide any noteworthy advance over those already published in my first book of case reports. I think I can offer an affirmative answer to this question for several reasons.

In the first place, the present volume (as well as the next two in this series) will place on record another large block of rather fully investigated cases, and this number, together with the records of those already published, should help to make clear that, whatever the best interpretation of these cases, we are confronted with a phenomenon that has occurred many times. No one should dismiss the claim to remember a previous life as a rare aberration. The larger number of cases also permits, as I have already mentioned, more valid delineations of patterns within groups of cases and in all of them taken together.

Second, nearly all the cases in the three volumes here considered have been followed for longer periods of time than were those presented in the first edition of my earlier book of case reports.[4] Most of the cases here included have been under observation since the early to mid-1960s, that is, for eight to ten or more years. With only occasional exceptions I have made two or more visits to the subjects and their families and also to the previous families concerned. Furthermore, in a large number of these cases my associates and assistants have visited the informants for the cases before, between, or after my own visits. With the exception of Francis Story, who needed interpreters (as I do) in Asia, these colleagues could themselves speak the language of the informants. They were thus in a position to gather information without the need to translate it on the spot for me and without the possibly distorting effect of a Westerner present at the interview.

Third, the present collection contains more cases than did my first book in which investigators have reached the scene within a few weeks or months of the main events—one of which is, naturally, the first meeting of the two families concerned, which usually provides the occasion for the verifications of the child's statements. For the majority of the cases we were able to begin our investigations not later than two years after the main events had occurred. This is far from ideal, but it does represent a considerable improvement over the delays in beginning investigation that we often had in the earlier years of this work. I shall later emphasize that the passage of time causes the informants' memories to fade quite unevenly; in general, however, their accuracy does diminish with time. When qualified scientists of the countries in which these cases frequently occur begin to study them, we shall have information about more cases in which the investigators reach the sites *before* the two families have met. The first two volumes of this

---

[4] The second edition of my first book of case reports (Stevenson, 1974a) includes results of follow-up interviews with eighteen of the twenty subjects, eight to twelve years after the initial investigations. But I published the original case reports after observations extending over only one or several years.

series include reports of five cases in which some written record of the subject's main statements was made before the two families concerned had met. These are the cases of Jagdish Chandra, Bishen Chand Kapoor, and Kumkum Verma in India, and those of Indika Guneratne and Sujith Lakmal in Sri Lanka.[5]

Fourth, the present reports contain much more information than did those in my first book about the behavior of each subject as related to the previous life and its correspondence to behavior of the identified previous personality. When I first went to Asia in 1961, I was not at all prepared by expectation or experience to study the behavior of the children subjects concerned. I believed that a case would consist only of statements made by the subject, or attributed to him by other informants, concerning imaged memories of the claimed previous life. In short, I focused attention at that time almost exclusively on the cognitive features of each case. (I was equally unprepared to see the importance of birthmarks, dreams before or during pregnancy, and many other aspects of the cases that now seem to me much more important than they did when I began this research.) I could not, however, avoid hearing the often vivid reports of unusual behavior (other than verbal) attributed to the child subject. And this behavior corresponded, I learned from other informants, with what they remembered about the conduct of the related previous personality. I recorded a certain amount of such information in my first book of case reports, and in the General Discussion of that work I insisted that adequate interpretation of the cases should take account of the child's personation of the related previous personality. Since then, however, I have given much more attention to information about behavioral traits of the subject and those of the previous personality, and possible correspondences between them. As the importance of such observations slowly penetrated my mental screens, I began to make more systematic inquiries and, when I could do so, direct observations of the nonverbal behavior of the children subjects. This book and the others in the series contain some of the first fruits of these efforts.

For many of the cases now reported I have included a section describing the behavior of the child related to the previous life and a tabular summary of the correspondences of that behavior with the behavior of the previous personality. About these correspondences I wish to make some disclaimers, which I shall repeat for emphasis from time to time in order to reduce misunderstanding.

First, I should acknowledge that informants' reports about one of the two persons concerned are not free of possible contamination by information concerning the other person. I have already mentioned that we have few cases in which the two families had not met before I or my associates reached

---

[5] For a list of all known cases in which a written record of the subject's statements was made before verification of them, see p. 144, n. 1 in the report of the case of Jagdish Chandra.

the scene of the case. This means that in many of the cases the two families concerned may have more or less mingled their memories of what the child said and did with their memories of what the previous personality said and did. However, such confusion of memories will not provide an adequate explanation for all cases even when the two families met before we reached them. For example, in some cases, the social gulf between the two families (as in the cases of Kumkum Verma and Dolon Champa Mitra, in this volume) or a hostile attitude toward the case on the part of one family (as in the case of Lalitha Abeyawardena, in the next volume of this series) has prevented anything more than brief conversational exchanges between the two families prior to our investigations. I do not think that in such exchanges the families could have shared much information about the behaviors of the persons concerned and thus have spuriously increased correspondences between the behavior of the subject and that of the related previous personality.[6]

Second, I in no way assert that the various noted behavioral traits are specific either for the child subject or the previous personality. They vary greatly as to the degree of specificity that can be assigned to them. Some traits, such as keeping a pet cobra (as did Sundari, the related previous personality in the case of Kumkum Verma, p. 213 below) are so unusual as to be almost unique. But these are rare; in most instances the behavioral traits, at least of the previous personality, are not particularly unusual and are sometimes quite commonplace. Disna Samarasinghe, Ratana Wongsombat, and Hair Kam Kanya (whose cases will be reported in the second and third volumes of this series) showed unusual behavior for small children, but much of it was banally typical of all pious old ladies in Southeast Asia. What makes such behavioral traits remarkable then is not their specificity for the previous personality, but their unusualness in the subject as compared with other children of the age at which the subject shows them, and particularly as compared with other children of his family. I have taken special pains to ask the informants to assess the behavior of the child subject in relation to his or her siblings, and I have usually heard that other children of the family have not shown the behavior in question, or at least not to anywhere near the same degree as the subject. There is naturally some risk here that once the members of the subject's family have identified

---

[6] The parents of subjects remembering previous lives with no related previous personality identified just as often report that their children also show unusual behavior apparently (and appropriately) related to the previous life the child seems to be recalling. A later volume of the present series will contain numerous examples of such cases. I included one case of this type (that of Ranjith Makalanda) in my first book of case reports (Stevenson, 1974a) and will report another (that of Wijanama Kithsiri) in the second volume of this series. In such cases the question of an imitation of a *particular* previous personality through normally acquired knowledge of him cannot arise. Cases of this type, however, suffer from other weaknesses, which I shall discuss along with the reports.

him as remembering a previous life, they will pay more attention to his behavior and see it as more discrete and unusual than would other observers.
This may well occur in some cases. If it does, however, we should not always
assign the distortions thus introduced to efforts, even unconscious, at improving the subject's character, for often the traits attributed to him, such as
avarice or snobbish pretensions to membership in a higher social class, make
the subject appear less lovable rather than more so.

Although the behavioral traits reported are not, for the most part, specific for either the child or the previous personality, the correspondences
reported are, with few exceptions, remarkably close. And since the behavior
of the child agrees so well with the imaged memories of the previous life, I
feel entitled to require even more strongly than before that interpretations
of a case take account of the child's behavior just as much as of his imaged
memories.[7]

Methods of Investigation

Although in my first book of case reports I described my methods of investigation in considerable detail and have not departed from them in
essentials, I think it will be helpful if I summarize here the more important
features of the methods used in this research. In doing so I shall emphasize
ways in which I have tried during recent years to profit from earlier mistakes and deficiencies.

The Types of Evidence Obtainable. I find it useful to group the evidence
bearing on these cases in the following four categories:

1. Statements by the subject directly recorded, or statements attributed to
him by firsthand informants, concerning imaged memories of the previous
life.

2. Statements by informants about the subject's recognitions of people,
places, or objects related to the previous personality, or, in a few cases,
direct observations of these recognitions by myself or my associates.

3. Information about the behavior (nonverbal) of the subject and other
persons concerned in the case. This includes reports about the manner and

---

[7] I wish to repeat here the explanation that I use the word *memories* without commitment
to a particular interpretation of how the subject acquired what he undoubtedly experiences as
memories of events that he believes happened to him in a previous life. For the subject these
memories are indistinguishable from others not in question. However, for us—the investigators
and the readers of these reports—the question remains all-important as to how the subject
acquired these particular memories. Are they real memories or only pseudomemories? I find it
helpful to distinguish the subject's imaged memories of cognitive knowledge and his behavioral
memories, by which I mean nonverbal behavior such as habits, interests, skills, phobias, philias,
and other attitudes.

circumstances of the subject's talking about the previous life. We note and analyze also the attitudes toward the case shown by the subject's parents, the family of the previous personality, and any other informant or person somehow importantly associated with it.

Especially valuable are reports and observations of the subject's behavior that seems to correspond with that of the previous personality. The subject's parents and other adult informants furnish most of the data in this category, but occasionally the subject himself reports details of it and sometimes also the investigators can observe directly the behavior in question exhibited in their presence.

4. Written materials such as diaries, letters, certificates of births and deaths, autopsy records, hospital charts, and newspaper reports.

I shall now describe further the gathering and analysis of testimony in each of these categories.

The General Strategy of the Interviews. In approaching a case of this type I usually start with the subject and his family. I gather all the testimony obtainable from them within the limits of the time available or their patience with my tendency to ask a great many questions about details.

If the child subject shows some willingness to meet and talk with us, and most do, the interpreters try to engage him in conversation about the memories of the previous life and other interests. Naturally the children vary greatly in their ability to talk easily with the interpreters, and the latter also differ in their skill in drawing the children out. They succeed better with some children than with others. In the list of persons interviewed given with each case report I have always included the subject, but I wish to make clear that for many of them the word *interview* hardly applies. In some cases we must content ourselves with seeing the child in his mother's lap or hovering close to her. But in other instances the child becomes affable and makes himself the best informant of his own case. Some children, listening to what their parents are saying, correct the faulty memories of their elders, sometimes with expressions of annoyance over the stupid errors from which they have saved us.

Private interviews are rarely possible in Asia. The distinction between public and private business as known in the West hardly exists in Asia, and certainly not in most villages. The arrival of a stranger in a village, and certainly that of a Westerner, signals to everyone the importance of dropping what he is doing in order to attend the interview. Even among well-educated and prosperous informants, husbands listen to the testimony of their wives (although the reverse occurs less commonly), and one cannot politely ask a host to leave the room (of his house) while one interviews a member of his family. Thus one witness frequently hears the testimony of another. We insist nevertheless on at least recording the testimony of each witness separately. (In a few rare instances my notes fail to distinguish which of two or more informants interviewed together said what.) I would certainly prefer to interview most informants alone, since this would increase the independence of the testimony of different persons. (It would not necessarily make the testimony completely independent, however, since the informants could still discuss between the interviews what they remembered and had told us—as they undoubtedly do anyway.) However, the public interviews that one must accept in most situations in Asia do have some compensating advantages. For one, the presence of other informed persons sometimes permits immediate correction of an error or the clarification then and there of some discrepancy between different accounts of the same event. And also the other observers often guide and restrain the person who is currently in our "witness box." They can sometimes deflate tendencies to dramatic exaggeration on the part of the main informant, and they can also discipline him if he slides into lazy summaries and omits important details. In a valuable experiment of errors in testimony concerning an enacted scene of a quarrel between a Welshman and an Englishman, Selbst (1952–53) observed that a joint report prepared by four witnesses together "was substantially more accurate than any of the individual reports."

Although we rarely have private interviews in Asia, we rather often have independent ones with some informants, sometimes important ones. This can happen when a significant witness is away, perhaps at work or out of the village, as we begin study of the case. We may then be able to seek him out at another place and obtain a statement from him before he has had a chance to learn about the depositions of other persons. Also, our interviews with members of one of the two families concerned nearly always occur without the presence of a member of the other family. If a member of the first family offers to join us as we leave to go to the other one, we usually decline his proposal politely unless we absolutely require him as a guide.

In addition to the main informants, who are the subject and his parents, I try to obtain information from other persons who were in a position to observe and remember what the child has said or done. Sometimes the subject has talked first and most with his grandmother. This can occur because the mother is busy with housework or the care of a younger sibling and the grandmother has the leisure to listen to the child's narrations. A sibling of the subject also often becomes his confidant; if the parents have scolded or derided him, he may pour himself out to a more sympathetic brother or sister. Uncles, aunts, and neighbors not living in the immediate household of the subject usually provide less valuable information. However, they have often witnessed one or a few details of what the subject has said or some unusual behavior he has shown, and so they can sometimes furnish valuable supplementary material. They also usually make more detached observers, and their testimony about prior acquaintance of the two families, about the reliability of the main informants, and about the behavior of the child often adds greatly to the relevant information on the case.

Some of the lists of persons interviewed given in the case reports that follow include many names. I do not wish to mislead anyone into thinking that I have interrogated all these people at great length. In many instances I have, but I have sought out others of the listed informants solely to corroborate or verify one or a few items. When they have volunteered more information, and have seemed competent to give it, I have listened to that also. The length of the lists of persons interviewed in some cases testifies chiefly to my insistence on independent verifications of the subject's statements. Statements not independently verified I have recorded and noted, but I do not like them and have made considerable effort to eliminate them.

A larger number of persons interviewed also tends to increase the authenticity of the case. By this I mean that as we increase the number of witnesses for a case we decrease the likelihood that we have overlooked some important defect in it. To take the most obvious possibility, if a case should be fraudulently contrived, the secret may be kept by a few informants agreeing to falsify evidence, but not often by a group or crowd of conspirators. And when a substantial number of persons testify that they have heard the child make statements about a previous life, it becomes more likely that he did so than when only one or two persons assert this. But multiple witnesses may strengthen a case in other respects. Usually they support the claim of the principal informants that the two families have never met before. On the other hand, sometimes the search for previous connections between the two families shows that in fact they have had some mutual friends or relatives even though the members of the immediate families concerned may never have met each other themselves. Information of this kind obviously has great importance, and we can often obtain it only by taking the trouble to trace and question a number of witnesses who otherwise have only minor roles in the case.

At the first visit to the subject's family we always obtain some preliminary information about the behavior of the child related to the previous life. The hope of obtaining additional information about the child's behavior provides an important motive for second and more visits.

After obtaining the testimony of the subject and his family, I then visit the family of the previous personality if it has been traced. If no one has yet identified a family corresponding to the child's statements, I try to do so myself if there seems reasonable prospect of success.

With the other family we seek information permitting independent verification (or refutation) of all the statements the subject has made about the previous personality. In this endeavor I give a high priority to identifying and dismissing the secondhand informants. They seem vulnerable to a

combination of faulty memory and a wish to oblige their visitors by furnishing affirmative answers. A particularly striking example of the importance
of pursuing firsthand testimony about verifications occurred in the case of
Mounzer Haïdar, to be included in the third volume of this series. Informants on the subject's side of the case described an unusually impressive
detail. According to them Mounzer said the previous personality had left his
watch in pawn with a baker in order to obtain bread for the Lebanese
partisans with whom he was fighting. Mounzer was also said to have given
the name of the village of the baker (a woman) with whom the previous
personality had exchanged the watch for the bread. I could confirm—with
good reasons for confidence—that the previous personality had obtained
bread from this baker. And one informant also assumed that he had left his
watch with her, while another agreed that the subject had given the correct
name of her village. But I wanted to meet the baker herself and hear what
she could say about the episode. For years she eluded me whenever I was in
Lebanon. At one time she went to Africa for a year or more, and I imagined
that she was fleeing from our interview. When she returned to Lebanon,
she was never at home when I called; this seemed like deliberate evasion.
Eventually Mr. Wadih Rabbath caught up with her and interviewed her
about the details that interested us. She denied receiving the watch as a
pawn from the previous personality and equally disclaimed any connection
with the village named (or said to have been named) by Mounzer in connection with her. She fully agreed that she had furnished bread for the
partisans to the person whose life Mounzer claimed to remember.[8]

At the previous personality's home we also obtain whatever information
we can about the behavior of the deceased person the child claims to have
been. In this we often meet difficulties. The members of the subject's family
generally talk freely about his behavior apparently related to the previous
life. They usually find it more amusing than annoying, and if the child
shows some unpleasant trait such as stinginess they may remark about it
without much concern. But informants for the previous personality can
rarely expose so openly the blemishes in his character. The tendency found
in the West to blacken the living and whiten the dead exists also in Asia,
although in my opinion less strongly. To some extent, however, this practice may more or less obstruct frank revelations about the behavior of the
previous personality. How can a widow, for example, who may have wished
her husband's death, admit after this event that he was a drunkard who beat
her? In instances of this sort I have found the testimony of neighbors or
other less involved informants extremely helpful. Yet they also may have

---

[8] For further information about this item, see the report of the case of Mounzer Haïdar in
the third volume of this series.

their biases, and I am inclined to use their statements as a corrective rather than as a substitute for those of the principal witnesses.

Readers of these reports may think I have given only matted black-and-white portraits of the previous personalities, but I have not deliberately aimed at this effect. Some drabness in the descriptions derives, however, from my determination to depict the previous personalities as accurately as I could—given the materials and informants available. If I found witnesses inclined to tint up their own accounts of the previous personalities, I washed out any color that other informants did not also put in. It seemed better to give half the truth than an unsorted mixture of truth and falsehood.

As I have already indicated, I am only interested in hearing what informants can tell me from their own experiences. Unfortunately, many persons cannot distinguish firsthand from secondhand testimony, or think my insistence on the difference a pedantic whim for which they need not humor me. Such persons often yield to the temptation to include in their statements what they have heard from other persons.

Human beings seem to have no trait more in common than that of being willing to talk about things of which they know nothing. If you add to this habit a courteous wish to accommodate a visitor, you can find—and not only in Asia—many people quite ready to narrate authoritatively events that they did not themselves observe. I remember once going to visit (in India) the aunt of a subject who had observed closely what the subject had said about the previous life. She seemed like a valuable informant. Her husband was present at the interview, and, after listening to a few words from his wife, he assumed control of the conversation and rapidly filled in all the details with an appearance of great clarity. During a short pause in his flow I disturbed his soliloquy by asking: "Were you there?" He then said that he had been in England at the time his wife had observed the child. With a little struggle I got him to remain silent while I continued to hear her testimony. This episode occurred in 1964, and since then I have been even more stern with secondhand witnesses. Unfortunately, this particular man has had many companions in his weakness. Informants often cannot understand why we should limit them to saying what they themselves saw and heard with their own eyes and ears. They want to oblige us and see no reason why their summaries of essential matters should not suffice instead of the fragments from firsthand witnesses that have to be fitted together later. A husband who has just given his account of a case may express astonishment when we ask to talk also with his wife. "Why do you want to see her?" he will sometimes protest. "Have I not just told you the whole story?"

Interpreters working with me have learned to instruct each informant to tell only what he himself saw or heard. But this may prove insufficient. A witness who starts well enough with a pledge to do so may soon insensibly glide into secondhand narrative. So the interpreters interrupt with the gentle, sometimes painfully retarding question: "Were you there?" After this the informant tries to control himself better, but may relapse once more—or repeatedly.[9]

Experience has taught me that the ability to keep to observations of which one has had direct knowledge has very little connection with formal education. I have had scientifically trained colleagues who would talk with the greatest freedom about matters of which they were totally ignorant; and the most restrained and limpid narrative I ever heard came from a simple, illiterate Arab peasant woman in Turkey. Although many of our Asian informants have little or no formal education, many of them can nevertheless give excellent accounts of what they have observed and can remain within the boundaries prescribed for their statements. They are often not ashamed to say: "I was not there," or "I do not remember." On the other hand, better-educated persons may find confessions of this sort humiliatingly incompatible with the role of a well-informed person, which they feel obliged to play in every situation.

All these considerations make me attach particular importance to the careful segregation of witnesses according to their competence to observe, remember, and narrate the facts. But even this does not suffice: an ordinarily excellent witness may sometimes make errors, and a generally unreliable one can sometimes supply truthful information about some points. This means then that we almost always have to evaluate each statement of each witness independently with regard to its worth for the case as a whole.[10] Here we find another advantage in multiple informants, since the statements of new ones assist greatly in evaluating those of their predecessors.

I will not say that all secondhand testimony has no value; an honest secondhand witness helps us more than a false or stupid firsthand one. I have noted in the tables of the case reports every instance in which I was aware of using secondhand testimony.

[9] The main grounds for dismissing secondhand informants are not that they improve the cases, but that they forget essential details or never bothered to learn them. "The secondhand narrator is very apt to have forgotten, or at least to have omitted, some of the chief evidential details" (Prince, 1931, p. 110).

[10] This is not my discovery. In the final years of the last century, Binet (1900) observed from his experiments how unreliable a guide the memory of one detail provided for that of another. He wrote: "In practice, these inconsistencies [in the accuracy of memories for different details] prove to us that it would be wrong to believe that if a person makes a correct response with regard to one part of something remembered, he would be equally correct on the rest; one often hears the veracity of a witness discussed in legal circles and if it happens that the testimony of a witness can be verified on one detail he seems to become more credible with regard to other details that cannot be verified. No doubt every case has to be examined separately; we can only offer general rules; however, we should concede as a general rule the partial inconsistency of memories and consequently one is not entitled to say that, given a series of memories *a, b, c, d,* etc., if *a* is found to be correct, that is evidence that *b, c, d,* etc., are also correct" (pp. 285–86; my translation).

Follow-up Interviews. I have been unable to overcome a habit of remembering many questions I should have asked only at the moment the airplane that is to take me to my next stop taxis down the runway for its takeoff. And my afterthoughts or the helpful suggestions of colleagues, together with new points mentioned by the family of the previous personality, nearly always impel me or an associate to make a second or third visit to the subject's family. And that may lead to second or more visits to the other family. Whenever possible I have tried also to visit the subject and his family (and sometimes the family of the previous personality) again after one or several years.

Such follow-up interviews have several advantages. They permit comparisons between the accounts given by informants at the first visit and those given at later ones. We usually find some discrepancies about details and should be suspicious if we do not. In nearly every case, however, the accounts given resemble each other in essentials. If we can then learn that the informants have not embellished their earlier versions, we may feel justified in concluding that these first statements were not themselves elaborations of still earlier ones. The informants usually have no warning of our later visits, so they have no time to prepare a rehearsed similarity of their accounts.

By the time of the later visits the informants have become somewhat accustomed to us, and as they appreciate our general harmlessness and occasional helpfulness [11] they begin to talk more freely. This seems to happen particularly with informants of the previous personality's family. At later interviews, panegyrics may become muted and one may be given glimpses of blemishes in the deceased and even allowed to learn about more serious defects. On a second or third visit the unhappy widow mentioned above may concede—especially if everyone else has already done so, and she knows it—that her husband drank alcohol and occasionally lost control and struck her.

Another and no less important advantage of the follow-up interviews comes from the opportunity to observe the development of the subject. I find it particularly important (and interesting) to observe how in most cases the imaged memories of the previous life fade as the child grows older,[12] and how the related behavioral traits often persist longer and sometimes last into the adult years, although most of these also gradually diminish and disappear under the influence of new experiences. From the follow-up inter-

[11] The parents of subjects in some of these cases may become perplexed about how to respond to their statements, importunate demands for visits to the other family, requests for material objects the parents cannot afford, and other oddities of behavior related to the memories of the previous life. When asked for advice, I have sometimes had the satisfaction of saying something useful derived from my experience with other cases.

[12] I have elsewhere acknowledged and discussed the great difficulties one encounters in appraising a claim to the preservation of the imaged memories after childhood. Nor can one always accept at face value a subject's claim to have forgotten the memories (Stevenson, 1974a).

views we can often observe the extent to which parental attitudes may accelerate or retard such fading of memories and related behavior.

The Conduct of Individual Interviews. In the initial interviews I try to let each informant first tell what he can spontaneously, with the least possible stimulation from questions. The experiments of Stern (1935) on *Aussagen* showed that questions about a remembered scene elicited twice the number of errors found in a spontaneously given report of the same details. This has no mystery. The most difficult words for any man to utter seem to be: "I do not know." When someone is asked a direct question, if he furnishes an answer—let it be any answer—he has the double satisfaction of pleasing the person he is talking to and suppressing doubts about his own knowledge of the matter under consideration.[13]

Stern conducted his experiments (in the first decades of this century) with the aim of examining and improving the truthfulness of testimony in legal conflicts. In these the adversaries may force answers from their own witnesses or opponents to a degree that may not occur in other situations such as the interviewing undertaken for the investigation of the present cases. Binet's experiments (1900) on the influence of the form of the question on the accuracy of the response bear on this point. He found errors in 27 per cent of the answers to indifferent questions, in 38 per cent of those to moderately suggestive questions, and in 71 per cent of those to strongly suggestive ones. Experiments such as Stern's and Binet's gradually influenced legal processes and also interviewing techniques in the social sciences. Among many social scientists, hesitations about the use of direct, closed, or leading questions developed through the stage of a phobia into that of a taboo.[14] Such proscriptions ignored the observations of Binet (1900) and Whipple (1918), who found that some items recalled by interrogation, although omitted in a spontaneous narrative, may be just as accurate as those freely given. On this point, Binet wrote: "There is another feature of errors of memory: they do not occur less frequently in spontaneous memories than in those that a person only recalls with someone else's assistance" (Binet, 1900, p. 284; my translation). Persons who persist in thinking that

[13] Stern (1935) correctly pointed out that "I do not know" can also provide a helpful release for lazy or evasive persons who do not wish to strain themselves to remember some past event or describe it if they do.

[14] This development occurred, or rather expanded, despite the opposition of Malinowski, who inveighed against the ban on leading questions. He stated: "The dread of leading questions as expressed over and over again in all instructions for ethnographical field work is, according to my experience, one of the most misleading prejudices." In a later passage he added: "It is absolutely impossible to work without leading questions, if many important features are not to be omitted, and as there is no earthly reason to avoid this type of questioning, it is directly erroneous to brand the leading questions" (Malinowski, 1916, p. 383). Malinowski properly accompanied his approval of leading questions by warning that one should only use them with informants previously identified as capable of giving reliable testimony.

all direct and leading questions are noxious should also study reports of some more recent experiments that have examined the influence of leading questions again and found them much less harmful than most authorities had supposed. In one series of experiments (Richardson, 1960; Richardson *et al.*, 1965, p. 187) leading questions stimulated answers that were slightly more accurate than nonleading ones. The experiments of Marshall and his colleagues (Marshall, 1969; Marshall *et al.*, 1971) confirmed the harmlessness of direct questions and their value in making reports more complete than an entirely spontaneous narrative. Marshall found that questioning increased the subjects' correct responses as compared with their free reports. Errors also increased under questioning, but the proportion of errors to correct responses did not (Marshall, 1969, p. 64).

Reports given under questioning are also more complete than those provided by free recall. Some experiments of Marston (1924) demonstrated that questioning subjects increased the completeness of their reports, as compared with those given in free recall, by (approximately) 25 per cent but decreased accuracy by 11 per cent.

Richardson *et al.* (1965) wisely pointed out that a proper communication of the interviewer's expectations may actually increase the validity of responses to questions. An exposure of the interviewer's knowledge of the subject under discussion may help the informant to gain confidence that he is talking to someone familiar with the topic. A distortion from the interviewer's expectation occurs only if the informant departs from what he would have said anyway by complying against his previous inclinations and offering an expected answer. This rather obvious wisdom returns us to the question of the extent to which my informants wished to modify their responses to please me. I shall defer consideration of this important topic to a later section of this Introduction.

The experiments I have just cited strengthened but did not initiate my own convictions about the value of properly placed direct and leading questions. My training in medicine has enabled me to escape the disabling fear some social scientists have had of deflecting the informant from an accurate report by the use of questions. The exigencies of medicine often require one to ask the patient outright such questions as: "Have you ever had gall-bladder disease?" and "Has the color of your urine changed?" To the art of posing such questions we have to add what science we can in weighing the answers. And so in my interviews for the study of these cases I come sooner or later to direct questions and sometimes to leading ones.

We need leading questions especially when trying to verify the existence of a particular object or the occurrence of a particular event in the life of the previous personality. Suppose, for example, that the subject has said that in the previous life his family had a red water jar. If our informants for the previous personality had all the time and patience needed, we could ask them to enumerate all the objects of their household. Perhaps after sunset they would spontaneously mention the red water jar. But this process would weary an unemployed person and certainly exasperate a farmer with a field to plow or a mother with eight children to cook for. And so we usually ask instead a question such as: "Did you (during the lifetime of the previous personality) have any water jars and, if so, what color were they?" Or we may say, more directly: "Do you remember whether you had a red water jar up to about ten years ago?"

Sources of Error in Information Obtained [15]

Errors in Recording. I have continued my practice of making notes as the informant (or interpreter) talks, and I think I manage to get down nearly every word and certainly every important one spoken by the interpreter. In recent years I have also developed the habit of noting the exact question asked when we come to the interrogation phase of an interview. In India, since 1964, I have usually had the assistance of both a principal interpreter and an assistant interpreter, who also made notes in Hindi. We could then later compare the Hindi notes with my English ones and detect the occasional omissions or discrepancies that occurred. In Turkey, Reşat Bayer and I have tape-recorded nearly all our interviews with the principal informants of cases since 1964. I have also made simultaneous notes in French of Reşat Bayer's translations (into that language) of what the informants were saying. In our hotel rooms later we could then compare my notes with the tape recordings, or, if time did not permit this, we could compare my notes with transcriptions and French translations later made by Reşat Bayer, after his return to Istanbul. In Sri Lanka, also, I have often had two interpreters with one making notes as I do and here again we could make comparisons and notice discrepancies or omitted details. I have only rarely had opportunities for dual recording in Thailand, Burma, and Lebanon, but the general experience confirming the accuracy and comprehensiveness of my notes in India, Turkey, and Sri Lanka has made me confident that we should attribute few errors, omissions, and discrepancies to mistakes in recording.

I have not overrated the value of tape recordings as instruments helpful in fieldwork. They tend to intimidate some uninformed and uneducated

---

[15] I have not thought it desirable, or even adequately feasible, to separate an exposition of methods from a consideration of the sources of error they contain. I think it better to share with readers my own understanding of these weaknesses and the measures I have used to reduce them before presenting the case reports that follow. If any reader prefers, however, he may defer studying this section until he has examined the case reports.

persons who imagine anxiously that their words will be given some quasi-legal importance and may even be used against them later. Worse still, tape recordings gather in a great deal of irrelevant talk. It seems impolite to reach over and press a button in order to stop the preservation of mere chatter; but one can put down one's pen and appear even more attentive to what is being said when one actually is not. Finally, recordings made in the presence of several persons talking successively—or, more often, simultaneously—can fail to distinguish who said what. And as I think this a most important part of the information, I do not like to lose it in a jumble of competing voices.

On the other hand, I now recognize more than I did earlier the value of tape recordings for documenting precisely what each principal informant said in his initial statement. We are now arranging to record on tape also the statements of all children subjects whom we reach while they are still talking about the previous lives they remember.

Errors in Translation. The methods of comparing notes or tape recordings made in one language with those made by myself in another have also, I think, assured that comparatively few errors occur in translation. I believe that for other reasons as well, errors of translation have become fewer in recent years.

In India, Sri Lanka, Turkey, and Lebanon I have, fortunately, had the same interpreters working with me over many years. They have become used to my methods and I to theirs so that we have worked out what have seemed to me satisfactory methods of reducing, if not eliminating, important errors in translation.

In the narrative stage of an informant's testimony I prefer to take down a verbatim translation of what he says. But often the informant will not wait for the translation and continues the flow of what he wants to say without regard to our needs. At such times the interpreter has a choice between diplomatically checking the informant and reminding him of the importance of a full translation, or giving me a summary. We adopt the expedient that seems best for the person we are interviewing. By the time we reach the stage of questions, the decompressed informant has said most of what he wants to say, and we can proceed more slowly and more precisely. I then record exactly what I ask in each question and what the interpreter gives me back as the informant replies.

I have not yet acquired any working knowledge of an Asian language, but I have learned some rudiments of several and in particular I now know something about the places where errors of translation seem most apt to occur. For example, the translation of words for colors offers opportunities for vagueness that have sometimes led to apparent discrepancies; but when greater care was taken in the selection of the translating words for the colors mentioned, it was found that these discrepancies did not really exist. Hindi speakers, I learned after much concern over my own eyesight, use the word *kala* to indicate the color of something that may be to my vision black, brown, or merely dark. Words for family relationships also provide many occasions for errors. Asian languages are generally much richer in words for family relationships than are English and most other European languages. Hindi has an especially lush growth of nouns for relatives who would all be known in English only by such rather general expressions as *uncle* or *aunt.* On the other hand, Asians may use the word *brother* to refer either to a male child of the same parents as himself (as we do in the West) or to almost any male of approximately the same age with whom the speaker has a friendly relationship. They may similarly call any older male relative, or even an older male friend of the family, by the general appellation *uncle.* And in a village all the older males with whom the informant is not feuding may be "uncles" to him. Awareness of these kinds of errors has led me to enquire often whether the informant is talking about a "real brother" or a "village brother." And in most instances I now also make a genealogical plan showing the exact relationships of the subject (or previous personality) and the people around him.

To give another example, I found very puzzling the tendency of interpreters to translate the Hindi word *marna* sometimes by "to beat" and sometimes by "to kill." Hindi speakers can discriminate these two meanings well enough, but careless translation into English may give a sense quite different from the one intended. Increasing familiarity with such sources of misunderstanding has made me gradually less vulnerable to them than I used to be. Nevertheless, I know they do sometimes occur, and when my associates and I try to understand discrepancies between the testimonies of different persons, or between those of the same informant given at different times, we often think first of some slip in translation.

We have also another defense against mistakes in translation. I refer to the not infrequent occasions when one of my Asian associates has gone without me to interview informants of a case. He is not then obliged to make instantaneous translations and can listen with attention undistracted except by the need to make his own notes or a tape recording. He can later at leisure translate what he has recorded, and we can compare this material with other testimonies.

All but one of the case reports (of the first three volumes of this series) have been read by at least one interpreter who worked with me on the investigation of the cases whose reports he read; some of the reports have been read by two or more interpreters (Mr. Tem Suvikrom died before he could read the draft of the report of the case of Ratana Wongsombat, for the third volume of this series, that I had sent him.)

Errors in Written Materials. The relevant documents include diaries, letters, certificates of birth and death, autopsy reports, horoscopes, hospital records, and newspaper reports. They have their main value in confirming or making more precise remembered dates for significant events and in otherwise supporting the oral testimony. In Asia written records are still often distressingly deficient, although many improvements have occurred in recent years.

I regret to say also that motives for falsifying birth (or other) records sometimes come into play. A village family in Turkey, for example, may desire that a son finish his two years of military service at a younger age than usual so that he can return to work in the fields. They may therefore claim that he is older than he really is. In India on the other hand, there exists an advantage for some persons in seeming to be younger than they really are. Government officials there are required to retire at the age of fifty-eight, but if they can successfully claim to be several years younger, they may in fact work on in the civil service until their sixties.

Corruptions of dates often occur when the birth of a child is first registered with the civil authorities. In some instances a parent postpones notifying the proper official about a birth for some months or even years, and when he finally gets around to registering it he has perhaps quite innocently forgotten the date, or even the year, of the child's birth. Further temptations for falsification of records occur in Lebanon, where the government levies a small but not negligible fine (in 1974, 20 Lebanese pounds, or approximately $8.00 U.S.) for late registration of a birth. I think it unfortunate that the fine applies to registration delayed more than three days after the child's birth. The authorities aim at encouraging, if not enforcing, immediate registration of births. But in fact, if the father postpones the registration for several weeks or months, he may find it simpler and certainly less costly to tell the mukhtar (village headman) that his child was born "the day before yesterday" when in fact it was born long before. In small villages, where everyone would hear of a birth, falsification of this type requires a dull or compliant mukhtar. Starting out as I did with some awe of written records and an assumption that they would usually be more accurate than competing unrecorded memories, I gradually came to realize that a written record deserves no more credence than the competence, including accuracy, of the persons furnishing the information and the clerk recording it. My reservations about written records acquired in Asia have spread to the evaluation of those in Europe and North America, where, although the general level of accuracy is much higher than in Asia, errors occur commonly enough to justify an examination of every document on its own merits, which means on those of the person or persons who made it.

In view of the foregoing considerations I do not feel obliged necessarily to accept the information of a written record over that of an informant, although in most choices I would do so. (I shall mention later some instances in which I have preferred an oral statement over a written document that seems to contradict it.) But in every case I try to obtain whatever written records show promise of clarifying or supplementing other information.

Errors on the Part of Informants. I shall discuss this topic with regard to deliberate falsification of evidence, loss of memories with the passage of time, some other factors influencing memories, and motivated distortions of subjectively honest recollections.

As for outright falsehoods, I wish that I were one of those saintly persons in whose presence only the truth can be spoken.[16] I have no need to say that I am not, but if other evidence of this were needed it could surely come from the fact that I have on a small number of occasions listened to informants telling me the most outrageous lies. Some persons obviously value their reputation more highly than truth and will tell falsehoods, for example, in order to maintain the fiction of the happy marriage of a couple who have barely spoken to each other for twenty years. I have not found many such, and I hope that I have not missed as many others. It may be asked how, given my confessed inability to compel informants to tell the truth, I can have any confidence that so few altogether have not done so. I cannot answer this with any certainty. The assurance I feel in the matter rests on my comparison of the testimonies of different informants. General falsifiers offer testimony which varies on many points from that of other witnesses whose testimonies accord—more or less—among themselves. They also tend to include less detail in their narrations than do informants telling the truth (Arntzen, 1970). This results, first, because the liar does not have the detailed images of real memories to draw upon for his account and, second, because he usually believes that the bare outlines of a report will suffice; he forgets, or never thinks, that someone may later question him about details.

These guides for assessment only help in sorting out the comprehensive liar. In addition to obligatory liars we must sometimes cope with facultative ones, persons who tell the truth until it impinges on important personal concerns. For example, one of my informants in Turkey had been tried on a charge of responsibility for a fatal automobile accident because he was suspected of driving while intoxicated. The assistance of supportive friends

---

[16] I believe such people have lived and may even exist today. In connection with two Asian cases informants have told me the case *must* be authentic because witnesses recounted it in the presence of venerated persons before whom everyone spoke only the truth. The case of Hair Kam Kanya (reported in the third volume of this series) earned this endorsement. And Francis Story once wrote of the case of Wijeratne (Stevenson, 1974a) that it had received a similar stamp of authenticity when Wijeratne's father gave an account of it to the monks of Pelmadulla, whose monastery was in the area where Wijeratne's family lived. No one would tell a lie, he said, to these revered monks. Persons of this renown seem much rarer in the West than in Asia, but occasionally someone arises among us with the capacity of eliciting the truth from everyone. The Curé d'Ars (St. Jean-Baptiste-Marie Vianney) provided a remarkable example in the willingness—sometimes the apparent compulsion—of sinners to travel many miles in order to confess their sins to him (Marshall, 1952; Pezeril, 1959). Staretz Amvrosy (Dunlop, 1972) and, closer to our own epoch, Padre Pio (Carty, 1963; De Liso, 1961) had their penitents under similar benevolent spells.

had won his acquittal, but the evidence I obtained about his sobriety on the occasion led to quite a different conclusion. His testimony to me on most of the details pertaining to the case that we were studying seemed reliable until we touched on the question of whether he had been drinking before the accident. At this point he saw no benefit to anyone and possible trouble to himself if he altered the account given at his trial, and so he stuck to it, even though he probably knew that I knew it was false. Such persons pose a special problem because the bulk of what they say stands up to challenge and comparison with other testimony, but one can never be entirely certain of having detected all the deviations that the informant's special needs may provoke. However, if they include falsehoods for no more than 10 per cent or even 20 per cent of the items for which they testify, they may not damage the record any more than those who introduce motivated errors unconsciously, and so I shall consider their detection with this group later.

Of all the informants contributing to the cases of the first three volumes in this series, I do not think I have classified more than ten as "general falsifiers." I have felt justified in ignoring the testimony of most of them and have omitted their names from the lists of persons interviewed in the investigation of the cases. However, in some instances I thought such rejection might seem to strengthen the case unfairly, especially if the person I labeled a liar had attacked other informants or challenged the genuineness of the whole case. I have therefore included the names and testimonies of these persons. To allow myself more freedom in castigating their offenses I have adopted pseudonyms for most of them.

I may here appropriately mention instances in which informants have asked for money or hinted at the pleasure that gifts would bring them. When I think that I have probably interviewed altogether several thousand persons in Asia, most of them of humble means and many living in desperate poverty, I find it surprising that so few have asked anything for themselves, and all the more so since they see that we spend much money on these researches and naturally think that we also make money from them. Most of our informants have no concept whatever of such matters as fixed salaries, research budgets, and expense accounts. And yet I feel sure that twenty would be an outside figure for the number of them who have actively sought some reward in money or gifts for their information. And of these only four have flatly refused to testify unless I paid them money.

In response to requests for money, but more often voluntarily and because it seemed fair, I have occasionally paid informants small sums, mainly to compensate for time lost from work. This seems only just when a laborer stays at home and loses the wages of half or a full day in order to meet me. So far as I can tell, such payments have not sullied the testimony in the case of this book or its companion volumes. Where a question about this may arise, I shall give pertinent details in the relevant case report.

Having broached the subject of lying by adult informants, I will digress briefly to weaken a myth that sometimes comes into the discussion of these cases. I refer to the claim made by some adults that you cannot trust children to tell the truth. Given the very young age at which most subjects of these cases first speak about the previous lives they claim to remember, a hypothesis of fraud on their part seems so farfetched as to be absurd. Apart from this, the belief that children are in fact untrustworthy has no basis in careful observation. Stern devoted much attention to this subject and concluded that, with rare exceptions, small children lie only when frightened, and even then usually only in a confrontation with an irrational adult (Stern and Stern, 1909; Stern, 1965). Arntzen (1970), from an extensive study of the reliability of children's testimony, concluded that they can provide accurate statements even in such highly emotional matters as their sexual abuse by adults.

The myth under criticism here says that children always lie, not that they never do. And freeing them from the effects of a foolish adult-centered generalization need not lead us into the opposite error of thinking them all innocent. If children are, on the whole, no less truthful than adults, we still have the duty of evaluating what a child says as carefully as what an adult says.

The idea of children's untrustworthiness may have developed carelessly from the fact that children *do* have rich imaginations, although I think we should have to define what we mean by this expression before we could judge them superior to adults in the capacity to imagine. Critics of cases of the reincarnation type have sometimes attributed them to fantasies on the part of the subjects. But in a large number of such cases the subject's statements have been verified, so that the word *fantasy*, which refers to images (and statements expressing them) that do not correspond with any publicly verifiable reality, is inappropriate. We may, if we wish, apply that word to some cases of the reincarnation type in which we have not traced any deceased person corresponding to the child's statements about a previous life. Even this, however, would be arbitrary, since other explanations may apply as well or better.

A topic quite separate from children's propensities for truthfulness is their suggestibility, but it also bears on the evaluation of these cases. R. Messerschmidt found that children between the ages of six and eight *are* more suggestible than those younger or older (Hull, 1933, pp. 83–85). And Stern (1935, p. 362) observed in his *Aussagen* tests that seven-year-old children succumbed to 50 per cent of suggestive questions, whereas older ones yielded to only 20 per cent of them. This is worth remembering, since a hypothesis that may apply to some cases supposes that the subject has a few genuine memories of a previous life to which details become added by the eager and influential questions of his parents. The child may accept the suggestions of the surrounding adults and the additional details then become cemented in his story by repetition. I have observed a small number of cases (none with verifiable details) in which it seemed to me that a crude block of inchoate statements had been sculpted into an appearance of memories of a previous life by the chiseling questions of the parents. But if we believe that major cases with abundant verifiable details are developed in this way, we are really returning to the theory of fraud (on the part of the parents), since, in all the stronger cases, the parents deny that they had any prior knowledge of the significant details narrated by their child.

Coming now to the topic of the fading of memories with time, I shall first remark that it needed no psychologist to tell us that most memories diminish in clarity with the passage of time. But it has taken much effort, from the experiments of Ebbinghaus (1885) on, to learn what little we know even now about the processes of remembering and forgetting. Numerous experiments since those of Ebbinghaus have demonstrated the loss of accuracy in memories with the passage of time (Bartlett, 1932; Dallenbach, 1913; Stern, 1935), and yet we have not learned with certainty whether memories tend to fade with the mere passage of time or because of intervening experiences that occur during that passage. An experiment of Jenkins and Dallenbach (1924) strongly suggested that subsequent experiences rather than the lapse of time alone produce most of the interference with memory.

In considering the strengths and weaknesses of memory one can find psychologists' experiments, like the scriptures of theologians, to support any desired position. Some experiments show how bad memory is, others how good it is or can be. Many scientists studying memory have used subjects and test materials not at all relevant to the topic of these cases, although appropriate enough to demonstrate some other particular aspect of memory processes. Accepting the charge of some selection of authors cited, I believe the following remarks relevant to the present cases and justified by various experiments and observations.

I think it important, in considering the effects of time, to distinguish complete omissions, partial mistakes in recall, and what Bartlett (1932) called "importations," by which he meant inventions of the experimental subject having no connection, unless by association, to the picture or story whose remembrance he was testing.

The experiments of Dallenbach (1913), Bartlett (1932), and Marshall (1969) all showed significant loss of detail with the passage of time. In Dallenbach's studies the loss of detail after forty-five days, as compared with recall immediately after exposure to the stimulus, amounted to approximately 27 per cent in one experiment and 23 per cent in another. I am not much concerned about loss of detail in the information I obtain about the present cases. I find it regrettable, but I think that in most instances the forgotten details would, if remembered, tend to enrich and strengthen the case. We are not in any trouble if the case as reported appears weaker than it may really be. It seems much more important to know, or estimate, the extent of errors in the residue left after simple omissions.

Bartlett (1932) gave no figures for the errors that came into the reproductions of his subjects with the passage of time, but he noticed a paucity of importations. Stern (1935) found in his experiments that the elapse of "some weeks" increased the number of errors in the statements of his subjects from 5 per cent (at immediate recall) to 10 per cent. Dallenbach (1913) reported an increase in errors from 14.1 per cent (at immediate recall) to 22.4 per cent after forty-five days, and in another experiment the errors over the same time interval increased from 11.4 per cent to 18.1 per cent. Dallenbach also found that much of the increase in errors occurred within a few days of the stimulus. He stated: "The increase of error is as great in the first five days as it is in the next forty" (Dallenbach, 1913, p. 329).

I should be quite content myself if the errors of my informants did not exceed those reported by Stern and Dallenbach. Most of the cases I have investigated could afford to lose 25 per cent of their details, these being rejected as inaccurate, without fatal injury. Unfortunately, too many other factors beside the passage of time influence the accuracy of recall of the details of these cases.

Since, other things being equal, memories do tend to fade with time, it may be of interest and value to record the interval that elapsed between the main events in the cases and the first written record of the principal statements made by the subject and other related items of his behavior. By "main events" I mean (usually) those occurring during and around the occasion of the first meeting between the families. Table 1 gives the data for those cases (in the first two volumes of this series) in which the families concerned had met before investigators reached the scene. For these fourteen cases the median interval was 3.5 months.

The mentioned experiments on the effect of time on memories give us general guidance only. The average result for a group of subjects tells us little about the best and worst of them or about members of other groups. And in assessing informants for these cases we need to know how many of them satisfy minimal requirements for having memories adequate to the occasion.

Although standard tests of intelligence include subtests of memory, these show quite variable correlations with other measures of intelligence. Moreover, the ability to remember one type of material correlates poorly with that for recalling another (Achilles, 1920). But, fortunately, we have some evidence—not likely to surprise anyone—that we remember personal experiences better than nonsense syllables and the other materials, often neutral to

TABLE I. *Interval between Main Events* * *of Case and First Written Report of Its Important Features*

Case	Interval	Relevant Written Record
Gopal Gupta	7 months	Field notes of Jamuna Prasad
Sunil Dutt Saxena	8 months	Field notes of I. Stevenson
Rajul Shah	2 months	Letter of V. J. Shah to Jamuna Prasad
Puti Patra	11 months	Field notes of P. Pal
Dolon Champa Mitra	4 months	Field notes of P. Pal
Veer Singh	12 years	Field notes of I. Stevenson
Ramoo and Rajoo Sharma	1 year	Field notes of L. P. Mehrotra
Shamlinie Prema	6 weeks	Field notes of I. Stevenson
Gamini Jayasena	3 months	Report of R. Perera
Disna Samarasinghe	2 months	Record written out by Disna's mother
Lalitha Abeyawardena	3 months	Field notes of V. F. Guneratne
Ruby Kusuma Silva	3 months	Field notes of I. Stevenson
Mahes de Silva	4 months	Field notes of G. Samararatne
Warnasiri Adikari	1 month	Field notes of F. Story
Median Interval	3.5 months	

* The period in which the subject has his first meeting with the family of the related previous personality. For the purposes of this table the date (exact or approximate) of this meeting is taken as the point for the beginning of the pertinent interval. In most cases this meeting of the two families concerned occurs during the period of the peak of the subject's talk about the previous life.

the point of tedium, that psychologists have so often offered as stimuli to subjects of experiments on memory (Meltzer, 1930). We do not need to alter this conclusion if we acknowledge that the difference may arise from the fact that, in the absence of special incentives, one ordinarily learns almost anything else better than nonsense syllables.

Some persons have much better memories than others. This platitude does no justice to the extraordinary range of the capacity for remembering exhibited by different persons. Some few persons seem to have almost unlimited powers of recall with retention of perfect detail after many years (Hunter, 1964, p. 154; Luria, 1968), while others have poorer memories than at least some of the higher subhuman animals such as dogs and elephants. Although we sometimes need to emphasize the failure of memory, we should not overlook its successes. Prince (1918, 1919) and Parsons (1962) published accounts of several cases in which the subjects gave evidence of detailed accuracy of memories six to thirty years after the original experiences.

Apart from the passage of time, observation and experiment have identified other important factors that impede or facilitate remembering and forgetting. Some of these relevant to the present cases are the unusualness of the remembered event or, conversely, its familiarity and repetition, and the pleasure or pain that its memory gives us.

William James (1890) was perhaps the first psychologist to make explicit the tendency we have to remember the unusual or what is new and interesting rather than what is habitual and ordinary. This certainly bears on the present cases. Children who talk about previous lives are unusual—even in Asia.[17] What they say and the way they say it often strike their parents as novel if not bizarre. After many repetitions the other members of the family may have heard enough, especially if the subject dwells at length on the superiority of his "previous family." But initially, and for a long time afterward, his family regard what he says as extraordinary, and hence they are likely to remember his statements more than those of other persons.

Although it may seem paradoxical to our tendency to remember an unusual event well, we also tend to remember well those that have become familiar through repetition. Our associations, an important aspect of remembering, tend to follow our experiences. Foley and Macmillan (1943) demonstrated this experimentally. In a word-association test they gave the same stimulus words to three groups of students studying law, medicine, and liberal arts, respectively. When the stimulus word could have different meanings for the members of the different groups, for example, such words as *expiration, complaint,* and *cell (sell)*, the students' associations tended to reflect their specialties. Goodenough (1946) obtained similar results when she compared the associations of men and women to "ambiguous" words. The stimulus word *ring*, for example, tended to evoke responses such as "boxing" from men and "wedding" from women. Our experiences, at least of the major paths of life, harmonize with our interests. Thus we try to choose our vocations because they interest us, and if others choose them for us, our interests generally become aroused if only slowly and passively. It follows from this that we should expect informants to remember different items or events with varying clarity. A case from the field of criminal detection illustrates this tendency neatly (Hatherill, 1971). A suspect in the murder of two young girls had been seen with them by some other children whose descriptions led to the suspect's being traced and his ultimate conviction for the crime. Two boys and three girls had seen the suspect, a soldier who drove a truck, while he had been talking with the girls who were murdered. Of interest here is the fact that the girls gave a good description of the driver, but had only blurred recollections about the truck; in contrast, the boys could not say what the driver looked like, but gave a detailed description of the truck. In the present cases, therefore, we should feel no surprise if a subject's mother remembers what he said

[17] Cases occur frequently in Asia, but we should remember that even there their incidence in the general population is low, and that a child who remembers a previous life stands out as quite exceptional. In certain unusual families several members have remembered previous lives. In one such family known to me in India, the father listened to several of his children talking about their previous lives. Eventually he became sated, and when a younger daughter began talking about *her* previous life, he suppressed her testimony. So her case was lost. But then a less conforming, still younger brother started talking about *his* previous life and persisted, so that we do know something about what he said. Yet families of this type, with several persons claiming to remember previous lives, are much rarer than those with just one such person. The majority by far of the subjects of these cases are unique in their families with regard to having memories of a previous life.

about the clothes and food of the previous life and his father what he said about having cattle, estates, and an automobile.

We also remember pleasant experiences better than unpleasant ones (Meltzer, 1930; Myers, 1915). And we remember statements that agree with our views better than those that do not (Levine and Murphy, 1943). These facts relate to errors in the memory of our informants due to the interference of their own wishes with what they are recalling or speaking about. I am now, therefore, considering the large and important topic of motivated errors of memory and am referring mainly to *unconscious* motivated errors. I have already acknowledged the existence of the regular and the occasional liar. So I shall be concerned in this place with the much larger problem of persons who wish to tell the truth but encounter internal opposition of which they are almost or entirely unaware.

We could estimate better the error due to unconscious motivations in the informants of the present cases if we knew that only one or two motives guided all of them. Unfortunately, although one motive—that of pleasing the interviewers—may influence (more or less) most of the informants, we find many others also in play, if less often. Sometimes contrary motives affect the different informants of the same case so that they may pull the case in opposite directions.

Before coming to motives that seem to me important, I shall first dispose of one to which, I believe, Western critics have given much more attention than it deserves. Some of them—viewing the cases from their armchairs—have seen Asia as filled with many persons yearning to convert the West to a belief in reincarnation. It would be difficult to wander farther from the facts. The average Asian is almost exclusively occupied with making a living for himself and his family. By Western standards he has a hard lot and must apply himself fully to earn enough just for subsistence. He has no more interest in persuading Westerners to a belief in reincarnation than has the average Iowa farmer or Munich brewer in converting Asians to Christianity. As a matter of fact, as I shall describe later, a large number of Indians (to take one group only) have never even heard of reincarnation, and many of those who have, seem never to have learned of any case of a child claiming to remember a previous life until one erupted, so to speak, in their own community. I cannot emphasize too strongly that these cases impinge unexpectedly and often in an undesirable way on the lives of the persons concerned. The nagging demands of a four-year-old boy that he be taken immediately to another remote village, his revelations of sordid murders or other crimes, his claim that he has in the "other" home electricity, good food, automobiles, and maybe a wife, cannot possibly increase the pleasure of a poor farmer who must listen to such talk in the morning before he leaves to till the soil and again at night when he returns weary from doing so. Although Asian people (at least among the groups of

them where these cases occur) do believe in reincarnation and although
this belief forms a general background for the cases, this fact has little bearing on the attitudes informants adopt toward a particular case. The belief
makes credible for them the statements of a child who talks about a previous life. It enables them to let him say what he wants about it without, as
often happens when a Western child talks of a previous life, thinking that
either he or they have lost their minds. But this does not necessarily mean
that they enjoy what they hear. I have marveled sometimes (and occasionally have recorded my wonderment in the reports that follow) at the
tolerance of some of the parents for their children's statements and behavior related to the previous lives. Here again the conviction, at least
among Hindus and Buddhists, that they may have earned the presence of
such a child in their midst by their own past conduct may increase the
patience of those who have to live with him.

Although I believe the desire to establish and propagate the truth of
reincarnation—as the informants see the matter—does not bias the testimony of many of them, I do not mean to say that it never governs any.
Now and again I have encountered an informant whose missionary zeal for
Hinduism or some other religion wrecked his testimony. One finds such
enthusiasts among the half-educated urban dwellers, never in the villages.

Coming now to the review of other motives that I think more common
and more important as distorters of testimony, I should emphasize first that
while some factors tend to promote and inflate the case, others influence
the families concerned to suppress it.

I have already mentioned the occasional thought of personal monetary
gain and given my opinion that it has an almost negligible influence on the
testimony. Covert aspirations to use the case for personal aggrandizement
may occur more often than the few brash actual attempts known to me.
But, if so, they never turn into practical success; I have not yet heard of
any profit from such an attempt at exploiting a case in Asia.

The wish for some fame, whether of local or international proportions,
excites the minds of a few informants. One can sometimes notice the
pleasure they derive from the publicity of a newspaper report about the
case or from the repeated visits of persons from the national metropolis
or from abroad. But I have not found this factor sufficient in any case to
account for major alterations of the evidence. The local attention quickly
evaporates. The visitors come for a few days; they return, but perhaps
not for one or several years, and then they stay only for a day or two. Such
attention and unpredictable descents would hardly justify slanting the
testimony of a case; in fact, they can have their inconveniences. Crowds
sometimes throng into the subject's house, investigators take time from
pressing duties, and the attention of visitors arouses the jealousy of gossip-
ing neighbors.

I do not think any of the preceding motives so important as the next that I shall mention. After the subject has made his statements and word of them has spread into the surrounding community, his parents often wish him to be shown correct. I have seen some of the subjects' parents become too attached to the confirmation of what the subject has said. They then view him and themselves in terms of either vindication or disgrace. I am always uneasy when I notice this attitude, because it can influence the informants to overlook the subject's mistakes and exaggerate his successes. And rarely it may stimulate a foolish prompting of the subject when we are talking with him directly.

After the families concerned have met, as I have mentioned, some blending of memories may occur in which the informants may credit the subject with more accurate information about the previous personality than he actually had shown before the families became acquainted. Here my reliance on independent verification provides some assistance. When we interview the members of the identified previous family, we learn from them about various details mentioned by the subject. For verification of past events and destroyed buildings or objects we usually have to depend entirely on their memories. But we can confirm many other details with our own eyes and ears. If the child has given names of relatives of the previous personality, we can often meet them; it may be assumed that a healthy person is the best authority on his own name. I would go even further and say that (unless he is in a state of dementia) he can be relied on to give correctly the names of members of his own immediate family. If the subject has said that his previous mother was called Gayatri Devi and I am unable to meet a real and seemingly relevant Gayatri Devi, I can usually accept her husband's statement that his wife is in fact called by that name. In addition, we can often examine houses and ask to see objects whose description the subject has given. This kind of direct observation accounts variously for between 10 and 20 per cent or more of all the items stated by the subject. And it often includes—in the proper names of people, for example—the most important information for identifying the particular deceased person the subject has been talking about. In this way the previous family becomes largely exonerated of the charge that *its* members have (after the two families have met) exaggeratedly attributed more correct statements to the child than he actually made. Thereby we place the main responsibility for the accuracy of what the child said before the two families concerned had come together on the subject's family.

I have already mentioned some factors—such as burdensome visitors—that may incline the subject's parents to suppress or minimize the case. Other ideas may start them in the same direction. One is the pervasive superstition—found widespread in South Asia, but not in western Asia—that those who remember a previous life die young.[18] No evidence known

[18] This superstition, extremely common in northern India and Burma, seems not to occur in Sri Lanka.

to me supports this belief, and I do not understand how it began or remains so strong. But strong it is (in some areas) and because of it parents may resort to a wide variety of devices to keep a subject from speaking about his previous life. Initially they only succeed in stopping him from talking about his memories, but since rehearsal tends to fix the memories, if the subject does not talk about them he may end by forgetting them altogether.

Parents may also dislike the particular content of the subject's remarks and behavior. If he claims to have belonged to a wealthier family or one of higher caste than theirs, his remarks may bore or annoy the other members of his family. Some of the subjects threaten to run away to the previous family, and this naturally wounds and frightens their parents. They may also talk about domestic quarrels, village feuds, odious crimes, and other distasteful topics. For all these reasons a subject's parents may think it best to silence him.

A similar variety of motives may incline the family of the previous personality to promote the case or to belittle or even deny it.

The pleasant thought that a loved deceased person has "come back again" warms and makes tearful many of the parents, siblings, and spouses of the previous personalities concerned. And this sense of reunion can lead to overenthusiastic endorsement of the case and to the tendency, already noted as sometimes affecting the parents, to minimize the subject's errors and to proclaim him accurate in every detail.

Yet not all members of the families of previous personalities react with pleasure to the possibility of a return by the departed. The idea of a lost member having come back may revive receding grief and bring the wish to withdraw from any reminder of the deceased loved one. This may lead to a refusal even to testify on the facts of the case. Some persons add to this the jealous thought that, if the case is authentic and one of reincarnation, a member of their family is now in the arms of another.

As I have mentioned above, some subjects insist on opening the doors of skeleton-containing cupboards; this sort of public exposure, and even the scattering about of information concerning less important family secrets, may vex the previous family and, in some instances, alarm them. The candid babbling of some subjects can particularly displease members of families who have preferred the fame of respectability to its reality. For such persons, denigrating the case may seem important in order to shore up a tottering structure of public esteem.

Some persons of wealthy families yield to still another motive for disparaging the case: they may suspect a claim from the subject's family to some of the property of the previous personality. Occasionally, a subject makes a possessive remark about the house or estate of the previous personality, blurting out as he surveys the property some such comment as "All this is mine." But no one takes such utterances seriously except miserly members of the previous family who fear someone else may do so. In a small number of cases, such as those of Dolon Champa Mitra and Sunil Dutt Saxena in this volume, irrational fears of this type seem to have led some members of the previous family to derogate the case or reject it altogether. Or does another deeper motive make some wealthy persons fear to confront a child born in poverty who claims he was once one of them? Are they afraid it is true—and that something similar could happen to them? For their part the parents of children rebuffed by wealthy families of previous personalities seem to take these rejections in good spirits.

The above review should make clear that numerous emotional forces can arise with variable strengths in the different participants of these cases. In the reports that follow I have tried to indicate my awareness of such motives when they seemed strong enough to bring about errors in the reporting of the subjects' statements or other features of the cases.

There remains to be discussed the need on the part of the informants to please me or my colleagues. I think this thought did variously affect the informants—nearly all of them. After all, they saw that I had come a long distance to visit them, so common courtesy required that I go away with what I came for. But what had I come for? In order to please someone you have to know, not just surmise, what he wants. And how can the informants judge—at least on first acquaintance—whether we have come to attack or fortify the case? Initially, they can only know that we have a strong interest in studying the evidence of reincarnation cases. If they wanted to please the average skeptical Western scientist, they would certainly help him to see how weak the case is. It cannot be obvious to many of the informants that I am not of this group, and yet most of what they tell me tends to support the authenticity of the cases. I am in fact not sure myself about what I would like to hear about any particular case. I have some interest in fraud and much curiosity about cryptomnesia and also about the subtle ways in which extrasensory perception works. I have found that my interest never flags when we encounter features of the cases that suggest these interpretations instead of supporting that of reincarnation. Without claiming that I always like what I hear, I do believe that I am willing to listen to anything that anyone cares to tell me about a case, and I have often gone out of my way (sometimes to the exasperation of my associates) in order to trace out some remote informant who might throw light on the possibilities of normal communication between the two families concerned in a case or who was reputed to speak unfavorably about it.

Even if some of the informants do perceive me as an example of the unbelieving Westerner finally matured and ripe for conversion to a belief in reincarnation by a demonstration of the perfect case, my Asian associates cannot invite any such judgment. And quite often, as will be seen in the case reports that follow, they have traveled to the sites of the cases and have interviewed the informants with, in all essentials, the same results that have come from interviews at which I was present. It seems to me that if any informants think they (or I) can gain something by their ameliorating a case in my presence, they cannot possibly believe this about their own countrymen when these come alone to visit them.

Although I cannot say how much the wish to accommodate me may have guided the informants, I can show that they never implemented any such intention perfectly. In many instances they certainly failed to say what I would have liked to hear. I will not deny that, once I am committed to the study of a case, I also become involved with the accuracy of the child's statements. (I do not think this means I am committed to the interpretation of reincarnation for the case if he is correct, but I know that I like to see him shown to be accurate.) Notwithstanding this inclination of mine, on numerous occasions informants for the side of the previous personality have failed—even when given the chance with a leading question—to verify some statement attributed to the subject. Often informants have not corroborated a recognition that another person had already attributed to the subject.

In one much larger matter the testimony obtained did not confirm one of my expectations, not necessarily a wish, for the cases. Before beginning these researches I had read extensively in the Western literature of theosophy and to a much smaller extent in works closer to the authentic scriptures of Hinduism and Buddhism. These had soaked me in the teaching of karma, so that without having at that time either the basis for a better judgment or the critical restlessness to seek one, I had become convinced that if field investigations found evidence of reincarnation they could not avoid also finding equally strong evidence of karma.[19] In fact we have found almost nothing whatever to support the idea of karma, and only four cases—out of hundreds now—in which the data even suggest it. Even in these four cases the idea of karma may be only the subject's rationalization for his situation as compared with that of the previous life he remembers. We have no evidence compelling us to believe that karma is the correct explanation, although it may be.[20] This outcome surprised but did not pain

[19] I am referring here to what I call retributive karma, the idea that moral conduct in one life leads to appropriate rewards and punishments in another terrestrial life. For a further, but still quite incomplete, discussion of the concept of karma, see Introduction to Cases in India, which follows this General Introduction, and also my article "Some questions related to cases of the reincarnation type" (Stevenson, 1974b).

[20] Numerous cases occur with marked differences in the social, economic, or other circumstances of the two personalities concerned. The four cases I have mentioned are the only ones in which such marked changes *may* be attributable to misconduct on the part of the identified previous personality. In the other cases we have no data about the conduct of the previous personality, or we have information that his conduct had been either completely blameless or not of the viciousness that would—according to the orthodox teachings of Hinduism and Bud-

me. It did, however, cause some worry to Francis Story, who before his death in 1971 accompanied me in the investigation of many cases in Southeast Asia and studied others by himself. A Buddhist by conviction from the age of sixteen, Francis Story often expressed to me his puzzlement and disappointment over the lack of evidence of karma in our data. He faced this bravely, and I never heard him guiding an interrogation in a way that would impel our witnesses to increase the yield of such evidence. But if they had wanted to please him—or satisfy my own expectations in this matter, grotesquely naive as I now see them—they could have done much more along this line than they did.

The same arguments tend to defend my interpreters from a suspicion sometimes heard that they have modified the testimony of informants to suit what they thought I wanted to hear or ought to hear. If so, those of Southeast Asia could almost stand under a charge of heterodoxy for not having worked into my notes more evidence of karma.

Such then seem to me the more important motives and influences that have led informants to give inaccurate responses during interviews. What can we say about the extent of their distorting effect?

The Validity of Data from Interviews

We have not yet conducted any systematic investigations of the validity of the information given in the investigation of reincarnation cases. However, analyses of the validity of data developed in other types of anamnestic interviews, not too far removed in type from those of the present cases, show that informants have a considerable accuracy of recall (Haggard *et al.*, 1960; Pyles *et al.*, 1935; Weiss and Dawis, 1960). Whether one judges the level of accuracy attained satisfactory will depend on the standards one sets. The investigation of Weiss and Dawis seems particularly pertinent to the present cases. They obtained information from handicapped individuals and from the relatives of such persons. The information elicited pertained to such matters as vocational records, medical histories, and education. They then checked the data obtained against available records of government agencies and employers. They found that the validity of information given for different items varied from 100 per cent for one item to less than 50 per cent for another. The median invalidity for the total sample of all items was 16 per cent with a range from 0 per cent to 55 per cent. The information obtained from the relatives (who correspond to the parents of the subjects and other informants of the present cases) proved as valid as

dhism—precipitate a downward slide to such inferior circumstances in the next life as the subject finds himself in. I wish to emphasize that I am not denying the existence of karma, only that any empirically derived evidence for it now exists and is known to me.

that given by the handicapped persons themselves. The items sampled all had important meanings for the persons interviewed. Some concerned events of the past (as opposed to information about current circumstances), and therefore the accuracy of the informants' memories affected the results.

In another investigation of the validity of interviews, Smith (1958) vindicated the claim of many mothers who say they know how they behave with their children. She found a quite adequate correlation between what the mothers she studied said about how they behaved with their children and what observers saw them actually doing.

We should naturally hesitate to apply observations of the validity of interview techniques made on Western subjects as support for that of interviews with Asian informants speaking through interpreters to a Western investigator. But I think that the citation of these reports is justified here as a corrective to the suggestion often heard that interviewers are helpless victims in the hands of self-misrepresenting informants.

The foregoing studies of the validity of information gathered in interviews show something else perhaps obvious enough without research: namely, informants vary widely not only as compared with each other but also with regard to their accuracy for different facts or events. This observation reinforces the need for the practice I mentioned earlier, that of evaluating not only each informant but each item of what he says.

The Analysis of the Data for Errors

I know of only one guide to the validity of material derived from interviews. Historians, lawyers, and psychologists all know its limitations, but we have nothing better. I refer to the comparison of one person's statements with those of others giving information on the same details. If witnesses B and C agree with A, they support his testimony provided theirs is independent of his. In the present cases we have to concern ourselves with independence of two types—that of the original observations and that of the communication of the observations to the investigators. I have already explained that we were able to have some private interviews, but, of the total number of interviews, few of them qualified as truly independent in the sense that no one but the informant, myself, and the interpreter was present. Other persons, whether themselves witnesses or not, were nearly always at the place of the interview. (I have already also mentioned that semipublic interviews have value as well as disadvantages.) The witnesses did, however, report a much more satisfactory number of independent observations. Many of our subsidiary witnesses had heard the subject make only one or two statements or had seen him make only one or two recognitions. And many of them were persons outside both families, so that their reports became correspondingly valuable. In addition, even the members of the subject's own family often reported different observations made independently. The subject, for example, would have told his father some details, and then his mother or grandmother other details after his father had gone to work.

We often have also in these cases the opportunity to check what an informant says at one time against what he says about the same details at a later interview. I have never deliberately tried to mislead an informant, but I have often asked one to cover the same ground again; this gives a chance to detect consistency of memories on the one hand, and tendencies to adornment and forgetting of the original report on the other. In such comparisons one finds many small discrepancies of details, and these tend to increase as the interval between successive interviews lengthens. But I have found accretions and distortions of the case with the passage of years much more rarely than I expected.[21]

I do not claim to have checked every statement furnished me against the criterion of its agreement with other testimony. There were numerous statements for which I had only one informant, and there was no one else to gainsay or support him on such items. I have, however, examined the statements of all the main informants as to their general reliability. And I have compared all testimonies on items reported by more than one informant. Except for harmless variations in phrasing—sometimes due to shifts in the interpreter's words as well as the original ones of the informants—I have in each chapter indicated all discrepancies in the column of comments in the tabular summary of the subject's statements.

We can supplement analysis of the informational content furnished by an informant with our observations of his demeanor and other indices of emotion as he talks. Data of this type play an important part in evaluating information given in medical (Stevenson, 1971) and forensic (Arntzen, 1970) interviewing. But I have found that these signs of emotion play a less important part in the assessment of material from the interviews on which the present reports are based. The informants, with some exceptions, have less confessional pressure than one finds in medical crises and less tendency to clandestinity than one finds in legal unpleasantnesses.

In connection with the topic of the informant's nonverbal behavior I think it worth adding something about the importance we should give to the confidence shown or asserted by the informant as he talks. Dallenbach

---

[21] Quite often subjects tell us at a later interview some item we did not hear about at an earlier one. This does not necessarily mean they have supplemented the case with the help of imagination. They may simply have forgotten to mention the detail at the earlier interviews and have been reminded of it by something said at the later one. "We not only tend to forget what we have once remembered but we also tend to remember what we have once forgotten" (Ballard, 1913).

(1913) found in his experiments that subjects made fewer errors in statements about which they expressed certainty, including willingness to take an oath about them, as compared with those about which they felt less assurance. But this effect tended to diminish with time, so that at the forty-fifth day the subjects made errors in no less than 19.5 per cent of the statements about which they expressed agreement to take an oath. Münsterberg (1908) found a similar, almost impertinently unrealistic disconnection between assertions of confidence concerning memories for stimulus pictures and actual performance in recall.

I have a considerable preference for an informant who presents himself diffidently as being unable to recollect everything exactly over one who pretends to quasi-eidetic imagery of all that happened. But, regrettably, some persons who apologize for having bad memories have them.

The monograph of Arntzen (1970), which reviewed and summarized much German research on the validity of testimony, gave me blended comfort and regret. I felt pleased that Arntzen and his coworkers had found no better guides to validity than those that I have employed; but I cannot help deploring that advances come so slowly in this field, because we need much better and quicker means than we now have for evaluating the worth of oral testimony.

In concluding this section I will add that I have aimed at offering enough information about the qualifications of the informants and the discrepancies in their testimony so that readers can at least participate in the judgment of the reliability of the evidence in the cases to be presented. To have given less information might have been misleading; to have given more would have made these volumes impossibly bulky. I am fully aware, however, that I have more information about the witnesses for the cases than I have recorded here. I hope therefore for the reader's indulgence in believing that I have done my best to offer him only information that I consider reliable or to say so when I think otherwise.

The Relative Worth of the Different Types of Data Given by Informants. Before leaving the important topic of sources of error, I wish to say something concerning my own judgments of the relative value—speaking generally—of the different items of evidence the informants provide. (I am considering here only those reports dependent on the memories of the informants giving oral testimony; by definition, written documents no longer depend on memory, although at one time, as they were being written, they did.)

I shall first make a few general remarks about places of weakness in the memories of many informants and then discuss the relative likelihood of error in the three main categories of information depending on oral testimony: the subject's recognitions, his statements, and his behavior.

Like everyone else, the informants for these cases show the least reliability in their placement of events in time. And the ordinary human weakness in this regard becomes augmented when, as is often the case, the informants have no clocks, calendars, newspapers, or other aids for reckoning
and remembering the units of time to which urban dwellers of the West
have become accustomed. It is not surprising, then, that the informants
often forget and confuse dates and the chronological order of events.

Informants also more commonly remember an event—say, a child's statement or recognition—than the circumstances surrounding it. I have found
them particularly weak in recalling who else besides themselves was present
on a particular occasion. I have often posed this question in the hope of
corroborating an informant's statement, and I do not think the vagueness
of the informants about such matters reflects a wish to avoid contradiction
by someone else. I think it derives in most instances from the fact that the
statement or other behavior of the child struck them as unusual and became registered in their memories, but the situation in which it occurred
did not.

The largest number of discrepancies in the testimony of these cases occurs
in connection with recognitions attributed to the subject. In principle,
recognition of persons, objects, and places related to the previous life could
provide some of the strongest evidence for paranormal processes in the
cases. In the first place, it is exceedingly difficult to recognize another person unless one has either seen him before or been told specific details about
almost unique features of his appearance. Polanyi (1958, 1962, 1966) included recognition of faces among the functions of "tacit knowing," or skills
that cannot be learned without practice.[22] If, then, a child is taken to another village where he has never been and there, without guidance of any
kind, can recognize and properly identify by name a person he has never
seen before, we have impressive evidence of some paranormal process.

Unfortunately, when these recognitions occur in most cases of this type,
a gulf yawns between the theoretical ideal and the actual events. The conditions rarely satisfy minimal standards of control. The best-regulated and
most successful series of recognition tests known to me occurred under the
supervision of the Ven. Piyadassi Thera in the case of Gnanatilleka (Stevenson, 1974a). She was taken into a separate room with only her parents and
four other observers present. The persons she was to recognize were mar-
shaled outside and then introduced into the room, usually singly but twice
in a group of three. At each person's entrance one of the observers in the
room asked Gnanatilleka: "Do you know this person?" If the persons concerned conducted all recognition tests in this manner, we could have more

---

[22] I consider the recognition of the friends of George Pelham by Mrs. Piper's control GP one
of the most impressive demonstrations of paranormal knowledge yet reported (Hodgson, 1898,
pp. 323–28).

confidence in them. But usually the two families come together at best without any planning and at worst with the subtlety of a collision. As the child and his family grope for the correct house in the strange village, curious onlookers notice them, and quickly the group swells to a crowd. When the two families do meet, someone often hastily asks the subject: "Do you see your 'mother' here?" If, then, all eyes turn to the mother of the presumed previous personality, no one can wonder that the child also looks in that direction and seems to recognize the woman everyone is staring at. Fortunately, this sort of mistake does not wipe out all value from scenes of this type. Someone may ask the child to give the mother's name, and we may have some important evidence if he pronounces it unaided. Also no bungling of the initial recognition can cancel the importance of the frequent reports of the child's unusual behavior with the persons recognized. Even if someone has cued the child with leading questions, and even if he has been helped by the glances of other persons in the direction of the person to be recognized, he is not thereby obliged to go and sit in the lap of that person, treat that person affectionately, and perhaps weep with joy at seeing someone who was a complete stranger a few minutes before.

Even when the participants conduct recognition tests with proper safeguards—and it would be quite unfair to say they have mishandled all such tests—more discrepancies occur in the testimony of recognitions than in that of the other two main categories of evidence. I puzzled over this for many years before I began to understand at least one of the reasons involved. It sometimes happens that the parent of a subject reports that he has recognized someone, and yet the person said to have been recognized (or other informants) denies this when questioned. (This has occurred even when the previous personality's family was in other respects favorable to the case and more eager than the subject's own family to emphasize its strong points.) As I began to enquire in more detail about the setting of recognition tests and to participate in a few myself, I became aware that the child may make his brief statement of recognition in a rather low voice that only the people close to him can hear. Thus the child may be held in the arms of his mother while someone asks: "Who is that?" and points at a woman twenty feet away. Under these circumstances perhaps only the child's mother can hear the soft response. This seems to me one important cause of discrepancies in the testimony about recognitions.

Another lies in the fact that the child has only one chance to make his statement of recognition, and persons not paying attention at that very moment may fail to hear what he says. Those who are not watching and listening closely when the child utters or mutters his recognition lose the right to an opinion about it, but may give one anyway. In general, I do not think the special experiments designed to demonstrate and examine errors in testimony are pertinent to an analysis of the evidence in spontaneous cases, including cases of the reincarnation type. I have argued this at length elsewhere (Stevenson, 1968). However, I think such experiments are clearly relevant to the recognitions accomplished by the subjects of these cases or attributed to them. The suddenness and brevity of the child's recognition often resemble what the witness of a highway accident or unexpected robbery confronts. In all these situations the observer experiences little or no warning, short duration of the event to be remembered, and (usually) the arousal of emotion—all factors tending to diminish the reliability of observation and memories. Planned experiments concerning the accuracy of witnesses [23] have shown how very inaccurate they can be *in such situations*. But I am unwilling to concede that the same defects affect testimony about other evidence in these cases, such as the subject's statements and his (nonverbal) behavior.

Although I have said above that the child has only *one* chance to make a recognition of a person connected with the previous personality, he may nevertheless make several related remarks at this time in response to differently posed questions. These may vary greatly in suggestive power. Thus one bystander may point to someone and ask the subject: "Who is she?" As the child answers, or immediately afterward, another person may insert something like: "Is she your mother?" thus throwing away the chance for the subject to respond correctly and without guidance. For instances in which such double questions may have accounted for discrepancies in reports of recognitions, see the report in this volume of the case of Ramoo and Rajoo Sharma (pp. 354–55).

Some of the foregoing considerations have led me to see the value of discriminating between differences in testimony that occur when one witness does not confirm what another has said, and true discordances, which occur when two witnesses both claim to remember some event—for example, a recognition—but disagree as to what actually happened. I therefore now distinguish omission discrepancies and discordant discrepancies in comparing the testimony of one informant with that of another.

If I were to draw only from my own experiences with recognition tests in these cases, I should think even less of this category of testimony than I do. From time to time I have arranged for recognition tests in cases where the child has not yet met members (or all the members) of the identified previous family. (For examples of my observations of recognition tests, see the reports of the cases of Indika Guneratne and Lalitha Abeyawardena in the second volume of this series. The third volume will include, in the report of the case of Faruq Faris Andary, an account of an attempt I made to arrange recognition tests that developed into a fiasco.) With two exceptions, subjects have failed to make any substantial recognitions when I

---

[23] For an excellently conducted and analyzed experiment of this type, see Selbst (1952–53).

have been present: Imad Elawar and Gnanatilleka succeeded (Stevenson, 1974a). Several reasons may account for this. The presence of someone who is more or less a stranger may inhibit the child and induce just enough anxiety to block his emerging recognition, assuming that he would recognize the people or places concerned if he were more relaxed. And if I and my colleagues or interpreters do not trouble the child directly, our presence may draw an even larger crowd than usually attends these events—and these crowds are rarely small on the best of occasions. This crush of onlookers may trouble the child further. On the occasion of the successful recognitions that Imad Elawar made in my presence, we were inside a house (that of the previous personality) and only eight persons were present, including Imad, myself, and the interpreter. It was a comparatively tranquil situation. At the time of Imad's first visit to Khriby his memories were still strong, whereas in some other cases where I have tried to observe recognition tests the subject's memories had already begun to fade. We must remember also that the older the child, the greater his distance in time from the people connected with the previous personality and the more likely it is that they have altered in appearance during the intervening years.

Many informants for these cases in Asia take a position exactly opposite to mine concerning the importance of the recognitions made by the subject. They frequently evaluate the entire case on the basis of whether the subject succeeded in making recognitions under conditions that satisfied them. I remember one secondary informant who dismissed an entire case—otherwise excellent, it seemed to me—because the subject had failed to recognize him. He had been a somewhat distant relative of the previous personality. In this instance vanity compounded an ordinary prejudice. Informants who complain of not being recognized may forget that their appearances have been changed by twenty years of aging since the previous personality died and that the child was surrounded by huge crowds when he was suddenly challenged to give the name of a person he failed to recognize. On the other hand, the importance that some cautious informants attach to recognition tests deserves respect because these persons are in the best position to know whether the subject received any cues for the recognitions they witnessed.

Although in general I give a low value to reports of recognitions made by the subjects of these cases, I am not prepared to discard all such reports as worthless. I have already mentioned that some aspects (especially the emotional components) of a scene of recognition may contribute important evidence even when the adult participants have not controlled the situation well with regard to absence of normal cues guiding the child. In addition, we also have some valuable reports of completely spontaneous recognitions, made by subjects without anyone asking them a question or otherwise inciting or guiding them. These may occur when a subject suddenly sees someone in a group or on the street and calls him by name or perhaps even by a nickname by which the previous personality knew the person hailed. The cases in this volume of Gopal Gupta and Sunil Dutt Saxena provide examples of this type of spontaneous recognition; so do those of Gnanatilleka and of Corliss Chotkin, Jr. (Stevenson, 1974a).

The potential importance of recognitions by the subjects of these cases provides one more reason for my hope that soon other qualified investigators who are natives of the countries where these cases occur will take up their study. Asian investigators could easily reach the cases earlier than I have been able to do and could also find more of them in which the two families have not yet met. Since the informants nearly always give us willing cooperation, most of them will gladly enter into planned recognition tests conducted by investigators. I predict that in the years ahead this category of evidence will increase in value.

Statements made by or attributed to the subject come next in merit among the types of evidence in these cases. Although sometimes the subject makes a particular statement only once or twice, more often he repeats the same claim over and over again, for example, giving many times the name he says he had and those of members of the previous family, or telling how he lived and died in the previous life. These repetitions tend to fix the memories of what he said in the minds of his parents and other informants. Furthermore, we are likely to find more informants for the child's statements than for his recognitions. Often he has made the same remarks about the house he claims he has elsewhere, together with his goats, bullocks, and wife, to many persons. If his parents show signs of satiety with his talk about the previous life, he may wander off to find a more attentive audience in neighbors. They offer the additional prospect of being seduced into taking the subject to the previous village if his parents have refused to do so. In the end, then, numerous persons may have heard the child make the same or similar statements about the previous life. In contrast, although throngs may observe his recognitions, there are few reliable witnesses of such scenes. Curious but inattentive and uninformed villagers constitute the bulk of such crowds.

Sometimes the subject bursts out with such unusual and unexpected remarks as to startle his parents, thus helping to fix what he said in their memories.

We may hear the subject himself repeat his statements about the previous life directly to us. If he starts talking about it at the age of, say, three (the average age), and we reach the case when he is no more than five, he may still have the previous life much on his mind and be able to tell us himself about the memories he has, or he may amend the statements of his parents as he listens to them.

With regard solely to fixation in the minds of observers, the behavioral traits reported for the child seem to me to provide our most trustworthy evidence in these cases. The recognitions occur in a flash; each can only occur once and for all time. And although the subject may repeat some of his statements about his imaged memories often (as I have emphasized above), he may state others on only one or a few occasions. But he usually shows the related odd behavior repeatedly from the ages of three to five and longer. In many cases the child's behavior noted to be unusual among his siblings continues up to the time of my investigation of the case and beyond. Sometimes my colleagues and I can observe it directly or, failing that, we can often hear of an illustrative episode that happened just a day or several days before our interview.

Unfortunately, other factors sometimes diminish the value of the informants' reports about the child's behavior. His statements about the previous life may guide the observers in the family to think they see traits concordant with the character of the previous personality that his statements have suggested. Family members may even promote, quite unconsciously, his playing the role he seems to have assigned himself. The risk of this becomes augmented when the part seems to have comic aspects, as when the subject recalls the life of an alcoholic and imitates his conduct. (For an example of this, see the case of Sujith Lakmal, in the second volume of this series. Although I am not suggesting that informants in this particular case exaggerated Sujith's unusual and amusing behavior, the temptation to do so existed.) The hazard of distorted reports of the subject's behavior becomes more likely after the two families have met and the child's family have learned something about the previous personality as remembered by his surviving relatives. A tendency to harmonize reports of the subject's behavior with traits the previous personality was known to have may set in. The difficulties become further compounded when we try to form a reasonably accurate picture of the previous personality. Sometimes many years have passed since his death, and during this time the formerly sharp outlines of his character may have become hazy in the memories of his contemporaries—altogether apart from the tendency I noted earlier for his relatives to cover his sins and parade his virtues.

The Recording of the Data in This Book

At the beginning of each case report I have provided a summary of the case and its investigation. (In some instances a short introduction drawing attention to salient features of the case precedes this summary.) These summaries derive only from information that I believe reliable. Although I do not detain the reader with many details about the sources of the information, I obtained it for the most part from the informants listed later.

The summary provides an aperçu of the case. Some readers may wish to skip from it to the sections that are concerned with the subject's behavior. Those more interested in the details of the case, however, will find them in the sections immediately following the summary. These provide information about the geographical factors and possibilities for normal communication between the two families; about the persons furnishing the information; about the identified previous personality; and particularly about the statements and recognitions attributed to the subject. I regard these last sections as the core of each report, for in them I give the best information I have about who said what under which circumstances. For ease in studying individual items I have ordered them in summarizing tables. Following these sections are reports of the behaviors of the subject and of other persons concerned in the case that may bear on its authenticity. Next are my own comments on the evidence of paranormal processes in the case. Finally there is for most of the cases some information about the subject's later development with special attention to the fading or persistence of imaged memories of the previous life and behavior apparently related to it. This method of presentation involves some repetition, but it has the advantage of providing details for those willing to grapple with them while also enabling those who are not to obtain a more superficial view of the cases.

As already mentioned, I have not included in the published record the testimony of a small number of informants who were caught in falsehoods or shown otherwise to be unfit for listing alongside the majority of witnesses who seemed to me reliable.

I have sometimes also not included in the tables of statements and recognitions some items about which the testimony of different informants was so discrepant or confused as to prohibit any valid judgment about who, if anyone, was correct. Similarly, I have omitted a few items—for example, some of the recognitions made by Kumkum Verma (in this volume) —for which I thought I had incomplete information about the circumstances in which they occurred. And I have omitted a few extremely general statements that, although correct, could be applied to many persons and therefore could contribute little to the case. Since all these dropped items are of statements or recognitions attributed to the subject of the case, their loss has in every instance a tendency to weaken the evidence of paranormality by reducing the number of items for which the subject might receive credit. For these reasons I have omitted probably fewer than thirty items from the case reports published in this book.

The reader thus has before him an almost complete list of the statements and recognitions attributed to the subject (or made by him) about the previous life as given to my colleagues or me. And he has in addition as complete a record as we could make of all the major discrepancies in the different testimonies. I have not counted (or listed) various minor inconsistencies in the words or phrases actually used by informants as they remembered what a child said, provided the content was exactly or substantially the same. The child himself may have said the same thing in slightly different ways at different times, or the parents, in sifting it through their memories, may have modified the words actually used by the child. Other variations in this category may have come from differences in the translations given by the interpreters. I have provided notes about the important variant testimony of different informants or of the same informant at different times.

Every item in the tables summarizing the statements and recognitions derives from a corresponding record in my own notes, in those of associates present at interviews with me, or in communications sent to me by associates concerning inquiries they made at times when I was not present.

The subject's statement was correct unless I have indicated in the columns of verifications and comments of the pertinent tables that it was not.

When I have listed more than one person as a verifier for a particular item, it can usually be understood that they gave concordant information confirming what the subject had said for that item. Sometimes, however, one verifier furnished more detail than another. When persons in a position to know the facts gave discordant testimony with regard to verifications, I have indicated this in the column of comments.

In the case of recognitions I have listed no informants in the verifications column of the tables. The informant for the recognition is also the person who knew at the time, or found out later, that the recognition was correct, partly or completely.

Under informants I have generally listed only one or two persons, even though in some instances another person, or several persons, corroborated the report of the one or two principal informants. I have already explained that these other informants were often not independent of the first ones either in their observations or in giving their reports; and to list them all every time would give a spurious appearance of greater strength to the cases. But I have named and given the testimony of some of these confirming informants, especially when they were partly or completely independent of the main informant, or when it seemed important to mention discrepancies in the statements of different informants for the same item.

A small number of informants have been listed among the persons interviewed but have not been included as informants or verifiers in the summarizing tables. Such persons provided miscellaneous information relevant to the case, such as comments assisting in judgments about the reliability of other informants, information about the subject's behavior or that of the previous personality, or other details pertinent to the evaluation and understanding of the case.

In some places I have enclosed statements attributed to the subject within quotation marks. Readers should remember that most such quotes are from my notes of what the interpreter said the informant said the subject said. When the subject is quoted, the passages are from my notes of what the interpreter said the subject said. In those instances in which the informants spoke English or French directly to me, the quotes are likewise from my notes. I do not want to mislead anyone into thinking that quotation marks always imply a word-for-word translation of what the child or other informant said to me or the interpreter.

For some items I have given a word or short phrase of an Asian language in order to bring out more clearly exactly what the interpreter reported the subject to have said at a point where some difficulty in translation or understanding might occur.

In the tables summarizing the subject's statements I have consistently used the past tense, as if the child had said, for example, "I had a wife," or "We used to have electricity." Although this provides consistency, it does not adequately reflect the frequent use by the children of the present tense in their statements, for example, "My mother's name *is* Podi Nona," or "I *come* from Budaun." I have, however, drawn attention to such phrasing in the text.

I have tried, sometimes without success, to avoid confusion in the use of pronouns when the subject and the previous personality are referred to in the same sentence or paragraph. To improve understanding I have sometimes added explanatory words in parentheses, which results in sentences such as "Her (previous) mother was better-dressed than her (present) mother." Readers should not interpret such asides as begging the main question raised by these case reports.

Readers should also remember that I have usually given as the statements of the subject the more or less final, well-articulated versions of what he said. Often a child begins fumbling at the age of two, or even less, to communicate his memories of a previous life.[24] At this time he does not have the linguistic capacity for adequate expression. He mispronounces words and often falls back on gestures to make a better impression on the (for him) obtuseness and slowly improving awareness of his parents concerning what he is trying to say. By the time my colleagues or I reach the scene of a case this stage has usually passed. The informants then give us the later, clearer versions of what the child has said about the previous life. But sometimes they have also given us some examples of his first crude efforts to communicate the same thought, and I have often noted these in the tables or text.

---

[24] I wish I had more reliable information about the age of first coherent speech by the subjects and the ages when they first spoke about the previous lives. Unfortunately, in asking about these, I neglected until recently to insist on the distinction between the imitative babbling of a child's early vocalizations and his first use of meaningful words and phrases.

In some of the case reports, I have listed the subject himself as an informant for certain items, giving the date of the record of what he said directly to us. Since in nearly every such instance the subject had already met the previous family, I attach no weight whatever to such statements as evidence that he said the same thing *before* the two families had met. For evidence on that point we must rely on his parents or other qualified informants. But since some critics have suspected the parents of these children of attributing more statements to them than they actually make, or of elaborating those they do make, it has seemed helpful to listen whenever possible to whatever the subject will tell us directly. Records of the subjects' statements will naturally increase in value as investigators reach the scenes of cases at earlier dates than they now usually do.

I have furnished the details, when known, about where and when each item occurred and special circumstances that may have stimulated it. The text contains a summary of this information, and the columns of comments in the tables give additional details about many individual items.

In the tables giving the statements and recognitions made by the subject, I have, as a general rule, grouped all the statements first and followed them with the recognitions. I have also grouped the statements, to the extent that they permitted this, by topic. I have departed from this plan in some instances—for example, when a subject made a statement immediately after a recognition and the two in effect form part of one episode; and when groups of statements, as well as one or more recognitions, were made on a particular occasion such as a visit to the previous family. The statements and recognitions made by Veer Singh and reported in this volume seemed best presented in this manner.

For items that are (or seem) distorted, incorrect, or unverified I have sometimes added my own interpretations, often only conjectures, about how the error occurred or whether or not the item, if unverified, seems plausible and likely to be correct. In these last comments I am not trying to explain away errors, but rather to understand them. I think that by studying errors we may penetrate more deeply into the processes of memory both of the children subjects and of the informants who relay what they have heard the subject say.

Readers may notice that for some cases women, especially the mothers of the subjects, contribute little to the testimony. This occurs through no wish of mine; instead, it represents a submission to the presumption of men —greater in Asia than in the West—that they know more than their womenfolk about important matters. One can do little to check the extravagance of this claim, even when it is put forward in connection with observations of small children, who spend much more time with their mothers than with their fathers. A further difficulty arises in this connection from the fact that Asian women, who generally have a much lower status than women in the

West, frequently lead sequestered lives and have less experience in communicating with strangers than have men. Consequently, when we do succeed in interviewing an important female informant, we often find her distressingly timid and sometimes almost mute with shyness.

Asian proper names give rise to many difficulties for Western readers, and I will comment briefly on some of these. In the first place, inconsistencies occur, even in the attempts of Asian people, to romanize the proper names of Asian languages. One finds many variant spellings in English of names that are obviously, or almost certainly, the same in the original Asian language. If I have offended anyone by misspelling his name or seeming to do so, I beg forgiveness. Second, marriages between cousins or between members of extended families occur rather commonly in parts of Asia, and this circumstance may account for some similarity in the names of marriage partners and in-laws and a liability to confuse them. Third, names of castes in India are adopted by some persons as family names, but are omitted altogether by others, so that these latter persons seem to have only what we in the West call first, given, or "Christian" names. Readers may notice some inconsistency in my use of caste names from case to case and even within one case report. I have tried to follow the usage of the persons concerned. Fourth, a wife sometimes does not take her husband's name after marriage. Often in Sri Lanka and Thailand, and nearly always in Burma, she may preserve afterward the name by which she was known before. (In a few places, in order to help the reader properly place a particular woman concerned in a case, I have arbitrarily attached her husband's name to hers even though she might not do this herself.) Fifth, in Sri Lanka, family names are often indicated by initials preceding the given name. In the case of Disna Samarasinghe, for example, R. M. Gardias and R. M. Romanis are (biological) brothers whose family relationship is indicated by the initials R. M. By a combination of these last two principles, the wife of R. M. Gardias is known as T. N. Alice. Her initials indicate her father's family; her husband's name figures nowhere in hers.

I have found it necessary or helpful to use some words from Asian languages both for certain common objects, titles, and occupations, and for some of the concepts of Asian religions. In the romanization of these words I have omitted all diacritical marks. I have spelled them consistently in this series of books even when local custom might dictate otherwise. For example, I have used the word *karma* (Sanskrit) in reference to cases of India and again for those of Sri Lanka although a purist crossing the Gulf of Mannar would think he should change to *kamma* (Pali). In the same way I shall in a later volume of this series use the word *mukhtar* (village headman) both for cases of Lebanon, where this spelling would be acceptable, and for cases of Turkey, where correct orthography would call for *muhtar*. I have defined lesser-known words of Asian languages in the Glossary (pp.

361–67 below) and have also explained many of them in the text. I adopted all these conventions in the belief that I am writing mainly for scientists in medicine, psychology, and anthropology rather than for individuals in philology or comparative religion.

At the beginning of each group of cases from a particular country I have included an introductory chapter on the belief in reincarnation and the characteristics of the cases of the region. Such a chapter is not the place to review all aspects of the religions of the peoples among whom the cases occur—even if I had the competence to do so, which I am far from claiming. I have therefore confined each introductory chapter almost entirely to features of the cultures bearing on the belief in reincarnation and on the cases.

A few of the case reports include accounts of the subject's statements concerning experiences that he claims to remember as occurring between the death of the previous personality and his own birth. These rarely contain any verifiable material. Most have the details of local mythology and the value only of culture-bound fantasies. I have thought it important to include them in the case reports, however, for two reasons. First, they form part of the record of the whole case, and I did not feel justified in suppressing them arbitrarily. Second, they may help to prepare the reader for similar accounts to be included in volumes succeeding this one in which the subjects have made more extensive statements about events occurring during the "intermission" between death and presumed rebirth.

References

Achilles, E. M. 1920. Experimental studies in recall and recognition. *Archives of Psychology* 80:1–80.

Arntzen, F. 1970. *Psychologie der Zeugenaussage: Einführung in die forensische Aussagepsychologie.* Göttingen: Verlag für Psychologie.

Ballard, P. B. 1913. Obliviscence and reminiscence. *British Journal of Psychology Monograph Supplement* 1:1–82.

Bartlett, F. 1932. *Remembering: A study in experimental and social psychology.* Cambridge, England: Cambridge University Press.

Binet, A. 1900. *La suggestibilité.* Paris: Schleicher Frères.

Carty, C. M. 1963. *Padre Pio the stigmatist.* Rockford, Ill.: Tan Books and Publishers, Inc.

Dallenbach, K. M. 1913. The relation of memory error to time interval. *Psychological Review* 20:323–37.

De Liso, O. 1961. *Padre Pio, the priest who bears the wounds of Christ.* London: James Clarke and Co. Ltd.

Dunlop, J. B. 1972. *Staretz Amvrosy.* Belmont, Mass.: Nordland Publishing Company.

Ebbinghaus, H. 1885. *Über das Gedächtnis.* Leipzig: Verlag Duncker und Humblot.

Foley, J. P., and Macmillan, Z. L. 1943. Mediated generalization and the interpretation of verbal behavior. V. 'Free association' as related to differences in professional training. *Journal of Experimental Psychology* 33:299–310.

Goodenough, F. L. 1946. Semantic choice and personality structure. *Science* 104: 451–56.

Haggard, E. A., Brekstad, A., and Skard, A. G. 1960. On the reliability of the anamnestic interview. *Journal of Abnormal and Social Psychology* 61:311–18.

Hatherill, G. 1971. *A detective's story.* London: Andre Deutsch.

Hodgson, R. 1898. A further record of observations of certain phenomena of trance. *Proceedings of the Society for Psychical Research* 13:284–582.

Hull, C. L. 1933. *Hypnosis and suggestibility.* New York: Appleton-Century-Crofts, Inc.

Hunter, I. M. L. 1964. *Memory.* Rev. ed. Harmondsworth, Middlesex: Penguin Books, Ltd.

James, W. 1890. *The principles of psychology.* New York: Henry Holt and Co. 2 vols.

Jenkins, J. G., and Dallenbach, K. M. 1924. Obliviscence during sleep and waking. *American Journal of Psychology* 35:605–12.

Levine, J. M., and Murphy, G. 1943. The learning and forgetting of controversial material. *Journal of Abnormal and Social Psychology* 38:507–17.

Luria, A. R. 1968. *The mind of a mnemonist.* Trans. L. Solotaroff. London: Jonathan Cape.

Malinowski, B. 1916. Baloma: The spirits of the dead in the Trobriand Islands. *Journal of the Royal Anthropological Institute of Great Britain and Ireland* 46:353–430.

Marshall, B. 1952. The curé of Ars. In *Saints for now,* ed. C. B. Luce. New York: Sheed and Ward, pp. 272–94.

Marshall, J. 1969. *Law and psychology in conflict.* Garden City, N.Y.: Doubleday and Co., Inc.

Marshall, J., Marquis, K. H., and Oskamp, S. 1971. Effects of kind of question and atmosphere of interrogation on accuracy and completeness of testimony. *Harvard Law Review* 84:1620–43.

Marston, W. M. 1924. Studies in testimony. *Journal of Criminal Law and Criminology* 15:5–31.

Meltzer, H. 1930. Individual differences in forgetting pleasant and unpleasant experiences. *Journal of Educational Psychology* 21:399–409.

Münsterberg, H. 1908. *On the witness stand.* Garden City, N.Y.: Doubleday and Co., Inc.

Myers, G. C. 1915. Affective factors in recall. *Journal of Philosophy, Psychology and Scientific Methods* 12:85–92.

Parsons, D. 1962. A non-existent building located. *Journal of the Society for Psychical Research* 41:292–95.

Pezeril, D. 1959. *Pauvre et saint curé d'Ars.* Paris: Editions du Seuil.

Polanyi, M. 1958. *Personal knowledge.* London: Routledge and Kegan Paul.

——— 1962. Tacit knowing. *Reviews of Modern Physics* 34:601–16.

——— 1966. *The tacit dimension.* Garden City, N.Y.: Doubleday and Co., Inc.

Prince, W. F. 1918. Experiences of Augustine Jones. *Journal of the American Society for Psychical Research* 12:718–27.

——— 1919. Some coincidental dreams. *Journal of the American Society for Psychical Research* 13:61–93.

——— 1931. Human experiences. *Bulletin of the Boston Society for Psychic Research* 14:7–328.

Pyles, M. L., Stolz, H. R., and Macfarlane, J. W. 1935. The accuracy of mothers' reports on birth and developmental data. *Child Development* 6:165–76.

Richardson, S. A. 1960. The use of leading questions in non-schedule interviews. *Human Organization* 19:86–89.

Richardson, S. A., Dohrenwend, B. S., and Klein, D. 1965. *Interviewing: Its forms and functions.* New York: Basic Books, Inc.

Selbst, G. 1952–53. Are witnesses reliable? An experiment in crime. *Obiter. Journal of the London School of Economics Law Society* 2:26–33.

Smith, H. T. 1958. A comparison of interview and observation measures of mother behavior. *Journal of Abnormal and Social Psychology* 57:278–82.

Stern, C., and Stern, W. 1909. *Erinnerung, Aussage und Lüge in der ersten Kindheit.* Leipzig: Verlag J. H. Barth.

Stern, W. 1935. *Allgemeine Psychologie auf personalistischer Grundlage.* The Hague: Martinus Nijhoff. (American edition. Trans. H. D. Spoerl, 1938. *General psychology from the personalistic standpoint.* New York: The Macmillan Co.)

——— 1965. *Psychologie der früheren Kindheit.* Heidelberg: Quelle und Meyer.

Stevenson, I. 1966. Cultural patterns in cases suggestive of reincarnation among the Tlingit Indians of Southeastern Alaska. *Journal of the American Society for Psychical Research* 60:229–43.

——— 1968. The substantiality of spontaneous cases. *Proceedings of the Parapsychological Association* 5:91–128.

——— 1970. Characteristics of cases of the reincarnation type in Turkey and their comparison with cases in two other cultures. *International Journal of Comparative Sociology* 11:1–17.

——— 1971. *The diagnostic interview.* 2d ed. New York: Harper and Row.

1973. Characteristics of cases of the reincarnation type in Ceylon. *Contributions to Asian Studies* 3:26–39.

1974a. *Twenty cases suggestive of reincarnation.* 2d ed. Charlottesville: University Press of Virginia. (First published in 1966 as *Proceedings of the American Society for Psychical Research* 26:1–362.)

1974b. Some questions related to cases of the reincarnation type. *Journal of the American Society for Psychical Research* 68:395–416.

Weiss, D. J., and Dawis, R. V. 1960. An objective validation of factual interview data. *Journal of Applied Psychology* 44:381–85.

Whipple, G. M. 1918. The obtaining of information: Psychology of observation and report. *Psychological Bulletin* 15:217–48.

Introduction to Cases in India

THE GREAT religions of the world each contain various elements that, however disparate and seemingly unrelated, belong more or less to a unified system. Since the doctrine of reincarnation forms such a central tenet of Hinduism, it may seem futile to attempt discussion of it apart from other aspects of the Hindu tradition. Nevertheless, I think Hinduism has many features that touch only tangentially on the question of reincarnation, and I shall confine what follows largely to those aspects of it that are directly related to the subject of this book.

This restriction still leaves much to be considered. Hinduism has no more important belief than that of reincarnation. Moreover, the belief itself arose in India several thousand years ago. Although the Rigveda does not mention it (Radhakrishnan, 1923, 1:113–16; Smart, 1964, p. 26), the Upanishads (Hume, 1921) present it in a form little different from what one finds among Hindus today.

The Distribution of the Belief in Reincarnation among Hindus

It has been widely believed both in the West and in India that Indians (I am speaking here of Hindus and not of the other religious groups, such as Moslems or Christians, of India), being a deeply religious people, attempt to practice their religion more than other peoples practice theirs. Lewis (1958) challenged this claim as an unsubstantiated myth, but Opler (1959), making a careful count of items of religious behavior in the day-to-day life of the people in a north Indian (Uttar Pradesh) village, found ample evidence that religion plays a large part in the life of ordinary Hindus. However, an examination of the types of religious behavior (and associated beliefs) of Hindus shows a wide range of knowledge, conduct, and beliefs, including that in reincarnation.

Throughout India all educated or partly educated Hindus, and probably all high caste Hindus, whether educated or not, know about the concept of reincarnation. For members of these groups, life consists of a continual cycle of birth, death, and rebirth (samsara). Terrestrial life is considered undesirable, and release from it (moksh, liberation) in union with God (Nirvana) [1] is the ultimate goal. This requires many lives of suffering and struggles at self-improvement in which one strives for the abandonment of carnal desire and the progressive realization of spirituality. One's conduct in one life determines one's character and circumstances in future lives and one's progress toward the final discharge from the cycle of rebirth.

The Hinduism of Indian villages, where most Indians still live, differs rather markedly from what a scholar working only with Hindu scriptures might expect. Dube (1955) was one of the first anthropologists to challenge the belief that Hinduism in villages corresponded with that of the educated classes in the towns and cities. He remarked: "Clearly, Hinduism as it is practiced in the village is not the Hinduism of the classical philosophical systems of India, for it possesses neither the metaphysical heights, nor the abstract content of the latter. It is a religion of fasts, feasts, and festivals, in which prescribed rituals cover all the major crises of life. Worship and the propitiation of gods and spirits follow the annual round of festivals and the ritual of the human life cycle. Disease and difficulty may also necessitate invoking assistance from these sources" (p. 93).

Several anthropologists have made systematic inquiries among Indian villagers concerning their religious beliefs and practice including their acquaintance with the traditional Hindu teachings on reincarnation. Carstairs (1957) reported that high caste villagers (in a village of Rajasthan) showed a thorough familiarity with the doctrines of reincarnation and karma even though only sixteen of his thirty-seven male subjects seemed to him assiduous in the practice of their religion. He observed, however, that some lower caste groups knew much less about the belief in reincarnation. Elder (1959) found in a village of Uttar Pradesh that 88 per cent of the persons he interviewed believed in reincarnation: in that village the percentage of "believers" was higher among the low caste groups, for example, Jats, Sudras, and scheduled castes (formerly untouchables), than among the Brahmins.

Other surveys, however, have shown a much lower incidence of the belief in reincarnation, especially among the lower castes. Harper (1959) reported from observations in a village of Mysore (south India): "Sanskritic gods figure prominently in the religion of the higher castes who are concerned with the acquisition of merit; lower castes frequently were completely unfamiliar with the term for, as well as the concept of, rebirth (punarjanma) "

---

[1] For some interesting notes on the possible origins and meaning of the word *Nirvana,* see Schopenhauer (1908, II: 583). For further accounts of different beliefs about reincarnation occurring in other cultures, see the corresponding chapters introducing cases of other countries in the volumes following this one. See also the comparisons made by Parrinder (1956) and Stevenson (1974b).

(p. 229). Lewis (1958) stated that only fourteen of twenty-five villagers (of a Delhi village) whom he questioned expressed belief in the doctrine of reincarnation. The belief was stronger among the Brahmins and the low caste groups, and weaker among the Jats (intermediate low caste). Cohn (1959) made similar observations among Chamars (a low caste group) in a village of Uttar Pradesh: "Chamars appear to lack many of the values and concepts which are associated with Hinduism of the Great Tradition. When I discussed matters of the afterlife with Chamars, I invariably heard the statement that they do not know what happens after death. They do not have any ideas about rebirth" (p. 207). Kolenda (1964), in a study of low caste villagers (Sweepers) in Uttar Pradesh, found that the persons she interviewed had a concept of reincarnation, but that they applied the idea of karma in a manner rather different from that of the traditional teachings. She stated: "While they understand and can explain the ideas of transmigration and karma, indicating the connection between sins in past lives and present life conditions, they refuse to admit that low-caste persons were less virtuous in past lives than members of castes which rank immediately above them" (p. 74). In a summary statement Kolenda added: "If the Sweepers accepted the full karma theory, they could be expected to explain their low-caste status as the result of the sinful past lives of the members of their castes, but they do not draw this conclusion" (p. 75).[2]

I have cited these observations on the diversity of belief about reincarnation among Hindus because I think an appreciation of this essential to proper evaluation of my case material. Many Westerners acquainted with India only through publications or visits to its big cities and tourist centers imagine that the country teems with millions of ardent Hindus eager to press the truths of their religion on the rest of mankind. If this were true it would have a bearing on our evaluation of the case reports, since enthusiasm for a case that seems to support the doctrine of reincarnation could impart an important bias to the reports of informants. I will not deny that this has happened in some cases. Some Hindus eagerly expound the merits of their religion, and in the cities one can listen involuntarily to tedious discourses on the subject. The lecturers are mostly little-educated Indians who know something of Hindu teachings but do not credit the foreign listener with such familiarity; better-educated persons seem to have less need to proselytize, or they think an interested foreigner is capable of asking for the information he lacks and wants. At the lowest extreme of education, informants—perhaps for different reasons—generally adopt a similarly modest

---

[2] Reports known to me of variations in the belief in reincarnation among Indians all derive from studies of *villagers*. We need information also from *city dwellers*. This might help to show whether differences in understanding the concept of reincarnation and in the belief in it depend on caste differences, education, or socioeconomic status, or on combinations of these factors.

attitude. Not a single villager has ever tried to instruct me in the concept of reincarnation. This does not show a lack of solicitude for me, but rather indifference to reincarnation, at least as a subject for propaganda. In my experience the villagers concerned with a case of the reincarnation type usually accept it pretty much at face value. They may like or dislike some aspects of the subject's statements and behavior and the associated involvement with the family of the previous life he claims to remember. But they are, with rare exceptions, quite detached from the case as an instrument for reinforcing their beliefs or converting others to them. Some villagers have asked me to state my own opinions concerning reincarnation, but never, it seems to me, with any wish to press me into a doctrinal alliance with themselves.

I mentioned above that some Indians of the cities and larger towns who are acquainted with the traditional teachings of Hinduism may show a zealous attachment to Hindu beliefs which villagers rarely express. Fortunately, the education of such persons often helps to make them better observers than the unlettered villagers, and this curtails, without always eliminating, the bias that religious enthusiasm can give to observations and reporting.

On the other hand, some upper class Hindus who have become Westernized (whether or not they have ever left India) tend to depreciate Hinduism in favor of Western materialism (I mean by this term *both* disbelief or skepticism regarding life after death *and* preoccupation with physical comforts and possessions). Although such persons may profess nominal Hinduism, privately (and sometimes publicly) they assert that it no longer has any effective meaning for them. When Indians of this group encounter a case of the reincarnation type, the evidence confronting them often shakes their doubts since it suggests that what they were taught in childhood may make some sense after all. Some of them (and other persons also) have approached the cases that have come to their attention with great resistance. They have sometimes tried to mislead or trick the subject into discrepancies or false statements and recognitions.

Having indicated the widely different beliefs and attitudes concerning reincarnation that one may find in India, I shall now briefly outline the main components of this belief as traditionally taught.

The Concept of Reincarnation in Hinduism

Each person after death is inevitably reborn in some form of terrestrial life, and he continues to be reborn until he succeeds in attaining moksh by appropriate religious practices. He may then become united (strictly, re-united) with God and cease to be reborn on earth.

An enduring soul, or jiva,[3] persists from one life to another and becomes associated with a new physical body in each incarnation. (This belief contrasts with the concept of anatta, or "no soul," taught in Theravada Buddhism.)

The soul may take birth in a physical body of either sex. It may also be reborn under certain circumstances in the physical bodies of subhuman animals. The belief in rebirth of humans in subhuman animal bodies derives from early periods in the history of Brahmanism and Hinduism. For example, in the Chandogya Upanishad we read: "Accordingly, those who are of pleasant conduct here—the prospect is, indeed, that they will enter a pleasant womb, either a womb of a Brahmin, or the womb of a Kshatriya, or the womb of a Vaisya. [All these are upper castes.] But those who are of stinking conduct here—the prospect is, indeed, that they will enter a stinking womb, either the womb of a dog, or the womb of a swine, or the womb of an outcast" (Hume, 1921, p. 232). Another ancient text, the Srimad-Bhagavatam, contains an account of the rebirth of a human as a deer (Sanyal, 1965, 2:187–91).

A variable interval occurs between the death of one physical body and the soul's next terrestrial incarnation. The discarnate soul passes this period in a subtle form, inhabiting one of a number of possible realms. Existence in these places is more or less pleasurable, and assignment occurs according to the merits of preceding earthly lives.

The balance of good and bad deeds determines the conditions and circumstances of the next incarnation. Hindus use the word *karma* in referring to these connections. The word literally means (in English) "action" or "doing," but has become more narrowly applied to actions whose effects are delayed until later in the same life or another one. One can find many statements of the belief in karma in Indian scriptures. For example, the Srimad-Bhagavatam states: "Renouncing the body on this earth by which actions are performed, a creature assumes another birth in the next life and in that new life he feels the consequences of the actions performed by him in his previous life" (Sanyal, 1965, 2:149).

The concept of karma requires some further consideration. The Hindu teaching on this subject does not require that a person receive the penalties or rewards for his conduct in the present or immediately following life. The conditions and circumstances of a particular life may derive from actions committed by the person in some life that occurred long before the one immediately preceding his present life. This codicil provides an explanation for those cases in which the subject is born in poverty but remembers the previous life of a person of virtuous character who lived,

---

[3] The word *jiva* corresponds to the English word *personality* and denotes the Self in association with the physical body. The atman is the eternal Self identical with Brahma (God). For a discussion of the identity of atman with Brahma, see Hume (1921, pp. 29–30).

according to his memories, just before the subject's present life. It is, however, both irrefutable and insupportable, at least by any present evidence, and thus has little interest for empirical science.

Some Western writers have seen in the doctrine of karma a fatalism that justifies apathy and sloth. The economic backwardness of India seems to them at least partly derived from a tendency toward passivity that the doctrine of karma may encourage. I think this is a wrong interpretation, certainly as a general rule. Karma may indeed provide a rationalization for inactivity as for many other deficiencies. (One can think of worse crimes justified by appeals to other religious beliefs.) But we should not mistake an ignorant or hypocritical excuse using a distorted concept for the original idea. Radhakrishnan (1937) stated the distinction in this instance clearly: "We cannot confuse belief in karma with an easy-going fatalism. It is the very opposite of fatalism. It deletes chance for it says that even the smallest happening has its cause in the past and its result in the future. It does not accept the theory of predetermination or the idea of an overruling providence" (p. 284).

The last moments of life before death indicate the nature of the next terrestrial life. One sometimes hears (or reads) this belief stated as if the last thoughts of one life *determine* the next life, and some Hindus behave when dying, or when with dying persons, as if this were so (Prabhavananda and Isherwood, 1944, pp. 97–101; Sanyal, 1965, 2:140); for an incident in a modern case illustrating this belief, see the account of the death of Seth Sri Krishna, p. 113 below). But this idea seems to me only a shallow interpretation of the belief that a man's thoughts both express and form his character. The dominant thoughts of a man's life often come into consciousness prominently at the moment of his death. They then indicate what his character has been and therefore what it may be in another incarnation. Such last thoughts before dying would not have come to the surface of the dying person's mind if longstanding habits had not already made him likely to think them. The distinction I am making here has a bearing on empirical evidence relevant to the question of karma, to which I shall return in a later section.

Although Hinduism does not enjoin anyone from wishing to be reborn under improved conditions in the next life, in fact not many Hindus seem to express such wishes. Few have been reported to me; perhaps more are uttered privately or held silently. But, if so, the mere fact of their covertness contrasts with the frequent and often quite open expression of wishes and plans for the next life that one can hear among the Tlingits of Alaska (Stevenson, 1966). The Tlingits often freely declare their wish to be free of a stutter, no longer to have flat feet, to have blond hair, and so on. Perhaps the persuasive belief in karma based on deeds and misdeeds as the sole determiner of the next life—to be sure, modifiable by other deeds—has led

Hindus to disbelieve in the efficacy of mere wishing. To this the Tlingits might reply that without some initial desire for self-improvement, and a corresponding belief in its possibility, there would be no energizing endeavor that could bring this about—no matter if this self-improvement is a later effect of benevolent actions or a more direct effect of wishes themselves.[4]

Jainism

Since one of the cases presented in this volume (that of Rajul Shah) occurred in a Jain family, it is necessary to say something about Jainism, particularly with regard to the Jains' belief in reincarnation (Glasenapp, 1933, 1964; Guérinot, 1926; Guseva, 1971; Jaini, 1940; Schubring, 1935; Stevenson, M., 1910, 1915).

Jainism has a history as ancient as that of Hinduism. It certainly arose long before the development of modern Hinduism, and, like Buddhism, seems to have developed within ancient Brahmanism as a reform movement in opposition to some of the corrupt doctrines and practices that had arisen among the Brahmins (Smart, 1964). The founder of "modern" Jainism was Mahavira, who lived in the sixth century B.C. and was a contemporary of Gautama Buddha (Nagrajji, 1970). However, Mahavira was himself the last (twenty-fourth) in a long line of saints (tirthankaras) who are said to have taught doctrines similar to those of Mahavira. Of these predecessors, only Parsva Natha, the one immediately before Mahavira, seems to have been a historical personage.

Jainism never spread outside India, as Buddhism did, but neither was it crushed inside India, as Buddhism was. It has persisted to the present day; in 1961 the religion had about two million members.[5] The influence of its adherents on Indian affairs far exceeds what we should expect from their small proportion of the Indian population. This derives first from the great wealth accumulated by Jains, who have mostly engaged in business, but also and perhaps no less from their generally high moral conduct. According to Jaini (1940, p. 73), the crime rate among Jains was, at the time of his writing, remarkably lower than that among Hindus, Mohammedans, and Christians in India.

The Jain religion has many features in common with Hinduism. It teaches reincarnation and also the doctrine of karma, although Jain ideas on

---

[4] Readers interested in learning about the ideas of other peoples who believe in reincarnation, but without a concept corresponding to karma, may find further information in the chapters introducing the cases of other countries in the later volumes of this series and also in Stevenson (1974b).

[5] *The Gazetteer of India* (1973. Delhi: Ministry of Information and Broadcasting) records the total population of Jains in India in 1961 as 2,027,281.

karma differ in some respects from those of Hinduism. For example, Jains disregard the intention of an act as influencing its effects. Thus accidentally stepping on an insect earns as much demerit (or almost as much) as pulling off its legs one by one with enjoyment. This belief leads Jains to support with fervor the practice of ahimsa (nonviolence). They are all strict vegetarians. Certain legalistic extremes in adherence to this doctrine should not detract from its extraordinary moral power. Jainism emphasizes positive good in, for example, service to others; its moral precepts begin but do not end with the concept of ahimsa. Stevenson (1915) referred to Jainism as "one of the most emphatic protests the world has ever known against accounting luxury, wealth, or comfort the main things in life" (p. 22). Also like Hindus, Jains believe that man is destined for continual rebirth until he attains moksh and union with God.[6] Jains believe in reincarnation in the bodies of subhuman animals.

Jains are divided into two main sects, the Svetambara and the Digambara. These developed around the issue of nudity as a device of asceticism and hence of salvation. Subsequently, other differences arose between the two groups—in particular, concerning the authenticity of the Jain canon. Although respecting the intense importance attached to sectarian differences by those directly involved in them, I do not think that those of Jainism have any bearing on our study of reincarnation cases among them; some relevance may appear later.

For the purposes of the present work the most important difference between the concepts of Jainism and those of Hinduism concerns the period between a person's death and his rebirth. The Jains believe that the soul cannot exist independently of a physical body until it has become completely purified and has attained moksh (Guérinot, 1926, p. 159; Jaini, 1940, p. xxiii; Radhakrishnan, 1923, 1:321). They believe that, at the very instant of death, a discarnate soul immediately attaches itself to a new physical body just conceived (Glasenapp, 1964, p. 174; Schubring, 1935, pp. 124–25). This body will then be born after the usual period of gestation, nine months (more or less). This belief of the Jains somewhat resembles that of the Druses; but the members of the two religions have different ideas about the occasion when the freshly discarnate soul becomes linked with a new physical body. The Druses believe that the soul of a deceased person becomes attached to a new physical body at the time of its birth, whereas the Jains think of the new connection as occurring *at the moment of conception.*

---

[6] Opinions differ as to whether or not Jains believe in God. Smart (1964) described Jainism as atheistic. Since Jains do not believe in a creator (or intervening) God of the kind envisaged in Hinduism and Christianity, it may be better to consider them nontheistic. Jaini (1940) equated the concept of God "to the highest ideal man can think of." Jains believe that men can perfect themselves and that a certain small number (their tirthankaras) have done so and become gods or nearly so. These, however, are not the same as a supreme God.

The Jain case (Rajul Shah) presented in this volume illustrates, and in a sense vindicates, the Jains' expectation that a subject with memories of a previous life should be born about nine months after the death of the previous personality. I have only studied two other Jain cases. In both of these the interval between the death of the previous personality and the birth of the subject was considerably longer than nine months. In such cases the Jains would hold, as do the Druses, that an "intermediate" physical life—as an infant, for example—must have occurred, but that this brief life, with no memorable content, did not figure in the subject's memories.

Characteristics of Reincarnation Cases in India

I have now under study more than 150 cases of the reincarnation type in India. But, of these, only 105 have so far been sufficiently well investigated (either by myself or by persons in whom I have confidence) to justify inclusion in an analysis of the characteristics of Indian cases. I have published elsewhere (Stevenson *et al.*, 1974) some preliminary results of this analysis and will merely summarize some of the main features of the cases here.

The cases are reported much more frequently in northern India than in southern India. I have information about only one case occurring south of a line between Bombay in Maharashtra and Visakhapatnam in Andhra Pradesh. I do not understand the reasons for this difference. It is, I must emphasize, one of *reported* cases. We have no knowledge whatever of the real incidence of these cases and will not have until we engage in systematic surveys of entire villages and mohallas (quarters of towns and cities) in different parts of India. Among probable causes of the difference in the incidence of reported cases in northern and southern India, variations in the belief in reincarnation are, I think, almost certainly *not* important. The people of southern India believe in reincarnation just as strongly as those of northern India. The newspapers of northern India seem to have shown more interest in publishing reports of cases than those of southern India.[7] I have myself worked much more in northern India than in southern India, and colleagues in the north have actively looked there for cases to investigate. These circumstances may have contributed to the markedly higher incidence of reported cases in northern India.

---

[7] In a personal communication, Dr. B. K. Kanthamani (1973), a native of southern India, assured me that in her opinion cases of the reincarnation type occur as frequently in southern India as in northern India. She attributed the difference in the incidence of reported cases mainly to differences in the methods of news-gathering used by the newspapers of the two regions. The northern newspapers have numerous local correspondents who can submit accounts of various events to central offices. The regional language newspapers of southern India do not have so many correspondents in small communities. I hope that further investigations will confirm or modify this interpretation.

In the 105 cases under review here, 60 have a male as subject and 45 a female. In 6 of the cases the subject remembered a previous life as a member of the opposite sex.

The cases occurred among members of most castes and of all socio-economic classes. That so many of them occur in villages is, I think, simply due to the fact that most Indians still live in villages. More precise information on the actual distribution of cases among different social and geographic groups could emerge from a systematic survey that I hope to undertake with my colleagues.

Hindus are endogamous within castes but exogamous with regard to gotras (lineages outside the immediate family but within the caste). Marriages are usually arranged between members of the same caste but of different gotras living in separate villages. The geographical area within which brides are sought varies with the wealth and opportunities of the families concerned. It seems likely that the practice of village exogamy has a bearing on the location of the homes of subjects and related previous personalities in the reincarnation type cases. The two families concerned nearly always live in separate villages or communities. But here again we suffer from extremely imperfect knowledge because of the essentially haphazard ways in which information about cases has been communicated. During my first visits to India I thought that subject and previous personality only rarely belonged to the same family. This contrasted markedly with the data from studies of the Tlingits of Alaska, among whom most of the subjects and related previous personalities are members of the same family, usually connected on the mother's side (Stevenson, 1966). However, my more recent experiences in India have made me revise this opinion. Some members of families with whom I have become friendly through the study of one case have felt trustful enough to tell me about other cases in the same families. These other cases had received no publicity in newspapers but had been quietly observed by the family members themselves. And in many of these "private cases" the previous personality related to the subject was a member of the same family—for example, a deceased grandparent, uncle, or aunt.

Although, as I mentioned earlier, Hindus believe that the soul sojourns in another plane of existence for a varying interval before reincarnating, few Indian subjects of these cases have anything to say about life during this "intermission period." A small number of subjects have, however, given reports of experiences occurring to them after death and before birth, and which they claim to remember after their presumed rebirths. Some, for example, claim to recall the cremations of their previous physical bodies and others, how they were directed to the home of the new birth. (See the report of the case of Jasbir in Stevenson, 1974a). Some report memories of visits to paradisal scenes and meetings there with sages or even with the gods of the Hindu pantheon. The majority of the subjects, however, claim no memories whatever of the "intermission period," and those who do often provide only scanty fragments about the experiences they claim to remember. (One hears much more detailed accounts of events claimed to be remembered between death and presumed rebirth from subjects in Burma and Thailand.)

A small number of Indian subjects, such as Swarnlata Mishra and Parmod Sharma (Stevenson, 1974a), claim to remember more than one previous life. And an equally small number recall a former life in which the previous personality himself remembered a life preceding his, although the subject does not remember that earlier life. The case of Bishen Chand Kapoor in this volume provides an example of this.

Cases of the reincarnation type seem to have a circular relationship with the belief in reincarnation. The belief permits the cases to come to expression since, when parents believe in reincarnation, they will nearly always allow a child claiming to have memories to talk about them. And the existence of the cases, whatever their ultimate correct interpretation, seems to provide strong support for the belief. Certainly the people concerned in a case usually believe that it does. But we should not therefore make the mistake of supposing that there is nothing more to be learned about the connections between belief and cases. Nothing demonstrates our ignorance of this subject more clearly than the durability in Southeast Asia of the belief in rebirth in subhuman animals and the almost total lack of evidence for it. Although nearly all Hindus with whom I have discussed this question believe firmly in the possibility, and indeed in the actuality, of reincarnation in subhuman animal bodies, only very rarely has one expressed to me an actual claim to remember a previous life as a subhuman animal. And even more rarely has anyone given me anything that I (or he) could consider evidence for the pretension. Given the nature of things, evidence supporting the idea of reincarnation in subhuman animal bodies would be hard to obtain. Even its most earnest exponents admit this. I find it puzzling, however, that the belief should have persisted so strongly in the complete absence of any sustaining data. The extreme paucity of claims to memories of lives as subhuman animals has the effect on me of weakening the idea that the subjects who remember previous lives as humans are simply engaging in fantasies. One would suppose that Indian children have just as much encouragement from the cultural influences working on them to claim to remember lives as subhuman animals as to remember lives as humans, and yet claims of memories of previous lives as subhuman animals occur with extreme rarity.[8] (For reasons that I am far from understanding,

---

[8] I do not think it likely that shame about an animal life has led to suppression of accounts of such lives if they seem to be remembered. Although within the Hindu system of beliefs an animal life results from previous misconduct as a human, a human remembering an animal life could always say that, having behaved well as an animal, he had earned restoration to human status.

claims to remember previous lives as subhuman animals occur much more commonly in Burma and Thailand, both Buddhist countries, than in India.)

I now return with some trepidation to the difficult subject of karma, the idea that one's conduct in one life influences the circumstances of a later one. This concept provides an attractive theodicy that seems to dissolve the apparent injustice we can all see in the unequal conditions of different persons at birth. Unfortunately for those who endorse the belief, it receives little support from the cases I have studied.

Looked at superficially, these cases may seem to invite the interpretation of karma. They often show wide differences between the socioeconomic circumstances (including the castes) of the subject and the related previous personality. A child born in a peasant's family may claim to remember the life of a rich man, and, conversely, a child of prosperous, educated parents may make statements about the life of a low caste person such as a Sweeper. For anyone who thinks these cases best interpreted as instances of reincarnation, the frequent socioeconomic differences between the two related personalities of a case are enough to humble the arrogant rich and to enhearten the downtrodden poor. And in addition to these vicissitudes of material fortune, we must consider the often drastic differences in emotional circumstances of the two related lives. As experienced by some of the subjects of these cases, a happily married man in his prime suddenly finds himself a helpless infant in the hands of negligent parents; or conversely, a man escapes by death from a termagant wife into the welcoming breasts of a new and doting mother. One is tempted to paraphrase Solon and say: "Call no man happy before his many deaths." But all these observations of differences between the circumstances of the two personalities do not mean that we can interpret them as due to the workings of retributive karma. They may well have this origin, but I have found almost nothing in the way of data to support this idea in the cases I have investigated. In this volume the case of Bishen Chand Kapoor seems at first glance an excellent example of retributive karma because he remembered (with verified details) a previous life as a rich young man who murdered a rival lover. And he was born into a poor family and has remained relatively poor all his life. He himself interpreted the difference in circumstances between the two lives as due to his misconduct in the previous life he remembered. His conclusion that he was born into a poor family in order to expiate the crime of Laxmi Narain (the previous personality whose life he remembered) has social value to the extent that it contributed to the reform of his own character; but it counts for little as evidence of the correctness of his conclusion or the existence of a process of retributive karma. He may have merely repeated the conventional formula by which Indians who know about the Hindu doctrines of reincarnation and karma try to explain the circumstances of their lives. Moreover, against the case of Bishen Chand Kapoor we can set many others in which the subjects remember previous lives as persons no less reprehensible than Laxmi Narain and yet were born into circumstances as good as those of the previous lives they remembered, or better. When I discuss these observations with intelligent Hindus, they tell me that in such cases the person concerned had performed good actions in *earlier* lives and that these outweighed the demerits of the misconduct in the life immediately preceding the present one. Such arguments, as I mentioned earlier, are unanswerable, but equally difficult to support with evidence.

In looking at the differences between the circumstances of the subject's life and those of the life of the related previous personality, one's attention can become harmfully fixed on the visible details of social and economic disparities. The easiest features to see may not be the most important ones. A person who seems to be "demoted" in economic circumstances from one life to another may thereby gain advantages that more than compensate for what he has lost. The poor man does not have the responsibilities and temptations to corruption that beset the rich one. In India millionaires are not appreciated just because of their wealth, as they often are in the West. Wealthy persons in India usually feel guilty about being rich and are aware that their possessions may hinder their spiritual progress.

We may eventually learn to penetrate these mysteries, and I hope that the investigators of the next century will study them with success. We could take a small step in this direction by abandoning the word *karma* or at least by trying to separate and specify the several processes that may be subsumed and confused by careless use of the word. I referred above to retributive karma, the idea of some kind of justice-dispensing process that guides a discarnate person to the conditions and circumstances of the next life according to the summed accounts of his good and evil actions. But it is quite possible to conceive of reincarnation without retributive karma, as do such groups as the Druses and the West Africans.[9] It is, however, difficult to think of reincarnation without at the same time imagining some continuity of personality between the previous personality that died and its related "successor" in the next life. Hindus allow for this also by pointing out that we make our character by our actions and that we carry that character over to our later lives. This idea also goes back at least as far as the Upanishads, where we can read: "One becomes good by good action, bad by bad action" (Hume, 1921, p. 112). If we now turn again to the data of the cases, we find abundant evidence of correspondences between the behavior of the subject and that of the related previous personality. And if we interpret cases in which such correspondences occur as instances of reincarnation, then they provide us with a basis for what we might call developmental

[9] For a summary of the Druse belief in reincarnation, see Stevenson (1974a). For information about the West African belief in reincarnation and further references, see the articles by Parrinder (1956) and Stevenson (1974b).

karma, by which I mean the tendency for habits of conduct to become fixed and to continue with the additional concept that, if we survive death and reincarnate, we shall find ourselves in the next life with the same habits that we developed in this one. I am assuming here under the word *habits* not only such superficial details as the way we dress or the manner in which we hold a knife and fork, but the whole range of our attitudes and emotions —our loves and our hates, our fears and our hopes—and also all our talents and skills; in short, most of the ingredients of what we call our personality.

Despite the scantiness of evidence bearing on the question of karma, this concept sometimes enters into the observation and reporting of the cases. Since Hindus do believe in retributive karma (whatever truth there is in the idea), their opinions about it may influence attitudes toward particular cases. Consider again, for example, those cases in which we find a marked difference in socioeconomic (or caste) circumstances between the subject and the related previous personality. If a subject born into a poor family remembers a previous life as a wealthy person, this suggests a "demotion" due to misconduct in a previous life, and both families may therefore wish to avoid publicity for the case. Two cases, one in India and one in Sri Lanka, in which subjects of very low caste were said to remember previous lives as unusually prominent persons have been suppressed and closed for investigation. I believe this happened because the families concerned could not bear public disclosure of the fact, as it seemed to them, that one of their high station had become déclassé. (In one of these cases—in which the subject was a Buddhist and the previous personality a Christian—religious biases also contributed to the extinction of the case.) Conversely, if a subject born in a wealthy, upper class family remembers a previous life as a poor person, both families may say he deserved a "promotion" and there may be associated pride in his achievement on the part of all concerned. Other considerations, however, may far outweigh such attitudes derived from judgments about karma. For example, although a wealthy family may admit that a child of a poor family has earned a "promotion" into its circle by meritorious conduct in a previous life, they may nevertheless find association with the low class family of the child's remembered previous life embarrassing and repugnant. Or, if the subject's family is poor and the previous personality's family wealthy, the latter may fear that the subject's family will make claims on them for financial support. (In this volume see the case of Sunil Dutt Saxena for an example of such conjectures—quite unjustified in that case—as a reason for rejecting the case.) Thus judgments about karma certainly sometimes enter into the attitudes adopted toward a case; but since many other factors are also influential, I have found it impossible so far to predict when considerations about karma may prove weighty enough to bias the observations and reporting by the informants.

"Announcing dreams" and birthmarks occur in the reincarnation cases of

India, but both happen less frequently there than in the cases of some other cultures—for example, those of the Tlingits of Alaska, the Burmese, and the Alevis of Turkey.[10] The lower incidence of birthmarks among Indian cases cannot be accounted for only on the basis of the somewhat less frequent occurrence of violent death among the related previous personalities in India as compared with its occurrence in the cases of these other cultures. The incidence of violent death in the previous personalities of Indian cases (46.2 per cent) is not far below that in other cultures (Stevenson, 1974b).

References

Carstairs, M. 1957. *The twice-born*. London: The Hogarth Press.

Cohn, B. S. 1959. Changing traditions of a low caste. In *Traditional India: Structure and change,* ed. M. Singer. Philadelphia: American Folklore Society, pp. 207–15.

Dube, S. C. 1955. *Indian village*. Ithaca, N.Y.: Cornell University Press.

Elder, J. W. 1959. *Industrialism in Hindu society: A case study in social change*. Unpublished dissertation. Harvard University.

Glasenapp, H. von. 1933. *Unsterblichkeit und Erlösung in den indischen Religionen*. Halle: Max Niemeyer Verlag.

    1964. *Der Jainismus: Eine indische Erlösungsreligion*. Hildesheim: Georg Olms Verlagsbuchhandlung.

Guérinot, A. 1926. *La religion Djaïna*. Paris: Paul Geuthner.

Guseva, N. R. 1971. *Jainism*. Trans. Y. S. Redkar. Bombay: Sindhu Publications, Ltd.

Harper, E. B. 1959. A Hindu village pantheon. *Southwestern Journal of Anthropology* 15:219–26.

Hume, R. E. Trans. 1921. *The thirteen principal Upanishads*. 2d ed. rev. London and New York: Oxford University Press.

Jaini, J. 1940. *Outlines of Jainism*. Cambridge, England: Cambridge University Press.

Kanthamani, B. K. 1973. Personal communication.

Kolenda, P. M. 1964. Religious anxiety and Hindu fate. In *Religion in South Asia,* ed. E. B. Harper, Seattle: University of Washington Press, pp. 71–81.

---

[10] I use the expression *announcing dream* to refer to a dream experienced by a pregnant woman, and sometimes by one of her close relatives or friends, in which, as it seems to the dreamer, a deceased person communicates his wish or intention to be reborn as the baby of the pregnant woman. For examples of such announcing dreams see my article summarizing the cases among the Tlingits of Alaska (Stevenson, 1966). The reports of several Turkish cases in the third volume of this series will include some additional examples.

Lewis, O. 1958. *Village life in northern India*. Urbana: University of Illinois Press.

Nagrajji, Muni Sri. 1970. *The contemporaneity and the chronology of Mahavira and Buddha*. Trans. Muni Mahendra Kumarji. New Delhi: Today and To-morrow's Book Agency.

Opler, M. E. 1959. The place of religion in a north Indian village. *Southwestern Journal of Anthropology* 15:227–34.

Parrinder, E. G. 1956. Varieties of belief in reincarnation. *Hibbert Journal* 55: 260–67.

Prabhavananda, Swami, and Isherwood, C. Trans. 1944. *Bhagavad-Gita: The song of God*. Hollywood: The Marcel Rodd Co.

Radhakrishnan, S. 1923. *Indian philosophy*. London: George Allen and Unwin, Ltd. 2 vols.

1937. Hinduism. In *The legacy of India*, ed. G. T. Garratt. London and New York: Oxford University Press. pp. 256–86.

Sanyal, J. M. Trans. 1965. *The Srimad-Bhagavatam*. Calcutta: Oriental Publishing Co. 5 vols.

Schopenhauer, A. 1908. *Die Welt als Wille und Vorstellung*. 2 vols. Leipzig: F. U. Brockhaus.

Schubring. W. 1935. *Die Lehre der Jainas nach den alten Quellen dargestellt*. Berlin: W. de Gruyter and Co. (English edition. Trans. W. Beurlen. 1962. *The doctrine of the Jainas*. Delhi: Motilal Banarsidass).

Smart, N. 1964. *Doctrine and argument in Indian philosophy*. London: George Allen and Unwin.

Stevenson, I. 1966. Cultural patterns in cases suggestive of reincarnation among the Tlingit Indians of southeastern Alaska. *Journal of the American Society for Psychical Research* 60:229–43.

1974a. *Twenty cases suggestive of reincarnation*. 2d ed. Charlottesville: University Press of Virginia. (First published in 1966 as *Proceedings of the American Society for Psychical Research* 26:1–362.)

1974b. Some questions related to cases of the reincarnation type. *Journal of the American Society for Psychical Research* 68:395–416.

Stevenson, I., Prasad, J., Mehrotra, L. P., and Rawat, K. S. 1974. The study of cases of the reincarnation type in India. *Contributions to Asian Studies* 5:36–49.

Stevenson, M. 1910. *Notes on modern Jainism*. Oxford: B. H. Blackwell.

1915. *The heart of Jainism*. London and New York: Oxford University Press.

The Case of Gopal Gupta

Summary of the Case and Its Investigation

GOPAL GUPTA was born in Delhi on August 26, 1956, the son of S. P. Gupta and his wife, Omvati Gupta. Gopal is the older child and only son of the family; he has a younger sister. At the time this case developed, S. P. Gupta was employed as manager of a filling station (petrol pump) in Delhi. Subsequently he opened his own business as a supplier of machinery parts.

Gopal's family noticed nothing unusual about his infancy except that he seemed to be somewhat late in speaking. His mother said that he began speaking at the age of between two and two and a half years.

The first indication that Gopal seemed to remember a previous life occurred not long after he had begun to speak. One day the family had a guest. Gopal gave the guest some water in a glass, but when someone asked him to remove the used glass Gopal startled everyone by saying: "I won't pick it up. I am a Sharma." [1] He then had a temper tantrum and broke several glasses. When asked to explain his rude behavior, Gopal said that he came from Mathura, where he had another father and two brothers, one of whom had shot him. He mentioned other details, including that he had quarreled with his wife and owned a company that had to do with medicines. He gave the company's name, Sukh Shancharak. He said that he had a large house and emphasized that he had many servants to carry away dishes and utensils. Gopal gave out all or almost all of this information on the evening of his first outbreak of anger over being asked to remove a used glass. His mother did not wish the matter gone into further, and his father seems at first to have been more or less indifferent to Gopal's statements.

Nevertheless, Gopal's father talked about his son's statements with some of his friends and with his employer, Mohan Lal Raizada, at the gasoline station where he worked. Sri Raizada remembered somewhat vaguely the shooting some years earlier of a businessman connected with the Sukh Shancharak Company in Mathura that seemed to correspond with Gopal's statements. Gopal's father also talked about his statements with Jwala

---

[1] Sharmas are a subcaste of Brahmins. The Guptas are of a lower caste, Banias.

Prasad, a building contractor who was constructing a house at that time for the Guptas. With the approval of Gopal's father, Jwala Prasad questioned Gopal extensively in 1963[2] about his memories of a previous life. Gopal's father was urged to verify more precisely what the child was saying. Gopal himself asked once or twice to go to Mathura, but showed no strong desire to do so.

The following year, in 1964, S. P. Gupta went to Mathura with his sister to celebrate a religious festival.[3] While in Mathura, but apparently not before going there, he remembered the possibility of verifying his son's remarks, and with the information Gopal had given he found the Sukh Shancharak Company that manufactured medicines. He sought out the company's sales manager, K. B. Pathak, and told him what Gopal had been saying, including some of the names and events he had mentioned. K. B. Pathak was rather impressed by the degree of similarity between Gopal's statements and events in the life and death of his former employer, Shaktipal Sharma. The latter had been one of three Sharma brothers who had worked together in the company. Shaktipal had been shot by his younger brother, Brijendrapal, on May 24, 1948. He died three days later, on May 27, 1948.[4]

Somewhat reluctantly S. P. Gupta gave his name and address to K. B. Pathak, who passed it on to the widow of Shaktipal Sharma. S. P. Gupta's visit aroused the Sharma family's curiosity, and they asked a friend in Delhi, Chaman Lal Kapoor, to make further inquiries there about what Gopal was saying. The first written document in the case consists of a letter written from Delhi by Chaman Lal Kapoor on November 15, 1964, to K. B. Pathak in Mathura. This letter briefly confirmed the report of what Gopal had been saying and mentioned some of the details of his statements. Gopal was then more than eight years of age.[5]

Following this report, Subhadra Devi Sharma, the widow of the murdered man, his sister, and the sister's son came to Delhi, where Gopal recognized them under circumstances described in Table 2. Subhadra Devi Sharma then invited the Guptas to visit her in Mathura. In January 1965, Shaktipal Sharma's older brother, Vishwapal, and his wife, Satyawati, visited Gopal in Delhi, and he recognized them. About this time, one of Shaktipal Sharma's sisters, Chandra Kumari Devi Shastri, visited Gopal, but he did not clearly

---

[2] If this date is correct (as I think it is) and that of Gopal's first speaking about the previous life approximately so, then several years had elapsed between Gopal's first mention of the previous life and the arousal of curiosity about whether Gopal was correct or not in what he was saying about it.

[3] Mathura is an important center in Hinduism, since Krishna was born there and spent at least some of his childhood nearby, at Brindaban.

[4] The date of the shooting was given variously by informants as May 24 and May 25, 1948. I verified myself, in the Registry of Deaths at the Mathura Municipal Board, the date of death of Shaktipal Sharma: May 27, 1948.

[5] The letter incorrectly gave his age as nine. He was, however, in his ninth year.

recognize her. One or two months later she and her husband invited Gopal and his family to the wedding of their son. They accepted, and on that occasion Gopal recognized spontaneously the younger brother, Brijendrapal, who had murdered Shaktipal Sharma. (See item 33, Table 2.) Subhadra Devi Sharma also attended the wedding reception, and she reminded the Guptas of her invitation for them to come to Mathura. They then decided to take Gopal there.

On March 21, 1965,[6] Gopal's parents took him to Mathura in a car. Gopal was at this time almost nine years old. Accompanying them were Jwala Prasad and his wife, and B. B. Das, another friend of S. P. Gupta. At Mathura, Gopal made a number of additional statements and recognitions that further established the correspondences between what he was saying and facts in the life and death of Shaktipal Sharma. Gopal has not returned to Mathura since 1965, and with one exception, no member of the Sharma family living there has visited him since then. He made about three subsequent visits to the homes of Shaktipal Sharma's sisters in Delhi, and then visits between the families in Delhi ceased. Later, Vishwapal Sharma wrote me (in a letter dated March 4, 1974) that he had again visited Gopal and his family in Delhi; but he found them unresponsive to further inquiries on his part, and nothing new concerning the case came out at this meeting.

Gopal's visit to Mathura attracted a considerable crowd and aroused much attention there. Shaktipal Sharma had been a leading figure of the community. In addition to being a prominent businessman, he had been active in civic affairs and at a comparatively young age had been elected chairman of the Municipal Board, a position approximately equivalent to that of mayor in a Western city. So Gopal's claim to be Shaktipal Sharma reborn excited interest in many persons of the city. Newspapers published reports summarizing the case and the visit to Mathura of Gopal and his family. In this way the case came to the attention of Dr. Jamuna Prasad, who then told me about it.

In October 1965, a team led by Dr. Jamuna Prasad interviewed eight informants about the case, including Gopal and his parents (in Delhi) and persons who knew Shaktipal Sharma well (in Mathura). Dr. Jamuna Prasad's team also gathered much information about personality traits reported for both Gopal and Shaktipal Sharma. Dr. Jamuna Prasad has made available to me translations of the notes of the testimony taken in 1965 for the preparation of this report.

In March 1969, in Delhi, I interviewed Gopal, his parents, and the two friends, Jwala Prasad and B. B. Das, who had accompanied them to Mathura. At that time I also obtained some correspondence in Hindi between

[6] This date is fixed most precisely by the short report of the case in the *Northern India Patrika* for March 26, 1965, which mentions that Gopal and his family had gone to Mathura on March 21.

S. P. Gupta and Subhadra Devi Sharma about the case, as well as the previously mentioned short letter by Chaman Lal Kapoor.

In October 1969, I had further interviews with Gopal and his parents
and also with seven relatives, a close friend, and an employee of Shaktipal
Sharma. I interviewed four of these persons in Delhi and the remainder in
Mathura, where I visited the Sukh Shancharak Company, saw the site of
Shaktipal Sharma's murder (on the company's premises), and then went
to his house along the route taken by Gopal and his family when they had
come to Mathura in March 1965.

In 1971 I visited Gopal and his family again to obtain some additional
information about details and to learn about Gopal's later development. I
also interviewed three persons who had, in 1965, made and reported some of
the first verifications of Gopal's statements. These were R. C. Chaturvedi
and his wife, Prabha, and Chaman Lal Kapoor, who was a friend of
K. B. Pathak, the sales manager of the Sukh Shancharak Company in
Mathura. In 1971 I also returned for another visit to Mathura, where I
interviewed Vishwapal Sharma, Shaktipal Sharma's older brother, and his
wife, Satyawati.

In 1973, on two separate visits to Delhi, I had a further meeting with
one of Shaktipal Sharma's sisters and one with Gopal's parents. Gopal himself was out of Delhi on a visit to Chandigarh when I called on his family
in 1973. In October 1974 I went to see him again when I was in Delhi, but
only his father was at home. Gopal and his mother were in Calcutta. I have
not met Gopal, therefore, since 1971.

Persons Interviewed during the Investigation

In Delhi I interviewed:

Gopal Gupta
S. P. Gupta, Gopal's father
Omvati Gupta, Gopal's mother
Jwala Prasad, building contractor and friend of S. P. Gupta
B. B. Das, friend of S. P. Gupta
Chandra Kumari Devi Shastri, Shaktipal Sharma's older sister and wife
   of M. D. Shastri
M. D. Shastri, Chandra Kumari Devi's husband and Shaktipal Sharma's
   brother-in-law
Chandra Kanta Devi Sharma, Shaktipal Sharma's older sister and
   R. S. Sharma's wife
R. S. Sharma, Chandra Kanta Devi's husband and Shaktipal Sharma's
   brother-in-law

Chaman Lal Kapoor, friend of K. B. Pathak (see below)

R. C. Chaturvedi, acquaintance of Chaman Lal Kapoor

Prabha Chaturvedi, R. C. Chaturvedi's wife and distant relative of Shaktipal Sharma

In Mathura I interviewed:

Vishwapal Sharma, Shaktipal Sharma's older brother

Satyawati Sharma, Vishwapal Sharma's wife

Kirtipal Sharma, Shaktipal Sharma's oldest son

Subhadra Devi Sharma, Shaktipal Sharma's widow

Asha Sharma, Shaktipal Sharma's niece by marriage

K. B. Pathak, sales manager of the Sukh Shancharak Company

R. A. Haryana, friend of Shaktipal Sharma

In addition to the above, in Mathura K. S. Rawat interviewed R. D. Shastri, an Ayurvedic physician and friend of Shaktipal Sharma. This interview occurred in 1965, and I have used a translation of notes of it furnished to me by Mr. Rawat. R. D. Shastri was not a firsthand informant for any statement or recognition made by Gopal; his main contribution to the case consisted of his testimony concerning the total lack of prior acquaintance between the two families.

Mohan Lal Raizada (S. P. Gupta's former employer and the first person to link Gopal's statements with the murder of Shaktipal Sharma in Mathura) would have been an important witness in the case, but he died in (about) 1965.

Gopal's parents speak no English, and this was also true of the majority of the other informants. However, several informants for the Sharma family are well-educated people, and they speak English fluently. Among these persons, I particularly include Dr. Vishwapal Sharma, Shaktipal Sharma's older brother, and Dr. R. S. Sharma, Shaktipal Sharma's brother-in-law, both of whom are physicians.

*Relevant Facts of Geography and Possibilities for Normal Means
of Communication between the Two Families*

Mathura is a large city (population: approximately 250,000) in Uttar Pradesh, about 160 kilometers south of Delhi and 60 kilometers from Agra. Being a religious pilgrimage center, it is often visited by people from Delhi.

S. P. Gupta said that he had never been to Mathura before the occasion in 1964 when he went there and, just incidentally, tried to verify Gopal's statements. B. B. Das, who accompanied the Guptas when they took Gopal to Mathura (in March 1965), said he had never previously visited Mathura; and Jwala Prasad, who also accompanied them, said that although he had been to Mathura, he did not know the section of the city where Shaktipal Sharma's business and house were situated. Gopal's mother, Omvati Gupta, had never been to Mathura before the occasion of taking Gopal there in March 1965. S. P. Gupta denied that his family had had any previous acquaintance with the Sharma family before the development of the case.

The geographical separation of the two cities where the families lived greatly reduced the likelihood of their meeting and becoming acquainted with each other's affairs. The pilgrims going from Delhi to Mathura or nearby Brindaban would ordinarily have little to do with citizens of Mathura except casually, during the course of their stay in Mathura, at hotels, restaurants, and similar public places. Apart from this, there were important differences both of caste and wealth between the two families that would have made it unlikely (although not impossible) that they would have social intercourse of an extent likely to lead to any exchange of information relevant to this case.

It is worth noting also that a period of more than eight years separated the murder of Shaktipal Sharma and the birth of Gopal Gupta, and that more than ten years had elapsed before Gopal began talking of the previous life. Although the shooting of Shaktipal Sharma by his brother was a rather sensational murder because of the prominence in Mathura of the victim, it was largely forgotten after a time except by members of his family. S. P. Gupta denied that he had even read of the murder in the newspapers. My inquiries revealed that the *Statesman* (New Delhi), one of the leading English-language newspapers of India, had not published a report of the murder of Shaktipal Sharma, and it seems unlikely that any other English newspaper had done so. (In any case S. P. Gupta and his wife did not read English.) A Hindi newspaper of New Delhi, *Nav Bharat Times,* did publish a report of the murder; but its files for the years before 1951 were destroyed in a fire of that year, so I could not learn what its report of the murder stated. I am confident, however, that it would not have contained all of the personal details of the life of Shaktipal Sharma that figured in Gopal's statements and recognitions. Shaktipal Sharma was conspicuous enough in Mathura, but a person of little or no renown in Delhi. I suspect that if he had died naturally, his death would not have been noted in the Delhi newspapers.

As already mentioned, Chaman Lal Kapoor, who lived in the same section of Delhi (Krishna Nagar) as the Guptas, had made inquiries on behalf of K. B. Pathak (the sales manager of the Sukh Shancharak Company) about Gopal's statements. Chaman Lal Kapoor, originally from Mathura, had lived in Delhi since 1959. He had some knowledge of the murder of Shaktipal Sharma (which had occurred during his residence in Mathura), but he did not know the Guptas in Krishna Nagar, Delhi. He asked his wife to make inquiries of R. C. Chaturvedi and his wife, Prabha. The latter came from Mathura, and she and her husband lived much nearer to the Guptas in Krishna Nagar than did Chaman Lal Kapoor. Prabha Chaturvedi was a distant relative of Shaktipal Sharma and had been close enough to him to call him uncle. She was quite familiar with the details of the murder of Shaktipal Sharma and even of the family quarrels that had led up to it. She and her husband had lived in Delhi since 1950 and in the Krishna Nagar section since 1962. Although the Chaturvedis lived only two blocks from the Guptas in Krishna Nagar, they had had no previous acquaintance. Nor had they any mutual friends of which the Chaturvedis were aware. Prabha Chaturvedi was quite sure also that she had never talked about Shaktipal Sharma to any neighbors in Krishna Nagar. Since he had died in 1948, more than ten years before Gopal began talking about the previous life, his murder would probably have subsided in the mind of Prabha Chaturvedi by that time; and I think it unlikely to have been a current topic of conversation for her in the 1960s. In addition, she and her husband had not moved into the Krishna Nagar section of Delhi until 1962, several years after Gopal began to talk about the previous life.

Prabha Chaturvedi had heard some rumors in the neighborhood about Gopal's memories of the previous life, but she had made no attempt to look into them until Chaman Lal Kapoor asked her to do so. She then went to the Guptas' home and met Omvati Gupta. (Gopal was not at home that day.) Gopal's mother told Prabha Chaturvedi about some of Gopal's statements, and she knew immediately that they were accurate with regard to the life of Shaktipal Sharma. She relayed this information back to Chaman Lal Kapoor, and he then wrote the confirming letter to K. B. Pathak that I have already mentioned. These three persons seemed reliable witnesses; on the basis of the information from them I do not believe that Prabha Chaturvedi was a conduit for the normal communication to Gopal of the information he had about Shaktipal Sharma and his murder. Proponents of the interpretation of such cases as instances of psychometry may nevertheless find relevant the fact that Prabha Chaturvedi, a person very well informed about the Sharmas of Mathura, lived only two blocks from Gopal Gupta during part of the time he was talking about the previous life.

I asked four members of Shaktipal Sharma's family (his widow, one of his sisters, his brother, and his son) about any contact they may have had with the Gupta family before the development of the case, and all denied that there had been any. Dr. Vishwapal Sharma, Shaktipal's older brother, was particularly emphatic on this matter. He resolutely denied (in a letter to me dated March 4, 1974) that any member of the family had known Gopal or his family before the development of the case. He considered the caste differences between the two families sufficient to preclude any social acquaintance. For many Indians caste differences would outweigh geographical ones in importance.

Since two of Shaktipal Sharma's sisters lived in Delhi after getting married, it is not inconceivable that they had had some contact with S. P. Gupta or his wife. I cannot say that they never bumped into each other in the crowded streets of Delhi. But I am confident that if such contact occurred it was impersonal and that there never existed any social connection between the two families during which Gopal might have learned intimate details of the life and death of Shaktipal Sharma. My assurance on this point derives, first, from the mentioned wide gap in caste and socioeconomic circumstances between the two families and, second, from the improbability that any member of Shaktipal Sharma's family could have passed on all the detailed information Gopal had at the age of two and a half without his parents' being aware of any occasion or occasions when he could have learned such details from one of them. A child of that age in India (and in most other countries) has no opportunity for contact with strangers in the absence of his mother, or at least no such opportunity of which she is unaware.

The Life, Death, and Character of Shaktipal Sharma

Shaktipal Sharma was born in Mathura on December 30, 1913. His father, Kshetrapal Sharma, had established and owned a large pharmaceutical company, the Sukh Shancharak Company, which manufactured Ayurvedic medicines and distributed them widely throughout India. He became a millionaire who could afford to own numerous houses and to give each of his sons an automobile. In the India of the 1930s only a very wealthy man could or would give each of his three sons a car. Like many rich fathers, Kshetrapal Sharma showed a mixture of indulgence and strictness toward his sons.

Shaktipal was the middle of three sons. Vishwapal was the oldest of the three, and Brijendrapal the youngest. There were also two sisters, both older than Shaktipal.

After completing his early education, Shaktipal Sharma attended a college in Mathura and then went on to Agra University, where he obtained a B.A. degree. He led a rather wild life at Agra University, and after one escapade the warden asked him to leave the student hostel. He then moved to private lodgings but continued his former dissolute habits. Later he received an M.A. degree from Nagpur University, but without having been in residence there.

After graduating from Agra University, Shaktipal Sharma married and had a family, but unhappiness clouded his marriage. His wife remained attached to the home and took little interest in public affairs or social life. He, on the other hand, relished these, and in addition to participating in the family business, he engaged in politics. His charm, gregariousness, and ability all helped him in commercial and public life. He achieved a considerable local success and became chairman of the Municipal Board of Mathura (roughly, mayor) when still a young man.

Shaktipal Sharma was an intelligent person with a good memory. He was an able linguist, could speak English, and also knew some Urdu and Sanskrit. He played the piano as a competent amateur. In addition to his main business interest and his political activity, he enjoyed buying and selling property and constructing houses.

At Agra University he had not applied himself diligently and seemed satisfied with rather mediocre scholastic attainments. But he had some ambitions for further education, to which his eventual attainment of an M.A. degree testified. And even later, after he had become fully involved in the business affairs of his family's company, he still wished to continue his education. He started work toward a doctoral degree but then abandoned it. He was also eager to study law and to do so in London, England. When he was about twenty-eight, he began to plan in detail to go to London and train there to become a barrister. His father opposed this project, but Shaktipal continued preparing for it secretly. He even paid a deposit for the courses he hoped to take in London and made arrangements to slip away quietly without telling his father. But just before he was due to leave India, he became ill; during the several months it took him to recover, his father learned of his scheme and canceled it by somehow having his son's passport annulled.

Not long after this episode Shaktipal Sharma's father died (on January 24, 1942), and he found himself one of the heirs of a prosperous business. His father had come to dislike the youngest of his three sons, Brijendrapal, partly on the grounds that he had married a Christian girl. He therefore excluded Brijendrapal from an inherited share in the pharmaceutical manufacturing business and left it exclusively to his other two sons. Shaktipal, however, felt that his younger brother should have a fair portion of the inheritance, and he allowed Brijendrapal to participate. But Brijendrapal seemed always in debt, and he constantly demanded more than his share of the profits. Quarrels between him and his older brothers became more frequent and more intense. The brothers evolved a plan for rotating the office of manager of the company among themselves. The two older brothers then came to believe that Brijendrapal had stolen funds from the company during his term as manager. This suspicion and Brijendrapal's repeated and unreasonable demands for money naturally led to increasing friction.

Inevitably the tension between the brothers reverberated in the domestic life of Shaktipal Sharma. His wife became unwillingly drawn into his disagreements with his younger brother. Since I am presenting this case with the real names of the persons concerned, regard for the feelings of members of the Sharma family inclined me to omit some of the details of these private discords which can contribute little further to the evidence of the case. However, in the interests of a larger truth on which these reports may bear, Vishwapal Sharma generously gave me permission to mention one detail of particular importance, first, because it was an unusually intimate one and, second, because Gopal had memories about it. This was that, in an effort to appease Brijendrapal, Shaktipal had asked his wife to let him have 5,000 rupees. (Wives in India often dispose of considerable sums of money, and it is neither uncommon nor improper for a husband to try to raise money from his wife in an emergency.) Subhadra Devi had refused, and this seems to have exacerbated the quarrel between Brijendrapal and his brothers.[7] Brijendrapal became increasingly hostile, and on May 24, 1948, he came into the Sukh Shancharak Company's office and showroom and, after exchanging angry words with his two older brothers, shot at them. One bullet entered the chest of Shaktipal Sharma. He was taken to the hospital, but the bullet was not retrieved; he died a few days later, in the hospital, on May 27, 1948. Brijendrapal was convicted and sentenced to prison for life. After some years of confinement, he was released on the grounds of being physically ill.

The piebald character of Shaktipal Sharma does not lend itself to facile summary. On the one hand, he behaved extravagantly, like so many spoiled sons of wealthy men; one informant told me that he "spent money like water." But on the other hand, he was generous both to his friends and the poor. Other persons easily exploited his unselfish inclinations. He enjoyed physical pleasures but did not give himself wholly over to them. I have already mentioned his frustrated ambitions toward higher education. And he took seriously his duties with the company he inherited from his father. The people of his community recognized his administrative skills by electing him chairman of the Municipal Board when he was less than thirty-five years old.

Concerning Shaktipal's interest in religion, I obtained different opinions. His widow described him as religious, but other informants thought he had no outstanding interest in religion. He was a vegetarian but not a teetotaler,

---

[7] It appears that to Gopal, later, Subhadra Devi's refusal to give Shaktipal Sharma the 5,000 rupees he asked for seemed a direct precipitant of Shaktipal's murder by his brother. She was naturally embarrassed by Gopal's revelations of this unhappy episode and retracted an early admission of the facts, but later acknowledged their truth. I must say in her defense, first, that although her refusal to give her husband money for Brijendrapal thwarted his efforts to buy off his intransigent brother, we cannot consider this an important cause of a quarrel deep enough to have enraged a man to kill his own brother; and, second, that the subsequent murder in a melancholy way confirmed Subhadra Devi's own judgment concerning the folly of trying to pacify a person like Brijendrapal with advances of money.

and imbibed wine freely although not excessively or indiscreetly. He enjoyed eating fruits, especially oranges, but otherwise his diet contained nothing extraordinary, for India has many vegetarians.

Statements and Recognitions Made by Gopal

In Table 2 I have listed the statements and recognitions attributed to Gopal by the informants of the case. I have omitted a few items for which the information was insufficiently detailed. I have placed all the statements in a group first and then listed the recognitions.

With a few exceptions noted in Table 2, Gopal made all the statements given there before he went to Mathura and also before his father had made (in 1964) the preliminary inquiries there that led to the first meeting between the two families.

Table 2 includes a small number of items for which Gopal himself was (in 1965) the informant—statements he made to members of Dr. Jamuna Prasad's team. These were made after his visit to Mathura.

Item 27 has a special status which deserves comment. It was communicated to me by Vishwapal Sharma (in a letter dated July 29, 1972) and subsequently verified by him (in a letter dated March 4, 1974). It is secondhand testimony, since he was not in Mathura at the time of Gopal's visit there. But he heard about the item from persons in whom he had confidence. These included R. A. Haryana, whom I interviewed, but who did not happen to mention the item to me. The item deals with the rather odd habit Shaktipal Sharma had of keeping financial records in a personal diary. Despite the fact that it rests on secondhand testimony, I consider that its endorsement by Vishwapal Sharma and its unusualness make it one of the more important details of the case.

Gopal made a few recognitions when members of Shaktipal Sharma's family visited him in Delhi. It was there that he first met and recognized Subhadra Devi Sharma, Shaktipal Sharma's widow, and Chandra Kanta Devi Sharma, his older sister. He also recognized in Delhi (in January 1965) Shaktipal Sharma's older brother, Vishwapal, and his wife, Satyawati. Then one or two months later, at the wedding reception for Shaktipal Sharma's nephew, Gopal recognized Brijendrapal Sharma, Shaktipal's younger brother and murderer (item 33). All the other recognitions occurred during Gopal's first and only visit to Mathura, on March 21, 1965.

In Mathura, Gopal showed a remarkable ability to recognize people in photographs, including two of Shaktipal Sharma in which his face could not be seen. Gopal also impressed the informants by his recognition of places in Mathura connected with the life and murder of Shaktipal Sharma. I went over this terrain carefully in 1969 and am satisfied that although

Gopal had, or might have had, some suggestions that could have helped in some of these recognitions, such suggestions would not account for other recognitions such as his correctly finding the house where Shaktipal Sharma lived, a place then quite unknown to his father and the other men accompanying them.

I think it noteworthy that Gopal was almost nine years old at the time he first accomplished all these recognitions. That is an age at which many of the subjects of these cases have already lost all the imaged memories of the previous lives they claim to remember and the ability to make related recognitions.

Gopal failed to recognize a number of persons (and photographs of persons) rather well known to Shaktipal Sharma. He did not recognize two of Shaktipal Sharma's brothers-in-law or one of his sons, Kirtipal Sharma. His recognition of Shaktipal Sharma's sister Chandra Kumari Devi Shastri was doubtful. Nor did he recognize K. B. Pathak, who had been an employee of the Sukh Shancharak Company for four years at the time of Shaktipal Sharma's murder.

Gopal's Memories of Events Occurring after Shaktipal Sharma's Death and before His Birth. After Gopal's visit to Mathura, a newspaper correspondent there wrote a report of the case that many Indian newspapers published. Numerous curious persons came to see Gopal, and some asked, even pressed, him to say where he had been during the eight years between the death of Shaktipal Sharma (1948) and his own birth (1956). In response to this urging, and perhaps only because of it, Gopal began telling about events during this period that he claimed to remember.

Gopal recounted experiences he remembered of life as a discarnate mind on a presumably intermediate plane of existence. He also gave some details of another short terrestrial life as an Indian boy named Sanjiv Kumar who had lived in London, England. The scope and size of this book prevent me from furnishing here the details of these claimed experiences. Suffice it to say, however, that although Gopal gave the names of two streets (one of them rather obscure) that actually exist in London and some other names and details of the life he said he had lived there, I have not been able to trace anyone corresponding to his statements about this "intermediate" life. I shall discuss a possible interpretation of it later.

Two Other Possibly Related Events Occurring after Shaktipal Sharma's Death and before Gopal's Birth

About a year after the death of Shaktipal Sharma (that is, in 1949), his older sister, Chandra Kumari Devi Shastri, dreamed that he told her: "I

TABLE 2. *Summary of Statements and Recognitions Made by Gopal*

Item	Informants	Verification	Comments
1. He was a Sharma.	Omvati Gupta, Gopal's mother S. P. Gupta, Gopal's father	Subhadra Devi Sharma, Shaktipal Sharma's widow	S. P. Gupta said Gopal said: "I am the son of a Sharma."
2. He had servants to remove utensils from the table.	Omvati Gupta	Kirtipal Sharma, Shaktipal Sharma's oldest son	
3. He came from Mathura.	Omvati Gupta S. P. Gupta	Subhadra Devi Sharma	S. P. Gupta said Gopal phrased this: "One of my fathers lives in Mathura."
4. He had a very big house in Mathura.	S. P. Gupta	I visited the large house of Shaktipal Sharma in Mathura in 1969.	This house, near the Sukh Shancharak Company's offices, was one of several owned by the Sharma family. (See also items 8 and 9.)
5. His company was called "Sukh Shancharak."	Omvati Gupta	I visited the Sukh Shancharak Company in Mathura in 1969.	S. P. Gupta in 1969 did not recall that Gopal had mentioned the name of the company, but the letter written by C. L. Kapoor on November 15, 1964 (to K. B. Pathak in Mathura) quotes Omvati Gupta as saying Gopal had mentioned the name of "his" company as "Sukh Shancharak."
6. His company dealt in medicines.	S. P. Gupta	Verified by me in 1969	
7. He had a showroom.	Jwala Prasad, friend of S. P. Gupta	I visited the showroom of the Sukh Shancharak Company in Mathura in 1969.	
8. They had another house outside the town with a garden.	S. P. Gupta	Chandra Kumari Devi Shastri, Shaktipal Sharma's older sister In 1971 I visited this large house with a garden in Mathura. It was formerly on the edge of the city, although	

	Informants	Verification	Comments
		Kirtipal Sharma Chandra Kumari Devi Shastri	within the municipal limits. The city has since grown well beyond it.
9. He had many big houses.	Jwala Prasad		Jwala Prasad said that Gopal had told him before they went to Mathura that he had many big houses. He compared the house Jwala Prasad was building (in 1963) for S. P. Gupta unfavorably with those he said "he" owned. The Sharma family had numerous houses, several of which belonged to Shaktipal Sharma.
10. His father used to recite Sanskrit couplets in a temple.	S. P. Gupta	Partially incorrect	This item belongs to the group recorded in 1965. According to Vishwapal Sharma, Kshetrapal Sharma (his and Shaktipal Sharma's father) knew Sanskrit and would cite Sanskrit couplets in conversation. But he was a member of the Arya Samaj movement of reform in the Hindu religion. He was therefore opposed to temples and would certainly *not* have recited Sanskrit couplets in temples. I suspect that the reference to temples was an addition (based on faulty inference) made by S. P. Gupta to what he heard Gopal say.
11. He had a car.	Jwala Prasad	R. A. Haryana, friend of Shaktipal Sharma Subhadra Devi Sharma	

NOTE: In this and similar tables, the *Informants* column lists the witnesses of what the subject did or said related to the previous life. The *Verification* column lists the informants for information verifying the accuracy of what the subject said or did with regard to the previous personality. In citing recognitions I have usually left the *Verification* column blank, since the person who was the informant for the recognition (nearly always himself a witness of this recognition) either knew that the recognition was correct at the time it occurred or later verified its accuracy. In most instances, I have asked a person who was recognized by the subject about the details of the recognition, including circumstances, other persons present, and whether there were leading questions put or simply requests to name the person to be recognized. I have included information on these matters under *Comments*, in the right-hand column. This column also contains some other information or explanatory material. Unless specifically noted to the contrary, the statements and recognitions made by the subject were verified as being correct or appropriate for the previous personality.

TABLE 2 (cont.)

Item	Informants	Verification	Comments
12. He went to the college in a car.	Jwala Prasad	R. A. Haryana Subhadra Devi Sharma	
13. He received the degree of M.A.	Gopal Gupta (1965) S. P. Gupta	Chandra Kumari Devi Shastri R. S. Sharma, Shaktipal Sharma's brother-in-law Vishwapal Sharma, Shaktipal Sharma's older brother	S. P. Gupta said Gopal said he received the M.A. degree from Agra University. Shaktipal Sharma received a B.A. degree from Agra University but earned an M.A. from Nagpur University.
14. He drank wine on the graduation day.	Gopal Gupta (1965)	Unverified	
15. He shook hands with Dr. Radhakrishnan at Agra University.	S. P. Gupta	Unverified	Dr. S. Radhakrishnan was a well-known Indian philosopher and later vice-president and president of India.
16. They (the drug company) used to give free medicine to poor persons.	Gopal Gupta (1965)	Vishwapal Sharma	
17. He was fond of the piano.	Gopal Gupta (1965)	Kirtipal Sharma	Shaktipal Sharma owned and played a piano.
18. They had a servant named Motu or Kallu.	Gopal Gupta (1965)	Unverified	Shaktipal Sharma had a neighbor in Mathura called Motu, but he was not a servant. The name Kallu was somewhat familiar to Vishwapal Sharma, but he could not definitely identify anyone with that name.
19. His workers were happy because he used to give them wine.	S. P. Gupta	Kirtipal Sharma	
20. He was one of three brothers.	Omvati Gupta S. P. Gupta	Subhadra Devi Sharma	S. P. Gupta said Gopal had given the names of the brothers, but in 1969 he had

forgotten these. K. B. Pathak, in his testimony of 1965, said S. P. Gupta had told him the names Gopal was giving for the brothers when he (Gopal's father) first went to Mathura and made inquiries and attempted verification. The names were not exactly correct, but were similar to the actual names of the brothers.

In her 1965 testimony Omvati Gupta said Gopal had said "he" had three brothers, not two.

Shaktipal Sharma was the middle of three brothers. His younger brother, Brijendrapal, shot him during a quarrel, and he died three days later.

Statement			Comments
21. His younger brother used to drink a lot.	Gopal Gupta (1965) S. P. Gupta	Chandra Kumari Devi Shastri	S. P. Gupta said Gopal had described the younger brother as a drunkard and a debauchee.
22. His younger brother had married a woman from Assam.	Omvati Gupta	Chandra Kumari Devi Shastri R. A. Haryana	
23. His younger brother wanted money for his wife.	Omvati Gupta	Subhadra Devi Sharma	I am not sure that Gopal made this statement before going to Mathura. Subhadra Devi Sharma did not say for what uses Brijendrapal demanded money from his brothers.
24. He asked his wife for some financial assistance, but she refused.	Omvati Gupta S. P. Gupta	Vishwapal Sharma S. P. Gupta	Gopal first mentioned this effort (on the part of Shaktipal Sharma) to borrow money from Subhadra Devi when his father questioned him about why he had been so cool toward Subhadra Devi when she had first come to see him in Delhi. Shaktipal Sharma had wished to obtain money from his wife to give (and appease) his younger brother, but she had resisted giving the money. Her refusal preceded

TABLE 2 (*cont.*)

Item	Informants	Verification	Comments
24. (cont.)			the intensification of the quarrel between the brothers which led to Shaktipal Sharma's murder. S. P. Gupta was a secondhand informant for the verification of this item. He said that when, during the visit to Mathura, he mentioned Gopal's statement about Shaktipal Sharma's request to his wife to give him money, Subhadra Devi had fainted. (Although my notes are not quite clear on this point, Gopal had apparently mentioned the exact sum, 5,000 rupees, that Shaktipal Sharma had asked his wife to give him for his brother.) Later, when she had recovered, Subhadra Devi confirmed to Omvati Gupta (who told S. P. Gupta afterward) that her husband had asked her for 5,000 rupees. Vishwapal Sharma was not present during Gopal's visit to Mathura, but he provided corroborating secondhand testimony of the fact that when Gopal had mentioned trying (as Shaktipal Sharma) to borrow money from Subhadra Devi, she had fainted. Apparently a blend of astonishment at Gopal's remark and chagrin over the revelation of a domestic secret altered the flow of blood to her brain. Vishwapal Sharma also confirmed the acknowledgment by Subhadra Devi of the truth of Gopal's statement, her later attempt to deny it, and her final return to admission of its correctness. (See text for further discussion of this important item.)
25. One of his brothers shot him.	S. P. Gupta Omvati Gupta	Vishwapal Sharma	In his 1965 testimony, S. P. Gupta said Gopal had said one of the brothers had

Claim	Informants	Verification	Comments
		Gopal Gupta (1965)	shot him. But in 1969 he stated that Gopal only said, before he went to Mathura: "There was shooting between the brothers," and not that he himself had been shot. Gopal himself said in 1965 that he had known that it was the *youngest* of the three brothers who had shot him. And this detail was also included in his mother's testimony of 1965. Brijendrapal Sharma, who shot Shaktipal, was in fact the youngest of the three brothers.
26. He was shot in the chest.	R. S. Sharma Kirtipal Sharma Vishwapal Sharma	Omvati Gupta Asha Sharma, Shaktipal Sharma's niece by marriage	Omvati Gupta said Gopal said he had been hit in the *right* side of the chest. S. P. Gupta did not remember that Gopal had said *before* he went to Mathura that he had been shot in the chest. He said that in Mathura Gopal had said he had been shot in the *left* side of the chest. This is also what Asha Sharma heard him say in Mathura. According to R. S. Sharma, Shaktipal Sharma was struck by the bullet in the left chest.
27. He kept a diary in which he also maintained accounts.	Vishwapal Sharma	Vishwapal Sharma	Vishwapal Sharma was a secondhand witness for this item. Gopal mentioned it during his visit to Mathura, and Vishwapal Sharma heard about it from a number of persons who had been present at the time of Gopal's visit, including R. A. Haryana. (It was not, however, included in the items mentioned to me by R. A. Haryana during my interview with him.) Vishwapal Sharma verified the detail to me in a letter dated March 4, 1974, in which he referred to "my absolute personal knowledge that . . . Shaktipal Sharma maintained a private and personal diary of accounts which I had occasion to look in as we were

TABLE 2 (cont.)

Item	Informants	Verification	Comments
27. (cont.)			then running a common business and enjoyed complete confidence of each other." Although the item derives from secondhand testimony, I consider the transmission of it by Vishwapal Sharma to raise its importance almost to the level of firsthand testimony; and because of the unusual and private nature of a diary in which financial and private accounts were also kept, I believe the item one of the more important in the case.
28. Recognition of Chandra Kanta Devi Sharma, Shaktipal Sharma's older sister	S. P. Gupta		This recognition took place at the Gupta home in Krishna Nagar, Delhi. Chandra Kanta Devi Sharma, her son, and her sister-in-law, Subhadra Devi (Shaktipal Sharma's widow), went together to visit Gopal. Chandra Kanta Devi Sharma asked Gopal: "Who am I?" After some reluctance to respond, Gopal pointed to S. P. Gupta's sister and then to his father and said that he (Gopal) had the same relationship with her as S. P. Gupta had with his sister. However, Chandra Kanta Devi Sharma did not notice or remember this statement. (See also comment for next item.)
29. Recognition of Subhadra Devi, Shaktipal Sharma's wife	S. P. Gupta		This item occurred during the same visit as that of the preceding one. Subhadra Devi went to visit Gopal with her sister-in-law, Chandra Kanta Devi Sharma, and the latter's son. When the two women were present at the Gupta house, Gopal would not say who the other woman was. He said goodbye (namaste) to Chandra Kanta Devi Sharma and her son, but would not say goodbye

88

to Subhadra Devi Sharma. During this meeting Chandra Kanta Devi Sharma's son had told S. P. Gupta who Subhadra Devi Sharma was, and Gopal could have overheard this remark, but he did not recognize her at the time.

Later, Gopal's father asked him if she had been his wife, and he replied, "I do not have a wife."

A few days later, when again asked who Subhadra Devi was, he said she was "my wife" and that he was angry with her because she had refused to help him financially when he had requested help. (See also item 24.)

30. Recognition of Chandra Kumari Devi Shastri, Shaktipal Sharma's older sister

Chandra Kumari Devi Shastri

This recognition occurred about a month after the visit to Gopal of Subhadra Devi Sharma and Shaktipal Sharma's younger sister. Chandra Kumari Devi Shastri went to visit Gopal and asked him: "Do you recognize me?" Gopal then said: "Yes. I recognize you. You are my father's sister" (Hindi: bua). Gopal added: "In our family we address our sisters as Bua." But this was incorrect, since Shaktipal Sharma had called his older sister Jiji, a common form of address for an older sister. Shaktipal Sharma did address his father's sister as Bua, and Gopal may have confused this person with Shaktipal Sharma's sister. I consider this recognition quite doubtful.

31. Recognition of Satyawati Sharma, Shaktipal Sharma's sister-in-law

Satyawati Sharma, Vishwapal Sharma's wife and Shaktipal Sharma's sister-in-law

Vishwapal Sharma

This and the following recognition occurred at the same time in January 1965, at the Gupta home in Krishna Nagar, Delhi. Gopal came out to the car where Shaktipal Sharma's brother and sister-in-law were sitting. Gopal went to Shaktipal's

TABLE 2 (*cont.*)

Item	*Informants*	*Verification*	*Comments*
31. (cont.)			sister-in-law first, and she asked him if he could recognize her. He said: "Yes, you are my bhabhi" (English: older brother's wife).
32. Recognition of Vishwapal Sharma, Shaktipal Sharma's older brother	Vishwapal Sharma		After making the remark just quoted in item 31 above, Gopal looked at Vishwapal Sharma and said: "Bhai sahib," which means "older brother" and was the form of address used by Shaktipal Sharma in speaking to Vishwapal Sharma. At the time Gopal made these recognitions, his mother had learned that Vishwapal Sharma and his wife were "from Mathura," but they had not told her anything else about themselves.
33. Recognition of Brijendra-pal Sharma, Shaktipal Sharma's younger brother	S. P. Gupta Vishwapal Sharma		S. P. Gupta, his wife, and Gopal were invited to a wedding reception in Delhi by one of Shaktipal Sharma's sisters. (This was the marriage of the son of M. D. Shastri and his wife, Chandra Kumari Devi, who was Shaktipal Sharma's older sister.) At the reception Gopal made some unintelligible gestures to his father, who, busy talking with other people, paid no attention to him. Afterward, as they were returning home, Gopal said: "Papa, did you see my brother?" S. P. Gupta said he had not, and Gopal replied that he had pointed him out to his father. Then he added: "Papa, he looked like a thief—guilty; and he has grown a beard also." Brijendrapal Sharma did not have a beard during the lifetime of Shaktipal Sharma. Vishwapal Sharma was a secondhand informant for a variant account of this recognition. He said that he and his wife

34. Recognition of way to Sukh Shancharak Company offices from Dwarkadish Temple in Mathura

S. P. Gupta
Jwala Prasad
B. B. Das, friend of S. P. Gupta

also attended this wedding reception and that his wife, Satyawati, overheard Gopal say to his father: "That man who is disguised [referring to Brijendrapal's beard] shot at me."

Gopal led the way, a distance of about 1.5 kilometers, from the temple to the offices and showrooms of the Sukh Shancharak Company (both were in the same building). He was followed by his father, Jwala Prasad, and B. B. Das, who stayed behind him. Gopal's father knew the way and tried to mislead him. Gopal walked ahead confidently and stopped at the building of the Sukh Shancharak Company.

There was, however, a sign at the front of the building, and Gopal's father thought that Gopal, who was then nearly nine years old, might have read the sign. He then asked him to find "his" previous house.

35. Recognition of Shaktipal Sharma's house in Mathura

S. P. Gupta
Jwala Prasad
B. B. Das

Gopal went into one lane and returned. He said: "There is a betel shop in front of my lane." Gopal's father and Gopal himself seem not to have noticed the betel shop, which, as I found myself in 1969, was just beyond and opposite the entrance to the lane leading to Shaktipal Sharma's house. After returning from the wrong lane, Gopal found the correct lane, went up it, and, stopping at a house, said: "Papa, here is my house." Although S. P. Gupta had visited the company building, he did not know where the house was. Nor did anyone else in the group. At this stage of the visit, there was no crowd of local people, and therefore no one to guide Gopal in finding the house.

TABLE 2 (cont.)

Item	Informants	Verification	Comments
36. Recognition of piano belonging to Shaktipal Sharma in Mathura	Omvati Gupta Jwala Prasad B. B. Das		Gopal touched the piano in the house and his mother reproached him. Gopal said: "Why should I not touch it? It belongs to me." He then played a little on it. (See further discussion of this episode in the text.)
37. Recognition of Shaktipal Sharma's bedroom	B. B. Das		Gopal went into one of the rooms of the house and said: "This is my bedroom."
38. Recognition of R. A. Haryana's photograph	Kirtipal Sharma		Gopal first recognized R. A. Haryana in a photograph. Someone asked Gopal: "Who is he?" and he replied: "Haryana."
39. Recognition of R. A. Haryana	Kirtipal Sharma		Later, R. A. Haryana came to meet Gopal and as he entered the room someone said: "Who is this man?" Gopal said again: "Haryana." This recognition has less value than the preceding one since he had shortly before seen the photograph mentioned in the preceding item. R. A. Haryana was not aware that Gopal had recognized him. Also S. P. Gupta said that Gopal had been unable to recognize R. A. Haryana when asked to do so. This recognition is therefore not endorsed by informants other than Kirtipal Sharma.
40. Recognition of a photograph of Shaktipal Sharma	S. P. Gupta		When Gopal entered the house of Shaktipal Sharma, he noticed a photograph of Shaktipal Sharma and spontaneously said: "This is my photograph." Subhadra Devi Sharma tried to persuade him that this was impossible since he was a small boy from Delhi, but he insisted that it was "his" photograph.

Item	Witnesses	Comments
41. Recognition of a photograph of Shaktipal Sharma's father	S. P. Gupta Kiripal Sharma	Subhadra Devi Sharma pointed to another photograph and asked Gopal whose it was. He said: "This is my father's photograph."
42. Recognition of a second photograph of Shaktipal Sharma	S. P. Gupta Jwala Prasad B. B. Das R. A. Haryana	R. A. Haryana brought an album of photographs to the Sharma house and showed some of them to Gopal. He showed Gopal a group photograph and asked him if he could recognize himself in it. Gopal correctly pointed to the figure of Shaktipal Sharma, although the face was covered in the photograph and only the lower part of the body was visible. According to my notes, R. A. Haryana said part of the face of Shaktipal Sharma was visible in the photograph, but I think the error is mine; the other informants indicated that only a portion of the body was visible, and not the face. The question was put to Gopal in an unfortunate way, since he knew he was expected to identify one of the persons in the photograph as Shaktipal Sharma.
43. Recognition of a third photograph of Shaktipal Sharma	S. P. Gupta R. A. Haryana	In this photograph Shaktipal Sharma was seen only from the back, and yet Gopal said it was of himself.
44. Recognition of a second photograph of Shaktipal Sharma's father	S. P. Gupta Asha Sharma	This was a photograph of Shaktipal Sharma's father taken after his death. Asha Sharma asked Gopal whose photograph it was. Gopal replied: "Pitaji." This indicated father well enough, although Shaktipal Sharma had called his father Babuji, which also means father. The expression *babuji* is not found in Delhi. Gopal called his father Pitaji or Papaji.
45. Recognition of Shaktipal Sharma's office at the Sukh	S. P. Gupta Jwala Prasad	Gopal found his way from the Sharma house of the preceding items to the Sukh

TABLE 2 (*cont.*)

Item	Informants	Verification	Comments
45. (cont.) Shancharak Company	Asha Sharma		Shancharak Company's building. He started to go back down the lane toward the main street and the front entrance of the company's office. Asha Sharma then told him it would be closed because of a holiday. She then left him near the back entrance to the building on a back lane. Gopal entered the building at the back and found his way to a large room of the company's building where he said: "This was my office." Asha Sharma, who was with but behind Gopal as he moved ahead, said he went to the showroom first, but in fact Shaktipal had his desk ("office") in the large room that also served as the company's showroom. Unfortunately, by this time a considerable crowd had gathered and some of its members might have guided Gopal by their remarks or other indications. This recognition therefore does not have the value of Gopal's finding the way from the front entrance of the building to the house earlier in the day, when there was no crowd and the few people with him did not themselves know the way.
46. Recognition of place where the murderer stood when he shot Shaktipal Sharma and where Shaktipal Sharma was when he was shot	S. P. Gupta Jwala Prasad Kirtipal Sharma Asha Sharma		Persons in the surrounding group who knew the facts tried to mislead Gopal, but he insisted he knew the correct positions of the murderer and his victim. There had been blood on the floor where Shaktipal Sharma had been shot, but the tiles had been taken up for examination by the police. The new tiles that had been laid down to replace the bloodstained ones might have given some indication of the site where the

murdered man had been when he was shot. But this could not have told anyone the position of the murderer when he fired at Shaktipal Sharma.

I inspected the site of the murder at the offices of the Sukh Shancharak Company in 1969.

am going to London." Shaktipal Sharma's family knew of his intense desire
to go to London, and his sister's dream might have had no other provenance
than her knowledge of her deceased brother's wish. But he, not she, had
wished to go to London, so her dream expressed his desire rather than hers.
The possibility remains that the dream emanated in some way from the
mind of the deceased Shaktipal, and it harmonizes very well with Gopal's
later claim that he had had an "intermediate" life in London. The two
families were still quite unknown to each other in 1949.

Omvati Gupta, Gopal's mother, had an unusually strong desire for fruit
juices, especially orange juice, during her pregnancy with Gopal. She did
not notice such a desire for fruit juices during her other pregnancy, or before or after the pregnancy with Gopal. It seems, however, that her husband
took unusually good care of his wife during her pregnancy with Gopal since
it had come after a long period without pregnancies. He therefore offered
her more fruit juice than usual at this time, and this fact may to some
extent account for her saying afterward that she especially wanted orange
juice. If we reject this explanation, we may consider that her craving for
orange juice also derived somehow from the mind of Shaktipal Sharma,
who particularly enjoyed fruits and especially oranges.[8] And, when young,
Gopal also had a special fondness for oranges.

Absence of a Relevant Birthmark on Gopal

Gopal had a birthmark consisting of a flat pigmented area about one and a
half inches in diameter around his umbilicus. He had no trace, however,
in 1969 when I examined him, of any birthmark on his chest, which was the
site of the bullet wound that had killed Shaktipal Sharma. Birthmarks
occur so regularly in subjects claiming to remember previous lives in which
they were shot or stabbed that a subject of this group without one arouses
my curiosity. I wish to reserve a full discussion of this topic for another
volume and will therefore mention here only that the length of the interval
between the death of the previous personality and the birth of the subject
seems to influence the occurrence (or absence) of birthmarks in these cases.
And the present case has (for Indian cases) a relatively long interval, one of
eight years, between the death of Shaktipal Sharma and the birth of Gopal.[9]

---

[8] For other examples of pregnancy cravings related to the appetites of the previous personalities and subjects of these cases, see the cases of Ruby Kusuma Silva and Bongkuch Promsin to
be published in later volumes of this series.

[9] Analysis of a small number of Indian cases has shown that the average interval between
death and presumed rebirth in cases in which the previous personality died violently is a little
less than three years; in cases in which the previous personality died naturally, it is a little
more than five years. The difference between these means is not significant.

Gopal's Behavior Related to the Previous Life

Circumstances and Manner of Gopal's Speaking about the Previous Life. As I have already mentioned, Gopal told most of the details that he remembered of the previous life on the evening that he behaved rudely when asked to remove a glass used by a guest. But he did thereafter supplement these early remarks from time to time with additional details.

For the most part Gopal used the past tense in talking of the previous life, but in Mathura (and occasionally at other times) he spoke of it in the present tense. For example, on reaching the house of Shaktipal Sharma in Mathura, he said: "This is my house." Inside the house he said: "This is my living room." When he touched the piano in the Sharma house and was reproached for doing so, Gopal retorted: "Why should I not touch it? It belongs to me." Later, in another room, he said, "This is my bedroom," correctly indicating the room where Shaktipal Sharma had slept.

Gopal showed some confusion of time sense when he said on at least one occasion: "I have a mother and father in Mathura." Shaktipal Sharma's father had died more than six years before Shaktipal Sharma himself did.

Events that offered some basis for comparison with the previous life sometimes stimulated his memories. When asked to do some household task, he would talk of "his" many servants of the previous life. And when Jwala Prasad was building a house for the Gupta family, Gopal made scornful comparisons between it and "his" bigger house in Mathura.

No informant told me that Gopal complained of being in a small body, but on at least one occasion he complained of being treated like a child. This occurred as he was leading the way from the Dwarkadish Temple in Mathura to the Sukh Shancharak Company's offices. His father (who knew this part of the way) tried to mislead him. Gopal said: "Don't consider me a child. I know the way."

Gopal's identification with Shaktipal Sharma seems to have been quite strong and was specially demonstrated when he insisted on bringing home from Mathura one of the photographs of Shaktipal Sharma the family there had shown him.

Gopal's Behavior toward the Members of the Previous Family. Before he went to Mathura, Gopal had once or twice asked his father to take him there, but he had never demonstrated any strong desire to go to the previous family such as many other children subjects of these cases have expressed. After he did go to Mathura in 1965, he never asked to return, and his father thought he had a positive repugnance for it.

Before the first contact between the two families, Gopal had mentioned having brothers in the previous life but had never said he had a wife. When

Subhadra Devi Sharma, Shaktipal Sharma's widow, came to visit Gopal in 1964 he treated her with great reserve, and when she left he refused to utter the friendly word *namaste,* which every Indian child learns to say to respected guests as they leave. After she departed, Gopal's father (who had learned her identity during the visit) asked Gopal if she was "his" wife. Gopal replied: "I do not have a wife." But some days later when his father pressed him again to say who she was, Gopal said: "She was my wife." S. P. Gupta then said: "Then why not say so?" to which Gopal replied: "I am angry." Asked for an explanation of this remark, Gopal said that he had asked her for some money and she had not given it to him. (See item 24, Table 2.) In 1965 Gopal told K. S. Rawat that he had not said anything about "his" wife because "she was of no use to me in my studies, etc."

Opinions of informants differed somewhat as to how Gopal behaved toward Subhadra Devi Sharma in Mathura, but they disagreed only on whether Gopal had shown positive rudeness or merely coolness toward her. No one claimed that he had gone to her with affectionate eagerness, as have many other subjects of these cases when they meet relatives who have been loved by the previous personalities. Gopal's lack of ardor for the wife of Shaktipal Sharma accords very well with the unhappy marriage she and Shaktipal suffered through and particularly with the difficulties that arose between them when Brijendrapal Sharma quarreled over money with his older brothers. Subhadra Devi became caught in a cross fire then, and however blameless her own conduct, it probably magnified her husband's disappointment with her.

Gopal showed a contrasting attitude of friendliness toward Chandra Kanta Devi Sharma, one of Shaktipal Sharma's older sisters. Gopal's father said that Gopal liked to visit her even when he did not care to visit Chandra Kumari Devi Shastri, Shaktipal Sharma's other older sister, who also lived in Delhi. According to Dr. R. S. Sharma, his wife had been Shaktipal Sharma's favorite sister, so Gopal's preference between the two sisters seemed to accord with Shaktipal Sharma's. But Chandra Kanta Devi Sharma herself, and also Shaktipal Sharma's widow, Subhadra Devi Sharma, said that Shaktipal Sharma had liked his two sisters equally. Gopal's preference for Chandra Kanta Devi Sharma could have arisen simply from her being more cordial toward him and his claim that he was her brother reborn. But Chandra Kumari Devi Shastri said Gopal's visits made her sad by reminding her of her brother so she had not encouraged him to come. It did not seem, therefore, that she accepted Gopal's claim to be their brother reborn less than her sister did.

In wanting to visit Chandra Kanta Devi, Gopal perhaps also wished to be near her husband, Dr. R. S. Sharma. Shaktipal Sharma had been particularly fond of this brother-in-law. Dr. Sharma stayed by Shaktipal Sharma after he was wounded, remained with him when he was in the operating room, and held his hand when he died a few days later.

Toward Brijendrapal Sharma, the younger brother and murderer of Shaktipal Sharma, Gopal showed an attitude of forgiving without forgetting. As I have mentioned, after he saw Brijendrapal at the wedding reception in Delhi, Gopal told his father: "He looked like a thief—guilty." (This presumably referred to the belief of the older brothers that Brijendrapal had stolen funds from the Sukh Shancharak Company during his term as manager.) In 1965 Gopal said that he did not love "his" younger brother much because he drank excessively. Then he added: "Of course, I had some love for him." On another occasion Gopal said he wanted to avoid Brijendrapal, but he has never expressed any intention or desire of revenge.

Gopal's Attitude toward Caste and Wealth. Gopal on numerous occasions insisted to his family that he belonged to the caste of Brahmins, a higher one than their caste, Banias. When young, he refused to touch eating utensils used by anyone except his father. He said he had had many servants to take away utensils. He would not drink milk from a cup anyone else had used, even, in this case, his father.[10]

Other Behavior of Gopal Related to the Previous Life. Both Gopal's parents said that he was unusually generous, even as a small child. He gave up toys in order to give alms to beggars, and once he gave a woolen coat to a poor schoolmate who had none. Since members of the Bania caste tend to be frugal if not downright penurious, Gopal's generosity seemed particularly impressive in the Gupta family.

On the question of whether Gopal showed more inclination to religious practices than other children of his age, I received conflicting testimony, and I think it probably correct to say that he had only average inclinations in this direction.

Gopal liked to dress well when a small child and wanted his parents to pay attention to their clothes also. He liked good food and wanted to eat bread, although the Gupta family would eat chapattis rather than bread. He enjoyed eating oranges very much. These dietary preferences corresponded to some extent with those of Shaktipal Sharma, who also relished good food. Oranges had been one of his favorite fruits. He did not prefer bread over chapattis, but he did eat bread. Both Shaktipal Sharma and

---

[10] The refusal of Brahmins to use or even to touch utensils that others have used does not derive, strictly speaking, from any religious injunction. It belongs rather to the general sense of superiority toward other persons felt and exhibited by most Brahmins. In Gopal this sense of superiority based on caste seems to have mingled with pride in wealth and perhaps in education.

Gopal were strict vegetarians, but, as Gopal's parents were also vegetarians, Gopal's habits in this respect were not remarkable in his family.

Contrary to the experience of many subjects who remember previous lives terminated by shooting, Gopal showed no phobia of firearms. Indeed, his father told me in 1969 that Gopal liked to play with toy firearms.

Some observers remarked that Gopal played a little on the piano at the home of Shaktipal Sharma in Mathura during the visit there on March 21, 1965. Three informants said he used both hands when he played the piano and that he gave them an impression of being able to play it competently. Perhaps the most important features of this episode lie in the interest Gopal showed in the piano, in his attempt to play it, and in his possessive claim that it belonged to him. If Gopal did in fact play the piano with some ability, as these observers said he had, then this would have constituted the exhibition of an unlearned skill, since Gopal's father said he had never in his life seen a piano before the visit to Mathura. Gopal's father had a harmonium, but Gopal had never shown much interest in it and had never tried to play it. Unfortunately, none of the observers of this episode was an expert in music, and none had taken particular note of what composition, if any, Gopal had played or had attempted to play. We are left then with a suggestion of the demonstration of an unlearned skill, but nothing more.

In Table 3 I have summarized the principal behavioral traits for which I found a correspondence between Shaktipal Sharma and Gopal.

The Attitude of Gopal's Parents toward His Memories of a Previous Life

In parts of Asia (especially India and Burma), many parents of children who claim to remember previous lives discourage them from talking about these lives either because of the rather widespread belief that such children die young or for other more personal reasons such as displeasure over the content of memories of the previous life and the related behavior of the child. But Gopal's father, although not his mother, actively encouraged him to talk about the previous life. As I mentioned earlier, Gopal's father had at first been indifferent to his references concerning a previous life, but later he became a strong partisan of the case. Nevertheless, S. P. Gupta put off any attempt at verifying Gopal's statements for several years after he first began to make them. Although Gopal first spoke about the previous life at the age of about two and a half, he was eight when the two families met and almost nine when he went to Mathura. After the trip to Mathura, however, S. P. Gupta seems to have enjoyed the ensuing publicity and the numerous visitors who came to visit and question Gopal or just to see him. The interest of some prominent persons of Delhi in the case added to his

TABLE 3. *Correspondences in Behavior between Gopal and Shaktipal Sharma*

Gopal	Shaktipal Sharma
1. Conscious of wealth and caste; reluctant to do any household work	Brahmin by caste; wealthy and somewhat spoiled; not used to doing any household work, because he had servants
2. Generous to others	Well known for his generosity
3. Fond of good food, especially oranges and other fruits	Enjoyed good food, especially fruits, of which oranges were among his favorites
4. Fastidious about clothes	Fastidious about clothes; very particular about the crease of his trousers
5. Interested in piano at Mathura	Owned and played a piano
6. Cool toward Subhadra Devi Sharma	Known to have been unhappily married to Subhadra Devi Sharma
7. Affectionate toward Chandra Kanta Devi Sharma	Fond of his sister Chandra Kanta Devi Sharma and also of his brother-in-law, Dr. R. S. Sharma

pleasure. In India ignorant persons often believe that a child who remembers a previous life has other paranormal powers, such as of healing or future-telling, and although, in my opinion, almost none of them do have such powers, credulous seekers often come to them and ask for blessings or predictions. Gopal attracted a share of such persons, and his father did not find their attentions uncongenial. But his mother did. She became vexed with the time consumed and, in her opinion, wasted by these visitors. In 1965 Gopal failed to pass into the next class at school, and his mother blamed the interruptions of visitors and other commotions connected with the case for his failure. She had a solicitous attitude toward Gopal's schooling and disapproved of its being interrupted by the attention he and others gave to his memories of a previous life.

Gopal's parents have both, at least to some extent, subscribed to the belief that a child who remembers a previous life has other unusual gifts. They seem to have expected Gopal to do unusually well at school without effort, and they therefore experienced a painful disappointment when he showed only average ability in his studies.

They also indulged his aristocratic tendencies to some extent. They allowed him, for example, not to help clear away utensils used for eating, since he objected to this so much. And they spoiled him in some other respects as well. In India parents often especially favor the oldest son, but I have the impression that both Gopal's parents tended to gratify him rather more than the oldest son of a family, even in India, can expect.

Indian parents believe that some children bring luck into the family. The fortunes of the Guptas did improve after Gopal's birth, and this enhanced their tendency to think of him as someone special. At one point their fantasies about him ran to the extreme of supposing that he was actually an incarnation of God, and this belief naturally increased their tendency to pamper him.

The Attitude of the Sharmas toward Gopal's Claim to Be Shaktipal Sharma Reborn

On the whole, the members of the Sharma family and other informants for the Mathura side of the case showed more reservations about accepting it as a clear-cut instance of reincarnation than did the Guptas. Several of the former drew attention to the gaps in Gopal's memories or his failure to recognize persons well known to Shaktipal Sharma. Nevertheless, Gopal had impressed nearly all of them with the accuracy of most of his memories. His recognitions of certain photographs, especially those of Shaktipal Sharma with his face not shown, and other evidences moved some of them to tears. And Subhadra Devi Sharma fainted when told about Gopal's memories of her husband's efforts to borrow money from her before his murder. The details of this had certainly never appeared in any newspaper or been otherwise spread around publicly. Shaktipal Sharma's older sister, Chandra Kanta Devi Sharma, found herself calling Gopal "Shakti," a strong indication that she regarded him as her brother reborn. Vishwapal Sharma, Shaktipal Sharma's older brother, was similarly convinced, from the evidence he had seen himself and what he had learned from others, that Gopal was his deceased brother reborn. And Shaktipal Sharma's old friend from college days, R. A. Haryana, expressed the opinion that Gopal was Shaktipal Sharma reborn. So did Shaktipal Sharma's niece by marriage, Asha Sharma, who witnessed in Mathura Gopal's ability to find his way from Shaktipal Sharma's house to the Sukh Shancharak Company and then to point out the correct location of the murderer and victim at the time Shaktipal Sharma's brother shot him.

All these testimonials say nothing about how Gopal obtained the information he showed about the life and death of Shaktipal Sharma. But they do show that persons not particularly disposed initially to believe a boy claiming to be Shaktipal Sharma reborn could come to accept that he was. And they were naturally in the best position of anyone to test Gopal's memories in range and accuracy. They had certainly nothing to gain by acknowledging the accuracy of the memories, since these included scenes by no means pleasant and creditable to their family.

Evidence of Extrasensory Perception on the Part of Gopal

Gopal's father believed that he had at times shown some capacity for extrasensory perception. When I asked for specific examples, however, those furnished by S. P. Gupta did not seem to substantiate his belief. On two occasions Gopal had given his father reassurance about matters troubling him, and although these did have happy outcomes I could not learn about any specific detail concerning them in Gopal's predictions. Gopal did seem to have paranormal knowledge of the sudden, quite unexpected death of S. P. Gupta's employer, Mohan Lal Raizada. And on another occasion he correctly predicted the visit to the Guptas of a man whose arrival was unexpected. However, since these were the best examples of extrasensory perception on the part of Gopal that his father could tell me about, I am sure that Gopal did not have, or at least did not exhibit in his family, impressive powers of extrasensory perception unless we regard his memories of the previous life as evidence of this.

Comments on the Evidence of Paranormal Processes in the Case

In some cases, even when the two families have lived in separate villages or towns, I have by inquiry and searching learned of one or more persons connected with the subject's family who had some knowledge of the previous family or who even had personal acquaintance with its members. But in the present case I have found no person known to the Guptas having any contact, even remote, with the Sharmas of Mathura. One of S. P. Gupta's friends (his employer) had read of the murder of Shaktipal Sharma in 1948, and he first suggested the correspondence of Gopal's statements with that murder. But he had no personal knowledge of the Sharma family. The evidence for this lies in the fact that S. P. Gupta had to make independent inquiries on his own when he went to Mathura in 1964 and tried to verify his son's statements with K. B. Pathak of the Sukh Shancharak Company.

If we accept the above and also the statements of both families concerned about their lack of acquaintance with each other, and if we further consider that Gopal first talked of the previous life at about the age of two and a half, I do not see how we can believe that he acquired his information through any normal channel of communication. If we further take into consideration Gopal's behavior related to the previous life and sustained over many years, we find ourselves almost forced to interpret the case as including at least some paranormal process.

The foregoing bias on my part toward a paranormal interpretation of the case does not include the "intermediate" life in London described by Gopal. Apart from the fact that Gopal did name two streets in London, I have not verified any of his statements about that life. The Guptas have no connections with England and know next to nothing about London. By the time Gopal began talking about the "intermediate" life, he was already nearly nine and could certainly have learned something about London at school or elsewhere. I find it curious, however, that he should have selected

London for the site of the "intermediate" life if he made it up from nothing. But a life in London accords very well with the earnestly expressed wishes of Shaktipal Sharma. I consider it worth speculating that perhaps Shaktipal Sharma had, after death, a hallucinatory "intermediate" life which he placed in London and which he "lived out" in a dreamlike state before reincarnating in the body of Gopal Gupta. Thus Gopal's memories of the "intermediate" life would be memories of Shaktipal Sharma's postmortem existence. In that case they would be memories, not of a real terrestrial incarnation, but of an imaginary one that corresponded with and to some extent fulfilled Shaktipal Sharma's desire to go to London.[11]

Gopal's Later Development

As I have already mentioned, Gopal never expressed a wish to return to Mathura after the visit in 1965, for which he showed no enthusiasm in the first place. But he seems to have retained his memories of the previous life despite his lack of interest in maintaining contacts with the previous family. Or perhaps he wished to avoid them *because* his memories had not weakened, since most of them were far from happy ones. The life of Shaktipal Sharma had some public successes and many carnal pleasures, but no one could describe it as filled with domestic tenderness.

The lack of further contacts between the Guptas and the Sharmas in Mathura may also have arisen partly from disagreements that occurred between the families following publication in newspapers of reports of the case that contained information offensive to Subhadra Devi Sharma. She never visited Gopal again in Delhi. Gopal did make several further visits to the homes of Shaktipal Sharma's sisters, who lived in Delhi. But such visits ceased altogether in 1967 or 1968.

In 1969 Gopal said that his imaged memories had not faded. But he might have forgotten the original images while actually only remembering what others told him he had said earlier.

In March 1969, Gopal's father said that his reluctance to do such domestic tasks as removing utensils after use persisted, but that it had diminished in strength.

Gopal had not in 1969 made up the year he had failed at school in 1965, so that he was still one year behind his contemporaries, a fact that continued to be a source of surprise and chagrin to his parents, who had expected brilliant academic achievements from him.

Gopal's rather weak performance in school had not diminished his own

[11] Hinduism and Buddhism teach that our thoughts while we are alive create the world that we shall inhabit after death. The *Tibetan book of the dead* gives a particularly explicit account of this belief. (W. Y. Evans-Wentz, ed. 1957. *The Tibetan book of the dead.* 3d ed. London and New York: Oxford University Press.)

opinion of himself; in 1969, when asked what he would like to become when he grew up, he said: "Prime Minister of India." He showed politeness toward us, but we could observe traces of his reluctance to work. One of our group wanted a pack of cigarettes and asked Gopal to go to the nearest shop and buy him one. Gopal immediately delegated this assignment to his younger sister. The average Indian boy of his age would have gone for the cigarettes himself out of respect for the male adult making the request. Gopal's passing the errand to his sister might have been a residue of the previous life with many servants, but probably it had persisted only because his parents had not obliged him to become respectful and obedient. To the extent that they have done this, they have not helped Gopal in his adjustment to the situation he finds himself in as much as they might.

Gopal told his father that he remembered the location of a treasure that he (as Shaktipal Sharma) had buried in Mathura, but the Sharmas would not let Gopal try to show where it was. Gopal said that he would find it when he grew up.

In 1971 Gopal (at the age of fifteen) was in the ninth class of school and doing average work. He was still one year behind his peers. He had little interest in studies and did not read much. He had adopted the attitude that good students, in which group he included himself, did not need to study assiduously. He was rather outspoken at school and not popular for this reason with some of his teachers.

Gopal continued to complain sometimes of the low standard of living in his family as compared with that of the life he remembered in Mathura. And he continued also to show reluctance for household tasks. In fact, his father said he did such work only if "forced" to do so. On the other hand, he had lost the caste snobbery that he had expressed when a small child. He said that to him caste was unimportant. He was not at this time particularly religious. Occasionally, he engaged in religious rituals with the intent to influence adversely other persons who had annoyed his father or himself. For these rituals he invoked Saraswati, the Goddess of Learning, who is not, so far as I know, especially well known as an assistant for Hindus practicing what in the West is known as black magic.

Gopal still claimed in 1971 that he had undergone no fading of memories of the previous life, although he said he wished to forget it. Evidently the unpleasant memories outweighed the pleasant ones. I did not then know, any more than I do now, how to evaluate his claim of preserving the memories of the previous life essentially intact. His memories had definitely not diminished to any marked extent at age nine, when he accomplished the series of recognitions credited to him both in Delhi and in Mathura; this fact puts him in the small group of persons whose memories of previous lives do not recede, as do those of most subjects, between the ages of five and eight.

In 1971 Gopal's father still tended to indulge him to an extent that, in my opinion, far exceeded the favoritism shown in India to oldest sons, and particularly to only sons. S. P. Gupta said Gopal was fearless and that firmness had no influence on his character. This, however, to the extent that it was true, might have resulted to some extent from a lack of parental control when Gopal was younger.

Yet Gopal, if he was in many respects independent, was also a youth with attractive features. By 1971 he had learned to speak English quite well, and his conversation impressed me as being well-mannered and intelligent.

In October 1973, I went out to Krishna Nagar again at the time of another stay in Delhi. Gopal was, unfortunately, away on a visit to Chandigarh, but I had a long talk with his parents. Gopal was then in the eleventh class of school, and his parents said he was doing better there both in conduct and in scholarship. According to S. P. Gupta, Gopal still remembered the previous life but talked little about it, and when his parents brought the subject up he would avoid it. When I asked if Gopal still thought of himself as a Brahmin, his father said that he did not like domestic work; but this, for a boy of seventeen, as Gopal then was, can hardly have made him conspicuous among other boys of the same age.

Gopal's father still preserved some traces of the unusual respect and almost veneration with which he had earlier regarded Gopal. And even his mother said wistfully that she thought she and her husband inadequate parents in relation to Gopal's superior qualities. Despite these attitudes Gopal's parents seemed to have a much more objective view of him than they had shown before. They had trimmed him down almost to ordinary human stature. I experienced some relief and a feeling of contentment that Gopal had every opportunity to develop normally from this time on.

In October 1974 S. P. Gupta told me that Gopal had failed in the eleventh class at school and would have to repeat it. He thought that Gopal had not forgotten any of his memories of the previous life, but mentioned that they might have been refreshed by reading an account of his case that had appeared not long before in a Hindi magazine. According to his father, Gopal showed a continuing taste for luxuries and some tendency to reproach his parents for their poverty compared with what he remembered about the previous life.

The Case of Sunil Dutt Saxena

Summary of the Case and Its Investigation

S UNIL DUTT SAXENA was born in Aonla, 32 kilometers from Bareilly, Uttar Pradesh, on October 7, 1959. Sunil's parents are Chadammi Lal Saxena and his wife, Rameshwari. He was the third son and sixth child in a family of nine children altogether. The family belong to the lower middle class. Sunil's father made a precarious living as a boutique owner and restaurant keeper and in other low-paying employment. His mother had worked as a teacher, but the needs of her family and difficulty in finding a suitable position interfered with her having any regular employment.

When Sunil could barely talk, at the age of about one year and nine months, his mother heard him saying repeatedly the word *budaun*. Budaun is a town about 35 kilometers from Aonla, but Sunil's repeated mention of it at first made no sense to his mother. At about this time he also began talking about a teacher, but what he said about him also conveyed nothing to his mother.

When Sunil was a little over three, he went (with his mother) to visit a maternal uncle in New Delhi. At the uncle's home there were furnishings —for example, a radio, a telephone, and a refrigerator—not present in Sunil's home, and he commented that he had these things. He was also observed there to be peremptory toward the servants of the house.

Not long after Sunil and his mother returned to Aonla he told her: "Mummy, I have come from Budaun. An old man brought me to this place very comfortably . . . in a tonga." [1] Thereafter he made additional remarks about details of a life he had lived in Budaun, where, it seemed, he had been wealthy, had owned a factory, a car, and a tonga. He said that he had had a wife and children there as well as servants. He particularly talked about a college that he had founded in Budaun and referred to its principal, whom he called Master Sahib. Sunil was reluctant to do any housework and told his mother: "Bring the servants for the work from my house." When asked to go to school, Sunil said he would go to his own school and be taught by Master Sahib. He repeatedly asked his parents to take him to

---

[1] A tonga is a small two-wheeled horse-drawn vehicle much used in India, now mostly for short distances within a city or town.

Budaun. During one period he was asking his parents to take him there every day.

In 1963, when Sunil was less than four, the family moved from Aonla to the city of Bareilly. There Sunil continued talking about the previous life at Budaun, especially to Govind Murari Lal, the family's landlord. Govind Murari Lal began to urge Sunil's father to take Sunil to Budaun to see whether he could verify his assertions. One of Govind Murari Lal's friends had heard of a certain Seth [2] Sri Krishna of Budaun and thought that perhaps Sunil was talking about him. Sunil continued his insistent requests to go to Budaun until finally, on December 29, 1963, his parents took him and his sister there. A friend, Rameshwar Giri Goswami, accompanied them. They went first to the home of Sheveti Prasad, a distant "uncle" [3] of Sunil's father. On the way there they stopped at the college founded by Seth Sri Krishna. Then they met members of the Seth's family and entourage. They also visited the former home of Seth Sri Krishna and that of his fourth wife, Sakuntala Devi. At each of these places, Sunil recognized people, places, or objects familiar to Seth Sri Krishna, and he thereby established beyond any doubt that, whatever the origin of his knowledge, he was talking about people and events that had figured in the Seth's life. Seth Sri Krishna had died in Budaun on April 24, 1951, eight years before Sunil's birth. He was in his early or middle sixties when he died. At the time of his death, he was probably the wealthiest man in Budaun and a notable philanthropist and public figure of the community.

After Sunil's visit to Budaun, S. D. Pathak, the former principal of the college founded by Seth Sri Krishna, and his intimate friend (the "Master Sahib" of Sunil's statements), came twice to visit Sunil in Bareilly. Sunil, however, did not return to Budaun, and other members of the Seth's family and business circle did not visit him in Bareilly. Sunil lost interest in going to Budaun after the trip there in December 1963. In the early 1970s he went to Budaun again to visit an older sister who was living there after her marriage.

The newspaper *Indian Express* published, on January 3, 1964, a summary of the case and an account of Sunil's visit to Budaun. This article came to my attention and I was, fortunately, able to begin my study of the case in August 1964, only eight months after Sunil's visit to Budaun. I spent four days on its investigation that year and returned in 1969 and in 1971 to study certain details again and to interview other witnesses.

In addition, Prof. P. Pal investigated the case in October 1964. He confirmed the main evidence that I shall present and also obtained some in-

---

[2] The term *Seth* is an honorific title given in India to prosperous businessmen. It roughly corresponds to the English word *tycoon* (derived from Japanese). Unlike *tycoon*, however, it has no derogatory connotation, being rather a term of respect.

[3] The quotation marks around *uncle* indicate that Sheveti Prasad was a distant relative and an honorary uncle rather than a real one in the Western sense.

formation about additional details that he made available to me for this report. The materials used in its preparation also include a rather long typewritten statement furnished by S. D. Pathak. This statement repeats what he told me during several interviews about his friendship with Seth Sri Krishna and his meetings with Sunil in Budaun and Bareilly.

Persons Interviewed during the Investigation

In Bareilly I interviewed:

Sunil Dutt Saxena
Chadammi Lal Saxena, Sunil's father
Rameshwari Saxena, Sunil's mother
S. C. Verma, friend of Chadammi Lal Saxena
Govind Murari Lal, Chadammi Lal Saxena's landlord and friend

In Budaun I interviewed:

Sheveti Prasad, Chadammi Lal Saxena's distant "uncle"
S. D. Pathak, former principal, Seth Sri Krishna Inter College, and close
   friend of Seth Sri Krishna
Sakuntala Devi, Seth Sri Krishna's fourth wife and widow
Shyam Prakash, Seth Sri Krishna's adopted son and Sakuntala Devi's
   third husband
S. P. Sinha, journalist and son of H. P. Srivastava, also a journalist and
   a close friend of Seth Sri Krishna
Narendra Mohan Pande, acting principal of Seth Sri Krishna Inter
   College
"Munshi" Shafatt Ullah, former clerk of Seth Sri Krishna
Shiv Narain Das, friend of Seth Sri Krishna
Ram Gopal Vaish, Shiv Narain Das's younger brother and also a friend
   of Seth Sri Krishna
Gopal Vaidyaji (pseudonym), Ayurvedic physician and friend of Seth
   Sri Krishna

In Katsari village, near Aonla in the Bareilly District, I interviewed:

Rameshwar Giri Goswami, friend of Chadammi Lal Saxena

In New Delhi I interviewed:

Jai Narain Saxena, Sunil's maternal uncle (by marriage)

In Lucknow I interviewed:

J. D. Sukla, former collector (magistrate) of Budaun and friend of Seth
   Sri Krishna

In addition to my own interviews with the above-named persons, Prof. P. Pal interviewed many of the same informants. He also took down a statement by Hari Prasanna Srivastava, a journalist of Budaun and close friend of Seth Sri Krishna. This informant had died before my second visit to Budaun, in 1969, but his son, S. P. Sinha, gave me helpful assistance then and in 1971. Professor Pal also had very brief interviews with Ram Prakash Agarwal (Seth Sri Krishna's son) and Gopi Ram, formerly a manager and, later, a partner in the Seth's business.

In August 1974, Dr. L. P. Mehrotra (at my request) interviewed two informants then living in Ajmer, Rajasthan. These were Seth Sri Krishna's brother-in-law, Sunder Lal, and his niece (Sunder Lal's daughter), Anandi. Dr. Mehrotra gave particular attention in the interviews to Sunil's reported recognition of Sunder Lal and his wife (item 36, Table 4). He also enquired, however, about other details connected with the case of which these informants seemed to have reliable knowledge.

Chadammi Lal Saxena and his family moved from Bareilly back to Aonla in January 1965, so that my second and third interviews with them in 1969 and 1971 occurred in that town.

Relevant Facts of Geography and Possibilities for Normal Means of Communication between the Two Families

Budaun is about 55 kilometers southwest of Bareilly. It is a large town, although not as large as Bareilly, and the chief municipality of a separate district. There is frequent bus service and also some railway service between Budaun and Bareilly and therefore considerable travel between the two cities. Aonla, where Sunil was born, is about 35 kilometers northeast of Budaun and about 32 kilometers southwest of Bareilly. Bareilly and Budaun therefore make a triangle with Aonla.

So far as I could ascertain, the two families had no prior acquaintance before the development of the case. Sakuntala Devi, widow of Seth Sri Krishna, on the one side, and Chadammi Lal Saxena, Sunil's father, on the other side, both denied any previous knowledge of the other's family. Chadammi Lal Saxena said he had never heard of the Seth or his college in Budaun until Sunil began talking about him. As already mentioned, a friend of Govind Murari Lal, the Saxenas' landlord, had heard of the Seth and suggested that he was the person Sunil was talking about. Another of the landlord's friends, Gopal Swaroop, actually knew Seth Sri Krishna and had stayed with him in Budaun. Sunil met this friend of the landlord, but not until the family had moved to Bareilly, by which time he had been talking about the previous life at Budaun for more than two years. I would, nevertheless, have interviewed this witness if he had been in the area, but he had moved away by the time of my investigations. Govind Murari Lal, the landlord, said he did not know anything about the Seth's affairs except what he learned as the case developed.

As already mentioned, Sunil's father had a distant "uncle," Sheveti Prasad, in Budaun, and earlier one of his aunts had lived there. He was close to this aunt in relationship and affection, and he visited her often until about 1955, when she died. After that he rarely went to Budaun to visit his "uncle," Sheveti Prasad. He had gone there once or twice in the ten years between 1955 and 1964. His "uncle" rather often visited Sunil's family in Aonla or Bareilly. He had visited them in Aonla in the summer of 1963, before they had moved to Bareilly. As a resident of Budaun, Sheveti Prasad was quite well acquainted with the public affairs of Seth Sri Krishna, who was one of the most prominent citizens of the city. He said he knew the Seth "very well," but Sunil's father said his "uncle" never discussed the Seth with them prior to the development of the case. He could conceivably have been the intermediary for the conveyance of some information about the Seth to Sunil normally or by extrasensory perception. I find it impossible to believe, however, that Sheveti Prasad could have transmitted normally to Sunil all the detailed knowledge he showed without Sunil's parents being aware of this. Sheveti Prasad also had some acquaintance with S. D. Pathak in Budaun, but (according to S. D. Pathak) his knowledge of the relationship between the Seth and S. D. Pathak did not extend to the fact that the former called the latter Master Sahib.

Apart from Chadammi Lal Saxena's assurance that Sheveti Prasad never talked with them (the Saxenas) about Seth Sri Krishna, we need to remember that almost the first word spoken by Sunil was *budaun* and that by the age of three and a half (when he would still be closely under his mother's surveillance) he was already communicating much detail about the previous life.

As for Sunil's mother, she told me that prior to the family's visit (with Sunil) to Budaun in December 1963, she had only been in that city once before. This visit occurred, as nearly as I can date it, about 1955, approximately four years before Sunil's birth. She had gone to Budaun to attend a wedding and had remained there two days. She had no relatives in Budaun who would have visited her and brought her information from that city.

Sunil's maternal uncle, Jai Narain Saxena, was at one time the personal assistant to the chief minister of the state of Uttar Pradesh. This naturally engaged him in politics, and he traveled with the chief minister during an election campaign. In this connection he had heard of Seth Sri Krishna in 1945–46, but he only knew about him and did not know him personally.

Shiv Narain Das, a businessman of Budaun and friend of Seth Sri Krishna, owned a cold storage plant in Aonla. His brother, Ram Gopal Vaish, was a partner in this enterprise. Between 1963 and 1965 Chadammi

Lal Saxena was employed at this plant.[4] Chadammi Lal Saxena knew that
Shiv Narain Das had an ornament shop in Budaun, but had no knowledge
that he had been a close friend of Seth Sri Krishna. He was certain that
Sunil had not met Shiv Narain Das prior to an occasion when he recognized
him and his brother in May or June 1965. (See items 54 and 55, Table 4.)
He himself, however, had known Shiv Narain Das and his two brothers,
Ram Gopal Vaish and Ram Rakshpal, prior to this event. Chadammi Lal
Saxena talked with his family (including Sunil) about these employers and
thinks he might have mentioned that Shiv Narain Das had an ornament
shop in Budaun. If so, this would greatly weaken the value of Sunil's statement about Shiv Narain Das owning an ornament shop, although it would
not necessarily account for his connecting him with the ornament shop
when he first saw him. In any case, Sunil had been talking about the
previous life for at least one year and probably for three years before his
father became an employee of Shiv Narain Das and his brother.

Other than the above persons I do not know of anyone who might have
acted as an intermediary for the normal communication of knowledge between the two families.

The Last Years and Death of Seth Sri Krishna

When Seth Sri Krishna reached middle age he seems to have experienced
rather intensely the conflicting influences of sex and religion that bother so
many men at that period of life. For many years he had no heir and then
finally adopted a son, Shyam Prakash. After this his third wife gave birth to
a son. But then she died and the Seth began to give more attention to business than his associates wished. They had in mind managing his affairs in
their interests instead of in his. Therefore they contrived to find him a new
wife. A beautiful and willing girl of sixteen was found whose allurements
seemed incompatible with vigilance about financial accounts on the part of
the Seth. The single obstacle to her marriage with the Seth was the fact that
she was already married to a barber of another city. But he proved a reasonable person and his sacrifice was made easier by giving him a large sum of
money. (One informant said the barber received 15,000 rupees.) So the
Seth married his fourth wife, Sakuntala Devi, in 1943.

---

[4] The dates I have given (1963–65) were offered by Ram Gopal Vaish in 1971, but he acknowledged that his memory might have been faulty. The first date (1963) is almost certainly
inaccurate since, according to Chadammi Lal Saxena, he and his family moved from Aonla to
Bareilly at the end of 1963. They were living there in the summer of 1964, when I first met
them. They returned to Aonla in January 1965. I believe that it was only after this date that
Chadammi Lal Saxena worked for Shiv Narain Das and Ram Gopal Vaish at their cold storage
plant. Their meeting with Sunil also must have occurred after this date. I believe Chadammi
Lal Saxena placed the date of the meeting between Sunil and Shiv Narain Das and his brother
accurately when he said it occurred in late May or June 1965.

Unfortunately, the barber then came to Budaun to blackmail the Seth. Word began to spread in the city about how the Seth had acquired his young fourth wife. The gossips began to censure him, and the awkward scandal sapped the Seth's popularity. At least some of the Seth's philanthropy of his later years, including the founding of the college that bore his name, had the motive of restoring the shine to his tarnished reputation with the citizens of Budaun. Yet he seems to have had genuinely generous instincts, and it would be quite unfair to think that his gifts derived only from ulterior reasons.

A person of the Seth's wealth and position could probably have endured public obloquy if he had enjoyed domestic tranquillity. But no one allowed this. Instead, his family and associates subjected him to the kind of harassment that has cured at least some rich men of the delusion that money brings happiness. Intrigues developed between his new wife and his adopted son on the one hand and his biological son on the other. Under these circumstances, he became irrationally suspicious and even began to think (on the hints of counselors) that his good friend S. D. Pathak was having an affair with Sakuntala Devi. Reassured on this point, he next discovered much stronger evidence that his adopted son had in fact been excessively friendly with her. In addition, everyone around him seemed conspiring to gain control of his money while he lived and after he died. He became pervasively mistrustful, so that at the end of his life he felt that he had no real friends.

To restore his health and waning sexual functions the Seth began to take Ayurvedic medicines, in short, aphrodisiacs. Although accounts of his death differ in some details, it is certain that after seeming to be reasonably well one morning, he suddenly became gravely ill and died by the evening of the same day. The description of his illness and death that Sakuntala Devi gave me suggests that he had a coronary artery occlusion and died of its consequences.

The Seth had become more pious as he grew older, and his religious concerns came out as he was dying. He looked at his young wife and then asked S. D. Pathak to turn his face away from her so that he would not experience cravings for her as he died.[5] Soon after saying this he passed away.

Before the Seth died, but I do not know when, he had said that he would be reborn, but he did not predict where or in what family. The statement, by itself, indicated nothing more than that the Seth had not lost his belief in the teachings of Hinduism, including the belief in reincarnation.

After the Seth's death rumors circulated in Budaun to the effect that he

---

[5] Hindus, Buddhists, and Druses attach much importance to the thoughts a man holds during the last few minutes of life as having a particularly strong, almost decisive influence on the conditions of the next life. For further details of these beliefs, see the chapters introducing the reports of cases among these religious groups and further references given there.

had been poisoned. I found people there willing to believe this gossip, but none who could confirm it; I myself believe it untrue.

With the Seth's departure, quarrels continued among members of his family and his business associates. Indeed they intensified. His widow, Sakuntala Devi, succeeded him as president of the college, but when she became openly intimate with the Seth's adopted son, Shyam Prakash (whom she later married), members of the Seth's family ousted her from the presidency of the college and also from the guardianship of the Seth's son, Ram Prakash Agarwal. This group also found grounds for dismissing S. D. Pathak as principal of the college on charges that, he said, were entirely false; he filed a lawsuit (which he ultimately won) against the governing board of the college. The same clique also began maliciously identifying S. D. Pathak with the story that the Seth had died of poisoning.

When he reached adulthood, Ram Prakash Agarwal succeeded to the control of his father's business and also to that of the college his father had founded.

Statements and Recognitions Made by Sunil

In Table 4 I have given the statements and recognitions made by Sunil relating to the previous life. Items 1–28 occurred before the two families had any known acquaintance. Items 29–53 occurred on the occasion of Sunil's visit to Budaun, on December 29, 1963. Items 29–32 occurred on the way to and at the Seth Sri Krishna College. Items 33–38 occurred at the home of Ram Prakash Agarwal, formerly the home of Seth Sri Krishna. Items 39–40 occurred at the home of Sheveti Prasad. Item 41 occurred at the mill (for making nut oil) owned by Seth Sri Krishna. Items 42–45 occurred at the home of Sakuntala Devi, fourth wife of Seth Sri Krishna. Items 46–51 also occurred during the visit to Budaun, in December 1963, but I am not sure exactly where. Items 52–53 occurred as Sunil was being driven about in Budaun. Items 54–55 occurred in Aonla in May–June 1965.

Sunil recalled the previous name of Seth Sri Krishna as Kishen; since Kishen is a short and familiar form of Krishna, Sunil was quite correct in giving this version of the name. He said his name was written on the board of the college "he" had founded. This referred to the name of Seth Sri Krishna placed at the entrance to the college, although there actually was no signboard there. (See item 30, Table 4.)

Informants credited Sunil with several recognitions in which he seemed to show paranormal knowledge of the identity of the persons recognized, but he failed to identify some other persons who were well known to Seth Sri Krishna. Thus his recognition of the Seth's fourth wife, Sakuntala Devi, was doubtful. He did not give her name or relationship, but he did look at her intensely and tears came into his eyes as he did so. He showed a rather ambivalent attitude toward her, not inharmonious with what I learned of the Seth's own feelings toward her. Sunil failed even more definitely to recognize Ram Prakash Agarwal, the Seth's son, and Shyam Prakash, his adopted son. In general, he seemed to be rather better at recognizing the Seth's old friends and employees than at identifying his close relatives. But he sometimes failed to recognize persons of the first group also. He did not, for example, recognize Narendra Mohan Pande, who was principal of the Seth Sri Krishna College in 1969. Narendra Mohan Pande, a teacher in the college during the Seth's lifetime, had been fairly well known to the Seth since he had tutored the Seth's son for about a year. Sunil also seemed not to recognize changes in the buildings of the college that had been made since the Seth's death.

Sunil's statement (item 28, Table 4) concerning how "he" had died in the previous life requires special discussion. He said that "he" had died after "his" wife had brought him some water with poison in it. He seems to have hinted at this to his mother rather than stating it explicitly, but in 1964 he was quite bold in making statements about poisoning both to Prof. P. Pal and to me. On other occasions Sunil showed fears and suspicions about poisons. For example, he warned his uncle against taking medicines when ill. On one occasion he said: "Sometimes when you are ill, the wife gives you medicine and something else which will never let you recover." When he heard that one of his sisters was to get married, he said: "Do not get her married because people get poisoned when they marry." On another occasion he said: "You should not marry. Your wife may kill you." He also advised people against taking water from others.

According to Sakuntala Devi, Seth Sri Krishna's widow, she had not brought him any water on the day he died nor had he taken any. He fell ill rather suddenly and died the evening of the same day. However, Seth Sri Krishna had been taking aphrodisiacs in an effort to sustain his failing sexual powers, and Sunil's reference to medicines brought in water and to how a wife may kill you could refer to memories of the Seth's efforts to satisfy the sexual desires of a young wife. The memories of taking aphrodisiacs may have become blurred with memories of the Seth's rather sudden illness and death in such a way as to give rise to a mistaken impression on the part of Sunil that the Seth's wife had actually poisoned him. I have found other subjects of these cases who have mixed up the details of the circumstances of the death of the related previous personality.[6] On the other hand, some other subjects have given details that seem to throw new light on an obscure death.[7]

[6] See, for example, the case of Warnasiri Adikari (F. Story and I. Stevenson. 1967. A case of the reincarnation type in Ceylon: The case of Warnasiri Adikari. *Journal* A.S.P.R. 61:130–45); also in the next volume of this series.

[7] See, for example, the case of Puti Patra (in this volume) and that of Ravi Shankar (I. Stevenson. 1974. *Twenty cases*).

TABLE 4. *Summary of Statements and Recognitions Made by Sunil*

Item	*Informants*	*Verification*	*Comments*
1. He had lived in Budaun.	Rameshwari Saxena, Sunil's mother	During my visits to Budaun, I saw numerous places that had been associated with Seth Sri Krishna, for example, his factory, residence, and cinema house, as well as the college and dharmashala he had established.	When Sunil was less than two (and just learning to speak), he repeatedly said the word *Budaun*. Seth Sri Krishna had lived in Budaun.
2. He was called Kishen.	Rameshwari Saxena	S. D. Pathak, close friend and employee of Seth Sri Krishna	Sunil only remembered the name Kishen, a short and familiar form of Krishna. In 1964 Sunil's mother denied that he had remembered the name of the previous personality, but I believe that she was thinking of his inability to remember the full name. In 1969 and 1971 she said he had remembered the name Kishen.
3. He had a cupboard for keeping cold water.	Jai Narain Saxena, Sunil's maternal uncle	Sakuntala Devi, fourth wife and widow of Seth Sri Krishna	Sunil did not know the word for a refrigerator when he made this remark in New Delhi. Seth Sri Krishna did not own a refrigerator, but he had a commercial ice cream machine from which he obtained cold water.
4. He had a radio.	Jai Narain Saxena	"Munshi" Shafatt Ullah, Seth Sri Krishna's clerk	Sunil did not know the word for radio; he pointed to one and said: "I had a thing like that." He made this remark in New Delhi. Sunil said on one occasion that "his" radio had toy monkeys on it, but I found no one who could verify this statement.
5. He had a telephone.	Jai Narain Saxena	S. D. Pathak	Sunil did not know the word for telephone; he pointed to one and said: "I had a thing like that." He made this remark in New Delhi.

6. He had an electric fan.	Rameshwari Saxena	Sakuntala Devi	Sunil made this remark in New Delhi.
7. He had a wife.	Chadammi Lal Saxena, Sunil's father	Sakuntala Devi	Sakuntala Devi was Seth Sri Krishna's fourth wife and survived him. (See also item 20.)
8. He had children.	Chadammi Lal Saxena	S. D. Pathak	Seth Sri Krishna had one son born to his third wife and one adopted son.
9. He had a black car.	Chadammi Lal Saxena Rameshwari Saxena	S. D. Pathak Sakuntala Devi	Although Sunil had mentioned before he went to Budaun that "he" had had a car, when he was there he told Ram Prakash Agarwal that he (RPA) had changed the car. Ram Prakash Agarwal then asked him what the color of the other car had been, and Sunil correctly replied: "Black." According to S. D. Pathak, the car was "greyish," not black; according to Sakuntala Devi, it was chocolate colored. I have sometimes found discrepancies in the translations of words for color from Hindi into English. In Hindi the same word (*kala*) is used for "black" and "dark" and sometimes becomes a source of confusion.
10. He had a bungalow (kothi).	Chadammi Lal Saxena	Shyam Prakash, Seth Sri Krishna's adopted son.	
11. A college was named after him.	Chadammi Lal Saxena	S. D. Pathak	Seth Sri Krishna built a college in Budaun, and it was called Seth Sri Krishna Inter College after him. (The name was later shortened to Sri Krishna College.) His widow, Sakuntala Devi, was president of the college for a time after her husband died. A portion of the bulletin of Sri Krishna College was given to me. Sunil had some difficulty remembering the full name of Seth Sri Krishna, and once, when asked what his name had been, he said it

TABLE 4 (*cont.*)

Item	Informants	Verification	Comments
11: (cont.)			was written on the signboard, presumably referring to the name of Seth Sri Krishna that was printed on the main college building above the entrance. (See also item 30.)
12. He had founded the college.	Chadammi Lal Saxena	Sakuntala Devi	See Comment for item 11.
13. The college was in Bara Mohalla.	Rameshwari Saxena	Incorrect	Sunil could not pronounce *b* when he first said this, and said "Para Mohalla." The college was not in a place called Bara Mohalla, and in fact no such mohalla exists in Budaun. There is, however, a Bara Bazar and perhaps Sunil got this name mixed up in his memories. This conjecture seems to be more likely because Seth Sri Krishna's factory and house (which were together) were only about 100 meters from the entrance to Bara Bazar. The college was farther away.
14. There was a principal at the college called Master Sahib.	Chadammi Lal Saxena	S. D. Pathak	S. D. Pathak was known as Master Sahib and Pathakji. He was principal of Sri Krishna College during the lifetime of Seth Sri Krishna.
15. The principal had [also] handled his personal work.	Chadammi Lal Saxena	S. D. Pathak	Sakuntala Devi denied that S. D. Pathak had worked for the Seth at his home. She said he had not been a frequent visitor at the house. Western readers may find this discrepancy difficult to understand if they do not know that in most large houses of India the women occupy separate quarters and do not necessarily know what their husbands are doing in the male sections of the house.

Item	Informant	Verification	Comments
16. He had a box of clothes.	Rameshwari Saxena Chadammi Lal Saxena	Sakuntala Devi	Not a very specific item; many Indians keep clothes in boxes.
17. He had a tonga.	Rameshwari Saxena	S. D. Pathak Sakuntala Devi	
18. The tonga had a black horse.	Rameshwari Saxena	Incorrect	According to S. D. Pathak and Sakuntala Devi, the horse was reddish brown. According to Shafatt Ullah, it was dark brown. (See comment for item 9 concerning occasional confusions in translating names for colors from Hindi to English.)
19. He had servants.	Rameshwari Saxena	Sakuntala Devi	Sunil made this remark in New Delhi. I did not learn how many servants Seth Sri Krishna had, but he was very wealthy.
20. He had married four times.	Rameshwari Saxena	S. D. Pathak	
21. One of his wives was dark, the other fair.	Rameshwari Saxena	Sheveti Prasad, Chadammi Lal Saxena's distant "uncle"	Seth Sri Krishna's third wife was dark. Sakuntala Devi, whom I met, was rather fair. Sunil seemed sometimes to think of Seth Sri Krishna's third wife as still living. But, in fact, she had died before the Seth had married a fourth time.
22. He had arranged a big fair in Budaun.	Rameshwari Saxena	S. D. Pathak J. D. Sukla, former collector (magistrate) of Budaun and friend of Seth Sri Krishna	This was the Ramlila, a pageant celebrating the life and exploits of Rama. Seth Sri Krishna had organized this festival in Budaun and had also given a gate to the city of Budaun for the Gandhi Park, where the Ramlila was held. I saw this elegant gate during my visit to Budaun in 1971.
23. He owned a cinema house.	Rameshwari Saxena	Sakuntala Devi	Seth Sri Krishna erected a building for a cinema but then was persuaded not to open it for that purpose (because of competition from another theater in Budaun);

TABLE 4 (cont.)

Item	Informants	Verification	Comments
23. (cont.)			he adapted it as a storehouse. Following his death, the building was used as a cinema.
24. He had built many houses (dharmashalas) for religious pilgrims.	Rameshwari Saxena	S. D. Pathak	I saw one of these dharmashalas in Budaun.
25. He had a factory and an engine.	Rameshwari Saxena	S. D. Pathak Shafatt Ullah	The factory extracted oil from nuts. I saw the outside of the factory during visits to Budaun, but I did not go inside.
26. Once he had fallen from a horse and his feet were twisted.	Rameshwari Saxena	Incorrect	Sakuntala Devi and S. D. Pathak remembered one occasion when Seth Sri Krishna had had an accident while riding in his tonga. He had fallen out of the tonga and had fractured his elbow. They recalled no injury to his leg. His wife said he had had no trouble in walking.
27. The horse died.	Rameshwari Saxena	Unverified	
28. Sakuntala gave him water with poison in it, and he drank it and died.	Rameshwari Saxena Sunil (1964)	Incorrect	Sunil made almost the same statement about the death in the previous life to me in August 1964, and to Prof. P. Pal in October 1964. See discussion in text for my reasons for believing him wrong in this statement.
29. Recognition of Sri Krishna College in Budaun	Chadammi Lal Saxena Rameshwari Saxena		As the rickshaw in which Sunil was riding passed the college, Sunil pulled the shirt of the driver and said: "Stop! This is my college." He was then allowed to get down and enter the buildings. The informants gave discrepant statements about who was with Sunil in the rickshaw when he made this remark. In 1969 his father said Sunil was with Rameshwar Giri Goswami when

he made the remark, and that he (Rameshwar Giri Goswami) had told it to him, which would mean Chadammi Lal Saxena and his wife were secondhand witnesses of the item, but would have heard about it almost immediately afterward as they were all close together. Rameshwar Giri Goswami did not mention Sunil's remark to me when I interviewed him in 1964, and I did not meet him again.

Item	Informants	Verification	Comments
30. Someone had removed the signboard bearing his name.	Chadammi Lal Saxena Rameshwari Saxena	Probably incorrect	Before coming to Budaun, Sunil said that his (previous) name was written on a board at the college. When he reached the college, he almost immediately commented on the fact that the board bearing the name had been removed. I heard somewhat discrepant testimony about the way the Seth's name was written at the college entrance. Firsthand informants for verifying this item said that the college never had a signboard at the entrance, but that its name had been written above the door at the entrance to the college. S. D. Pathak said the words *Sri Krishna Inter College Budaun* had been written there, but that they had been eroded to illegible faintness by the time of Sunil's visit, in December 1963. Narendra Mohan Pande (who was acting principal of the college in 1969) said he thought the words at the college entrance had become illegible *after* Sunil's visit. Even so, Sunil at the age of four could not have read the words. A puzzle remains as to why Sunil said there had been a signboard at the college when (it seems) there had not been one. There had been a signboard at Seth Sri

TABLE 4 (*cont.*)

Item	Informants	Verification	Comments
30. (cont.)			Krishna's mill, and this read "Govindra-Sri Krishna Oil Mill." (Govindra was the Seth's father.) Perhaps Sunil got this signboard and the words written at the college entrance mixed in his memories.
31. Recognition of peon at the college	Rameshwar Giri Goswami, friend of Chadammi Lal Saxena		Apparently a spontaneous recognition, but I did not learn the details.
32. Recognition of which part of the college Seth Sri Krishna had built	Rameshwar Giri Goswami Chadammi Lal Saxena		Narendra Mohan Pande denied that Sunil had recognized any alterations in the college buildings. (See text for my reasons for thinking he wished to discredit the case.)
33. Recognition of Seth Sri Krishna's bedroom in his house	Rameshwari Saxena Chadammi Lal Saxena		At the Seth's house, Sunil went upstairs by himself and then came and called to his mother to come up, saying: "This is my kothi." His mother and two other women then went upstairs. Sunil entered a room where there was no bed, but a wooden cot. He said: "This is my sleeping room." The room had been the Seth's bedroom.
34. Recognition of "Munshi" Shafatt Ullah, an old Moslem clerk	Chadammi Lal Saxena Rameshwari Saxena		Sunil recognized this person by name. Rameshwari Saxena said Sunil had recognized an old Moslem servant, but she did not recall the name spontaneously. It is of interest that "Munshi" Shafatt Ullah was with Seth Sri Krishna, and helping him, on the day he suddenly became severely ill and died. *Munshi* means clerk in Hindi, and Shafatt Ullah was called "Munshi" Shafatt. When I interviewed him he denied knowing that Sunil had recognized him. (See text for discussion of his testimony.)

Item			Comments
35. He built the bungalow.	Rameshwari Saxena	S. D. Pathak	This statement occurred in reply to a question as to who had built the bungalow. Seth Sri Krishna's father had started the bungalow, but Seth Sri Krishna had built most of it.
36. Recognition of Seth Sri Krishna's sister and brother-in-law	Chadammi Lal Saxena Rameshwari Saxena	Chadammi Lal Saxena	According to Chadammi Lal Saxena, Sunil did not give their names but did show a close relationship with them by touching their feet, a sign of deference in India. Rameshwari Saxena said Sunil had indicated the relationship of sister with Seth Sri Krishna's sister, and that he had mentioned the correct relationship of Seth Sri Krishna with her. Seth Sri Krishna's brother-in-law had asked Sunil: "Who am I?" and Sunil had replied: "You are my jija." His use of the word *jija* showed knowledge that the brother-in-law was the sister's husband, not the wife's brother. These two kinds of brother-in-law are distinguished by different words in Hindi. In 1974, Dr. L. P. Mehrotra heard discrepant testimony about this item from Seth Sri Krishna's brother-in-law, Sunder Lal, and his niece (Sunder Lal's daughter), Anandi. Sunder Lal stated that Sunil had recognized his wife (since deceased) by calling her Jiji without guidance, but that he had not recognized him (Sunder Lal). His daughter, however, although she was not an eyewitness, remembered that her mother had told her that Sunil had recognized both her and her husband.
37. Recognition of a photograph of Seth Sri Krishna	Chadammi Lal Saxena		Sunil was shown a photograph of Seth Sri Krishna and his father and was asked who these persons were. He said that one was himself and one was his father.

TABLE 4 (cont.)

Item	Informants	Verification	Comments
38. Recognition of a photograph of Seth Sri Krishna's father	Chadammi Lal Saxena		See comment for item 37.
39. Recognition of S. D. Pathak, former principal of Sri Krishna College	Chadammi Lal Saxena Sheveti Prasad S. D. Pathak		S. D. Pathak asked Sunil: "Do you recognize me?" Sunil replied: "Yes," S. D. Pathak then said: "What is my name?" and Sunil replied: "Pathakji." This was the familiar name by which S. D. Pathak was known. Sunil and S. D. Pathak both became tearful. S. D. Pathak said that Sunil gave his name as Pathak and also Master Sahib. His description of the recognition presented it as spontaneous, Sunil having spotted him in a group of people who had come to the house. Master Sahib was Seth Sri Krishna's special name for S. D. Pathak. (See item 50 for a similar use of a special name.) Sheveti Prasad gave discrepant testimony about this recognition, saying that Sunil's father asked him if he could recognize Master Sahib in the group of people at the house. This may have happened since, although Sunil's father had not met S. D. Pathak, he had heard Sunil refer so often to Master Sahib that it might have occurred to him to ask Sunil if this person was in the crowd somewhere. Sunil sat contentedly in S. D. Pathak's lap.
40. Recognition of Seth Sri Krishna's adopted son, Shyam Prakash	Chadammi Lal Saxena Rameshwari Saxena Shyam Prakash		This recognition occurred in the home of Sheveti Prasad. Chadammi Lal Saxena said that Shyam Prakash came into a room where Sunil was eating. As soon as Sunil saw him he left his food, ran toward him, and sat in his lap. Rameshwari Saxena

		said Sunil wept when he saw Shyam Prakash. Shyam Prakash stated that Sunil said, when he saw him, that he remembered him, but that Sunil did not give his name. The recognition, if it can be called such, was entirely through behavior and did not include a specific identification by Sunil.
41. Recognition that an engine in Seth Sri Krishna's mill had been moved from the room where Seth Sri Krishna had placed it	Chadammi Lal Saxena	This episode occurred while Sunil was going around the mill with Sri Krishna's son, Ram Prakash Agarwal. Chadammi Lal Saxena was not an eyewitness of the recognition, and therefore a secondhand witness. Shafatt Ullah told me that the engine had not been moved in the factory, but that it had been sold and removed completely. (I believe it had been replaced by a new, electric engine.)
42. Recognition of lion ornaments	Chadammi Lal Saxena Sakuntala Devi	Sakuntala Devi had two ornaments brought in. They were models of lions. Sunil said of them: "I had this silver one made, but the brass one I purchased from the market." According to Sakuntala Devi, Sunil said he had purchased them both.
43. Recognition of a clothes box belonging to Seth Sri Krishna	Sakuntala Devi	Sunil said: "I want to see my box." Sakuntala took him to the room where it was. Sunil recognized this box from among five or six other boxes.
44. Recognition of Seth Sri Krishna's turban	Sakuntala Devi	When he had identified the correct box (preceding item), Sunil pulled out a turban inside it and said: "This is my turban." He then asked about "his" other clothes and learned they had been given away. Sunil became annoyed at this information and said to Sakuntala Devi: "You are a bad woman."

TABLE 4 (cont.)

Item	Informants	Verification	Comments
45. Recognition of a scripture book read by Seth Sri Krishna	Sakuntala Devi		Seth Sri Krishna had been reading these scriptures the day he died.
46. Recognition of photographs of Seth Sri Krishna, Sakuntala Devi, and Ram Prakash Agarwal	Sakuntala Devi Shyam Prakash		Sunil, when shown a photograph of three persons, said: "This is myself, this is my son, and this is my wife." These were correct answers for Seth Sri Krishna. Shyam Prakash said that he only heard Sunil recognize Seth Sri Krishna, not the other two persons.
47. Recognition of an Ayurvedic physician, Gopal Vaidyaji (pseudonym)	Chadammi Lal Saxena		Gopal Vaidyaji asked Sunil if he recognized him. Sunil said: "Yes, you gave medicines to people." Chadammi Lal Saxena also mentioned that at the time of this recognition Sunil correctly gave details of an occasion when Seth Sri Krishna (in the company of Gopal Vaidyaji) had been teased and insulted at a public fair. Prof. P. Pal heard from S. D. Pathak in 1964 that Sunil had alluded to this episode when he had met Gopal Vaidyaji. Unfortunately, when I asked S. D. Pathak in 1971 about Sunil's remark and the related event, he could remember neither. Gopal Vaidyaji (in 1964) told me he recalled the episode when the Seth had been insulted, but he denied that Sunil had said anything to him about it or had otherwise recognized him. But he had earlier told Sheveti Prasad that Sunil had made a correct statement to him about the incident at the fair. I think he was lying to me about this as well as in his denial that Sunil had recognized him. (See text for my reasons for discrediting his testimony, and also the following item.)

Item	Informants	Verification	Comments
48. He had gone to a fair with Gopal Vaidyaji.	Chadammi Lal Saxena	Gopal Vaidyaji	Gopal Vaidyaji asked Sunil if he (meaning Seth Sri Krishna) had gone somewhere with him. Sunil replied: "Yes, we went to a fair together." Gopal Vaidyaji recalled the fair but denied that Sunil had recognized him (item 47) or made the statement about the fair. His testimony was shown to be unreliable, and I think he was purposefully denying the facts. (See text for further details of his testimony.)
49. Recognition of H. P. Srivastava	Shyam Prakash S. D. Pathak H. P. Srivastava, journalist and friend of Seth Sri Krishna		When Sunil saw H. P. Srivastava, he said spontaneously "Jai Ramjiki" (English: "Let Ram flourish"), which was a special greeting Seth Sri Krishna had used with him. And yet Sunil was unable to give the name of H. P. Srivastava when asked to do so. Prof. P. Pal obtained the corroboration of this episode from H. P. Srivastava in 1964. I had not interviewed him earlier in 1964, and he died before my visits to Budaun in 1969 and 1971. Seth Sri Krishna had specific familiar greetings for different friends.
50. Recollection of "Suklaji," a friend of Seth Sri Krishna	S. D. Pathak Shyam Prakash		H. P. Srivastava asked Sunil if he recalled "Sukla." Sunil immediately said, "Suklaji," to correct him and give the style according to which this man had been referred. Sunil then said: "Yes, I remember him." Sunil could not pronounce *s* clearly and lisped: "Thuklaji." The suffix *ji* is an honorific frequently added to names in India as an indication of special respect for the person named.
51. Recognition of a photograph of J. D. Sukla	H. P. Srivastava		Testimony recorded by Prof. P. Pal in 1964. H. P. Srivastava showed Sunil a group photograph with about sixteen

TABLE 4 (cont.)

Item	Informants	Verification	Comments
51. (cont.)			people in it. Sunil correctly identified J. D. Sukla in the photograph.
52. Recognition of gates at Gandhi Park donated by Seth Sri Krishna	Chadammi Lal Saxena		Told to Prof. P. Pal in 1964. Gandhi Park, a rather large square in the center of Budaun, is used for such festivals as the annual Ramlila, a theatrical re-enactment of the life of Rama. The park has four gates, and Seth Sri Krishna donated one of these. I saw the park and this gate during my visit to Budaun in 1971. The donor's name is indicated on the gate.
53. Recognition of dharmashala donated by Seth Sri Krishna	Chadammi Lal Saxena		Told to Prof. P. Pal in 1964. I saw this dharmashala during my visit to Budaun in 1971.
54. Recognition of Ram Gopal Vaish	Ram Gopal Vaish, friend of Seth Sri Krishna		Ram Gopal Vaish and his older brother, Shiv Narain Das, went to visit Chadammi Lal Saxena at his home in Aonla. Chadammi Lal Saxena was employed by them in their cold storage plant at Aonla, and they needed to ask him some questions outside regular work hours. When they arrived at the house, which they had never previously visited and where their visit was totally unexpected, Sunil opened the door and immediately went to tell his father: "Ram Gopal and Shiv Narain Das have come." Ram Gopal Vaish did not actually hear Sunil say this to his father so he was a secondhand witness of it. This recognition, according to the best estimate I can make, occurred in May–June, 1965. Shiv Narain Das, who went with his brother to visit the Saxenas, said that Sunil did not recognize Ram Gopal Vaish

when asked directly if he knew who he
was, although he (Shiv Narain Das) said
that he himself was recognized by Sunil.
(See the following item.) Possibly two
separate occasions were confused by the
informants. Perhaps also Shiv Narain Das
did not hear Chadammi Lal Saxena report
that Sunil had given both the brothers'
names. And it is also possible that Sunil
did not recognize the brothers as reported
by Ram Gopal Vaish.

55. Recognition of
Shiv Narain Das

Shiv Narain Das, friend of
Seth Sri Krishna
Ram Gopal Vaish

Shiv Narain Das asked Sunil: "Do you
recognize me?" Sunil said: "Yes, I know
you," but did not give his name. Sri Shiv
Narain Das then said: "Tell me where I
live and what my business is." Sunil then
replied: "I know you. You have an ornament shop." This was true, as Shiv Narain
Das had had an ornament shop during
Seth Sri Krishna's life.

129

In Table 4 I have listed Sunil's statements in the past tense. This does not communicate how vividly he seemed to be living in the past life when he spoke of it. He almost invariably used the present tense, saying, for example: "I have a cinema." "There is a college named after me." "I have married four times." "I have a radio." And in Budaun he made such remarks as "Stop! This is my college" (when the party had come to Sri Krishna College) , and "Everything belongs to me" (when they were at the bungalow the Seth had built) .

A Group of Dissident Witnesses

Careful readers of Table 4 will notice that in several instances some witnesses denied what others affirmed. I could not help remarking that those who challenged what others asserted were all employees or dependents of Ram Prakash Agarwal, Seth Sri Krishna's son.

When Sunil visited Budaun, in December 1963, Ram Prakash Agarwal at first received him cordially and even invited him and his parents to his house for dinner. And he made a more or less public statement to the effect that "the boy seemed to have the soul of my father." Later, however, he reversed his position on the case and adopted a negative attitude toward it. He avoided meeting me both in 1964 and 1969. He did meet Prof. P. Pal in October 1964, but only briefly. He denied to Professor Pal that Sunil had shown any particular knowledge of his father's life or property, such as the factory or residence.

The acting principal of Sri Krishna College, Narendra Mohan Pande, also belittled the case. He expressed surprise that Sunil had not recognized him, since he had tutored one of the Seth's sons for about a year. He denied that Sunil had made any correct comments about the buildings of the college and that he could find his way around it unaided. He said Sunil had claimed to recognize another teacher who, however, was not even employed at the college during the Seth's time. Sunil, he said, also stated incorrectly that he had seen Narendra Mohan Pande sitting in the principal's chair (he had not been principal during the Seth's lifetime) . Narendra Mohan Pande himself, however, gave incorrect statements about the construction of the buildings, at least according to another one of my informants. I felt also that he was evasive in his testimony and less than frank with me.

Another employee of Ram Prakash Agarwal, "Munshi" Shafatt Ullah, denied that Sunil had recognized him, although Sunil's parents both testified that he had. In this case perhaps they were wrong. Possibly also, as sometimes happens in these recognitions, Sunil spoke softly, within the hearing of his parents, but not loud enough so others could hear. I have the impression that Shafatt Ullah falsely denied that Sunil had recognized him, but I cannot be certain of this. His testimony on other items accorded well with that of other witnesses. He made it clear, however, that he thought S. D. Pathak might have developed the case fradulently, although he did not suggest how S. D. Pathak could have accomplished this. Such a project undertaken by S. D. Pathak would have meant hiring Sunil's parents and maternal uncle (minimally) and training Sunil himself for his part in a hoax.

A third associate of Ram Prakash Agarwal gave much more contradictory testimony. I refer to the Ayurvedic physician whom I have identified as Gopal Vaidyaji. He had known the Seth well, and he met and questioned Sunil. He made statements that disagreed markedly with those of Sunil's father and the latter's "uncle," Sheveti Prasad. Apart from his testimony on his meeting with Sunil (item 47, Table 4), I had ample reason to doubt the reliability of what he was saying on other matters because he contradicted himself in at least two places and made other improbable assertions. He told me, for example, that Sheveti Prasad had been coaching Sunil to pretend that he was the Seth reborn. (But S. D. Pathak found that Gopal Vaidyaji was saying that he [S. D. Pathak] was Sunil's instructor in fraud.) Moreover, Sheveti Prasad said that Gopal Vaidyaji had confirmed in at least one detail the account of his meeting with Sunil that was given me by Sunil's father. Sheveti Prasad also said Gopal Vaidyaji had come around to his house to discuss the case and had told him he was convinced of its genuineness. I interviewed Sheveti Prasad in Budaun in the absence of his nephew, so that he did not have to agree with him about this recognition or to say that Gopal Vaidyaji had given him an account of it different from the one he gave me. I have concluded, therefore, that Gopal Vaidyaji was trying to conceal the facts of the case from me and trying to discredit it, if need be, by lies.

I have already mentioned that Ram Prakash Agarwal, the Seth's son, changed his publicly stated opinion of the case from a favorable to an adverse one. And if I am correct in my judgments of the value of the testimony of his three associates, they may have found it expedient to adopt his second view of the case. As to why Ram Prakash Agarwal changed his opinion about it, my informants could only offer speculations. These included the suggestion that Ram Prakash Agarwal anticipated some claim on the part of Sunil's family for money or even a share of the Seth's property. But the conduct of Chadammi Lal Saxena in no way encouraged this concern. Ram Prakash Agarwal may also have feared unpleasant revelations by Sunil about the private affairs of the family. The Seth's last years, as I have already mentioned, far from being placid, were marred by plots and quarrels of a kind that his family could not have wished made more public than they already were.

I think S. D. Pathak advanced the most plausible reason for the reversal of Ram Prakash Agarwal's attitude toward the case. S. D. Pathak was then engaged in a lawsuit against the board of the college, which had, in his opinion, unjustly dismissed him. (Subsequently, as has been mentioned, he won this suit.) Sunil's claim to be Seth Sri Krishna reborn could not be admitted officially into the court proceedings. However, in a comparatively small city like Budaun many people would know that Sunil was said to be the Seth reborn, and they would know also something about the evidence he had furnished; therefore, his affectionate behavior toward S. D. Pathak could well have had some influence on the outcome of the trial. It must therefore have seemed unwise to Ram Prakash Agarwal to countenance the case in any way. S. D. Pathak told me that Ram Prakash Agarwal had reversed his position on the case on the advice of his lawyers and that his faction had begun to circulate a story to the effect that he (S. D. Pathak) had secretly tutored Sunil for two years before presenting him as a pretender to be the Seth reborn.

Sunil's Behavior Related to the Previous Life

Circumstances and Manner of Sunil's Speaking about the Previous Life. Sunil's memories were often stimulated by some occasion that reminded him of objects or events of the previous life. Thus, although he had been saying "Budaun" when less than two years old and talking about a school when less than three, he had not said anything really coherent about the previous life until he visited his maternal uncle, Jai Narain Saxena, in New Delhi. He was then about three years old. There the affluence of his uncle, who had servants, an electric fan, a radio, a telephone, a refrigerator, and a car, stimulated Sunil to say that he had all these things himself. And after he and his mother had returned to Aonla, he made his first clear statement to the effect that he "had come from Budaun." When Sunil's uncle sent him an English book to read, he said: "I would like to read it in my own college in Budaun." He also said: "I will read it with Master." (But he had used the expression "Master" before this.) When the family moved from Aonla to Bareilly and school was proposed for Sunil, who was then about four, another burst of memories occurred. He told his father that he wanted to study in his own school with "Master Sahib" and said he would show them "his college."

On another occasion, when Sunil was taken to a Ramlila Festival,[8] he wept and begged to go to Budaun, saying that he had built a gate with pillars in a park on the occasion of a Ramlila Festival. (See items 22 and 52, Table 4.)

---

[8] The Ramlila Festival includes a theatrical reenactment of the victory of the god Rama over Ravana, the king of the Rakshasa (demons).

Further memories, including various recognitions, came to him during his visit to Budaun.

Sunil evidently had considerable pressure to talk of the previous life and would do so spontaneously when eating or walking.[9] I have already remarked on his frequent use of the present tense in referring to the previous life.

In August 1964, at the age of nearly five, Sunil still talked easily about the previous life. Dr. Jamuna Prasad engaged him in a long discussion about his memories, enquiring about various aspects of the life of Seth Sri Krishna and about Sunil's current attitudes. Sunil mentioned a number of new details about the Seth's affairs that were not previously noted, or at any rate not previously told to us by his parents. I have not listed these in Table 4 since it is possible, perhaps even probable, that Sunil had picked up much additional information about the Seth's life and property at the time of his visit to Budaun. Three points, however, deserve mention. First, Sunil said that he did not care to return to Budaun then, but that he would go back when he was grown up. (Here he clearly acknowledged that he was a child.) Second, he showed some effort to vindicate the character of the Seth against criticisms he had heard or conjectured. He said that he had done "nothing wrong as Sethji," and that "people liked him." Finally, Sunil seemed mixed up about whom Sakuntala had married after the Seth's death. He thought that she had married S. D. Pathak and expressed anger at this. But this (mistaken) idea did not prevent him from expressing affectionate regard for S. D. Pathak to us.

Sunil had a strong sense of the present ownership of past possessions and of the continuation of past relationships. He would say, for example, "I would like to read in my own college," and, "Come to my house. My wife will prepare tea." When S. D. Pathak came to visit Sunil in Bareilly, Sunil characteristically ordered his (older) sister to prepare tea and his (also older) brother to go to the market and buy pastries. Sunil helped in the preparation of the tea for S. D. Pathak, but drank milk himself. S. D. Pathak said: "How is it that you have given us tea, while you are enjoying milk?" Sunil replied: "You know that I do not take tea." Seth Sri Krishna had abstained from tea and coffee, and Sunil's parents said that Sunil never took tea.

[9] The children subjects of these cases show a wide range in the ease or freedom with which they talk of the previous lives they claim to remember. (I am not referring here to the *amount* of detail stated about it.) Some, like Wijeratne (I. Stevenson. 1974. *Twenty cases*) and Sunil, talk quite spontaneously whether or not anyone is present and listening to them. At the other extreme are subjects like Suleyman Andary of Lebanon (I. Stevenson, 1973. Some new cases suggestive of reincarnation. III. The case of Suleyman Andary. *Journal* A.S.P.R. 67:244–66; also in the third volume of this series), who had clear memories of a previous life when he was about eleven and then kept them largely to himself (out of fear of derision, it seems) until he was about thirteen. In between are children who will talk if questioned, but who rarely make spontaneous comments about the previous life. For another example of a subject talking when no one was listening, see the case of Kumkum Verma later in this volume (p. 230).

In Budaun, Sunil's sense of proprietorship showed even more strongly. When the family group was passing the college, Sunil pulled the rickshaw driver's shirt and said, "Stop! This is my college." In the house owned by Seth Sri Krishna he went to the somewhat thronelike seat used by the Seth and sat in it. He called his mother to see the Seth's room upstairs. When he was offered something to eat and accepted, his mother asked him why he took food from strangers. He replied: "No, Mummy, this is my house and everything belongs to me." He also said he had had the telephone installed. Later, when Ram Prakash Agarwal came in a car to bring Sunil from Sheveti Prasad's house to his own, Sunil said, "Mummy, my car has come." In some of these statements Sunil evidently showed simultaneously an awareness of the present (for example, in telling his "mummy" about the house and car) and an awareness of the past as still somehow present (for example, in saying that the house and car were still his). On another occasion he showed a clearer sense of the change that had taken place in him when he told his father: "I have become a small boy in your house. I used to put on clothes bigger than yours." (It is, incidentally, a fact that Seth Sri Krishna was a larger man than Chadammi Lal Saxena.)

Sunil's Behavior toward Persons Known to Seth Sri Krishna. Sunil's behavior toward some of the persons who had known Seth Sri Krishna accorded very well with what I could learn of the Seth's relationships with these persons. I shall describe in detail only two of these relationships, those about which I have the most information.

As already mentioned, the Seth had a close, intimate friendship with S. D. Pathak, the principal of the college the Seth had founded. At one time he brought S. D. Pathak to live in his home, and they ate and read together as well as worked together. The Seth's friendship with S. D. Pathak survived well an attempt by enemies to alienate them by suggesting that S. D. Pathak had had an affair with the Seth's young wife, Sakuntala Devi.

Sunil showed a marked attachment to S. D. Pathak from the moment he recognized him in the crowd of persons who came to Sheveti Prasad's house. Although S. D. Pathak was a total stranger to the child, he embraced him for several minutes and wept. He sat happily in his lap, although he resisted being picked up by other persons. He wanted "Pathakji" to go along with him when he visited other persons in Budaun and deferentially offered him a chair when others neglected this. On the occasion of S. D. Pathak's later visit to Sunil in Bareilly, Sunil again treated him affectionately and respectfully. He ordered his family to prepare tea and wanted to detain his guest until finally S. D. Pathak was only able to leave by pretending that he would go for a walk and return later. When Sunil heard that S. D. Pathak had been dismissed from the principalship of the college (after the Seth's death) he said: "I will start another school here and you will work."

S. D. Pathak was much impressed by Sunil's spontaneous recognition of him and by his using the familiar expression "Master Sahib" to address him. He became convinced that Sunil was in fact his deceased friend, Seth Sri Krishna, reborn. He told Sunil: "You have come after many years." Sunil replied: "I tried my best to come earlier and repeatedly requested my father to bring me here, but he did not care to bring me." [10]

Sunil's attitude toward Sakuntala Devi, the Seth's fourth wife, was quite different. Even before Sunil had gone to Budaun, he made remarks expressing doubts about her, and one day he told his father that she might have remarried. Sakuntala Devi told me that when they met in Budaun he looked at her intensely and tears came into his eyes. But he did not embrace her; Sunil's father said that he behaved coolly toward her and refused to sit beside her. At one point Sunil said in his father's hearing: "She is not my wife." He became angry when he learned that she had given away some of the Seth's clothes; he said she was "a bad woman" and "I will not take you with me." She had not proposed that he should. At one point she did say that he could stay with her and that she would get him admitted to a school in Budaun. To this he replied, according to S. D. Pathak, that he would start another school in Bareilly and "Master Sahib" would teach him there.

Sunil was evidently vexed that Sakuntala Devi had remarried, but gradually he became reconciled to this. At other times he expressed annoyance that she had been turned out of the Seth's house after his death. (The Seth's son, Ram Prakash Agarwal, became his main heir, and his widow and adopted son, who then got married, had to move elsewhere. This information came out at the time of Sunil's visit to Budaun.) After Sunil returned to Bareilly, he was sad for about a week; when asked about this, he replied that it was because he had left so much wealth there and "they" (the Seth's family) had invited them (Sunil's family) for only one dinner; "they" had sold his cattle; "they" had dismissed "Master Sahib" (from the principalship of the college) ; and "they" had turned out his wife. During this same period, after the return from Budaun, Sunil said that he would like to hear Sakuntala Devi's songs, but he also hated her.

Other Behavior of Sunil Related to the Previous Life. Sunil showed a number of behavioral traits that distinguished him from the other children of his family and that also corresponded with similar traits reported for Seth Sri Krishna. For example, Sunil disliked tea and preferred to drink milk, although other members of his family enjoyed drinking tea. As already men-

---

[10] The above conversation is quoted from the written statement furnished in September 1964 by S. D. Pathak. Sunil's father confirmed that Sunil had requested to go to Budaun and had even talked of going by himself (when grown up) if not taken at the time. His mother said that at one time he was asking to go to Budaun "every day" and urging her to pack a meal for the trip.

tioned, he told S. D. Pathak that he never drank tea. During one of my visits to his home Sunil was offered tea and refused it emphatically. But by 1969 he had begun to drink tea sometimes, mainly because, the family having sold their cow, they had less milk.

Sunil had an interest in religion greater than that of his siblings. He wanted to purchase small statues of gods. He sometimes fasted on Tuesdays [11] when he was still a small child. Sunil's fasting greatly impressed his mother. In Budaun he carried out a little religious ceremony (puja) before eating a meal which, other guests told Chadammi Lal Saxena, exactly resembled a ritual Seth Sri Krishna had practiced before meals. He did not practice this little puja ceremony before or after this one occasion in Budaun where the unusual situation seems to have stimulated his behavioral memories. Seth Sri Krishna's brother-in-law, Sunder Lal, told Dr. L. P. Mehrotra, that Sunil's exact reproduction of Seth Sri Krishna's procedure for this puja had convinced him that Sunil was the Seth reborn. It seems to have impressed him more than Sunil's recognition of the Seth's sister, Sunder Lal's wife (item 36, Table 4).

Sunil disliked household work and resented being asked to do any. Once he said to his mother: "I used to sit only on the gaddi [12] and now you want me to work." He referred to "my servants" as if those of Seth Sri Krishna were still available to him. He showed an authoritarian attitude toward servants and was ordering them around when he was only three or four years old. He expected his older sister to carry his books to school. When S. D. Pathak went to visit Sunil and his family in Bareilly, Sunil acted as the host, dispatching his older brother to buy pastries and instructing his older sister to prepare tea for "Master Sahib." In general Sunil, when a small child, considered himself superior to other persons. He would not greet older visitors with deference, as a small child in India ordinarily would. He acted as if they should show respect toward him rather than the reverse.

Sunil disliked only menial or household chores. He was not opposed to *all* work. He enjoyed studying and showed an interest in schools. He expressed an interest in building a school or college in Bareilly. He said: "I will start a school in Bareilly. Master Sahib will be with me to teach me."

He early showed an unusual interest in money. When only fifteen months old his mother opened a box in which some money was lying and Sunil wanted to take it out. Once (when not yet six) he warned his father about being cheated by rickshaw drivers, advising him to settle the fare before

---

[11] Tuesday is a fast day for many Hindus, being the day for special worship of Hanuman, an important god in the Hindu pantheon.

[12] The gaddi is a slightly elevated table or seat on which the owner or manager of a business sits and from which he directs the business. He also receives the money and puts it in the till near him. Literally the word *gaddi* means the cushion on which the businessman sits, but the meaning has become extended to imply the place where he sits.

starting a journey in order to avoid disputes later. Sunil's father said Sunil was a miser and pointed to the fact that when he obtained a scholarship he deposited the money in the bank and did not give any to his mother. On the other hand, he sometimes was generous in buying gifts for other persons.

Sunil had expensive tastes and a fondness for comforts and luxuries. He wanted more than the other children to buy an electric fan, something of a luxury in India, and he tended to select other costly articles to purchase.

Sunil showed an interest in smoking tobacco. Once when he saw adults smoking a hookah he began to cry and said: "No one offers me a hookah."

Finally, Sunil had a quality of suspiciousness in his attitude toward some persons connected with the previous life. He seemed particularly distrustful of Sakuntala Devi, Seth Sri Krishna's fourth wife and widow.

The foregoing traits all corresponded with similar ones reported for Seth Sri Krishna. My chief informants for the character of the Seth were S. D. Pathak, the principal of the college he founded, and Sakuntala Devi. In Table 5 I have summarized these various traits reported for Sunil and

TABLE 5. *Correspondences in Behavior between Sunil and Seth Sri Krishna*

Sunil	*Seth Sri Krishna*
1. Disliked tea	Never drank tea
2. More interested in religion than the other children in his family	Had a separate room in his house for worship; often read the scriptures and was reading them on the day he died; his wife said that "his greatest interest was God"
3. Reluctant to do any household work; tendency to order his siblings around and to give work to others to do	Had servants who did all menial work for him; treated his servants and employees well, but was clearly a man used to telling other persons what to do; his wife said that "he did not like to do any work by himself; he did not even open his letters"
4. Interested in schoolwork and in schools and colleges, even expressing an interest in building one in Bareilly	Had founded a college in Budaun and took much interest in it personally
5. Concerned about money and frugal in his habits	Had amassed a fortune and conserved it carefully but was not a miser
6. Generous toward other persons	Engaged much in public philanthropy and in helping the poor
7. Had expensive tastes and a fondness for comforts and luxuries	Had great wealth and equipped his house with all available modern conveniences
8. Expressed an interest in smoking a hookah	Smoked a hookah
9. Demonstrated a particular style in performing a religious ceremony (puja) before a meal	Had a habit of performing a particular puja before meals which, observers said, corresponded exactly to Sunil's style
10. Somewhat suspicious toward some persons connected with the previous life	Became suspicious of the persons around him toward the end of his life

for the Seth. I do not claim that the traits listed for the Seth were specific to him. His character resembled that of numerous other prosperous Indian businessmen and, for that matter, businessmen of many countries all over the world. I only wish to emphasize that Sunil showed behavior that was both unusual for a child of his age and at the same time compatible with that of an Indian businessman.

In two respects Sunil's behavior did *not* correspond with that of Seth Sri Krishna. First, Sunil was rather fussy about being well dressed, but the Seth's widow, Sakuntala Devi, said that the Seth was not particularly concerned about clothes. Second, although Seth Sri Krishna (at least at the end of his life) was a vegetarian, Sunil ate meat and fish. He had to go to the home of an uncle to eat these, since members of his immediate family were vegetarians.

Other Relevant Behavior Noted in Sunil

According to Sunil's father he learned to speak unusually early, developed a large vocabulary quickly, and had a good memory. In some respects he showed knowledge and wisdom beyond his years. He sometimes pointed out his father's mistakes to him. Sunil has always impressed me as being of definitely superior intelligence, an opinion that his excellent performance in school supports.

Sunil's family have never observed any significant evidence of extrasensory perception on his part. When I asked his mother about this in 1964, she gave a categorical denial. I questioned his parents about it again in 1971. At that time they said he had not shown any evidence of telepathy, but they did describe two instances in which Sunil had correctly predicted events in the family which, they seemed to think, he could not have known about normally at the time. Once when his father was looking for a job, Sunil said that he would obtain one on a Wednesday, and this happened. On another occasion he predicted the day on which he (Sunil) would receive a scholarship. But in both these instances some normal knowledge of the forthcoming events may have influenced Sunil's statements. His family certainly did not offer any evidence of paranormal powers on the part of Sunil in other aspects of life that corresponded in richness with all the detail he communicated about the life of Seth Sri Krishna.

The Attitude of Sunil's Parents toward His Claim to Remember a Previous Life as a Wealthy Man

Sunil's parents, as they viewed the case, tried to lessen the shock to him of believing that he had died rich and been reborn poor. They accepted his claim that he had been rich and had had many luxuries in the previous life, and they tried to make him as comfortable as they could within their very humble means. They indulged him more than their other children. On the other hand, they did not spoil him. His mother did ask him to do work, and he was expected to do well at school. They made every effort, it seemed to me, to help Sunil accept the fact that however affluent he believed his position might have been in a previous life, he had now to live with them and conform, as they had, to the circumstances in which they found themselves while working toward their improvement. With this attitude of gently, but firmly, confronting Sunil with the need to adapt to his situation, they seem to me to have helped him more than parents of some other children of these cases who have unwisely favored them.

Comments on the Evidence of Paranormal Processes in the Case

I have already mentioned that several witnesses belittled the case or denied statements made by other witnesses. Hints of fraud were circulated in Budaun and even mentioned openly to me by two informants. These were Shafatt Ullah and S. D. Pathak, the former accusing the latter of tutoring Sunil to simulate the Seth's memories and conduct.

In this case it seemed extremely important to interview a large number of witnesses, and I think that I eventually succeeded in tracing everyone who could throw any light on the case and who was living and willing to talk with me. If all the witnesses in Budaun had failed to confirm the main evidence given by Sunil's parents and his father's "uncle" (Sheveti Prasad), the case would have become exceedingly weak. Even the abundant confirmation of S. D. Pathak did little to strengthen it against the testimony and public denials of the associates of Ram Prakash Agarwal. For S. D. Pathak had as much to gain—his lawsuit perhaps—from the confirmation of Sunil's accuracy and genuineness as his opponents had to lose. Under these circumstances, the testimony of Sakuntala Devi and her husband, Shyam Prakash, became particularly important. I do not think Sakuntala Devi could have benefited by endorsing Sunil as the Seth reborn. Indeed, in view of some of his statements about her (although I do not know how many of these she heard), and his ambivalence toward her when they met, one could easily have forgiven her if she had withheld approval of Sunil's claim to be her husband reborn; but she did not. The case also received the endorsement of H. P. Srivastava (interviewed by Prof. P. Pal), whom Sunil impressed much by spontaneously uttering the exact words of a special greeting that Seth Sri Krishna had always used with him. His testimony seemed quite uninfluenced by the partisan spirit that may have swayed other witnesses. And we can say the same for the independent testimonies of the brothers Shiv Narain Das and Ram Gopal Vaish, whom I interviewed separately about their being recognized by Sunil. I have myself concluded that the case is genuine, although I am not prepared to say that all the items denied by the dissenting witnesses happened exactly as the affirming ones stated.

If we can set aside the hypothesis of fraud, as I believe we should, we need then to consider possible ways in which Sunil might have acquired his knowledge of the Seth's life by normal means, but outside the awareness of his parents. I have already mentioned that I found one person who knew the subject's family and who also had some acquaintance with the previous personality and his affairs. I refer to Sheveti Prasad, a distant relative ("uncle") of Sunil's father. He visited Sunil's family about once a year in Aonla or Bareilly at about the time Sunil began talking of the previous life. Although Sheveti Prasad had known the Seth, Sunil's father said that he had never discussed the Seth with them prior to the development of the case, and it seems extremely unlikely that Sunil ever heard him make any reference whatever to the Seth. Other persons who knew Sunil and knew about the Seth seem to have had neither the detailed knowledge of the Seth the case requires nor sufficient contact with Sunil to transmit it to him. In short, my own survey of the possibilities for normal transmission of information to Sunil leads me to the conclusion that this did not occur or, at any rate, not to an extent that could account for the detailed knowledge Sunil showed of the Seth's possessions and affairs. I think some of his statements and recognitions in which he showed knowledge of special names or forms of greeting (items 39 and 50, Table 4), and also one quite spontaneous recognition (item 49), require reference to some paranormal process for their adequate interpretation.

We must include the behavioral features of the case in any comprehensive explanation of it. Sunil showed the attitudes of an older, wealthy man accustomed to luxuries and to having other people do his bidding. In these respects and in a number of other smaller details of behavior his conduct corresponded closely to that of Seth Sri Krishna, the events of whose life fitted the statements made by Sunil. It seems to me that the strong personation and the behavioral correspondence between the two personalities support the idea that Sunil did not simply obtain his information about the Seth by extrasensory perception. If he did, then he also obtained detailed information about the Seth's habits and attitudes by extrasensory perception and incorporated these ingredients in constructing a secondary personality. But this was not an imaginary secondary personality, for his statements clearly matched facts in the life of a particular deceased man, Seth Sri Krishna. I do not insist that the unusual behavioral traits exhibited by Sunil had a specific reference only to Seth Sri Krishna and could not have applied to other wealthy Indian men. I have already said that they could. But if we combine the personation by Sunil of a wealthy Indian man with his correct statements about the Seth, then it seems to me difficult to avoid saying that somehow he had at least partially reproduced the personality of Seth Sri Krishna. I wish we knew how to distinguish a facsimile of a previous personality from its actual continuation in a new physical body.

I could obtain no substantial evidence that Sunil had any powers of extrasensory perception apart from the memories of the previous life. But even if he had such powers of extrasensory perception, why should he choose the deceased Seth, of all people, as a person to imitate and model himself after? The Seth was wealthy, to be sure, and Sunil enjoyed luxury; so he might have imagined that in a former life he had all the wealth that he saw in his maternal uncle's home, but not in his own. However, the Seth also had many encumbering troubles, and his wealth had brought him sorrow as well as pleasure. Sunil's memories of the Seth included his anxieties as well as his fortune and status, so he did not enjoy a completely carefree fantasy. Moreover, his parents did not indulge him wholly in the idea that he had servants and therefore need do no work. They had no refrigerator, car, telephone, or radio; if he was just pretending to remember a previous life, this was bringing him into conflict with the real world just as much as it was removing him from it.

Sunil's allegations that the Seth was poisoned remain completely unverified, and I believe him to be in error in these suspicions. They may have arisen in several ways. First, the Seth did die rather suddenly. Apparently fairly well in the morning (certainly well enough to go down to the college), he was dead by nightfall. Since the different factions of his family, friends, and employees had feuded around and about him, he might well have conjectured (as he was dying) that someone had poisoned him. And such a suspicion could have been carried into the memories of Sunil. Second, Sunil might, through extrasensory perception, have acquired knowledge of the rumor that had circulated in Budaun after the Seth's death, according to which the Seth had died of poisoning. Some promoters of this rumor even named S. D. Pathak as the perpetrator. (This alone would not account for Sunil's saying the poison was in some water his wife brought him to drink when he was feeling ill on the day he died.) Very rarely subjects of these cases show some capacity for contact by extrasensory perception with the surviving members of the related previous family.[13] Although Sunil had never shown any important evidence of extrasensory perception to them, his mistaken idea about poisoning might have been an instance of it. And third, we must not forget the possibility that some of the rumors about the Seth's having been poisoned might have reached Sunil along normal channels of communication, although I have explained my reasons for thinking this unlikely.

[13] See, for an example, the case of Shamlinie Prema in the next volume of this series.

Sunil's Later Development

In 1969 Sunil, then ten years old, was no longer speaking about the previous life spontaneously, although he would answer questions if someone asked him about it. I had a fairly long talk with him (through interpreters), during which it became apparent that he had lost some of the memories of the previous life and no longer showed his intense identification with Seth Sri Krishna. But he could still place the people whose names we mentioned to him in somewhat correct relationship to the Seth. He knew that Sakuntala Devi was the Seth's wife, but he said that Shyam Prakash was his son and Ram Prakash Agarwal his adopted son, thus reversing their correct relationships to the Seth. He had no desire to go to Budaun and persisted in the suspicion that Sakuntala Devi had poisoned the Seth.

Although imaged memories of the previous life seemed to have faded in Sunil's consciousness, some of his behavior related to it persisted. He was still frugal and even stingy (his father said) in handling money. Although he had become more willing to do at least light work, he still passed on to others as much work as he could, they being more fitted for it than he, so he seemed to think. And he still tended to think of himself as better than many other persons and sometimes quarreled because of his expectation that he should dominate others. On the other hand, he had dropped his stance of superiority toward adults and no longer neglected to greet older visitors to the family respectfully.

In 1969, Sunil was in the sixth class at school and stood second in his class. He enjoyed studying and also showed an interest in business affairs.

In November 1971, he was in the eighth class and again second in the class. His father said that if he had not been ill at the time of the examinations, he would have gained the first place. At that time he retained few traces of the behavior that had previously distinguished him from the other children in the family. He had stopped complaining of household tasks and did his fair share of these. His parents still indulged him a little in not making him wash his own clothes although they asked the other children to do this. Sunil was developing into a responsible person. As he was the oldest son remaining at home, when his father was out of the house he attended to anything that called for a man. His interest in religion had persisted, but at this time his parents did not consider him more religious than their other children. Some slight traces of suspiciousness in his nature remained. He was still reluctant to take water in a glass that had been used by others or to eat any food prepared outside the house. But the former arrogance toward other persons had entirely disappeared. He said he would like to enter a business when he grew up.

Sunil's imaged memories seemed to have become further attenuated.

When questioned, he could place "Master Sahib" as a "headmaster," but did not further identify him. He said he had not seen him (S. D. Pathak) recently and expressed no desire to do so. He said he had no wish to go to Budaun.

In short, in 1971 Sunil had almost completely forgotten about the previous life and had also almost entirely lost those features of his behavior in earlier childhood which had set him apart from his siblings and which corresponded closely to similar traits reported for Seth Sri Krishna. He showed every evidence of developing into a normal young man, and one of unusually high intelligence.

I did not meet Sunil and his family between 1971 and 1974 although I exchanged letters with his father each year and enjoyed learning that Sunil continued progressing well in school and at home.

In 1974 I was able to visit Sunil and his family again and had a long talk with them at their home in Aonla on October 13. Sunil had then just turned fifteen. He had failed in the tenth class at school and was having some difficulty in passing the required supplementary examination. He had never had such troubles at school before, and I do not understand adequately why he was having any in 1974.

Sunil said that he still remembered the previous life, but did not think about it spontaneously. When I questioned him about details of the Seth's life, he got some right and some wrong but was more often right than wrong.

Chadammi Lal Saxena said Sunil still showed traces of his former distaste for household chores. He was aware that the family's poverty—their overall economic situation had not improved in the years I had known them—distressed Sunil; but he credited Sunil with tactfulness in no longer openly expressing his chagrin.

Sunil was old enough in 1974 for me to ask him whether he thought there was any advantage to remembering a previous life. He rather firmly replied that there was none so far as he could tell and even some disadvantage. At this point he became tearful as he told us how much the comparison between the wealth of the Seth's life and the straightened circumstances of his (Sunil's) family had troubled him. But he had no explanation of why, considering his case as one of reincarnation, such a great change in circumstances had occurred.

3.   The Case of Jagdish Chandra

Introduction

THE case of Jagdish Chandra is one of the best authenticated of all reincarnation cases. It belongs to the small group in which the subject's statements were written down before verification was attempted and before the two families concerned had met.[1] The case is now (1974) rather old, and the subject has reached middle adulthood; this report can therefore include much information about his adult life and particularly about the persistence of influences apparently related to the previous life and their gradual blending with those of his family.

Summary of the Case and Its Investigation

Jagdish Chandra [2] was born on March 4, 1923, the son of K. K. N. Sahay and his wife, Jamuna, in Bareilly, Uttar Pradesh. He was the third of three sons born to his parents. At the age of about three and a half he began to talk of a previous life he said he had lived in Benares (this city is now called Varanasi). His father, being a lawyer and a person thoughtful about evidence, wrote down what his son told him of the previous life and then sent a letter to a national newspaper asking readers to verify the boy's statements

---

[1] The following cases belong to the group in which some or all of the subject's memories were recorded in writing before verification: (1) Jagdish Chandra (the present case), (2) Bishen Chand Kapoor (Vishwa Nath; this volume), (3) Kumkum Verma (this volume), (4) Indika Guneratne (next volume of this series), (5) Sujith Lakmal (next volume of this series), (6) Swarnlata Mishra (I. Stevenson. 1974. *Twenty cases*), (7) Imad Elawar (I. Stevenson. 1974. *Twenty cases*), (8) Georg Neidhart (G. Neidhart. 1956. *Werden wir wieder geboren?* Munich: Gemeinschaft für religiöse und geistige Erneuerung e.V.), (9) Prabhu (R. B. S. Sunderlal. 1924. Cas apparents de réminiscences de vies antérieures. *Revue Métapsychique*. July–August: 302–7), (10) Heinrich Gerber (unpublished case of Germany), (11) Sunil Opanayake (unpublished case of Sri Lanka), (12) Nasser Murad (unpublished case of Lebanon).

[2] Like many Indians, Jagdish Chandra does not use a family or caste name in ordinary circumstances, and so I have not indicated one for him.

if they could. This soon led to replies from residents of Benares who quickly identified a man, Babu Pandey,[3] as corresponding closely to what Jagdish Chandra had said about the father he remembered. Babu Pandey's son, Jai Gopal, had died some years before, and he was identified as the previous personality Jagdish was claiming to have been.

Babu Pandey, as will be seen later in this report, never admitted that he was Jai Gopal's father. A suggestion was made that he had been Jai Gopal's grandfather, but he was in fact his father, as I shall explain later.

K. K. N. Sahay committed some further details of Jagdish's statements to writing and also had them verified by various people before he took Jagdish to Benares in August 1926, on a visit for further verification and possible recognitions by Jagdish of people and places in Benares. Subsequently, he published a detailed account of the case in a pamphlet from which I shall reproduce extracts.[4]

In 1939, S. C. Bose visited K. K. N. Sahay and talked with him and with Jagdish, then sixteen years old, about the case. Bose subsequently published a report of the case.[5] His report, however, is based largely on what he was told by K. K. N. Sahay and therefore contains little that is not included in Sahay's report.

In adulthood Jagdish Chandra himself wrote out (in 1960) an account of his memories of the previous life, and later he kindly placed this at my disposal. This autobiographical account of the case does not add greatly to its evidence. It is valuable, however, for its description of the feelings of the subject and particularly of his strong attraction to the previous family. It belongs to the small group of autobiographical accounts written by persons who have remembered previous lives with verified details.

I first learned of the case in 1959 when a person helping me in India sent me a copy of K. K. N. Sahay's booklet. I began my own study of the case in 1961 when I had interviews in Bareilly with Jagdish Chandra and his two older brothers, Keshav Chandra and Gokul Chandra. In the same year, I visited Benares and there interviewed Kamla Pandey, a younger sister of Jai Gopal Pandey, the previous personality of the case. Also present during this last-mentioned interview were another sister of Jai Gopal (Minto Pandey Tiwari) and his stepmother, the second wife of Babu Pandey, father

[3] *Babu* is not a given name, but an honorific. It was first applied in the British days of India to clerks, but then became more widespread. Almost anyone of the "gentleman" class could be called Babu. Servants often called their employers Babu or Babuji. After Indian independence the word became generally replaced as an honorific by *Sri*, although it is still sometimes used. I do not know how Babu Pandey acquired the appellation.

[4] K. K. N. Sahay. 1927 (ca.). *Reincarnation: Verified cases of rebirth after death*. Bareilly: N. L. Gupta.

[5] S. C. Bose. 1960. *Jatismar katha*. Satsang, Bihar: Privately published. (English translation by E. J. Spencer; unpublished typescript.)

of Jai Gopal. (Jai Gopal's mother [6] had died in 1960.) His stepmother was an old lady of ninety at the time of my interview and remembered few of the facts of the case. In 1961 I also discussed the case with S. C. Bose, who had visited the family in 1939. In 1964 I again interviewed Jagdish Chandra in Bareilly about his memories of the previous life and talked once more with his older brother, Keshav, about the case. In 1969 I had further interviews with Jagdish Chandra and members of his family, this time including his mother. And in 1971 I again visited the family and talked further with Jagdish Chandra and his brother Keshav concerning certain details of the case. In 1973, being dissatisfied that some apparently verifiable statements made by Jagdish had not yet been verified, I went to Benares again. In March of that year I had an interview with Minto Pandey Tiwari, Babu Pandey's oldest daughter. I was also able to examine parts of Babu Pandey's house and property that I had not earlier inspected. In 1972 and 1973 I had two interviews with R. N. Sahay, a paternal uncle of Jagdish Chandra, but found that he knew little at first hand about the case. He was a student in Agra at the time of his older brother's investigation of the case in 1926.

The main evidence in this case had been collected many years before I began to study it. I was able to add little to what Jagdish Chandra's father had already found and published, although I did learn about some additional details and made some more verifications. For the most part, however, I concentrated on studying the correspondences in behavior between Jagdish Chandra and Jai Gopal (so far as the behavior of the latter could be known or inferred) and the evolution of the emotional components in the memories of Jagdish Chandra.

Persons Interviewed during the Investigation

In Bareilly I interviewed:

Jagdish Chandra
Gokul Chandra, Jagdish Chandra's older brother (by about twelve years)
Keshav Chandra, Jagdish Chandra's older brother (by about ten years)
Jamuna Sahay, Jagdish Chandra's mother

In Satsang, Bihar, I interviewed:

S. C. Bose, who had visited the family in 1939

---

[6] Babu Pandey had had two wives simultaneously. This was rare among Hindus (although common among Moslems of India and elsewhere), but it was legal in India until disallowed by law in 1956. Earlier in his life he had had yet another wife, but she had died childless some (or many) years earlier.

In Benares I interviewed:

> Kamla Pandey, Babu Pandey's younger daughter and Jai Gopal's younger sister
>
> Minto Pandey Tiwari, Babu Pandey's oldest daughter and Jai Gopal's younger sister

In Delhi I interviewed:

> R. N. Sahay, K. K. N. Sahay's younger brother and Jagdish Chandra's paternal uncle

All the other major witnesses in the case, K. K. N. Sahay (Jagdish Chandra's father), Babu Pandey (Jai Gopal's father), and Jai Gopal's mother, had died before 1961.

Jagdish Chandra, his older brothers, and his uncle all spoke excellent English, as did S. C. Bose. I needed interpreters with the other informants.

Relevant Facts of Geography and Possibilities for Normal Means of Communication between the Two Families

Bareilly and Benares (Varanasi) are both large cities of the state of Uttar Pradesh, in northern India. The state, however, is very large, and these two cities are approximately 500 kilometers apart. Bareilly is in the western section of the state and somewhat to the north, while Benares is in the southeastern section. Bareilly is a commercial and industrial city, and also the center of a large agricultural district. Benares is on the river Ganges. It is famous as a place of pilgrimage for Hindus who come in large numbers every year to bathe in the river from embankments or piers called ghats.

K. K. N. Sahay's wife had never been to Benares before the case developed. He himself had been there, but had no detailed knowledge of the city. In his report, he said he had "no friends or relatives at Benares." This was not true unless he meant close relatives, since a cousin and her husband lived in Nuddesar, in Benares (this is a section of the city 4 kilometers from Babu Pandey's home, which was by the ghats on the river). When K. K. N. Sahay first took Jagdish Chandra and other members of his family to Benares for verifications, they stayed in the home of Manni Lal Saxena and his wife (K. K. N. Sahay's cousin). Neither of them had ever visited Bareilly, and although they lived in Benares, they had never heard of Babu Pandey before the case developed. Jamuna Sahay, Jagdish Chandra's mother, with whom I talked in 1969, said she herself had no relatives in Benares; she also denied that their family had ever had (prior to the development of the case) any visitors from Benares.

Apart from the great geographical distance separating the two families, they belonged to different castes, and castes in the India of the early 1920s formed more of a barrier to social relations than they do now. Babu Pandey was a Brahmin, while K. K. N. Sahay belonged to the Kayastha caste. As will be seen, some of the more striking behavior of Jagdish Chandra as a child consisted of appropriate expressions of Brahmin habits and attitudes which seemed most unusual in a Kayastha family.

Jagdish Chandra was just a little over three years old when his memories of the previous life burst into expression. His older brothers assured me that up to that age he spent nearly all his time within the compound of the family house in Bareilly. (I have visited it myself several times and noted that it is surrounded by a rather high wall.) Whenever Jagdish Chandra went out of the compound, he would invariably be with a servant or an older member of the family. Thus it would have been almost impossible for a stranger or anyone else to have had access to the child without his parents being aware of this.

The Published Report of K. K. N. Sahay

I shall now quote the principal portions of the report published by K. K. N. Sahay. In doing so, I have rearranged to some extent the order of paragraphs in the report so that the reader will first learn what Jagdish said (and what was verified) before he was taken to Benares, and will then read about the first visit to Benares. I have interpolated in brackets occasional explanatory words or comments. I have also harmonized some inconsistencies in spelling and made some minor improvements in the English.

I had gone to my village, Kama, where a message was received from home informing me of the serious illness of my wife. I returned on the 6th June [1926] and remained in the house for six days and did not go to the [law] court. My wife had a very high fever which took many days to lower down. It was on the 6th that [my son] Jagdish Chandra asked me to get a motor car. I replied that I shall get one soon. The baby [Jagdish was then three years and three months old] grew impatient and asked me to get one soon. I asked him where I should get it from. He said that I should get his car. I asked him where his car was. He replied that it was at the house of Babuji.[7] I again asked him [who Babuji was], and in reply he said that he lived at Benares, and was his father.

After ascertaining some additional statements, K. K. N. Sahay sent a letter to the editor of the *Leader* (a well-known English-language newspaper of northern India). This letter, titled "Enquiry about Babuji Pandey of Benares," was published in the issue of June 27, 1926, as follows:

---

[7] In Hindi *ji* at the end of a name is an honorific roughly equivalent to the word *respected* in the phrase "my respected father."

Sir,

I shall feel highly obliged if you publish the following . . . account in an early issue of your esteemed paper.

My son, Jagdish Chandra, gives the story of his previous life in a very connected form. He gives his father's name as Babuji Pandey, place of residence Benares, describes the house of Babuji in Benares, and makes particular mention of a big gate, a sitting room, and an underground room with an iron safe fixed in one of the walls.

He also describes the courtyard in which Babuji sits in the evening. He describes that Babuji and the people who collect there drink bhang [Indian hemp used as an intoxicant]. Babuji has malish [a type of massage] on his body and paints his face with powder or earth before his bath on washing his face in the morning. He describes two motor cars and one phaeton with a pair [of horses] and says that Babuji had two sons and one wife and all have died. Babuji is all alone. He also described many private and family matters.

I have no friends or relatives at Benares; my wife has never been there. I never heard before of Babuji.

I invite all gentlemen who may feel interested to ascertain the truth of the story given by the boy in a scientific spirit.

(signed) Kekai Nandan Sahay
Bareilly, U.P.

In his report K. K. N. Sahay lists the names of seven persons in Bareilly who had talked with Jagdish Chandra and who were presumably witnesses to some or all the details that he was stating about the previous life in Benares. K. K. N. Sahay sent a second letter (dated June 30, 1926) to the editor of the *Leader*. It was published under the title of "Corroborative Testimony" in the issue of July 5, 1926, as follows:

Sir,

I shall feel obliged if you give an insertion to the following in an early issue of your esteemed paper. I have received several inquiries regarding the story of his previous life which my son, Jagdish Chandra, had been telling, an account of which was published in your columns on the 27th June.

In order that an inquiry may be made in a scientific manner, I took the following steps:

The boy began to tell his story on 6th June and completed it by the 11th by replying to questions I put to him. I then asked the members of the Bareilly bar and other friends to examine this phenomenon and to advise me if the case is worth further inquiry. Friends and members of the bar continued to come and talk to the boy and it was decided on the 16th that no man should be sent to Benares as it would afford a loophole for skeptics. They may argue that suggestions regarding the house and other details of Benares have been conveyed by the messenger to the boy. So a letter was sent to the Chairman, Municipal Board, Benares, and on receipt of his reply letters were sent to the press. I have also requested some of the leaders of India to send their representatives so that the boy may be taken with them to Benares to point out on the spot the things mentioned by him. As the boy has told so many things to me which have been corroborated by letters received from gentlemen whom I do not know, I am convinced the boy will be able to point out many things on the spot which will satisfy the inquirers. An extract from the letters is given below. Munshi Mahadeva Prasad, Advocate and Chairman, Municipal Board, Benares, wrote: "On receipt of your letter I made the necessary inquiries and found that most of the things told by your boy are quite true. In fact, they are all correctly related except that Babuji Pandey's son, Jai Gopal, died about two years and a half ago.[8] The rest of the facts are all correct—about the phaeton, ekka [horse-drawn cart], horse, malish, goondas,[9] bhang, and the rest. Babu Pandey, for that is the name of the person referred to by your boy as Babuji, is well known to me, having been also my client for the last many years, and I could see on the mere first reading of your letter that he was the person meant by the boy. So I sent my man to Babu Pandey to make the necessary inquiries. Then his men, learning of this, came and took away [your] letter from me. Now they may be going to Bareilly to enquire and corroborate the facts for themselves. Babu Pandey is otherwise known here as Pandit [10] Mathura Prasad Pandey and lives at Pandey Ghat,[11] Benares City."

Pandit Uma Kant Pandey, Vakil [lawyer] of Benares, wrote: "I saw your letter in the *Leader* of today. Babu Pandey is a friend of mine. [He was also a relative.] I have seen this boy [i.e., the previous personality] who is reborn in your family. The descriptions given by him are in the main correct. Pandeyji does not possess a car, though he used one or two. I am informing [others] about the boy and we shall very soon go to see him at your [place]."

The date of birth of my son Jagdish Chandra is the 4th of March, 1923. I have applied for copies of the death entries [certificates] of both Jai Mangal [a brother of Jai Gopal mentioned by Jagdish Chandra] and Jai Gopal to the Chairman, Municipal Board, Benares, and for a copy of the birth entry of Jagdish Chandra to the Municipality, Bareilly. A comparison of these two will be of interest to . . . scientific enquirers. I have been asking people to ascertain the facts soon as old people have been constantly telling me that such memories last only for a short time. At present the boy remembers everything. It is possible after the lapse of some time he may forget.

(signed) Kekai Nandan Sahay
High Court, Bareilly

[8] This is incorrect according to other information. It would place Jai Gopal's death at the end of 1923 or the beginning of 1924, and therefore *after* the birth of Jagdish Chandra. Laxmi Kant Pandey (see p. 154 below) gave the date of Jai Gopal's death as October 1922.

[9] Goondas are servants who can apply force to refractory or reluctant customers or visitors of their employers. Their duties correspond to those of "bouncers" in an American bar, or even to those of "trigger men" among gangsters in America.

[10] *Pandit* is a title often given to Brahmins, or assumed by them, when they are scholars or sages. Babu Pandey was neither of these by far. But the title has come to be given or adopted by many Brahmins without regard to their scholarly attainments.

[11] Babu Pandey was a panda, or supervisor of a bathing ghat (pier), by the river in Benares. The pandas look after the ghats and assist the pilgrims who bathe at the ghats under their care. Pandas may charge money for their assistance, but some have exploited the pilgrims greedily, and goondas have often influenced ungenerous customers to give more freely.

After the publication of my [letters] in the press the public became greatly interested in the matter. For a full two months I had a number of visitors . . . who wanted to hear the story from the lips of the baby. The baby became quite tired of this and began to refuse to see people or to talk in their presence. I therefore wrote to Mr. V. N. Mehta, District Magistrate, Benares, for his help before I could make up my mind to visit Benares with the boy. I was afraid of the crowd as it confounded the child very much. He [Mr. Mehta] very kindly promised his help. . . .

The statements of Jagdish Chandra were recorded by Mr. Ram Babu Saxena, Magistrate 1st Class, Bareilly, on the 28th July, 1926 [i.e., before Jagdish Chandra was taken to Benares]. An extract from the statements is given below.[12]

"My name is Jai Gopal.[13] My father's name is Babu Pandey. Our city is Benares. The Ganges River is near my house. The gate of the house is similar to the gate of Kuarpur in Bareilly.

"My brother was Jai Mangal. He was bigger than I am. He died of poisoning. Our aunt made him vomit. I call Babu Pandey as Babu Pandey and not my 'uncle.' My aunt[14] lives with me.[15] There is a soldier at my gate. Babu Pandey keeps his money in an iron safe. It is on the left-hand side, sunk in the wall and high up.

"Babuji likes rabri [an Indian sweet]. In the evening people take bhang.

"Whenever Babuji washes his face, he massages it with clay. He has a phaeton. It is drawn by two horses. He also has a motor car. My aunt wears golden bangles. She wears earrings. Babuji wears a ring. My aunt covers herself with a long veil. The Dash Ashwamadh Ghat is there. The Ganges is nearby. My aunt makes

[12] The statement is in Hindi in K. K. N. Sahay's report, having been recorded verbatim as the child spoke. Dr. L. P. Mehrotra made the translation given here.

[13] Note Jagdish Chandra's use of the present tense and his fixation on the name of the previous personality. Many of the children subjects of these cases remain strongly attached to the name of the previous personality. Ismail Altinkiliç (whose case is reported in the third volume of this series) provided a particularly vivid example. In his case, Ismail's father actually yielded to the boy's refusal to respond to the name his parents had given him and changed his name officially to that of the previous personality, Abit. But other children remember the previous name without attachment, and many do not remember it at all. We need a special study to investigate the reasons for these differences in remembering names and clinging to them.

[14] Jagdish Chandra used the Hindi word *chachi*, which means "paternal aunt," provided the aunt is the wife of the father's *younger* brother. It turned out that Jai Gopal called both his mother and his stepmother Chachi. In the large households of extended families in India small children may often hear an adult addressed by an older child (or an adult) using a term of relationship. The child may then adopt this same term in imitation, even though it does not express his correct relationship to the person he is thus addressing. In his own family Jagdish Chandra called his mother Maa, the Hindi word for mother. Probably he vaguely sensed an inconsistency in calling the woman who was his mother Chachi, or Aunt, and not calling the head of the house Uncle, and so he explained in the preceding sentence that he called Babu Pandey by the name Babu and not Uncle.

[15] Note that here Jagdish Chandra spoke clearly of at least one "aunt" being still alive. This contradicts K. K. N. Sahay's statement (p. 149 above) that Jagdish Chandra had said of Babu Pandey's family that "all have died." In fact Jai Mangal and Jai Gopal, Babu Pandey's two sons, had died, but two of his wives were living and two daughters (Minto and Kamla) had been born since the deaths of the sons.

bread. I wear a loin cloth when I take my bath. Uma Kant is my uncle [mother's brother]. Uma Kant went to the Temple of Vishwa Nath. Babuji has dark glasses. Babuji listens to the songs of a prostitute named Bhagwati."

This completes the verbatim transcript (as translated into English) of Jagdish Chandra's remarks. K. K. N. Sahay's report continues as follows:

Pandit Laxmi Kant Pandey, Attorney, Benares, introduced himself by correspondence as an old neighbour [who was also a relative] of Babu Pandey possessing intimate knowledge of facts regarding him. Before we left for Benares, the following facts were written to him and verified as correct:

1. That Babuji's wife was called "chachi" [literally "aunt," the wife of the father's younger brother].

2. That "chachi" cooked food for the family although Pandeyji had means sufficient to engage a cook.

3. That "chachi," although an elderly female, observed purdah in her house and had a long ghungat [veil]. Jagdish said that "chachi" drew the ghungat or veil over her face when the goondas came inside the house.

4. That "chachi" wore gold ornaments on her wrists and ears.

5. That "chachi" had marks of smallpox on her face. [K. K. N. Sahay stated that this item was verified by a man from Benares named Bechu. See reference to him below.]

6. That Babuji liked rabri.

7. That Babuji took opium every day.

8. That Babuji wore gold rings on his fingers.

9. That Babuji's son, Jai Mangal, had died of poisoning and there was a suspicion of such a cause at the time of death.

Babuji's wife sent a man named Bechu [16] in August to Bareilly with an invitation asking me [K. K. N. Sahay] to come to Benares to show the child to her. Several letters from Babuji were also received [earlier] to this effect. This Bechu had a talk with Jagdish and admitted the following [additional] facts:

1. That Babuji smeared his face with ashes after washing his face every day.

2. That the iron safe was fixed in the wall to the left.

3. That Bhagwati, a prostitute, was called in for dancing and singing on occasions of different ceremonies in the family. He also certified that Bhagwati had a swarthy colour and a loud voice as Jagdish described her.

The final part of K. K. N. Sahay's report describes the details of his visit with Jagdish Chandra to Benares:

I started [for Benares] on the 13th August [1926] in the afternoon . . . and reached there the next morning. I did not give any previous intimation and stayed [with Manni Lal Saxena, his cousin's husband] at Nuddesar which is 4 kilometers from Babu Pandey's house. I thought I would not be harassed by the

---

[16] Regrettably, K. K. N. Sahay did not state what connection or relationship Bechu had to Babu Pandey and his wife that put him in a position to verify additional facts about the affairs of Babu Pandey. I infer that he was probably a trusted servant of the type who, in the India of those days, would have been sent on a mission of this kind.

crowd there. Unfortunately, the news leaked out and my house was besieged from the morning by a big crowd. I had to apply for the police to keep out the crowd but they did not leave us in spite of the police. B. Hanuman Prasad, a legal officer, Dr. Ganesh Prasad, Mr. Tandon, an Income Tax officer, and several other respectable people came to see us. Pandit Laxmi Kant Pandey also came to see us. The baby [Jagdish] recognized him at once. At first the baby said that he was Uma Kant. On his refusal he said that he was then Laxmi Kant as both brothers were similar in features. At this time there were some 100 spectators surrounding the house.

The boy also mentioned the relationship which Pandit Laxmi Kant had with Babu Pandey with some accuracy. In the evening Mr. V. N. Mehta, the Collector [a senior magistrate], reached Babu Pandey's house before us with eight constables and the city kotwal [chief of police]. Babu's house is near the river [Ganges] and the main road is about 2 furlongs [0.4 kilometers] away. One has to pass through a maze of lanes to reach his house. The boy pointed out the way through the labyrinth of lanes up to the house of Babu. On reaching there the number in the crowd swelled to over a thousand. In the room of Babu himself the boy found 35 men seated on the floor close together. The boy got upset and refused to reply. After a few minutes Mr. Mehta left the house as he had another engagement. Then the boy was taken to the other house where he pointed out the place where bhang was prepared. After this Mrs. Mehta also left. The boy was taken inside the zenana [female quarters of a house in India] where he pointed out "chachi" and said that he had come to her house.

As the crowd kept us surrounded till late it was decided to bring the boy quietly without intimation some other day.

I then took the child to Babu's house in the afternoon of 18th, a Tuesday. There was a local fair, the Durga-gi-ka Mela, and a large number of people had gone there. Jagdish then talked to Babu Pandey, repeated the entire story, and asked Babu to ask any questions he wanted. Babu did not ask any questions.

The boy was taken to the Dash Ashwamadh Ghat which he recognized from a distance. He took his bath twice with great pleasure in the arms of a panda whom he recognized at first sight. He was not at all upset with the sight of the swelled volume of the Ganges in August which flowed so violently, making a terrific noise. The volume of the Ganges did not bother him and he behaved as one who was very familiar with the site.[17] The panda offered him a betel [aromatic leaf chewed in the East] which Jagdish refused, saying that he being a bigger panda [i.e., one of higher status] could not accept from one who was a smaller panda.[18]

The boy also recognized the Vishwa Nath Temple, the Harish Chandra Ghat,

[17] S. C. Bose stated in his previously cited report that K. K. N. Sahay told him that when Jagdish Chandra went into the swollen water of the Ganges, "it seemed as if he and the river were old friends, though . . . he had never bathed in any river to our [i.e., his parents'] knowledge." There is no substantial river near Bareilly, and the inhabitants rarely have a chance to bathe in rivers.

[18] Although Jai Gopal was only a boy and not a panda by vocation, his father (Babu Pandey) was one, and Jai Gopal (and later Jagdish Chandra) identified himself with Babu Pandey. See also the section below on the vocation and character of Babu Pandey.

and the Dufferin Bridge. He had mentioned this bridge in reply to Mr. J. Nott-Bower, the District Superintendent of Police, Bareilly, before we left for Benares. I took Jagdish to the Benares Hindu University which he called Vishwa Vidalaya and said it was under construction in his time. . . .

I learned from Pandit Laxmi Kant Pandey that Jai Gopal died in October, 1922. Jagdish was born, as has been stated before, on 4th March, 1923. Jai Gopal was some ten or eleven years old [at the time of his death].[19] Besides this, Pandit Laxmi Kant Pandey's view is that this boy was the grandson of Babu, the son of his daughter who lived at his house and died, leaving this boy to Babu to bring up.[20] I also think that this explanation is quite in keeping with the account given by Jagdish Chandra except that he calls his grandfather his "father." It may be that, as his mother left her child to her father to bring up, the child did not know any other father except Babu Pandey.

Jagdish had given out two very disparaging facts regarding his father [of the previous life]. In the beginning some people heard about them and the rumor was carried to the ears of Babu Pandey. The attitude of Babu Pandey was definitely obstructive. The interest taken in the case by the District Magistrate [Mr. V. N. Mehta] had also frightened him into thinking that in case he admitted the truth, the disparaging facts would also be believed against him. But we have got the testimony of such high and respectable witnesses that this attitude of Babu Pandey cannot falsify the truth of the story of the boy. Every bit of the story was separately corroborated[21] before we left Benares.

Jagdish has a mark on each of his ears. The mark is in the upper part of the ear and looks as if a hole has been closed. People say that in Benares it is customary to wear earrings in the upper part of the ear.

The Vocation and Character of Babu Pandey

Before commenting on K. K. N. Sahay's report, I shall describe the activities of Babu Pandey. Hindus consider the Ganges River to be sacred, and they believe that Benares is the holiest of a number of places of pilgrimage along its banks. It is said that persons who die in Benares are not reborn, a destiny to which devout Hindus aspire. Every year thousands of pilgrims come to Benares, and nearly all bathe in the holy water of the Ganges. To do this they go to the ghats (piers with steps to facilitate bathing) along the river.

---

[19] In 1964 Jagdish Chandra told me that in 1958, during one of his later visits to Benares, surviving members of Babu Pandey's family told him Jai Gopal was only seven years old when he died. But the figure given by K. K. N. Sahay (obtained and written down much closer to the actual date) is probably more accurate. My efforts to obtain copies of records of the deaths of Jai Gopal and Jai Mangal from the Municipal Board, Benares, led to no discovery of such documents. It appears that they either have been lost or, more likely, never existed. The deaths of young children in India attract little official attention.

[20] See, however, my discussion of this point on p. 156 below.

[21] I think that K. K. N. Sahay meant to say here that Jagdish Chandra's statements were verified as well as corroborated before they left for Benares.

Access to these is controlled by the pandas, who are Brahmins having the privilege and responsibility of supervising the ghats and helping the pilgrims. In fact many of the pandas became licentious and shamefully exploited the pilgrims. They extorted money from the visitors; and if a pilgrim showed obstinacy, the goondas would maul him until he saw the reasonableness of paying what was demanded. Earnest Hindus deplored such conduct fully as much as sincere Christians disapproved of the selling of indulgences by the Roman Catholic Church in the sixteenth century.

Babu Pandey was a rather important and wealthy panda. His own pride of position apparently passed to his son Jai Gopal and became expressed in the rather haughty remark (p. 153 above) of Jagdish Chandra when he met another panda in Benares. He said in effect: "I should not take anything from a lowly person like yourself."

Comments on the Report of K. K. N. Sahay

K. K. N. Sahay mentioned the uncooperative attitude of Babu Pandey with regard to the verification of Jagdish Chandra's statements. During Jagdish Chandra's first visit to Benares, Babu Pandey said nothing and asked nothing. He did not admit a relationship—through reincarnation—with Jagdish Chandra, and did not even clarify what his relationship with Jai Gopal had been. Babu Pandey had several excellent reasons for his reticence.

The least important of these was a fear that Jagdish Chandra's family might exploit the claim that he was Jai Gopal reborn in order to extract money from Babu Pandey. In fact, as Babu Pandey could easily have ascertained, K. K. N. Sahay was very well off himself and also, so far as I have learned, a person of the utmost rectitude.

A more important obstacle to Babu Pandey's cooperation were the "disparaging facts" given out by Jagdish Chandra, which K. K. N. Sahay alluded to but did not specify in his report. Babu Pandey was upset by the interest taken in the case by the district magistrate. This is not at all surprising. Jagdish Chandra later told me what one of the "disparaging facts" was—namely, that Babu Pandey had killed a pilgrim for his money and that the body had been put down a well which had then been covered over. I have not verified this unfortunate event with information from other sources, but, assuming the accuracy of Jagdish Chandra's memory of it, certainly it was something that would have interested the district magistrate of Benares very much indeed. Wells are often covered over in India when another, better source of water becomes available. So a covered well by itself attracts no attention. But such a well could easily be opened up in order to verify a suspicion that it contained a human body.

Babu Pandey thus found himself in a most delicate situation. If he endorsed Jagdish Chandra, he ran the risk of the boy blurting out the "disparaging facts." If he refused, on the other hand, to accept the impressive evidence of the boy's accuracy on many details, he could have aroused suspicions that might have led to further inquiries by the police and district magistrate. He chose the somewhat risky third alternative of remaining silent, but this had the effect of annoying Jagdish Chandra, who suggested to his father that they leave Benares, which they did. One can readily imagine the relief of Babu Pandey on seeing them depart.

A further embarrassment for Babu Pandey arose from the fact, already mentioned, that according to Hindu tradition, persons who die in Benares are not supposed to be reborn. And here was a boy from Bareilly tending to prove the contrary. As a panda, Babu Pandey derived his income largely from the offerings, whether voluntary or forcibly extracted, of the pilgrims coming to Benares—to bathe and perhaps to die. Any discredit to the religious traditions of Benares could naturally have diminished Babu Pandey's income.

The uncooperative attitude of Babu Pandey explains, I think, at least one (and possibly more) of the very few details stated by Jagdish Chandra about which he seemed to give incorrect information. Babu Pandey was the real father of Jai Gopal, and not the grandfather, as was given out in Benares and accepted by K. K. N. Sahay. Both Kamla Pandey and Minto Pandey Tiwari, Jai Gopal's sisters, told me he was Jai Gopal's father. Although they were born after Jai Gopal's death, they presumably had learned the facts of his parentage from their (and Jai Gopal's) mother and perhaps also from Babu Pandey himself. He died about 1933–34.

Another of Jagdish Chandra's statements that was wrong may have been so due to a childish misunderstanding. Babu Pandey did not actually own any automobiles, but he did hire them and especially in order that his son could be driven around the city. (Automobiles, rare in India in the 1970s except in the big cities, were a very great oddity there in the 1920s.) For a child, as Jai Gopal was when he died, and as Jagdish Chandra was when he first talked about the previous life, it would be natural to confuse frequent use with actual ownership.

For some years I thought that Jagdish had also been wrong in stating that Babu Pandey had had a wife who had died. Babu Pandey had had two wives living at the time Jai Gopal died and when Jagdish Chandra first visited Benares a few years later. I confirmed from Kamla Pandey in 1961 and Minto Pandey Tiwari in 1973 that Babu Pandey had had these two wives. The older one (who had been childless) was present during my interview with Kamla Pandey. The younger one, the mother of Jai Gopal and (later) of Minto Pandey Tiwari and Kamla Pandey, had died earlier, in 1960. I thought these two wives accounted for all Babu Pandey's adventures on the sea of matrimony. But in 1973 I learned from Minto Pandey Tiwari that her (and Jai Gopal's) father had had a third wife. She must have died before the first visit of Jagdish Chandra to Benares and possibly even before Jai Gopal's birth. Jagdish Chandra, in his autobiographical report, written much later, said that he had remembered as a child that Babu Pandey had two wives and that he (Jagdish Chandra) had distinguished them in his memories. K. K. N. Sahay seems not to have understood from the remarks of Jagdish that there were two persons whom he called Aunt, actually Jai Gopal's mother and his stepmother. Since Jagdish Chandra referred to them both by the same word (*chachi*), it is not surprising that his father did not understand that two "aunts" were in question.

Additional Details Remembered by Jagdish Chandra as a Child

In his written report and in my interviews with him, Jagdish Chandra described a number of additional details that, he said, he had remembered about the previous life when he was a child. These items do not have the same value for evidence as do those recorded by his father, but they have some interest nevertheless. I have already mentioned one of them, the memory that Babu Pandey had two wives. There were thirteen additional details in this group. I have included them in the summary to follow of all the statements about the previous life made by Jagdish Chandra as a child.

Jagdish Chandra told me in 1961 that when he first visited Benares (in 1926) the site of the burial ghats [22] stimulated in him memories of the funeral of Jai Gopal. He then recalled seeing the body of Jai Gopal taken out for the funeral and mourners chanting around it. In his memories he could not make out what they were saying. He did not recall the cremation or any other details of the interval between the death of Jai Gopal and his own birth.

Statements Made by Jagdish Chandra

In Table 6 I have listed all the statements about the previous life made by Jagdish Chandra when he was a child. The most important of these are those recorded and verified by his father before the two families concerned had met. The next most important are those recorded before the two families had met, but verified afterward. There are a few statements re-

---

[22] In Benares funerals and cremations take place at the ghats, near the river. The bodies of adults and older children are cremated. Those of younger children may be buried; sometimes they are sunk with weights in the river. Jai Gopal's body was probably cremated.

TABLE 6. *Summary of Statements Made by Jagdish Chandra*

Item	Informants	Verification	Comments
1. His name was Jai Gopal. **	K. K. N. Sahay Jagdish's father	Mahadeva Prasad, lawyer of Benares	Babu Pandey himself, evidently because he wished to deny the genuineness of the case, never admitted that he was Jai Gopal's father.
2. Babuji Pandey was his father. **	K. K. N. Sahay	Mahadeva Prasad Kamla Pandey, Jai Gopal's younger sister Minto Pandey Tiwari, Jai Gopal's younger sister	
3. He lived in Benares. **	K. K. N. Sahay	Mahadeva Prasad	
4. His home was near the river Ganges. **	K. K. N. Sahay	Mahadeva Prasad Also verified by me	The Pandey house, above Pandey Ghat, is about 150 meters from the Ganges River.
5. The house had a gate. *	K. K. N. Sahay	Verified by me (See comment.)	I was shown the large and heavy double doors at the entrance to the house; a child could easily consider these a "gate."
6. A soldier stood outside the gate. *	K. K. N. Sahay	Minto Pandey Tiwari	There were two guards (probably goondas) with lathis (a type of heavy stick or baton). I presume they were usually posted at the entrance "gate." A child could have mistaken them for soldiers.
7. He was a Brahmin.	Gokul Chandra, Jagdish Chandra's older brother	K. K. N. Sahay	Jagdish Chandra never said directly that he was a Brahmin. He said: "I am Jai Gopal Pandit." But, since Pandit is an honorific title used only by Brahmins, the statement implies clearly that he regarded himself as having been a Brahmin in the previous life, and as still being one.
8. There was an iron safe fixed high up and in the wall on the left-hand side of the underground room.**	K. K. N. Sahay	Bechu, cited by K. K. N. Sahay	K. K. N. Sahay did not state Bechu's relationship with Babu Pandey's family, but he was most probably a trusted servant or other confidant.

Statement	Informant	Verification	Comments
9. There was marble flooring in the house.	Jagdish Chandra	Verified by me in 1973	A portion of the upstairs had some elegant marble flooring in a check pattern.
10. Babu Pandey was a panda.	Jagdish Chandra K. K. N. Sahay	K. K. N. Sahay	Although this could have been inferred from the other remarks of the boy, it seems not to have been specifically recorded by K. K. N. Sahay before the first visit to Benares. He mentioned in his report that Jagdish Chandra had there met and recognized a panda who, he said, was of a lower rank than himself, meaning in the previous life.
11. There were goondas where he lived.**	K. K. N. Sahay	Mahadeva Prasad	K. K. N. Sahay simply mentioned in his report allusions by Jagdish Chandra to goondas ("bouncers"), but Jagdish Chandra himself wrote (in his autobiographical report) that he remembered that Jai Gopal's father had employed goondas, which is very likely from all the other evidence.
12. The goondas brought gifts [from the pilgrims] on big brass plates.	Jagdish Chandra	Unverified	Although not specifically verified, this detail is quite plausible.
13. Babuji's wife was called Chachi.**	K. K. N. Sahay	Laxmi Kant Pandey, attorney of Benares and Babu Pandey's friend and relative	*Chachi* means "aunt." In the extended families and joint households of India a child may hear his older cousins calling his mother Chachi and, from imitation, may develop the habit of calling her Chachi also.
14. "Chachi" wore gold ornaments on her wrists and ears.**	K. K. N. Sahay	Laxmi Kant Pandey	
15. "Chachi" did the cooking although Babu Pandey could afford a servant.**	K. K. N. Sahay	Laxmi Kant Pandey	This statement was perhaps stimulated by Jagdish Chandra's noting the contrast between his family, who employed a cook,

* Recorded in writing before verification was attempted.
** Recorded in writing and verified before the two families met.

TABLE 6 (cont.)

Item	Informants	Verification	Comments
			and conditions in the life at Benares. Orthodox Brahmins are often so fastidious about the preparation of their food that they will not allow their wives to delegate this responsibility to mere employees.
16. "Chachi" made bread.*	K. K. N. Sahay	Minto Pandey Tiwari	Minto Pandey Tiwari said her (and Jai Gopal's) mother made bread; she said the family had no servants for cooking.
17. "Chachi" observed purdah and had a long veil.**	K. K. N. Sahay	Laxmi Kant Pandey	
18. "Chachi" was pockmarked on her face.**	K. K. N. Sahay	Bechu, cited by K. K. N. Sahay	See comment for item 20.
19. There were two persons called "Chachi" (Aunt) in the home.	Jagdish Chandra	Kamla Pandey	
20. The younger of these, with the pockmarks, was his mother.	Jagdish Chandra	Kamla Pandey Jagdish Chandra	Kamla Pandey told me that her (and Jai Gopal's) mother was the younger of the two wives of Babu Pandey. I did not independently verify that this mother (who had died by 1961) had pockmarks, but Jagdish Chandra told me in 1969 that he himself had verified that the younger of Babu Pandey's two wives (Jai Gopal's mother) was pockmarked, but that the older was not.
21. Babu Pandey had a wife who had died.*	K. K. N. Sahay	Minto Pandey Tiwari	Babu Pandey had a wife who had died before the time of Jagdish Chandra's first visit to Benares. He had two wives living in 1926.
22. Babu Pandey had two sons who had died.**	K. K. N. Sahay	Laxmi Kant Pandey	Jai Mangal died first, and then Jai Gopal.

Item	Informants	Verification	Comments
23. His brother was called Jai Mangal.**	K. K. N. Sahay	Laxmi Kant Pandey Minto Pandey Tiwari	
24. Jai Mangal was larger than he.*	K. K. N. Sahay	Minto Pandey Tiwari	Jagdish Chandra told me that Jai Mangal was younger than Jai Gopal. But Minto Pandey Tiwari said Jai Mangal was the oldest child of the family and therefore he would have been larger than Jai Gopal. For this item it appears that Jagdish Chandra was better at remembering a detail than at verifying it.
25. Jai Mangal died of poisoning.**	K. K. N. Sahay	Laxmi Kant Pandey	There was a suspicion, not a certainty, of accidental poisoning in the death of Jai Mangal.
26. There were no daughters in the family.	Jagdish Chandra	Kamla Pandey Minto Pandey Tiwari	Minto Pandey Tiwari and Kamla Pandey were both born after the death of Jai Gopal. They all had the same mother.
27. He had a car.*	K. K. N. Sahay	Incorrect as to ownership	K. K. N. Sahay said that Jagdish Chandra referred to two cars. Babu Pandey in fact owned no cars, but Uma Kant Pandey said that "he used one or two [cars]." According to Jagdish Chandra, Jai Gopal's mother told him a car was borrowed from one of Babu Pandey's friends and used to drive Jai Gopal around almost whenever he wished.
28. The car was red.	Jagdish Chandra	Unverified	Jagdish Chandra told me that Jai Gopal's mother had told him (Jagdish Chandra) the car Jai Gopal was driven around in was red. I did not verify this independently.
29. Babu Pandey had a phaeton and a pair of horses.**	K. K. N. Sahay	Mahadeva Prasad	

* Recorded in writing before verification was attempted.
** Recorded in writing and verified before the two families met.

TABLE (cont.)

Item	Informants	Verification	Comments
30. There was an ekka.**	K. K. N. Sahay	Mahadeva Prasad	An ekka is a horse-drawn cart.
31. Babu Pandey wore gold rings on his fingers.**	K. K. N. Sahay	Laxmi Kant Pandey	
32. Babu Pandey had black spectacles.*	K. K. N. Sahay	Unverified	
33. Babu Pandey received pilgrims in the big hall of the house.	Jagdish Chandra	Minto Pandey Tiwari	Minto Pandey Tiwari said that her father received pilgrims in the male quarters of the house. As I saw for myself, these contained a very large hall that was undoubtedly the place where Babu Pandey received visitors.
34. They went swimming in the Ganges daily.	Jagdish Chandra	Unverified	This is very probable; the house is close to the ghat on the river.
35. He wore a loin cloth when he went swimming.*	K. K. N. Sahay	Unverified	This is very probable.
36. Uma Kant was his mother's brother.*	K. K. N. Sahay	Unverified	
37. Uma Kant went to Vishwa Nath Temple.*	K. K. N. Sahay	Unverified	There is a well-known temple of Vishwa Nath in Benares.
38. There is a ghat called Dash Ashwamadh.*	K. K. N. Sahay	K. K. N. Sahay	The Dash Ashwamadh ghat, which I visited in 1974, is one of the more prominent ghats in Benares.
39. Babu Pandey was fond of wrestling.	Jagdish Chandra	See comment.	I did not independently verify that Babu Pandey was fond of wrestling, but this could be inferred from the fact that the family had its own akhara, a small arena for wrestling. (See next item.)
40. They had an akhara.	Jagdish Chandra	Verified by me in 1973	The Pandey akhara is about 100 meters in front of the house, above the river Ganges.

A memorial stone to Babu Pandey and his last two wives is on one of the surrounding walls.

Statement	Informant	Verification	Comments
41. Babu Pandey had malish on his body.**	K. K. N. Sahay	Mahadeva Prasad	Malish is a type of massage.
42. Babu Pandey painted his face with powder or clay in the morning.**	K. K. N. Sahay	Bechu, cited by K. K. N. Sahay	K. K. N. Sahay quoted Bechu as saying Babu Pandey "smeared his face with ashes after washing" it "every day."
43. Babu Pandey used to sit in the courtyard in the evenings.*	K. K. N. Sahay	Minto Pandey Tiwari	Babu Pandey sat outside the house for an hour in the evenings.
44. Babu Pandey and his friends drank bhang.**	K. K. N. Sahay	Minto Pandey Tiwari	
45. Babu Pandey liked rabri.**	K. K. N. Sahay	Laxmi Kant Pandey	Brahmins particularly relish sweet foods such as rabri, a sweet or dessert made from milk and sugar.
46. Babu Pandey took some arsenic in his rabri.	Jagdish Chandra	Unverified	Arsenic was formerly much taken as a "tonic" and rejuvenator.
47. Babu Pandey took opium every day.**	K. K. N. Sahay	Laxmi Kant Pandey	
48. A prostitute, Bhagwati, came to the house for dancing and singing.**	K. K. N. Sahay	Bechu, cited by K. K. N. Sahay	
49. She was dark complexioned and had a strong voice.**	K. K. N. Sahay	Bechu, cited by K. K. N. Sahay	
50. He died of enteritis or cholera.	Jagdish Chandra	Unverified	Jagdish Chandra told me that Jai Gopal's mother had told him Jai Gopal had died

* Recorded in writing before verification was attempted.
** Recorded in writing and verified before the two families met.

TABLE 6 (*cont.*)

Item	Informants	Verification	Comments
50. (cont.)			of "liver trouble," but that there was uncertainty about the correct diagnosis. I was unable to trace any official records in Benares of Jai Gopal's death.
51. He had a phonograph.	Jagdish Chandra	Unverified	Jagdish Chandra said that on his first visit to Benares, in 1926, he had asked about Jai Gopal's phonograph. It was remembered, but had been removed from the house. I did not verify this item independently.

corded and not verified or not reported as being verified. And I have included also the statements later written down by Jagdish Chandra himself in adulthood. Only one of these was corroborated to me by another informant, but a few others have been verified.

For convenience in studying Table 6 I have grouped the items according to topic.

There are fifty-one items in all. A total of thirty-six were recorded in writing before verification was attempted, and, of these, at least twenty-four were verified before the two families had met. I think probably more items were in fact verified before the first visit to Benares. K. K. N. Sahay in his report says that "every bit of the story was corroborated [23] before we left for Benares." I believe he forgot, or did not think it important to note down, the details of each verification. He perhaps believed the case strong enough with the details that he did write down.

I have included a number of statements for which I have listed Jagdish Chandra as the informant. All these derive either from his autobiographical account of his memories (1960) or from interviews I have had with him during the years 1961–71. For item 7 Gokul Chandra was my informant in 1969. All other items derive from the report of K. K. N. Sahay, and their recording therefore dates from 1926–27.

Comments about the Content of Jagdish Chandra's Imaged Memories

A colleague who read an early version of this report commented on the type of items that formed the major content of Jagdish Chandra's memories of the previous life of Jai Gopal. It seemed to this colleague that the memories related much more to the activities of Babu Pandey than to those of the child Jai Gopal. I believe the memories appear to be more narrowly focused (on Babu Pandey) than they actually were. The case may be better understood if it is realized that in India children begin to participate at a very young age in the social and vocational activities of their elders to the extent that they are able. Thus Jai Gopal would have engaged in the swimming and wrestling of the ghat pandas when quite small.

The automobile that figured so prominently in Jagdish Chandra's memories (and persistent demands that his father get "his" automobile from Benares) derived from the interest and activities of Jai Gopal, since, according to Jagdish Chandra (I did not verify this independently), Babu Pandey rented or borrowed automobiles for the main (or sole) purpose of having his young son driven around Benares.

---

[23] Since this remark was made in the context of replying to the refusal of Babu Pandey to endorse the case, I think he meant to say "verified" here, or perhaps "corroborated and verified."

Recognitions Made by Jagdish Chandra in Benares

The report by K. K. N. Sahay mentions that Jagdish Chandra recognized a number of people and places in Benares when he was first taken there. The most notable of these was certainly the indication Jagdish Chandra gave of the way from the main street to Babu Pandey's house by the river. The distance is about 0.4 kilometers and an extraordinary tangle of narrow streets and alleys connects the main, through road and the lanes along the river behind the ghats. I traversed this route in the company of Prof. B. L. Atreya in 1961. We got lost in trying to find our way back to the street and emerged about 100 meters from the point at which we had entered the lanes. That Jagdish Chandra did indicate the way through this maze of lanes was confirmed to me by his older brothers, Gokul and Keshav Chandra, and by his mother. They all had accompanied Jagdish and his father to Benares in 1926. Jagdish's older brothers were about thirteen and fifteen at the time. Jagdish was in their arms [24] as the party went from the street to Babu Pandey's house. Members of his family were quite certain that Jagdish Chandra independently indicated the way to the house through the alleys. There were, however, some people surrounding and following them. Reports differ as to their number. It is possible that murmurs and hints from such persons may have guided the child, but his older brothers and mother did not think so. Nor did his father, K. K. N. Sahay, according to what he wrote in his report.

Birthmarks on Jagdish Chandra

K. K. N. Sahay's report stated that Jagdish Chandra had a mark on each of his ears. These were located in the upper parts of the ears and had the appearance of closed holes in the skin. These marks must have been quite small, because I could find no trace of them when I carefully examined Jagdish Chandra's ears in 1961 and again in 1964. Unfortunately, it seems that in 1926 no one verified specifically that Jai Gopal had worn earrings through holes in the upper parts of his ears. In 1961 (when I was in Benares) Jai Gopal's stepmother (who then was ninety and had an enfeebled memory) and his sister Kamla Pandey (who was born after Jai Gopal's death) could not say whether he had worn earrings or not.

---

[24] Discrepancies occurred here in the testimony of Jagdish Chandra's two older brothers. In 1964 Keshav Chandra said that he had carried Jagdish as they walked through the lanes from the main road to the ghats and the house of Babu Pandey. In 1969 Gokul said Jagdish had been with him, and their mother agreed. Possibly on such a long walk (of nearly half a kilometer) each older brother carried the younger one at different times.

I have myself seen many Indian men wearing earrings through holes pierced in the upper part of the ear, or pinna. Jagdish Chandra told me that the pandas of the Benares ghats specially favored wearing earrings in the upper part of the ear, and his father said in a footnote of his report: "People say that in Benares it is customary to wear earrings in the upper part of the ear." I have not obtained further confirmation of this custom as specially common in Benares during the earlier decades of the century.

Jagdish Chandra's Behavior Related to the Previous Life

Circumstances and Manner of Jagdish Chandra's Speaking about the Previous Life. K. K. N. Sahay's report described the extremely rapid outpouring of Jagdish Chandra's memories once he began to talk about the previous life. The flow seems to have started when he saw an automobile, which reminded him of the one of the previous life in which Jai Gopal had been taken for drives. Once he began to talk about the previous life, Jagdish Chandra apparently said almost everything he could remember within a few days. He did, however, have some additional memories during the visit to Benares later the same summer, these being apparently stimulated by seeing places and people connected with the previous life. The rapidity of Jagdish Chandra's expression of the memories contrasts with the usual reports of parents of these subjects, who say more often that the memories come out gradually over months and sometimes over several years.[25]

The fact that Jagdish Chandra expressed so many memories within a few days does not mean that they only entered his consciousness at that time. Often subjects have the memories and do not tell anyone about them until specially stimulated or until they judge the people and time appropriate for them to talk about them. Jagdish Chandra's father was an educated man and also a person of more than average curiosity. He was interested in his son's statements, and he observed Jagdish Chandra's odd (for their family) behavior with a gentle, somewhat amused tolerance. His acceptance contrasted markedly with the superstitious fears of many Hindu parents who believed, as many still do, that a child who remembers a previous life will die young and should be prevented by various measures from talking about it. Thus an unusual father encouraged Jagdish Chandra to talk about the previous life and also saw the importance of making written records and obtaining independent verification of the information narrated by his son.

---

[25] But Jagdish Chandra is not alone in this feature. Two other examples of the rapid outpouring, within a short period, of nearly all the memories of the previous life occurred in the cases of Gopal Gupta (this volume) and Sunetra Rodrigo (to be published later).

Habits and Attitudes of Jagdish Chandra Related to the Previous Life. When Jagdish Chandra was between three and five years old, he showed some habits of eating and dress that distinguished him in his family. K. K. N. Sahay, although he carefully recorded his son's statements, wrote very little in his report about his son's behavior related to the previous life apart from his requests for a car. But I was able to learn much about Jagdish Chandra's behavior as a child from his brothers and mother and also from what he himself remembered of his conduct as a child. His brothers were sufficiently older than he to be able to observe and remember his behavior as a small child.

The principal traits noticed were the following:

1. Insistence on eating first, before other members of the family. It was the custom—still often observed—to invite Brahmins to begin eating a meal first. Orthodox Brahmins expect such deference when they eat with members of other castes, and Jagdish Chandra was simply insisting on his rights, as he saw them, from the previous life.

2. Refusal to eat with non-Hindus or to eat food touched by non-Hindus. This would be a trait of an orthodox Brahmin.

3. Fondness for sweets and especially for rabri. Brahmins are known to like sweet foods such as rabri. Pandas in Benares were especially fond of rabri.

4. Reluctance to eat salty foods. Brahmins generally dislike salty foods.

5. Refusal to eat garlic, onions, eggs, and meat. Garlic and onions are avoided by Brahmins. The reason is said to be a wish to avoid the flatulence which often follows the eating of these foods and which might disturb them during their long sessions of religious exercises. Jagdish Chandra's family were vegetarians, and so his refusal to eat meat was not unusual in his family.

6. Liking for bhang. For a small child to request the intoxicant bhang was, to say the least, most unusual.

7. Preference for wearing a loin cloth. A loin cloth was worn by the pandas during their wrestling matches and in swimming. Jagdish Chandra in his deposition mentioned that in the previous life he had worn a loin cloth when taking a bath. (See p. 152; see also item 35, Table 6.)

Other Behavior of Jagdish Chandra Related to the Previous Life. When he was a small child, Jagdish Chandra showed a markedly hostile attitude toward men with beards. He would not give water to bearded men or tolerate them near him or his food. This attitude derived from the dislike of Moslems on the part of orthodox Brahmins. More Moslems than Hindus are bearded, and in India a tendency can easily arise to think that anyone with a beard is a Moslem. As a child Jagdish did not enquire into such distinctions. He simply disliked all men with beards. His older brother Keshav

Chandra confirmed to me that Jagdish had had this trait as a small child. Keshav recalled that once a Hindu teacher with a beard had come to their home. When this man mentioned that he would take meals with the family, Jagdish insisted that he must not eat in the kitchen, but outside. This episode occurred when Jagdish Chandra was less than six years old.

Both in his written account and in my interviews with him Jagdish Chandra emphasized the strong desire he had as a child for a car. It seems that in June 1926 the longing for a car somehow stimulated the flow of memories of the previous life. His father was moderately well off, but did not then own a car. Young Jagdish had seen cars owned by persons who visited the family. The longing—one may easily call it a craving—for a car persisted in Jagdish Chandra into adulthood and was still strong in 1969. Jagdish's older brother Keshav corroborated the unusually intense interest his brother had in cars. This attachment to cars corresponds to the experiences of Jai Gopal, who was driven in a car borrowed by his father nearly every evening and apparently enjoyed such drives immensely.[26] Jagdish Chandra told me that he (as Jai Gopal) would cry if the car did not come to take him for a drive. And Jagdish Chandra persistently demanded that his father either purchase a car or bring "his" car from Benares. Jagdish Chandra's father in fact yielded to the importunities of his son and, more or less to appease him, purchased several cars one after the other in the 1920s. Jagdish Chandra's mother told me in 1969 that these new cars had not been altogether agreeable to Jagdish. Once, she said, when his father was looking at a new car with a view to purchasing it, Jagdish had said: "Don't purchase this car. Send for my car in Benares."

Jagdish Chandra wrote in his report (1960) that as a child he would sometimes roll on the floor dressed in a loin cloth, asserting to his family that this was a sort of loosening up before wrestling. Unfortunately, his older brothers and mother, at the time I talked with them, could not remember this behavior. Jagdish Chandra himself thought that he had perhaps only tried this once or twice before his family had stopped him. This playing at wrestling would have related to the wrestling that went on at the home of Babu Pandey, who had an akhara (wrestling arena) specially constructed in front of his house.

Jagdish Chandra did not show one trait that one might have expected in view of all the others that related to the previous life he recalled. He had little or no interest in swimming, although Jai Gopal had swum often. When Jagdish Chandra first went to Benares, he went into the river off one of the ghats, and his father mentioned in his report that he seemed com-

---

[26] I have not independently verified the facts of Babu Pandey's use of a car. Jagdish Chandra told me that Jai Gopal's mother had confirmed to him that whenever Jai Gopal wanted to go for a drive, a car was sent for and he was driven around. It seems that Jai Gopal was rather pampered.

pletely at ease in the huge river. But afterward Jagdish Chandra seems not
to have sought occasions for swimming. Perhaps he would have shown more
interest in swimming if, as a child, he had had more opportunities. Jai
Gopal lived within a few feet of the ghat and river; but Bareilly is not near
any important river or lake, and one would have to go a considerable distance from there to swim.

Jagdish Chandra's Relationship with the Previous Family. As with so many
of the subjects of these cases, Jagdish Chandra had a strong desire to go to
Benares and visit the previous family. His mother told me in 1969 that
when he would hear a locomotive whistle he would ask if that was the train
that would take them to Benares. Jagdish Chandra told me that it was only
on his insistence that his father took him to Benares. (But, judging from
K. K. N. Sahay's report, I think he had considerable curiosity on his own
to meet the other family and continue verifying his son's statements.)

As I have mentioned, Babu Pandey (although he had earlier invited the
Sahay family to come) treated them coolly in Benares. I have already explained his probable reasons for wishing to remain as aloof as possible from
Jagdish Chandra, whose revelations of private matters were embarrassing
and might have led to serious consequences for him. Babu Pandey's attitude
spread to his womenfolk, whether from direct instructions or ordinary
wisdom we do not know, and they also behaved distantly toward Jagdish. He
felt rebuffed, and even substantially hurt. He nevertheless continued to be
interested in the family. In 1937 he was again in Benares, being then
fourteen years old. He felt a strong attraction to the previous family and a
wish to see the house and people there again. So he went to the Pandeys'
house but did not go in or meet the residents at that time.

In 1949 he returned to Benares, and on this occasion he entered the house
and introduced himself. Babu Pandey had died in the meantime. The
women of the household—the two wives of Babu Pandey and Jai Gopal's
sisters (born after his death) —welcomed him affectionately. Afterward he
continued to visit the family every four years or so, and always with
pleasure. He said the family of Babu Pandey became fond of him and on
his subsequent visits embraced him and wept. That he was welcome in their
family was confirmed to me by Kamla Pandey in 1961.

On the occasion of a later visit to Benares, Jai Gopal's mother did not
recognize him, evidently because she was old. This too was painful to Jagdish Chandra. He expressed himself to me as saddened by the separations
he had experienced through death and afterward from persons he had loved.
In one of our earlier conversations he told me that he had not married
because he wished to reduce the number of his close relationships, hoping
thereby to diminish the suffering incurred in the inevitable partings of our
existence. Later, in 1969, he modified his stated reasons for not marrying

and attributed this rather to a detachment, almost an indifference, with regard to life. He denied being depressed, although he seemed more conscious than the average person of the transience of human life and endeavors. But in 1971 a woman he found attractive subdued all these doubts and hesitations, and he married her.

Some of Jagdish Chandra's attachment to the previous family seemed to be associated with the house and car in Benares, although much of it was undoubtedly related to the people there. He told me in 1969 that he had felt troubled because he had had to ask permission to enter the house of Babu Pandey at the time of his visit to Benares in 1949. But he said this had helped him in the end to become less attached generally to possessions. Nevertheless, his interest in the house persisted, and during a visit to Benares in the mid-1960s he had gone to see the house and meet the family. He last visited Benares in 1969.

Comments on the Evidence of Paranormal Processes in the Case

K. K. N. Sahay was a prominent and respected lawyer of Bareilly. When his son began to talk of a previous life, he called in various colleagues of the bar, who themselves interrogated Jagdish Chandra. Then he openly published details of the case in a newspaper before trying to get in touch with the previous family. Thus I believe that a fraudulent contrivance of this case by him is out of the question. We can also firmly exclude any mingling of memories of the two families so that they afterward came to think the child remembered more of the previous life than he actually did. The principal items of the statements made by Jagdish Chandra concerning the previous life were written down before verification was begun, and most of them were in fact verified before the two families had met. The great physical distance between the families, their separation through membership in different castes, and the close surveillance of Jagdish Chandra when he was a child make it virtually impossible that he could have picked up all the detailed information he showed about Babu Pandey and his family without someone being aware of the person who was passing such information on to the child.

And, finally, even if Jagdish Chandra had somehow acquired normally the informational details about the previous life which he verbalized, we should still have to account in this case, as in so many others, for the strong behavioral traits related to the previous life. No Kayastha parent would consider for a minute drilling (or allowing anyone else to drill) his child in the habits and manners of Brahmins. Such an idea seems quite preposterous to me, but I think it important for the reader to let himself consider fully even the most improbable alternatives before he decides that a case such as this might in the end be best interpreted as reincarnation.

Jagdish Chandra's Later Development

In earlier sections of this report I have given considerable information about Jagdish Chandra's adulthood, particularly to the extent that he appeared to be affected, even in his later life, by memories of the previous life and by the ties he felt to the persons he remembered in that life. Thus I shall only add here some observations concerning the fading and persistence of imaged memories and related behavioral traits in Jagdish Chandra.

Absence of Fading of Memories. Within about six months of his first visit to Benares, Jagdish Chandra (according to his older brother Keshav) began talking less about the previous life. Thereafter he gradually mentioned it less and less, until by the age of six or seven he had stopped speaking spontaneously about it. But Jagdish Chandra claimed to me in 1964 and again in 1969 that his memories of the previous life were still rather clear; thus they had not undergone the fading that occurs in the majority of cases of this type.

His claim in this respect seems to contradict a statement in S. C. Bose's report of the case mentioned earlier. Bose wrote that when he talked with Jagdish Chandra in 1939 (when Jagdish Chandra was sixteen years old), he told him: "I don't remember anything of all that now." When I asked Jagdish Chandra about this, he replied that S. C. Bose had not really conversed with him. This accords in fact with what Bose wrote in his report, for he seems to have exchanged just a few words with Jagdish Chandra and to have done so while leaving the Sahay house after talking with K. K. N. Sahay. It seems likely that Jagdish Chandra said falsely that he had forgotten everything in order to avoid further questioning by S. C. Bose. I have found in other cases that if a child subject dislikes an interrogation or the person asking questions, he may pretend to have forgotten the previous life.

If Jagdish Chandra's original memories did not fade, we may attribute this to the fact that as a child he reviewed them so often in telling them to others. His father never discouraged him from talking about the previous life and seems indeed to have derived some small entertainment from his son's Brahmin attitudes and habits.

The Diminution of Behavioral Traits Related to the Previous Life. In contrast to the absence of fading of imaged memories in this case, or the claim of such absence of fading, many of Jagdish Chandra's strong behavioral traits mentioned earlier diminished in childhood after the age of six, although a few continued into middle adulthood.

In Table 7 I have listed the more important traits related to the previous life shown in childhood by Jagdish Chandra, together with indications of their fading or persistence in later years.

K. K. N. Sahay made no effort to interfere with his son's memories or other behavior related to the previous life. And to some extent he even indulged him, as in the matter of purchasing a car. Jagdish Chandra's intense interest in cars persisted strongly into middle adulthood. But his antagonism toward bearded persons gradually softened and had ceased by the time he was an adult. His distaste for onions receded when he was still a young child; but he did not eat eggs until he was twenty-three, and he was still abstaining from meat in 1971.[27] He also took no alcohol.[28] His fondness for sweets lasted into middle adulthood, although not the special desire for a particular sweet, rabri, that he showed in childhood.

Jagdish Chandra showed no inclination to develop his life along the lines of Babu Pandey. (Since he was not a Brahmin, the vocation of a panda would be closed on him; but I am referring to the less creditable side of Babu Pandey's life.) He went to Lucknow University, trained as a lawyer, and practices law today in his native city of Bareilly.

[27] The distaste for meat could have derived from the influence of his family, since they were vegetarians.

[28] Jagdish Chandra's abstention from alcohol did not derive from any influence in the previous life. Babu Pandey probably indulged in bhang, and I think it very likely that he took milder intoxicants like alcohol also.

TABLE 7. *Summary of Behavioral Traits of Jagdish Chandra Related to the Previous Life*

Trait	Persons Confirming Occurrence of Trait	Fading or Persisting Later	Comments
1. Insistence on eating before other members of the family	Keshav Chandra, Jagdish Chandra's older brother	Ceased gradually in childhood	
2. Refusal to eat with non-Hindus or allow non-Hindus to touch his food	Keshav Chandra	Ceased gradually in childhood	
3. Dislike for bearded persons (Moslems)	Keshav Chandra	Ceased by adulthood	In the previous life this had a basis in religious antagonisms, but Jagdish did not make such a distinction. This trait provides an excellent example of a generalized response apparently related to a previous life.
4. Fondness for sweets, especially rabri	Keshav Chandra, Jamuna Sahay, Jagdish Chandra's mother, Gokul Chandra, Jagdish Chandra's older brother	Diminished in middle adulthood	
5. Reluctance to eat salty foods	Keshav Chandra	Ceased after the age of six	Gokul Chandra could not remember that Jagdish had disliked salty foods.
6. Refusal to eat garlic and onions	Keshav Chandra	Ceased after the age of six	Jamuna Sahay could not remember that Jagdish had refused to eat onions.
7. Refusal to eat meat	Keshav Chandra	Persisting into middle adulthood	The Sahay family were orthodox vegetarian Hindus, so this trait was not unusual in the family. It would, however, also be characteristic of Brahmins.
8. Refusal to eat eggs	Keshav Chandra	Persisted until the age of twenty-three	When Keshav Chandra returned to India after a long stay in England, he persuaded Jagdish Chandra to eat eggs.

9. Liking for bhang	Keshav Chandra Gokul Chandra	No information	In childhood Jagdish Chandra expressed a wish for bhang. In adulthood he has actually tried it only once.
10. Preference for wearing a loin cloth	Keshav Chandra	Diminished after the age of six	
11. Rolling on floor preliminary to wrestling	Unconfirmed	Probably expressed only for a short period	
12. Interest in cars	Jamuna Sahay Keshav Chandra	Persisting strongly into middle adulthood	Jagdish Chandra's father purchased cars and also motor bicycles during Jagdish Chandra's early childhood and thus perhaps reinforced the interest in cars his child already showed.
13. Interest in swimming	K. K. N. Sahay	Manifested only once, on occasion of first visit to Benares	Differing opportunities for swimming may account for the failure of Jagdish Chandra to show interest in swimming.
14. Interest in previous family	Jamuna Sahay	Persisted strongly into middle adulthood, then diminished	

4

The Case of Bishen Chand Kapoor

Introduction

THIS case is an important one for several reasons. First, much of what the subject said about the previous life was recorded in writing before verifications were attempted.[1] (The person who did this was K. K. N. Sahay, who was at the time also investigating the case of his son Jagdish Chandra, the subject of the preceding report of this volume.) Second, I have been able to assemble a considerable amount of information about the previous personality of the case and compare this with information obtained about the conduct of the subject both in childhood and in adulthood. Since the subject, Bishen Chand, was born in 1921, I have information about his development up to middle adulthood. Third, since the previous personality was wealthy and the subject was born in poverty, the case, if considered best interpreted by reincarnation, is outstanding as an instance of "demotion" with regard to socioeconomic circumstances. Because the previous personality was a sensuous dissolute and a murderer, the case naturally stimulates conjectures among Hindus and Buddhists about the contribution his misbehavior may have played in bringing about the "demotion." Beyond mentioning this last aspect here, however, I do not intend to discuss it in the present report; it is best considered when a large number of cases can be examined together.

Summary of the Case and Its Investigation

Bishen Chand Kapoor was born in Bareilly, Uttar Pradesh, on February 7, 1921. His parents were B. Ram Ghulam Kapoor, a railway clerk, and his wife, Kunti Devi. He had an older brother, Bipan Chand (born about 1914), and an older sister, Kamla (born about 1908). A younger brother died in early childhood. Bishen Chand's mother visited the temple of Vishwa Nath in Benares before conceiving him, and, from a sense of gratitude for her pregnancy, she called her son Vishwa Nath. He was known

---

[1] For a list of cases in which a written record was made before verification of the subject's statements, see p. 144, n. 1 above.

by this "pet name" during childhood but gradually adopted his correct name of Bishen Chand.[2]

When Bishen Chand was only ten months old and just barely able to speak, his family heard him uttering the word *pilvit* or *pilivit*. Pilibhit is the name of a large town about 50 kilometers east and slightly north of Bareilly, but the family had no connections there and the name conveyed nothing to them. Gradually, as Bishen Chand gained the power of speech, he began to speak of a previous life in Pilibhit. He mentioned many details of the previous life, including the name he said he then had, Laxmi Narain, and that of a man he described as "uncle," Har Narain. He said his father was a zamindar.[3]

When Bishen Chand was about four years old, his father took him and his older brother, Bipan Chand, to a wedding party at Golda, another town beyond Pilibhit. As they were returning to Bareilly, Bishen Chand heard the station of Pilibhit announced. He then demanded to get off the train, saying he "used to live here." His request was refused, and he cried on the way back to Bareilly.

Some eighteen months later B. Ram Ghulam happened to mention the statements of his child about a previous life to another man, who in turn informed K. K. N. Sahay, who was just then (in the summer of 1926) investigating the case of his own son, Jagdish Chandra. Sahay became interested in Bishen Chand's case also. He went to see Bishen Chand and wrote down some of his statements about the previous life in Pilibhit. He persuaded B. Ram Ghulam to undertake with him a visit to Pilibhit for the verification of the child's statements. Bishen Chand (and his older brother, Bipan Chand) went with the two men to Pilibhit on August 1, 1926. In Pilibhit, Bishen Chand recognized various places and made additional statements about the previous life. The statements and recognitions were found to correspond almost exactly with facts in the life of a young man called Laxmi Narain, who had died in 1918, a little more than two years before the birth of Bishen Chand. In a report published in 1927 K. K. N. Sahay[4] included many details of the statements and recognitions relating to the previous life made by Bishen Chand before and during the first visit to Pilibhit.

---

[2] In the published report of K. K. N. Sahay, from which I shall quote below, the subject is referred to as Vishwa Nath, the "pet name" he was given in childhood. I have not changed this given name in quoting Sahay's report. The family or caste name is Kapoor, but, as is customary in India, I shall not use it in referring to members of the family. Similarly, I shall refer to Bishen Chand's older sister simply as Kamla, without giving her full married name, Kamla Mehrotra.

[3] Zamindars were formerly large landowners and tax-collectors in India, and thus wealthy persons.

[4] K. K. N. Sahay. 1927 (ca.). *Reincarnation: Verified cases of rebirth after death.* Bareilly: N. L. Gupta.

In the middle 1930s S. C. Bose visited K. K. N. Sahay and learned some details of the case. He later published a summary[5] of it, which, however, contains little not included in K. K. N. Sahay's own account.

I first learned of the case from reading Sahay's pamphlet in 1959 and thought it might be feasible to make some further investigations of it. I was unable to begin, however, until 1964. In that year I had two interviews with Bishen Chand's older brother, Bipan Chand, and a short one with his sister-in-law, Bipan Chand's wife, Shyam Rani. Later in the same year Prof. P. Pal met B. Ram Ghulam, Bishen Chand's father, in Bareilly. B. Ram Ghulam, although eighty-two years old, seemingly still possessed an excellent memory. Professor Pal took down, as B. Ram Ghulam spoke, a long statement that confirmed and supplemented the information published by K. K. N. Sahay and also obtained by me from other informants. (B. Ram Ghulam died in 1966; his wife, Bishen Chand's mother, had died in 1948.) Finally, in 1969 I met Bishen Chand himself and had a long interview with him at his home in Bareilly. (He worked during the week as an excise tax collector in another town, Rampur, which accounted for my inability to meet him during an earlier visit to India.) In 1971 I met him again, and we had a further long talk about his memories and the possible connections between the previous life and events in his life. After that meeting we exchanged some letters. Then in 1974, when I was again in Bareilly, I met Bishen Chand once more and for the last time prior to publication of this volume.

Persons Interviewed during the Investigation

In Lucknow I interviewed:

Bipan Chand Kapoor, Bishen Chand's older brother
Shyam Rani, Bipan Chand's wife
Kamla, Bishen Chand's older sister

In Bareilly I interviewed:

Bishen Chand Kapoor

In Pilibhit I interviewed:

Rajendra Mohan, Laxmi Narain's second cousin

In Bareilly Prof. P. Pal interviewed:

B. Ram Ghulam Kapoor, Bishen Chand's father

---

[5] S. C. Bose. 1960. *Jatismar katha*. Satsang, Bihar: Privately published. (English translation by E. J. Spencer; unpublished typescript.)

Relevant Facts of Geography and Possibilities for Normal Means of Communication between the Two Families

Bareilly is a large city (now of perhaps 500,000 persons) in western Uttar Pradesh. Pilibhit is a large town (of perhaps 50,000 persons) approximately 50 kilometers east of Bareilly. The cities are (and were in 1926) joined by a railway line (as well as a road), and there is naturally much traffic between them.

Bishen Chand's family had no connections whatever with Pilibhit or the family to which he referred. Members of Bishen Chand's family had, however, on at least one occasion (already mentioned) passed through Pilibhit on the train. According to Bipan Chand, however, they had never stopped there prior to the first visit for the verifications of Bishen Chand's statements in 1926.

During the visit for verifications in Pilibhit, K. K. N. Sahay learned that B. Upendra Narain, the brother of the previous personality's mother, lived in Bareilly with his wife. His house, I ascertained later, was in the quarter of Bareilly where the school that Bishen Chand attended was situated. But the two homes (of B. Ram Ghulam and B. Upendra Narain) were about 2 kilometers apart. B. Upendra Narain's sister, Laxmi Narain's mother, was still living in Pilibhit during the first half of 1926, but she would come to Bareilly from time to time to visit her brother; not long after Bishen Chand's first visit to Pilibhit she moved to Bareilly and remained there with her brother. It is therefore conceivable that information about Laxmi Narain might have been diffused in Bareilly from Laxmi Narain's mother and uncle,[6] and might then have somehow reached Bishen Chand and furnished him with the materials for imagining that he had been Laxmi Narain in a previous life. I think we can be certain, however, that the route of any such normally transmitted information was completely unknown (up to August 1, 1926) to B. Ram Ghulam and K. K. N. Sahay. If they had known of the existence in Bareilly of the uncle of the previous personality, or of the occasional visits to Bareilly of his mother, they would certainly have sought them out to verify the statements of the child before undertaking a trip to Pilibhit to do so. I regard the fact that they went first to Pilibhit as almost proof of complete ignorance on the part of Bishen Chand's family of any facts connected with the life of Laxmi Narain.

Further evidence of a lack of prior acquaintance between the two families comes from the fact (as will be seen from Sahay's report) that Bishen Chand's family definitely identified the family to which he referred only

[6] These persons by no means conclude the list of those who knew Laxmi Narain and who lived in Bareilly. As will be seen in K. K. N. Sahay's report, a teacher of Laxmi Narain's time in Pilibhit, Sita Ram, had since moved to Bareilly and in 1926 was teaching in a school there.

when, during the first visit to Pilibhit, he recognized Laxmi Narain and his father in a photograph that was shown to him there. They then learned that Har Narain was Laxmi Narain's father, not his uncle.

In addition to the foregoing, B. Ram Ghulam stated that Bishen Chand had begun to talk about Pilibhit and his life there when he could still not speak clearly. Even at the age of ten months he was muttering *pilvit* indistinctly. And he was talking in some detail about the previous life when still under three years old, an age when he would be most unlikely to have come into contact with any strangers without this fact being known to his parents.

The Life and Character of Laxmi Narain

Readers will find the detailed account given later of Bishen Chand's statements and recognitions more intelligible if I here describe the life and character of Laxmi Narain, the previous personality to whom the statements of Bishen Chand referred. I have not myself interviewed any member of Laxmi Narain's family who knew him. In 1971, I met in Pilibhit Rajendra Mohan, a grandson of Laxmi Narain's paternal uncle, and therefore Laxmi Narain's second cousin, but Rajendra Mohan was born several years after Laxmi Narain's death. I have therefore had to base my account of him on the information furnished by K. K. N. Sahay and by Bishen Chand's father and older brother, who had talked with members of the previous family and with other persons of Pilibhit who remembered Laxmi Narain.

Laxmi Narain was the only son of a wealthy landowner, Har Narain, who spoiled his son and encouraged him in a taste for luxury and extravagance. Laxmi Narain dropped out of school after the sixth class, which ordinarily is completed by students at the age of about twelve. But B. Ram Ghulam learned that Laxmi Narain left school after the death of his father, which occurred when the boy was seventeen or eighteen years old. He must have been a most desultory student if he had only reached the sixth class at the age of seventeen. Laxmi Narain probably continued afterward with some private education or self-instruction, and apparently learned Urdu.[7]

When Laxmi Narain's father died, he left his son a substantial inheritance. Thereafter, Laxmi Narain freely indulged his fondness for good food, fine clothes, beautiful women, and alcohol. He seems to have had no settled occupation other than these pleasures; at one time he worked in the

---

[7] Urdu, a variant of Hindi, is written in Arabic script and includes many words of Persian or Arabic origin. The British favored Urdu during their dominance in India and required civil servants to use it. Since Laxmi Narain worked in the railway service at one time, I infer that he must have known Urdu as Bishen Chand claimed he did.

railway service, although we do not know for how long. He engaged in a lawsuit with relatives over family property and won the suit.

Har Narain had been a generous person and had given freely to charities. Consequently, his fortune was much diminished when he died. Laxmi Narain continued its dispersal. At his death, his mother had almost nothing to live on and was forced eventually to move in with her brother, B. Upendra Narain. The family house became dilapidated and was partly in ruins by 1926.

Laxmi Narain had a special attachment for a prostitute, Padma, and regarded her as reserved for himself. He also seems to have had a quick temper. One day he saw another man coming out of Padma's apartment. Instantly he seized a gun carried by his servant who was with him and shot the man dead. Laxmi Narain then hid in the house or compound of his home. Probably through bribery the case against him was hushed up, and after a time he emerged from hiding. If an allusion to a lawsuit in K. K. N. Sahay's report refers, as I think it does, to legal maneuvering connected with this murder, it occurred in 1918. Soon after this event Laxmi Narain moved to another town, Shahjahanpur (also in Uttar Pradesh), where he remained until his death in December 1918, at the age (probably) of thirty-two.

The reader should not suppose that the life of Laxmi Narain was one of unrelieved vice. On the contrary, the testimony of contemporaries tells about his great generosity. He was known sometimes to give his own food to beggars. B. Ram Ghulam learned that Laxmi Narain had given 500 rupees (an enormous sum in those days) to a Moslem watch dealer as an advance with which to begin his business (item 18, Table 8).

Laxmi Narain had strong religious inclinations. Bipan Chand had learned (from his father, who had got this information from Laxmi Narain's mother) that Laxmi Narain would worship austerely for ten to fifteen days, keeping himself secluded in the thakurdwara (shrine room) of the house during this period and even having his meals there. After this period he would devote the rest of the month, with equal earnestness, to debauchery. At the opening of a new month he would return to the first phase of the cycle.

K. K. N. Sahay learned from B. Upendra Narain, Laxmi Narain's maternal uncle, that Laxmi Narain had "remembered his previous birth [life] up to the age of six years. He said that he came from Jahanabad. [There are places of this name in Bihar and in West Bengal, near Calcutta.] But as the parents of Laxmi Narain thought that publicity would be harmful for the life and welfare of the boy, it was kept secret and no verification was made." Bipan Chand told me many years later that the previous personality whose life Laxmi Narain remembered had been a rajah's son. But he did not then remembered any other details of what Laxmi Narain was said to have remembered of that life. Bishen Chand had no memories of the previous life remembered by Laxmi Narain.[8]

The Published Report of K. K. N. Sahay

I shall next quote almost the entire report of the case published by K. K. N. Sahay. To facilitate reading and understanding the report, I have changed the order of one section, omitted some irrelevant material, and here and there modified the phrasing without changing the meaning. Much of the published report consists of a reprinting of two long letters sent by Sahay to the national newspaper, the *Leader*. The dates of publication of these letters as given in Sahay's report are August 12, 1926, and August 30, 1926.

Vishwa Nath [Bishen Chand] was born on February 7, 1921 in Mohalla [quarter] Khannu, Bareilly, [Uttar Pradesh]. He began to ask about Pilibhit when he was a year and a half old. He asked the distance between Pilibhit and Bareilly and wanted to know when his father would take him there. When he was three years old he began to give a detailed account of himself. The parents were afraid and tried to hide these strange facts. There is a superstition that such children do not live long and the sooner they forget the better for them.

I very recently heard of this case from Thakur Moti Singh, Vakil [attorney] and ex-member, Legislative Council, and went to see B. Ram Ghulam [Vishwa Nath's father] and Vishwa Nath on June 29, [1926]. I persuaded B. Ram Ghulam to go to Pilibhit to verify the facts and offered to accompany him.

I had taken down the story of Vishwa Nath on my first visit to him and had to verify only the following facts. . . . He had given his uncle's [of the previous life] name as Har Narain,[9] Caste Kayastha, Mohalla Ganj, City Pilibhit, and his age [as] twenty years [at death]. He said he was unmarried. He said his neighbour was . . . Sunder Lal, who had a green gate, a sword, and a gun, and had nautch [dancing] parties in the courtyard of his house. He described his own house as a double story building with separate apartments for ladies and gentlemen. He described singing parties and feasts which were frequently held at his house. He also described his great fondness for wine, rohu fish, and nautch [dancing] girls. He said he had studied up to the Class VI in the Government School near the river and knew Urdu, Hindi, and English. He described a thakurdwara [shrine room] in his house. . . .

We [B. Ram Ghulam, Bishen Chand, and Sahay] went to Pilibhit on Sunday, August 1, [1926]. We went directly to the Government High School, Pilibhit, which the boy did not recognize as his school. The present building of the

---

[8] For another instance of a subject who remembered the life of a person who in turn remembered a previous life, see the case of Mounzer Haïdar, to be published in the third volume of this series.

[9] Har Narain was the father, not the uncle, of Laxmi Narain. For a possible explanation of how the word *uncle* became attached to him by Bishen Chand, see p. 185 below.

School is new and was recently erected. I requested the Headmaster, Sahib Babu[10] Asharfi Lal, to help me in the investigation which he kindly did and accompanied [us] to the various places.

When we reached the gate of the late Sahu[11] Shyam Sunder Lal, the boy got down from the tonga [carriage] and recognized . . . the green gate of Sunder Lal. He also pointed to the courtyard where nautch parties were held. This was corroborated by the neighbouring shopkeepers. I saw the gate myself. It had a green varnish which had grown faint by lapse of time. Then we went to the house of the late Debi Prasad, Rais,[12] which the boy recognized as his house. He shouted that that was the house of Har Narain. Har Narain was the son of Debi Prasad. Portions of this big old house have fallen and the building has been abandoned by the family. The neighbours told us that the place had undergone a great change. The boy recognized the building . . . and the place where they used to drink wine, eat rohu fish, and hear the songs of nautch girls. The boy was questioned regarding the situation of the staircase which he pointed out correctly, among the heap of bricks and mud. He then recognized the zenana apartments[13] and specially mentioned a room on the upper story which ladies occupied.

An old and faint photograph of Har Narain and his son was brought by the sole surviving member of the family, Babu Brij Mohan Lal, who lives in a separate house. In the presence of a big crowd the boy put his finger on the photograph of Har Narain and said, "Here is Har Narain and here I," pointing to the photograph of a boy seated on a chair in the photograph. This was most remarkable and immediately established his identity as Laxmi Narain, son of Babu Har Narain.

We next took him to the old Government High School which the boy at once recognized as his school and went round it. He swiftly began to ascend the staircase which is situated in the right-hand corner. I and three men followed him up. On reaching the topmost roof he pointed out the River Deuha which was flowing on the back side.

The boy was next questioned about the place where Class VI was held in his time. He pointed out a room which was admitted to be correct by his two old class-fellows of Class VI, Babu Bishambar Nath, whose old photograph was recognized by the boy, and Babu Ram Ghulam[14] of Pilibhit who came out of the assembled crowd. The old class-fellows asked him the name of the teacher. He described him as a fat bearded man whose name was given by the crowd as M. Moin-ud-din of Shahjahanpur. In the house [of the previous personality] he

---

[10] *Sahib* is an honorific meaning approximately "Sir." *Babu* was (and is) also used as an honorific for respected persons.

[11] A sahu is a businessman, especially a private banker.

[12] The British often conferred the honorary titles of Rais (or Raisahib) and Rajah on a wealthy or otherwise prominent person whom they wished to honor or whose support they wished to cultivate.

[13] These are the female quarters of a house. In fact, Bishen Chand used the Urdu word *masurate* instead of the Hindi word *zenana*, familiar in his family.

[14] This former schoolmate of Laxmi Narain should not be confused with B. Ram Ghulam, Bishen Chand's father.

had correctly pointed out the old thakurdwara which he had mentioned before.

The boy was given a pair of tablas [drums] on which he played with ease. His father, B. Ram Ghulam, informed me that the boy never [previously] saw the tablas in his lifetime. The name of the prostitute with whom the boy associated in his previous life was repeatedly asked by . . . people [in the crowd]. He reluctantly mentioned the name "Padma" which the people certified as correct.

. . . Laxmi Narain, son of Babu Har Narain, died at Shahjahanpur on December 15, 1918, at 6 A.M. of fever and lung trouble. His age at the time of death was 32 years and 11 days. He died after a protracted illness of five months. I am indebted to B. Upendra Narain, the maternal uncle of Laxmi Narain, for the above information. He also writes [15] that the boy, Vishwa Nath, has narrated several incidents which were forgotten by members of the family. . . .

The character of Laxmi Narain was very gay. He loved wine, flesh, and women.

The mother of Laxmi Narain is living [16] at Bareilly with her brother, B. Upendra Narain. The boy was taken to her and she put the following test questions to the boy Vishwa Nath and became convinced that he is the reincarnation of her late lamented son.

Q. Did you fly kites?

A. Yes.

Q. With whom did you contest [in kite flying]? [17]

A. I contested with every kite that came in my range, but particularly I contested with Sunder Lal.

Q. Did you throw [away] my achar [pickle]?

A. I did throw [away the] achar but how was it possible to eat worms? You wanted me to eat worms, hence I threw your achar away.

NOTE: The mother says that once her pickles got rotten and she had worms in the jars. She threw the worms [out, but] kept the pickles in the sun. Laxmi Narain threw the pickle [away] much to her annoyance.

Q. Did you ever enter into the service?

A. Yes, I served for some time in [the Oudh] Railway.

Q. Who was your servant?

A. My servant was Maikua, a black, short-statured Kahar.[18] He was my favorite khansama [cook].

[15] Since B. Upendra Narain lived in Bareilly at this time (1926), this reference to writing can only mean that K. K. N. Sahay persuaded him to write out a report of what he knew of the life of Laxmi Narain, as well as an account of some additional statements made by Bishen Chand on later occasions of meeting the previous family. I shall refer to some of these occasions below.

[16] It is my understanding that at this time (August 1926) Laxmi Narain's mother had not yet moved to Bareilly and so could be better described as "staying" with her brother in Bareilly, rather than "living" with him, which she did later.

[17] Contests with kites are a favorite sport in India and other parts of South Asia. A contestant tries with his kite to entangle or cut the string of an opponent's kite.

[18] Kahars are a low caste group who work in kitchens or at other domestic services.

Q. You used to sleep on a bamboo charpoy[19] with no bedding. [This] question [was put] by B. Balbir Singh of Killa, Bareilly.

A. You never saw my bed. I had a good bed with an ornamental plank towards the head side and had a qalin [thick cover] on [it] and [I] kept two pillows under the head and two under my feet.

Q. What did I teach at Pilibhit? [This question was put by Sita Ram, a teacher of the Government School, Bareilly, who was formerly a teacher at Pilibhit.]

A. You taught Hindi.

Bishen Chand called Har Narain . . . his Tau [uncle]. There is a gentleman living in the quarter [of Bareilly] who is universally called Har Narain Tau [i.e., "Uncle" Har Narain]; hence the epithet imperceptibly suggested itself to the child.[20]

The boy remembers the name of Sahu Shyam Sunder Lal as Sunder Lal.

B. Jwala Prasad, Vakil [attorney of] Bareilly, referred to his diary. He finds that in 1918 he defended Laxmi Narain of Pilibhit in a criminal case under Section 193, Indian Penal Code, which was the offshoot of another case which took place at the house of Padma [the] prostitute, in which Laxmi Narain took part and gave evidence.

Additional Statements and Recognitions Made by Bishen Chand

K. K. N. Sahay performed a most valuable service in writing down some of Bishen Chand's statements *before* beginning their verification. He actually recorded (or at any rate published) less than half of Bishen Chand's statements. To those he did mention, we can add others that Bishen Chand made during the visit to Pilibhit and soon afterward, and still others about which I learned from the interviews with Bishen Chand's father, brother, and sister. These additional statements, together with one made to me by Bishen Chand himself, I have included in Table 8 along with those recorded by K. K. N. Sahay. These additional statements do not have the same force as evidence as those he noted before verification. Nor do they have the same value as the other items that he recorded within a few weeks of the visit to Pilibhit (August 1, 1926) when he sent letters to the newspaper that were published on the dates mentioned earlier. Skeptics may consider the

---

[19] A charpoy is a simple bed with four short wooden posts and with jute cord or sometimes canvas strips for the occupant to sleep on. It is the usual bed of poor persons in India and sometimes more prosperous ones also. The statement was deliberately made to Bishen Chand to test his knowledge of the luxury in which Laxmi Narain lived.

[20] Some Indian children pick up the habit of using for a parent the name Uncle, for example, which they hear other older children of the same extended family using to address the parent. In this way it is conceivable (although unverified) that Laxmi Narain had the habit of calling his father Uncle. (For another example of this, see the use of the relationship word *chachi* by Jagdish Chandra in the report of his case earlier in this volume.) There are thus two possible explanations for Bishen Chand's referring to Har Narain as "Uncle."

TABLE 8. *Summary of Statements and Recognitions Made by Bishen Chand*

Item	Informants	Verification	Comments
1. His name was Laxmi Narain.	Bipan Chand, Bishen Chand's older brother Kamla, Bishen Chand's older sister	K. K. N. Sahay	K. K. N. Sahay did not mention that Bishen Chand had given the name of Laxmi Narain before the first visit to Pilibhit.
2. His "uncle" was Har Narain.*	K. K. N. Sahay	Incorrect	Bishen Chand referred to Laxmi Narain's father as "Uncle" Har Narain. But Har Narain was Laxmi Narain's father, not his uncle. (See p. 185 for a possible explanation of this error.)
3. He was of the Kayastha caste.*	K. K. N. Sahay	Bipan Chand Rajendra Mohan, Laxmi Narain's second cousin	Bishen Chand's family are of the Kattri subcaste of the Kshatriya caste. Laxmi Narain's family are of the Kayastha caste.
4. He lived in Pilibhit.*	K. K. N. Sahay	K. K. N. Sahay	
5. He lived in Mohalla Ganj.*	K. K. N. Sahay	Incorrect	According to Rajendra Mohan, Har Narain's house was in Mohalla Sarai Khan, not in Mohalla Ganj, although there is a Mohalla Ganj some distance away in Pilibhit. A mohalla is a quarter or subdivision of a town or city.
6. His father was a zamindar [wealthy landowner].*	K. K. N. Sahay	B. Ram Ghulam, Bishen Chand's father K. K. N. Sahay	B. Ram Ghulam said (to P. Pal) that Har Narain was a prominent person of Pilibhit who had the courtesy title of Rajah. K. K. N. Sahay stated that Laxmi Narain's family were zamindars.
7. His father died before he did.	K. K. N. Sahay	B. Ram Ghulam Bipan Chand	This and the following item were not independently verified.
8. A large crowd attended his father's funeral.	B. Ram Ghulam	B. Ram Ghulam	Har Narain was popular in Pilibhit for his charities. A huge throng of mourners followed his bier.

9. His father gave him silk clothes. *	K. K. N. Sahay	Probable, but not specifically verified	In view of the wealth of Laxmi Narain's father, this statement is almost certainly correct.
10. He studied up to the sixth class in the government school.*	K. K. N. Sahay	B. Ram Ghulam K. K. N. Sahay	
11. His school was near the river.*	K. K. N. Sahay	K. K. N. Sahay	This refers to the river Deuha, which flows past Pilibhit.
12. His English teacher in the sixth grade was fat and wore a beard.	K. K. N. Sahay	K. K. N. Sahay	In his report of the case K. K. N. Sahay mentioned only that Bishen Chand (at Pilibhit) described a teacher (of Laxmi Narain) as fat and bearded. The other details were reported by S. C. Bose in his report cited earlier; but he obtained his information about the case from K. K. N. Sahay.
13. He knew Urdu, Hindi, and English.*	K. K. N. Sahay	B. Ram Ghulam	B. Ram Ghulam verified only that Laxmi Narain had studied Urdu, not English. But see comment for item 12. S. C. Bose quoted K. K. N. Sahay as also verifying that Laxmi Narain had studied English in school, although K. K. N. Sahay did not mention this in his own report of the case. Since Laxmi Narain worked in the railway service (in the British period), it can be assumed that he must have known some Urdu and English.
14. His house had two stories.*	K. K. N. Sahay	K. K. N. Sahay	K. K. N. Sahay's report mentioned a staircase recognized by Bishen Chand and an upper story where the women's quarters were.
15. His house had separate apartments for men and	K. K. N. Sahay	K. K. N. Sahay	In the houses of wealthier persons it was customary for women to live in separate

* Recorded in writing by K. K. N. Sahay before verification of Bishen Chand's statements was begun.

TABLE 8 (*cont.*)

Item	Informants	Verification	Comments
15. (cont.) women.*			quarters called zenana apartments. But Bishen Chand referred to these with the word *masurate*, not *zenana*.
16. There was a thakurdwara [shrine room] in the house.*	K. K. N. Sahay	K. K. N. Sahay	Many Hindu houses, especially large ones, have such shrine rooms, and so this detail is not very specific. In fact, the modest home of B. Ram Ghulam also had a thakurdwara.
17. He used to listen to and watch nautch girls.*	K. K. N. Sahay	K. K. N. Sahay	Nautch girls sing and dance in private or public places. They correspond roughly to the night club dancers of Western cities.
18. He established a Moslem watch dealer in business in Pilibhit.	B. Ram Ghulam	B. Ram Ghulam	See text for details of this gift.
19. He used to drink wine with Padma out of the same glass.	Bipan Chand	Unverified	I cannot find in my notes that this detail was specifically verified, but the known facts of Laxmi Narain's friendship with Padma make it almost certainly correct.
20. His "uncle" Har Prasad had a green house.	B. Ram Ghulam	B. Ram Ghulam	Har Prasad was actually a close friend, not a real brother, of Har Narain. But since in India close friends are often called brother, it would have been natural for Laxmi Narain to refer to Har Prasad as his uncle.
21. Har Prasad's mistress was called Hero.	B. Ram Ghulam	B. Ram Ghulam	
22. His own mistress was called Padma.	K. K. N. Sahay	K. K. N. Sahay	It seems that Bishen Chand did not mention her by name before he first went to Pilibhit.

Item			Comments
23. He had a neighbor, Sunder Lal.*	K. K. N. Sahay	K. K. N. Sahay*	From K. K. N. Sahay's report I infer that the house of Sunder Lal was close to that of Har Narain, but he does not say so explicitly.
24. Sunder Lal's house had a green gate.*	K. K. N. Sahay	K. K. N. Sahay	
25. Sunder Lal had a sword.*	K. K. N. Sahay	Unverified	
26. Sunder Lal had a gun.*	K. K. N. Sahay	Unverified	
27. Sunder Lal had nautch [dancing] parties in the courtyard of his house.*	K. K. N. Sahay	Unverified	This probably is correct, in view of the friendship between Sunder Lal and Laxmi Narain.
28. He used to drink wine.*	K. K. N. Sahay	K. K. N. Sahay Bipan Chand	
29. He liked to eat rohu fish.*	K. K. N. Sahay	K. K. N. Sahay	
30. He competed in kite flying with Sunder Lal.	K. K. N. Sahay	K. K. N. Sahay B. Ram Ghulam	
31. He worked for a time with the Oudh Railway.	K. K. N. Sahay	K. K. N. Sahay	
32. He once threw away some of his mother's pickles.	K. K. N. Sahay	K. K. N. Sahay	See the quoted report of K. K. N. Sahay for details of this item (p. 184).
33. His servant was called Maikua.	K. K. N. Sahay	K. K. N. Sahay	According to Bipan Chand, Bishen Chand gave the name of Laxmi Narain's servant before he went to Pilibhit; but since K. K. N. Sahay did not indicate this in his report, I have not listed it thus here.
34. Maikua was of the Kahar caste.	K. K. N. Sahay B. Ram Ghulam Bipan Chand	K. K. N. Sahay	Bipan Chand said that Bishen Chand mentioned Maikua's name before going to Pilibhit, but B. Ram Ghulam said he

* Recorded in writing by K. K. N. Sahay before verification of Bishen Chand's statements was begun.

TABLE 8 (*cont.*)

Item	Informants	Verification	Comments
34. (*cont.*)			mentioned it at Pilibhit, without, however, denying that he had given the name before.
35. Maikua was dark and short.		K. K. N. Sahay	
36. Maikua was also a cook.		K. K. N. Sahay	
37. His bed was an elegant one with a heavy covering and four pillows.		K. K. N. Sahay	
38. He won a lawsuit against some relatives.	Kamla Shyam Rani, Bipan Chand's wife	B. Ram Ghulam	Bishen Chand's sister, Kamla, remembered having heard him say that the lawsuit was against Laxmi Narain's father; this is most unlikely, since Laxmi Narain had a good relationship with his father, who died when Laxmi Narain was only in his late teens. Shyam Rani said that Bishen Chand had referred to a lawsuit against a maternal uncle which Laxmi Narain had won. Although she was (almost certainly) a secondhand witness for the item, I think her version of what Bishen Chand said much more likely to be correct than Kamla's. There had actually been protracted lawsuits, not just one engagement, between Laxmi Narain and some of his relatives. (See text for an account of how Bishen Chand expressed some of the emotional residue of these legal battles in his attitude toward the women of the branch of the family with whom Laxmi Narain had quarreled.)

Statement	Informants	Verification	Comments
39. He shot and killed a man who was coming out of Padma's house.	Bipan Chand Bishen Chand (1969)	Bipan Chand	The lawsuit of 1918, mentioned at the end of K. K. N. Sahay's report, probably arose out of this episode.
40. He was drunk at the time of the murder.	Bishen Chand (1969)	Unverified	
41. After the murder he hid out in the garden.	Bipan Chand	Unverified	Bipan Chand said Bishen Chand had said he had hidden in the house.
42. His mother sent food to him when he was hiding.	Kamla	Unverified	This is probably correct if Laxmi Narain was hiding in the garden.
43. He took a job in Shahjahanpur.	Kamla	Kamla	After the murder had been hushed up, it must have seemed wiser for Laxmi Narain to leave Pilibhit. He moved to Shahjahanpur, another town of Uttar Pradesh.
44. He sent rice and oranges to his aunt.	Kamla	Kamla	
45. He died in Shahjahanpur.	B. Ram Ghulam	K. K. N. Sahay	
46. He was unmarried.*	K. K. N. Sahay	Unverified	
47. He had been under the treatment of Hanumant Vaidya, an Ayurvedic physician of Shahjahanpur, before he died.	B. Ram Ghulam	Unverified	When B. Ram Ghulam went to Shahjahanpur to verify this, he found that there had been an Ayurvedic physician of this name there, but that he had died by the time of B. Ram Ghulam's visit. Therefore, he could not verify whether he had in fact treated Laxmi Narain. Ayurvedic medicine is the traditional medicine of India and is still practiced in many parts of the country.
48. He was twenty years old when he died.	K. K. N. Sahay	Incorrect	Laxmi Narain was thirty-two when he died according to his uncle, B. Upendra Narain.

* Recorded in writing by K. K. N. Sahay before verification of Bishen Chand's statements was begun.

TABLE 8 (cont.)

Item	Informants	Verification	Comments
49. Recognition of Sunder Lal's house in Pilibhit	K. K. N. Sahay		K. K. N. Sahay's report (see text of this above) suggested that the carriage might have stopped before Bishen Chand recognized the house, but S. C. Bose, quoting K. K. N. Sahay, stated clearly that the boy recognized the house spontaneously.
50. Recognition of Har Narain's house, which had also been that of Laxmi Narain	K. K. N. Sahay		Bishen Chand seems to have also recognized this house, or rather its ruins, spontaneously. Both this recognition and the preceding one lose some force from the fact that the boy knew he was being taken to Pilibhit for recognitions. This must have implied to him visits to the house where Laxmi Narain had lived and also the houses of his friends.
51. Recognition of Har Narain and Laxmi Narain in an old photograph	K. K. N. Sahay		These recognitions first clearly identified Laxmi Narain as the son of the person Bishen Chand was calling "Uncle" Har Narain.
52. Recognition of the place where the staircase in Laxmi Narain's house had been	K. K. N. Sahay		The house was in such ruins that Bishen Chand's recognition of where the staircase had been was considered paranormal.
53. Recognition of room where treasure had been buried	Bipan Chand		Bishen Chand did not show the exact place where treasure had been buried, but his indication of the room led to a further search and the treasure was found. It consisted of gold coins.
54. Recognition of shrine room (thakurdwara) of Laxmi Narain's house	K. K. N. Sahay		This was not an important recognition, since even in a house in ruins there might have been some fragments of decorations or Hindu idols that would have quickly

		suggested that the room was used for worship.
55. Recognition of the house of Lalta Prasad, a merchant	B. Ram Ghulam	During the visit to Pilibhit, someone pointed to a certain house and asked Bishen Chand whose it was. He said: "That of Lalta Prasad, the merchant."
56. Recognition of the former shop of Ismail, the watch repairer	Bipan Chand	On the way through the bazaar in Pilibhit, Bishen Chand stopped the tonga, got down, and went to a particular shop. He looked at it intently and said that it was the shop of his friend Ismail, where he had had his watch repaired. Ismail had died by that time, and the shop had changed hands some years earlier. There was no sign at the shop indicating the name Ismail. Bishen Chand's family verified that the shop had formerly been that of Ismail, a watch repairer. He was probably the same Moslem watch dealer referred to in item 18.

items reported many years later in interviews with Professor Pal and myself during the 1960s as mere embellishments added later by the witnesses. The testimonies of Bishen Chand's father, brother, and sister were (with the usual small discrepancies about details) concordant in three independent interviews, but I cannot exclude the possibility that this agreement arose from their having discussed the case together, perhaps often, over the years.

The murder of a rival lover by Laxmi Narain is the most important additional detail not described in K. K. N. Sahay's report—although it is hinted at there, in the reference to a criminal court case. Bishen Chand's statements about this murder were well known to his brother and sister. Bishen Chand himself said in 1969 that he still vividly remembered the incident. I believe that K. K. N. Sahay knew all about the murder in 1926, but that he did not publish it out of a wish not to offend surviving members of Laxmi Narain's family and perhaps also out of consideration for Bishen Chand's family.

Summary of Statements and Recognitions Made by Bishen Chand

We have thus altogether forty-eight statements about the previous life made by Bishen Chand (listed in Table 8). Of these forty-eight, K. K. N. Sahay wrote down twenty-one before verification was attempted; of these twenty-one statements, fourteen were verified. In one statement (item 2) Bishen Chand gave a correctly relevant name (Har Narain) but incorrectly identified the relationship to Laxmi Narain of the person named. Bishen Chand wrongly referred to Har Narain as "uncle," when he was in fact Laxmi Narain's father. As already mentioned, this error may have derived from a childhood habit of Laxmi Narain's carried over into the memories of Bishen Chand (see p. 185). Six other items were not verified, or else K. K. N. Sahay's report and the later informants did not mention the verification. Some of these were almost certainly correct, but we cannot say this except from inference. Bishen Chand made all but one of the remaining twenty-seven statements either during the visit to Pilibhit or in subsequent meetings soon afterward between the families and other persons concerned. Bishen Chand himself told item 40 to me in 1969.

Nearly all Bishen Chand's statements that could be verified were correct; in fact only two were completely wrong. These were his statements about the mohalla (quarter) of Pilibhit in which the house was located (item 5) and the age of Laxmi Narain at the time of his death (item 48).

The informants for the case, principally K. K. N. Sahay, stated that Bishen Chand had made eight recognitions during the visit to Pilibhit. Of these, the most important probably was his indication of the place where Laxmi Narain's father had hidden some treasure (item 53). After the death of Har Narain it was thought that he had left a treasure hidden somewhere, but no one knew, or told, where.[21] Laxmi Narain's mother asked Bishen Chand where the treasure was, and he led the way to a room. The treasure was found later in this room. The informant for this event, Bipan Chand, did not say that Bishen Chand was able to show the exact spot where the treasure was hidden, but his indication of the correct room was a sufficient stimulus for a new and successful search. Bipan Chand learned from his father that the treasure consisted of gold coins.

Bishen Chand's Behavior Related to the Previous Life

The Attitudes of Bishen Chand toward Laxmi Narain's Family and Friends. Bishen Chand showed much affection and consideration for Laxmi Narain's mother. When he returned from Pilibhit he tried to persuade his father to invite her to live with them. He would say: "Papa, she would not cost you much. She wears a plain sari and a petticoat and spends the greater part of the day in prayers and worship." When Laxmi Narain's mother came to visit Bishen Chand and his family, they found that he had described her correctly.

Following Bishen Chand's first visit to Pilibhit at the age of five and a half, he established affectionate relations with Laxmi Narain's mother and remained in touch with her until he was fifteen years old. When she moved to Bareilly and stayed with her brother, Bishen Chand used to visit her often, taking meals at the house of Laxmi Narain's uncle and sometimes even sleeping there. He insisted that he wanted to live with her. And he sometimes went alone to visit her at her brother's house.

Later Laxmi Narain's mother moved to Lucknow with her brother, who was transferred there by the railway for which he worked. Once she came back to Bareilly from Lucknow and stayed in B. Ram Ghulam's home for a few days visiting with Bishen Chand and his family. When the time came for her to return to Lucknow, Bishen Chand did not want her to go. When she left anyway, Bishen Chand told the rickshaw puller he would give him double fare if he would bring back news of her safe arrival. (He was

---

[21] People in Asia frequently place money, jewelry, or other valuable property in the ground or in hidden recesses of the walls and floors of houses. The motives for such concealment include distrust of banks, dislike of taxes, concern about inflation, fear of thieves, and simple miserliness. The owners usually intend to tell someone where the treasure is before they die, but sometimes they die without doing so. In the present case it seems that Har Narain, before he died, told Laxmi Narain where the treasure was, but Laxmi Narain told no one else before *he* died. The habit of burying or concealing money and other valuables is not confined to persons of wealth. For another example, see the report of the case of Disna Samarasinghe in the next volume of this series.

evidently too young to realize that the rickshaw puller would take Laxmi Narain's mother only to the railway station, not all the way to Lucknow.)

Bishen Chand expressed a definite preference for Laxmi Narain's mother over his own. This was remarked on by both his older brother and sister in their testimony and was acknowledged by Bishen Chand himself during my interviews with him. However, he was unable to identify just what he preferred about Laxmi Narain's mother.

As already mentioned, Laxmi Narain had engaged in a lawsuit with his uncle and other relatives which he had won. Bishen Chand showed evidence of preserving the bitterness of this quarrel. Once when some of the daughters-in-law of Laxmi Narain's uncle (I do not know just how many) came to visit him, they offered him some sweets which he refused. Then they offered him a rupee which he also refused. When they offered him two rupees, Bishen Chand rebuked them: "You wanted to take my blood, and now you are tempting me with money."

Bishen Chand met Padma, Laxmi Narain's favorite prostitute, when he was a child. Padma came to visit him with her younger sister, Ganga. Bishen Chand went to Ganga and sat in her lap. Ganga was about six years younger than Padma and therefore not much older than the age of Padma when Laxmi Narain had died. At this meeting Padma said: "You are a small child. I have grown old." (Bishen Chand's sister, Kamla, was a secondhand informant for this remark.) Considering the fact that only eight years had passed since Laxmi Narain had died, Padma's remark suggests a touch of female vanity. It is unlikely that she was yet thirty-five at the time she first met Bishen Chand.

Later, when Bishen Chand was a young man, he met Padma again under circumstances that I shall describe later.

Bishen Chand showed evidence of remembering the moral worth of persons known to Laxmi Narain. Before his father and K. K. N. Sahay took him to Pilibhit, B. Ram Ghulam mentioned within Bishen Chand's hearing his intention of purchasing a watch. Bishen Chand said: "Papa, don't buy. When I go to Pilibhit I shall get you three watches from a Moslem watchdealer whom I established there." By the time they visited Pilibhit, the Moslem watchdealer had moved away. But persons of the area who had known him confirmed Bishen Chand's claim. They said the watchdealer had been much indebted to Laxmi Narain for an advance of 500 rupees and that, had he been there, he would gladly have turned over to Bishen Chand, not three watches, but his entire stock of watches (see item 18, Table 8).

In contrast, when someone at Pilibhit mentioned that a certain merchant, Lalta Prasad (see item 55, Table 8), had been given the honorary title of Rajah (since the death of Laxmi Narain), Bishen Chand remarked contemptuously: "Lalta Prasad made a Rajah!"

Under the heading of this section I shall mention also Bishen Chand's attitude toward the house in which Har Narain and Laxmi Narain had lived. When he reached it, Bishen Chand entered and walked around it as if it was his own. The house was a large one, almost of palatial size, but it had deteriorated much since the death of Laxmi Narain, eight years before. One staircase particularly had apparently collapsed and disappeared to such an extent that observers considered Bishen Chand's pointing out of the place where it had been as some evidence of paranormal knowledge. (See K. K. N. Sahay's report quoted above.) When Bishen Chand saw the decayed condition of the house, he wept bitterly and said: "Nobody cared even to repair the house after my death!" He did not stop to consider the unfairness of this complaint; in fact the generosity of Har Narain followed by the prodigality and squandering of Laxmi Narain had left the surviving members of the family almost destitute and therefore unable to maintain a mansion.

Other Behavior of Bishen Chand in Childhood Related to the Previous Life. The behavior of Bishen Chand between the ages of approximately three and seven showed a number of features corresponding to the behavior of Laxmi Narain and distinguishing Bishen Chand from other members of his family. Bishen Chand frequently expressed disdain in those years for the humble condition of B. Ram Ghulam's home. B. Ram Ghulam was a poor man who could with difficulty support his family from the meager earnings of a clerk in the railway service. Bishen Chand reproached his father for his poverty, demanded money, and cried when he did not receive it. He said: "Even my servant would not take the food cooked here." He blamed his father for not building a house. He tore cotton clothes off when they were put on him and demanded silk ones. He said he always wore costly, silken clothes and that he would not give the clothes that were worn in his family even to his servants (of the previous life). According to his older sister, Kamla, Bishen Chand talked about the previous life every day during these years of early childhood. If so, he must have made himself something of a bore, to put it mildly, with his constant invidious comparisons of conditions now and then. I think it meritorious that, according to his older brother, Bipan Chand, his parents and older siblings never scolded Bishen Chand or attempted to suppress his flow of memories and derisive remarks which can rarely have included anything the people listening wanted to hear.

B. Ram Ghulam and his family were members of the Khattri group of the Kshatriya caste. They were the strictest of vegetarians and would not eat meat, fish, or even onions. Laxmi Narain and his family had been members of the Kayastha caste and therefore eaters of meat and drinkers of alcohol. Bishen Chand began to ask for meat when he was about five or six years old. He was naturally refused and took to eating meat secretly at the house of other persons who served it. He was fond of fish also and talked of the rohu fish he used to eat.

B. Ram Ghulam and his family were teetotalers, but on one occasion they had some brandy in the house for medicinal purposes. This was found to be diminishing, and Bishen Chand's sister, Kamla, caught Bishen Chand drinking it. When this matter was discussed with him, he said: "I am used to drinking." Kamla thought Bishen Chand was between four and five at the time of this episode. He himself said, in talking to me, that he thought he was perhaps six then.

B. Ram Ghulam said that when Bishen Chand was a small child (of less than five and a half years) he said to his father: "Papa, why don't you keep a mistress? You will have great pleasure from her." His father, although much surprised at this remark, somehow managed to ask his son quietly: "What pleasure, my boy?" Bishen Chand replied: "You will enjoy the fragrance of her hair and feel much joy from her company." [22] On the occasion of the family's first visit to Pilibhit, the superintendent of police there, who was with the party on that occasion, asked Bishen Chand: "Now tell us about your wife and children." To this Bishen Chand candidly replied: "I had none. I was steeped in wine and women and never thought of marrying."

During the same age period of which I am here writing, Bishen Chand would narrate with pride the story of the murder committed by Laxmi Narain. He boasted that the influence of Laxmi Narain's family had enabled him to escape punishment.

When he was a child (and later) Bishen Chand had a quick temper. Both his sister and brother affirmed this, and Bishen Chand himself acknowledged it a fault. Bipan Chand said his brother, when young, was inclined to hit people who annoyed him. Although I relate this trait to the previous life, I do not have evidence that Laxmi Narain was quick-tempered other than the fact that, according to Bipan Chand, he killed Padma's lover in a flash of anger.

Bishen Chand did not develop two of Laxmi Narain's strong interests. The latter's favorite pastime had been kite flying. Bishen Chand did a little kite flying when young, but did not continue. His father would not permit this, apparently out of a fear that his son might fall off a roof, from which kites are sometimes flown by city children in India.

---

[22] It may seem unlikely that a small child would make the remark I have quoted. At my request, Prof. P. Pal rechecked his notes of the interview he had had with B. Ram Ghulam, and he assured me that according to B. Ram Ghulam, Bishen Chand, when a small child, used words that showed he understood the difference between a mistress and a wife. Professor Pal interpreted the child's knowledge as derived paranormally, such as from memories of a previous life. Several other subjects of these cases have overtly manifested sexual interest in the partners of the previous life or persons who resemble them. (For another example, see the case of Imad Elawar in I. Stevenson. 1974. *Twenty cases.*)

Laxmi Narain was also a markedly religious person, at least in the practice of religious exercises. Bishen Chand, according to his brother, has shown only an average interest in religion. Bishen Chand himself claimed no more when I talked with him.

Unusual Skills and Knowledge Shown by Bishen Chand in Childhood. The informants for this case credited Bishen Chand with showing as a child two skills which, they said, he had not been taught. K. K. N. Sahay mentioned in his report, already quoted, that Bishen Chand played with ease on tablas (during the first visit to Pilibhit), although he had never seen them before. (I do not know from independent sources that Laxmi Narain played the tablas, but his fondness for singing and dancing is well enough established for it to be most probable that he could do so.) Bishen Chand's brother, Bipan Chand, confirmed that Bishen Chand had been very fond of playing on tablas (as a child) and that other members of the family knew nothing about this musical skill.[23]

Bishen Chand said that he continued playing the tablas up to the age of about eight and then stopped. He also confirmed that no one had taught him how to play the tablas. Without more knowledge concerning the possibility that Bishen Chand might at least have heard someone else playing the tablas in another family, we should draw conclusions about his exhibition of this skill very cautiously. But I think it can be admitted that Bishen Chand showed an interest in playing the tablas not manifested by other members of his famly and that he exhibited a skill at it, which was, at least to them, not explained by their knowledge of his exposure to instruction in music.

As already mentioned, Laxmi Narain had probably acquired a fair competence in Urdu, since he was employed in government service. Bipan Chand said that Bishen Chand, when a child, had been able to read Urdu before being taught it. B. Ram Ghulam did not say that Bishen Chand could read Urdu without instruction. He did, however, mention Bishen Chand's unexpected use of two Urdu words when he was a child. In referring to the ladies' quarters of the house in Pilibhit, Bishen Chand used the Urdu word *masurate* instead of the Hindi word *zenana,* familiar in his family. Also, pointing to a door of the house in Pilibhit, he said: "There was a kofal [lock] on this." The word *kofal* is an Urdu word used by the upper class people of Pilibhit. The Hindi word for lock, used in Bishen Chand's family, is *tala.*

Another surprising use by Bishen Chand of special words occurred when

---

[23] When I first heard about the playing of tablas, I conceived it as a very primitive skill amounting to a mere tapping on a drum. I revised this opinion after watching Dr. Jamuna Prasad play the tablas with great dexterity during a musical performance at his house in 1969. I then realized that playing well on the tablas requires discipline and practice.

Laxmi Narain's mother came to visit Bishen Chand in Bareilly with her sister-in-law (B. Upendra Narain's wife) and Bishen Chand recognized them.[24] According to B. Ram Ghulam, Bishen Chand called each by the name used in Laxmi Narain's family. Thus he called Laxmi Narain's mother Bahu, whereas he called his own mother Amma. And he called B. Upendra Narain's wife Mimi, whereas she would have been called Mami in his family.[25]

Correspondence of a Disease that Afflicted Both Bishen Chand and Laxmi Narain

In my first book of reports of cases of the reincarnation type (I. Stevenson. 1974. *Twenty cases*) I mentioned some correspondences between diseases of subjects and similar diseases in the related previous personalities. (The cases of Sukla, Marta Lorenz, Norman Despers, and Derek Pitnov provided examples of such matched symptoms or diseases.) Such a correspondence occurred in the case of Bishen Chand. In this instance I have no independent verification that Laxmi Narain suffered from the disease in question; nor have I any corroboration that Bishen Chand himself suffered from the disease that he remembers having in childhood. The reader should understand therefore that I report this detail solely from information given by Bishen Chand himself. It was mentioned first during correspondence with him and subsequently in an interview which Mr. Parmeshwar Dayal had with Bishen Chand in Bareilly on February 6, 1974. (I had asked Mr. Dayal to record a statement from Bishen Chand about this matter for me.)

Bishen Chand stated that as a small child he suffered from a disease of his eyes which caused them to become irritated and to swell. (I would suppose that the eyelids became swollen, not necessarily the eyeballs themselves.) At the time Bishen Chand was having this illness, Laxmi Narain's mother, who was by then living in Bareilly, dreamed that Bishen Chand was having trouble with his eyes. She remembered that her son, Laxmi Narain, had had a disease of the eyes, and early the next morning she sent a servant with an ointment (from the pharmacopoeia of Ayurvedic medi-

---

[24] Bipan Chand said that Bishen Chand first met Laxmi Narain's mother in Pilibhit, but I think he is mistaken about this. Bishen Chand himself said the first meeting took place in Bareilly. K. K. N. Sahay did not mention a meeting with her during the visit to Pilibhit and indicated in his report that she first met Bishen Chand in Bareilly. The testimony of B. Ram Ghulam clearly suggested this also, since he mentioned that Bishen Chand recognized her at his house. On the other hand, K. K. N. Sahay referred to Bishen Chand's "being taken to" Laxmi Narain's mother. Possibly two different occasions are in question: one when they first met and one later, when Laxmi Narain's mother put test questions to Bishen Chand.

[25] *Mami* is the correct word for the wife of the mother's younger brother, who is mama. Probably the word *mimi* started as a childish distortion and became fixed as a pet name. Its deviation from the correct word makes Bishen Chand's use of it noteworthy.

cine) that had been effective in curing Laxmi Narain of a disease of the eyes. Laxmi Narain's mother sent this medicine without waiting to ascertain whether Bishen Chand really had an eye disease or, if he did, whether it was the same as that from which Laxmi Narain had suffered. She simply assumed both of these details after having her dream. The servant who brought the ointment to Bishen Chand's home said that Laxmi Narain had suffered from an eye disease and that the ointment had helped him. Bishen Chand's father was impressed; he applied the ointment to Bishen Chand's eyes and the disease was cured. It returned about once a year during subsequent years until Bishen Chand was twelve or thirteen years old, and then it stopped. Each time Bishen Chand had the disease, the ointment was applied and it relieved the condition.

It does not appear likely that Bishen Chand or anyone else can furnish further particulars about the illness in question that will help us to understand it better. He himself conjectured that for Laxmi Narain the eye disease—assuming it was similar to that of Bishen Chand—derived from his intoxication with alcohol or was made worse by that habit.

Since the disappearance of this disease in Bishen Chand's early teens, he has had no major trouble with his eyes apart from some impairment of vision with increasing age (probably presbyopia), which has been corrected with spectacles.

Comments on the Evidence of Paranormal Processes in the Case

As I mentioned in introducing this case, it seems to me an unusually strong one with regard to authenticity. K. K. N. Sahay, a lawyer detached from the subject's family, recorded many of the subject's statements and then took the child and members of his family to the place of the previous life for verifications. I regret that K. K. N. Sahay did not explore further the possibility of some contact between young Bishen Chand and members of Laxmi Narain's family who were living in Bareilly. Unfortunately, I myself reached the case too late to do any detailed investigations of this aspect of it with the previous family, although I did enquire about it with Bipan Chand, Bishen Chand's older brother. In view of the early age at which Bishen Chand began to talk of the previous life, I should think it extremely unlikely that he could have acquired by normal means all the information related to the previous life that he showed between the ages of two and a half and five and a half. He was five and a half when first taken to Pilibhit.

In this case, as with many others, a full interpretation of all the facts requires some understanding of the subject's behavior apart from the information he exhibited about the previous life. Bishen Chand, when a small boy, showed the habits and attitudes of a spoiled, rich young man, and, in addition, of one belonging to a caste different from that of his family. He expected them to adapt their ways to his rather than that he should adjust to them. His father tolerated his alien behavior and gradually guided his son toward important modifications. But I cannot imagine any motive his parents could have had for promoting the sort of attitudes that Bishen Chand showed as a child. Or can someone seriously suppose that B. Ram Ghulam wanted to hear his son boast of a murder he had committed and scoff at his family for their poverty?

Bishen Chand's Later Development

At the age of about seven, Bishen Chand began to forget the imaged memories of the previous life. By the time he had reached adulthood, almost all had faded. When I first met him, in 1969, he remembered only one incident of the previous life—Laxmi Narain's murder of Padma's visitor.

As with many other cases of the reincarnation type, Bishen Chand's behavioral traits related to the previous life persisted longer than the imaged memories of it. As he grew older, however, he gradually adjusted to the circumstances of his life. He gave up some of the habits he had shown in early childhood. For example, he stopped playing tablas at about the age of eight. He also eventually accepted the fact that his family could only afford to give him low-priced clothes and not silk ones. He continued eating meat and fish into middle adulthood. At the age of twenty-five he married a girl of his caste who, like his parents, was a vegetarian. She would not permit her husband to eat fish and meat at home, so he was obliged to satisfy this craving at restaurants or in the homes of friends.

Bishen Chand went farther in school than Laxmi Narain had gone, continuing up to the tenth class. He became proficient in Urdu and also learned a fair amount of English. He entered government service and earned a modest living as an excise officer.

He continued to show a quick temper into his years of middle adulthood, but the tendency to physical violence noted in his childhood diminished in his teens and ceased by the time he was sixteen to eighteen years old. As he grew older he also showed a repentant attitude after losing his temper and would sometimes weep afterward.

He had weaker interests in women and in alcohol than Laxmi Narain had shown. With regard to alcohol, since his family did not take it, he had no easy opportunity to satisfy the taste for it that he had manifested in childhood, and so he gradually lost the desire for it. He seems to have had the usual interest and experiences with women before marriage, but showed nothing like the excesses of Laxmi Narain. After his marriage, at the age of twenty-five, he remained faithful to his wife. This he told me, and his brother, Bipan Chand, supported the claim.

Bishen Chand told me of an episode that illustrated the persistence in his early adulthood of vulnerability to alcohol and women. The unusual circumstances could hardly have been improved upon to bring out the old habits of Laxmi Narain. The incident occurred in 1944, when Bishen Chand was twenty-three years old. At that time he was working in the Central Excise Office in Tenakpore, a town 80 kilometers north of Pilibhit, in Uttar Pradesh. One day, quite unexpectedly, Padma and two or three other women came into the office where Bishen Chand was working. He had not seen Padma since the time of their first meeting, when he was about six. (In 1944 she would have been about fifty-two years old.) Bishen Chand recognized her and said: "Are you Padma?" She said: "Yes." Thereupon he embraced her, but was then so overcome with emotion that he fainted. In those days, Padma was living in the hills nearby at a village called Naikot, three miles from Tenakpore. On the evening of the same day, Bishen Chand went out to her home equipped with a bottle of wine and carrying the design of renewing the companionship which Laxmi Narain had enjoyed up to some twenty-six years before. When Padma saw him, however, she reproached him. "I am an old woman like your mother," she said. "Please go away. You lost everything in your previous life. Now you want to lose everything again." And she broke the bottle of wine and sent him off. In 1971 Bishen Chand told me that apart from his secret imbibing of medicinal alcohol as a child, he had never drunk alcohol before or after this episode. But the intensity of his aroused affection for Padma made him eager and willing to drink with her on this particular occasion.

Bishen Chand did not meet Padma after the above incident in 1944. In 1970 Dr. L. P. Mehrotra searched for news of her in the Tenakpore area and learned from her nephew that she had died at the end of 1945, thus not very long after the above meeting with Bishen Chand. So I have not been able to obtain her account of the rather dramatic meeting that Bishen Chand described to me. Two years after his last meeting with Padma, Bishen Chand married and has since apparently lived an exemplary conjugal life.

As I have already mentioned, when Bishen Chand was small he boasted about the murder committed by Laxmi Narain and otherwise also showed the behavior of a wealthy and arrogant young man. But as he grew older he began to reflect on the circumstances of his life, those of birth into poverty, and a ceaseless struggle to earn a meager living after he became an adult. He continued to compare his situation with that of Laxmi Narain, but now in a rather different spirit. Gradually his attitude changed. He assigned no specific date to this reform. The above incident with Padma no doubt contributed to his ruminations but was not decisive. However,

TABLE 9. *Summary of Behavioral Traits of Bishen Chand Related to the Previous Life*

Trait	Persons Confirming Occurrence of Trait	Fading or Persisting Later	Comments
1. Liking for meat and fish	Bipan Chand, Bishen Chand's older brother	Persisted into middle adulthood	He surreptitiously ate meat and fish as a child and was still eating these foods outside his home in adulthood.
2. Fondness for alcohol	Kamla, Bishen Chand's older sister	In childhood only, except for one episode at the age of twenty-three	
3. Precocious sexual interest in women	B. Ram Ghulam, Bishen Chand's father	No unusual sexual interest in adulthood	
4. Desire for expensive clothes	Kamla Bipan Chand	Acceptance of need to wear inexpensive clothes complete by adulthood	
5. Interest in music	Bipan Chand	Persisted into middle adulthood, but Bishen Chand gave up playing a musical instrument (tablas) at about the age of eight	
6. Ability to read Urdu	Bipan Chand	Fading of this skill could not be assessed; Bishen Chand studied Urdu, and so presumably his innate skill blended with what he learned of Urdu later	
7. Interest in kites	Bipan Chand	Faded in childhood	Bishen Chand's father suppressed his interest in kites on the ground that (under the conditions in the city) it was dangerous.
8. Quickness of temper	Bipan Chand	Persisted into middle adulthood, but tendency to physical violence faded in the late teens	I have no independent verification of the conjecture that Laxmi Narain had a bad temper habitually. The only instance of his losing his temper known to me occurred at the time he murdered a rival lover.

as a result of brooding over the contrast between his situation and that of the previous life, he decided that he had been born into poverty because of his conduct in the previous life, especially the murder that Laxmi Narain had committed. Remorse replaced haughtiness. In view of his changed attitude, I think it of particular interest that in 1969 Bishen Chand told me he had forgotten all but one of the events of the previous life. Everything else, he told me, he remembered only from what his father had told him. As I have mentioned, the original memories of the previous life had begun to fade after the age of seven; but he still remembered with vivid clarity the murder of Laxmi Narain's rival lover.

In 1969, when he was forty-eight years old, Bishen Chand still had some nostalgia, if I may call it such, for the previous life. He remembered himself as happier in that life than he was in the present one. He said that the wealth of Laxmi Narain had given more freedom to enjoy life and also to help others. He thought of himself as being generous (as was Laxmi Narain), and regretted that his very limited means gave him little or no scope to demonstrate this virtue. These aspirations to an improvement in material conditions were not accompanied by a desire for the extravagant living that Laxmi Narain could indulge himself in. He described his taste in clothes as simple, and his manner of saying this impressed me with its sincerity. I felt myself in the presence of a person who had learned that material goods and carnal pleasures do not bring happiness. Moreover, Bishen Chand's aspirations for another life, should he have one, centered, not on a desire for wealth, but on one for mental qualities such as superior intelligence, although he tinged this with a hope of fame through some superior attainment.

To facilitate review and understanding of all the behavior of Bishen Chand related to the previous life I have listed the more important traits in Table 9 along with remarks about their fading or persistence in the years after childhood. I wish to remind readers that I have not myself interviewed any member of Laxmi Narain's family who knew him. My conception of his character derives from remarks in K. K. N. Sahay's report together with the information furnished by Bishen Chand's older brother and father and Bishen Chand himself.

5

The Case of Kumkum Verma

Summary of the Case and Its Investigation

KUMKUM [1] VERMA was born on March 14, 1955, the second daughter and third child of Dr. B. K. Verma and his wife, Subhadra, who lived in Bahera, a village of northern Bihar, not far from the city of Darbhanga.

Kumkum was two and a half years old when she began to talk connectedly. At the age of about three and a half, she began speaking of a previous life she said she had lived in Urdu Bazar, Darbhanga. She gradually told many details about the life at Urdu Bazar, especially referring to her son, Misri Lal, and grandson, Gouri Shankar, as well as to events of the previous life. She mentioned that she had died "because of an altercation" and said that a daughter-in-law had poisoned her. Kumkum further indicated that she had belonged to a blacksmith's family. She also manifested at this time some behavioral traits, for example, extreme frugality, which impressed her family as typical for persons of that class.

Sometimes when remembering the previous life, Kumkum would say: "Call me Sunnary." Since the word *sunnary* means "beautiful," her family at first thought she was asking to be called beautiful. Later they learned that the woman identified as the person to whom Kumkum was referring had been called Sunnary. (I have adopted the more common spelling, Sundari.)

Kumkum's parents did not encourage her to talk about the previous life, but neither did they suppress her efforts to do so. She found a willing listener in her paternal grandmother and in her paternal uncle's wife, who spent some time in Bahera with Kumkum's family during Kumkum's early childhood. This aunt, Swarna Probha Verma, made written notes of many details mentioned about the previous life by Kumkum. Since Swarna Probha Verma's notes were recorded before any verification of Kumkum's statements, they put the case in the small class that I have listed above (see p. 144 n. 1). Swarna Probha Verma made her notes when Kumkum was about three and a half years old. The first verifications of her statements did not occur until Kumkum was about four.

---

[1] Kumkum's correct name is Sindhuja, but I shall use the name by which she was known to family and friends.

Kumkum's family ignored her requests to be taken to Urdu Bazar in Darbhanga. She had already shown strong emotions at times in talking about the previous life, and they were afraid that she might become ill, and perhaps even die, if she met the previous family, supposing that it existed and could be found. So no attempt at verifying Kumkum's statements occurred until 1959, by which time she was four years old. Dr. Verma, Kumkum's father, then told a friend who lived in Darbhanga, Harish Chandra Mishra, about her statements, and he decided to look into their truth. He was a senior official of the Darbhanga Raj Estate, the large property of the Maharajah of Darbhanga. He sent one of his employees, Mohammed Jan, to Urdu Bazar in search of a Gouri Shankar who was a blacksmith. Mohammed Jan was a Moslem who lived in Urdu Bazar. After some inquiries, he found and brought Gouri Shankar's father, Misri Lal Mistry,[2] to Harish Chandra Mishra. (Misri Lal had thought his son, then a boy in his midteens, had committed some crime for which he was wanted by the authorities, and so he had come himself to find out what the trouble was.) Misri Lal was able quickly to verify as correct everything Kumkum had been saying about her life in Urdu Bazar. The statements and behavior of Kumkum corresponded closely with the facts in the life of his mother, Sundari, who had died in Darbhanga in (about) 1950, about five years before Kumkum's birth. Misri Lal wanted to see Kumkum, but her parents would not permit this. Later Misri Lal's son, Gouri Shankar, went by himself to Bahera and met Kumkum there under circumstances that I shall describe below. Dr. Verma never allowed Kumkum to go to Urdu Bazar to meet the previous family. He himself went there once, in 1961. He met members of the previous family and also photographed some objects and persons he thought Kumkum might recognize.

Later someone informed a newspaper about the case, and an account of it appeared in the *Indian Nation,* of Patna, Bihar, for March 5, 1961. Still later the case came to the attention of Prof. P. Pal, who in October 1963 visited both families and made a thorough investigation of it. He wrote a long report of his interviews, which he made available to me. Professor Pal also obtained from Dr. Verma an English translation of portions of the notes of Kumkum's statements that Swarna Probha Verma, Kumkum's aunt, had made when Kumkum was about three and a half years old.

In 1964 I was able to have a long interview in Delhi with Swarna Probha Verma and her husband, N. K. Verma, about the case. N. K. Verma had been in England during much or all of the time Kumkum was talking of the previous life, but his wife seemed to remember very well what Kumkum had said. Her statements in 1964 coincided closely, although not exactly,

---

[2] Mistry is a trade name (not a caste name) applicable to skilled artisans such as blacksmiths. It is not a family name and thus is not taken by the women of the family or those sons who do not adopt the father's trade.

with the notes she had made in 1958. Apart from this single interview, I was unable to carry the investigation of the case any further that year.

In 1965, a team led by Dr. Jamuna Prasad visited Darbhanga and Bahera and made a further investigation of the case. They recorded the testimony of seven informants, including Kumkum herself, whose memories by then had faded considerably.

In the following year, another team under Dr. Jamuna Prasad's direction returned to northern Bihar to study the case with regard to the similarities and differences in the behavior of the two persons concerned. The case was particularly well suited to the investigation of these aspects because of the scanty contact the two families had had with each other.

In the autumn of 1969 I visited northern Bihar and, with the assistance of Dr. Jamuna Prasad and Dr. L. P. Mehrotra, resumed investigation of the case. We had detailed interviews with all the main informants. Kumkum, who was by this time more than fourteen years old, had lost nearly all her memories of the previous life.

Since 1969 I have occasionally exchanged letters with Dr. B. K. Verma in which he has answered questions about details of the case and also shared with me news about Kumkum and her family.

As a result of these extended and intensive studies, the case has been under almost constant observation since 1963.

Persons Interviewed during the Investigation

In Bahera I interviewed:

Sindhuja (Kumkum) Verma
B. K. Verma, Kumkum's father
Subhadra Verma, Kumkum's mother
Gangawati Devi Verma, Kumkum's paternal grandmother
Jugal Kishore Das Verma, Kumkum's paternal grandfather

In Darbhanga I interviewed:

Harish Chandra Mishra, special officer of the Darbhanga Raj Estate and
    friend of B. K. Verma
Misri Lal Mistry, Sundari's son
Gouri Shankar Mistry, Misri Lal Mistry's son
Saro Devi, Misri Lal Mistry's wife
Ram Chandra, younger son of Jhapu Mistry, Sundari's second husband

In Delhi I interviewed:

N. K. Verma, B. K. Verma's brother and Kumkum's uncle
Swarna Probha Verma, N. K. Verma's wife

Nearly all the above persons had also been interviewed in 1963 by Professor Pal and in 1965 by the team led by Dr. Jamuna Prasad. Professor Pal interviewed one informant, Indradeb Jha (a driver of the Darbhanga Raj), whom I did not meet. Notes and transcripts of all these interviews have been used in preparing this report.

An informant whose testimony could have been important, Jhapu Mistry, Sundari's second husband, had died in 1961.

A particularly important document in the case is an English translation of notes made in 1958 by Swarna Probha Verma, Kumkum's paternal aunt. She wrote down many of Kumkum's statements soon after Kumkum made them. Since the extracts given me probably contain only a part of the recorded statements, I have tried to borrow the original notebook, but without success. It was loaned to someone who did not return it and has apparently been lost. The extracts from it (in translation) sent to me include eighteen statements made by Kumkum about the previous life which were later verified.

Relevant Facts of Geography and Possibilities for Normal Means of Communication between the Two Families

Darbhanga is a large city of northern Bihar less than 80 kilometers from the frontier of India with Nepal. I estimate its population at 200,000. Bahera is a village about 40 kilometers from Darbhanga, but in the same district. It is a village of intermediate size and has perhaps 4,000 inhabitants. The villagers are largely engaged in agriculture, and the Vermas own some land in the area of Bahera. In addition, Dr. B. K. Verma practiced as a homeopathic physician in the village. He is an educated man who speaks English well. He spent time studying at the Viswa-Bharati of Rabindranath Tagore, where he took his degree. He is also an author of novels and shorter works. N. K. Verma, his brother, was an official of the central government in Delhi. I insert this information here to bring out the contrast between the Verma family and that of Sundari, whose members had little or no formal education.

Sundari's family lived in the Urdu Bazar section of Darbhanga. Urdu Bazar gets its name from the large number of Moslems in this quarter, which is mainly a commercial district where many small businessmen, artisans, and craftsmen live and work. Sundari's family, being members of a relatively low artisan class, would have been unlikely—one might almost say unable—to have any social relations with persons of the status and education of Dr. Verma and his family.

Dr. Verma said that he had never been into the Urdu Bazar section of Darbhanga prior to the first verifications of Kumkum's statements in 1959.

He had friends in Darbhanga, since it is the commercial and administrative center of that part of Bihar. I have already mentioned that one of these was H. C. Mishra, a senior official of the Darbhanga Raj Estate in Darbhanga. He, however, had never heard of Misri Lal Mistry and seems even to have been unclear about the existence of the Urdu Bazar. Even his employee Mohammed Jan, whom he sent to make inquiries and who lived in Urdu Bazar, had not heard of Misri Lal Mistry. Dr. Verma said he did not later discover any common friend he shared with Sundari's family.

Misri Lal told me that he had never been to Bahera for any reason until 1968, when he went there on business, and even then he did not visit the Vermas. His son, Gouri Shankar, said that he had never been to Bahera prior to the occasion in 1959 when he went to see and visit Kumkum after hearing that she was talking about the life of his grandmother.

The Life and Death of Sundari

The principal informant about the life and death of Sundari was her older son, Misri Lal. His account of her life has, except for the usual small discrepancies about details, remained consistent over the six years during which he has told the story to various investigators. Other informants, chiefly his son, Gouri Shankar Mistry, and Sundari's stepson Ram Chandra, have supplemented or at times corrected the account of Misri Lal. Sundari's second husband, Jhapu, died in 1961, before the investigation of the case had begun.

Sundari was born about 1900.[3] Her family was a moderately prosperous one of the village of Bajitpur, which lies across the river Bagmati from Darbhanga. When she grew up, she married a member of the blacksmith caste, Bikan Mistry. By him she had two sons, Misri Lal (born about 1918 or perhaps a little earlier) and Shiv Nandan. She had no daughters. She and her family lived in Urdu Bazar, Darbhanga. Around 1926 Bikan Mistry died, and his wife then raised the two children by herself. She obtained money from the sale of her ornaments and from the earnings of an assistant of her husband who continued to work the family smithy. After a

---

[3] Most dates of births and deaths in this case are approximate. I tried unsuccessfully to obtain a copy of the registration of Sundari's death from the Municipal Office in Darbhanga. Probably it was not recorded, as often happens with deaths of lower class persons in India. The dates used in this report have been chosen as reasonably accurate by comparisons of the accounts of different informants and by calculations from reported ages of various persons at the time of events described. It is unlikely that any date is wrong by more than three years and also unlikely that any except that of Kumkum's birth is exactly right. Misri Lal and his wife calculated that Sundari died in 1950, the date I have adopted, but Dr. Verma, who must, however, have derived his information ultimately from Sundari's family, thought she had died in the summer of 1949.

few years, probably around 1930, her straitened circumstances more or less forced her to accept a proposal of marriage from Jhapu Mistry, a distant cousin of her first husband. She married him and took her two sons to live with her in her new home, which was also in Urdu Bazar and about 200 meters from the first house. Jhapu Mistry had two sons and a daughter by his first marriage.

On the grounds of needing money for the maintenance of his stepsons, Jhapu Mistry sold property that had belonged to Bikan Mistry and Sundari. He also at least partially dismantled Bikan Mistry's house and used the bricks thus obtained for his own house.

Misri Lal married from his stepfather's house in (about) 1938. The following year he joined the Indian Army as a blacksmith and served in it until about 1945. His wife, Saro Devi, lived part of the time with her parents and part of the time with her mother-in-law, at Jhapu Mistry's house. She had one son, Gouri Shankar, who was born about 1941. Sundari was much attached to her older son, Misri Lal, and preferred his wife to the wife of her other son, Shiv Nandan. Shiv Nandan had two sons, but Gouri Shankar was her favorite of the three grandsons.

Misri Lal sent money home to his mother from his earnings in the army, and she then rebuilt the old house in Urdu Bazar that Jhapu Mistry had partly taken down. On Misri Lal's return from the army in 1946, he settled in this house with his wife and child. His mother would often visit him, and occasionally she spent one or more nights at his home. Misri Lal said that toward the end of his mother's life she came to his home several times a day.

It gradually occurred to Misri Lal that his stepfather, Jhapu Mistry, had misappropriated his father's money, and a few years after his return from the army he became so angry about this that he began a lawsuit against him. Sundari had not been happy in her marriage with Jhapu Mistry, which may account to some extent for the attention and affection she gave her older son and his family. Her stepson Ram Chandra said that she took good care of him, but she obviously preferred her own sons.

In fairness to Jhapu Mistry I should state that according to Ram Chandra, Jhapu Mistry had not only supported Sundari's children by her first husband when they were young but had actually contributed money to the rebuilding of her old house, which Misri Lal and his wife occupied after he returned from the army in 1946. But Sundari evidently believed that, on balance, her son's grievances against Jhapu Mistry were justified.

Sundari became so alienated from her second husband that in 1950 she found herself willing to be a witness in her son's suit against his stepfather. She engaged in the quarrel only reluctantly, however, and told Misri Lal (as he said in 1965) that he should abandon his lawsuit and allow divine justice to correct his wrongs. Her agreement to serve as a witness on his side must surely have envenomed her relationship with Jhapu Mistry. Misri Lal advised her to move to his house at least until after the suit was settled, but she did not do so. One morning, a few days before the trial of Misri Lal's suit against his stepfather, Sundari was at Misri Lal's house. She mentioned to her daughter-in-law Saro Devi that she had not been well the evening before, but that she seemed much better. She then returned to Jhapu Mistry's house. From there she sent word that she was ill and asked Saro Devi to come and nurse her. Saro Devi went to see her mother-in-law who, after a time, said she felt better and told her she could go. Neither she nor her husband imagined that Sundari was seriously ill. They were therefore astonished when the next morning some other persons, not of the family, said that Sundari had died during the night and that preparations for the funeral had begun. Jhapu Mistry had sent no word to Misri Lal about the death of his mother. Misri Lal suspected poisoning and wanted an autopsy. Relatives and a doctor dissuaded him on the grounds that an autopsy would mutilate the body and cause "unnecessary troubles." Sundari's sons then yielded and took the body of their mother down to the burning ghat. When the body was half-consumed in the cremation fire, Jhapu Mistry (or, according to one informant, Jhapu Mistry's cousin) disturbed the solemnity of the occasion by remarking in a too audible voice: "How will he [Misri Lal] proceed with his case now that his mother is dead?" This was a very cogent, if tactless, remark, since the exploitation of Bikan Mistry's property, if it occurred, took place during the minority of Misri Lal and his younger brother. So Sundari was the principal, and perhaps the only, adult witness of her second husband's use or misuse of her first husband's assets. The convenience to Jhapu Mistry of Sundari's sudden death just before the trial kindled the conjectures in the mind of Misri Lal that his stepfather or someone in the latter's household had poisoned his mother.

It has not been possible to determine the cause of Sundari's death beyond the fact that it occurred unexpectedly. This much was conceded by Jhapu Mistry's son Ram Chandra. In 1969 Saro Devi, Sundari's daughter-in-law, did not subscribe to the theory of poisoning, but Misri Lal persisted in his suspicions. Dr. B. K. Verma said in 1965 that he had heard some hints in the Urdu Bazar quarter of Darbhanga that Misri Lal's mistress had poisoned Sundari. Subsequently, according to this allegation, Misri Lal attributed the poisoning to his stepfather in order to protect his mistress. But this seems extremely improbable since his mistress did not live in Misri Lal's house and would have had no access to food at Jhapu Mistry's home, where Sundari spent the last night of her life. Sundari's condition deteriorated suddenly while she was there; if anyone poisoned her, it must have been a resident of that house.

The Character of Sundari

Sundari had many attractive qualities. She was particularly fond of children and took great pleasure in feeding and clothing them. She often played games with them, especially a game called andi, which is played with castor seeds and somewhat resembles marbles played by Western children. She was cheerful in demeanor and seems to have borne her domestic misfortunes bravely.

She made a pet out of a cobra which she fed and allowed to sleep in her room. The cobra no doubt had some deterrent effect on thieves and was considered a suitable guardian of the iron safe Sundari kept in her room at the house in Urdu Bazar. It had never bitten anyone.

A devout person, she passed much time in religious exercises and obligations. She would not eat without worshiping Shiva. She regularly observed the fortnightly fasts, or Ekadasis, of Hinduism. She never went to theaters except to see religious dramas presented in the local moving picture theater of Darbhanga. She attended meetings where slokas were sung. She brought her sons prasad [4] and even woke them up in the middle of the night to give it to them. I gained the impression that Misri Lal's piety fell short of wishing to have his sleep interrupted for religious practices, but he nevertheless appreciated his mother's devotion to God and to him. Certain imperfections in his conduct seem never to have weakened Sundari's affection for her son. He admitted to Dr. B. K Verma (but not to me) that his mother scolded him for a tendency to voluntary unemployment and an appetite for alcoholic restoratives.

Sundari knew prosperity in her childhood and during her first marriage. She passed through a period of financial hardship after the death of her first husband, but during her second marriage she was again prosperous and had servants to help with domestic labors. In her times of good fortune she was close to being wealthy. She was generous, however, to the point of being careless, and she gave money unsparingly to beggars and to young girls to help them get married.[5] She loaned money without interest. She freely allowed her daughters-in-law to borrow her gold ornaments for special occasions. Despite her liberality, Sundari seems to have managed money well. She used the funds that Misri Lal had saved from his salary in the army to rebuild the partly destroyed house of her first husband so that Misri Lal and his family could use it after his discharge and return to Darbhanga.

[4] When food is offered to a Hindu god in worship, a portion of the offering may be given to other persons. Such a gift is called prasad.

[5] The requirements of dowries in India often make it extremely difficult for a girl of a poor family to marry even today.

Statements Made by Kumkum

In Table 10 I have listed all the statements made by Kumkum related to
the previous life. All the statements for which the informant was a person
other than Kumkum herself were made before verification of any of them
occurred. Among these, the eighteen statements recorded in writing by
Swarna Probha Verma when Kumkum was only three and a half years old
have more value than the others. Srimati Verma was also an informant
(during an interview with me in 1964) of items that were not included in
the extracts from her notebook sent to me.

I do not know the chronological order of Kumkum's early statements
and have not attempted to list them in sequence. In order to facilitate
reading and correlation of the items, I have grouped them according to
topic.

For some items I have listed Kumkum herself as an informant with a
date. Kumkum made these statements to investigators in 1963 and 1965,
and I have included them for completeness. They indicate that she was
having memories of the previous life up to the age of eight or ten. They
also show that she was much freer in talking about the previous life to
strangers—that is, the interviewers—than are many subjects of these cases.

The distribution of Kumkum's statements over different themes deserves
comment. She was never reported to have mentioned Sundari's second son,
Shiv Nandan, or his two sons. She talked only of Misri Lal and his son,
Gouri Shankar. Sundari is known to have preferred Misri Lal and his wife
to her other son and daughter-in-law and also to have preferred Gouri
Shankar to her other grandsons. In addition, Kumkum mentioned Sundari's
first husband, Bikan Mistry, only once (item 36), and she also mentioned
Sundari's second husband only once, in connection with her allegation that
he had poisoned her. These omissions of Sundari's husbands from Kumkum's preoccupations accord with what we might have expected from inferences concerning their place in Sundari's life. Sundari's first husband
died around 1926, long before she did, and her marriage to her second
husband was so unhappy that she turned her attention and affection to one
of her sons and a grandson. So, for different reasons, memories of both her
husbands might be less persistent than those of her favorite son and grandson.

In the comments of Table 10 I have indicated that some of the details
mentioned, for example, ponds, iron bars, etc., are not specific and could
apply to many places, especially of the Darbhanga area. (Collectively, all
the items, and especially the proper names, could apply to Sundari and to
her only.) This lack of specificity of some details raises the possibility that
some of Kumkum's memories referred to Jhapu Mistry's house, although

most of them probably referred to that of Misri Lal, which he inherited from his father, Bikan Mistry. Both houses had ponds, windows with iron bars, brick walls, and tile roofs. And they both also had guava, jilapi, and date trees. There seems to have been a black-and-white spotted cow only at Jhapu Mistry's house. And the plum tree, snake, sword, and iron safe were at Bikan Mistry's house. Ponds were excavated at both houses, but the pond could not be seen from the windows at Jhapu Mistry's house, only at that of Bikan Mistry. Also, Sundari had nothing to do with paying laborers for the excavation of the pond at Jhapu Mistry's house, but she did pay them for the excavation at Bikan Mistry's house. There are, then, far more items of objects and events relating to the house of Bikan Mistry as compared with those relating to the house of Jhapu Mistry. It is evident that Kumkum's memories cluster around the last twelve years of Sundari's life, when, although unhappy in her marriage, she had companionship with her son, daughters-in-law, and grandson.

Recognitions Made by Kumkum

As I have already mentioned, Kumkum's family opposed her meeting members of the other family and, despite her urgings to go to Urdu Bazar in Darbhanga, they never allowed her to do so. However, in 1962 Gouri Shankar went out to the village of Bahera, where he met Kumkum in the street. Most of the informants credited her with having recognized Gouri Shankar spontaneously. Unfortunately, their accounts of exactly how she recognized him, as she seems to have done, are somewhat discrepant. And Gouri Shankar himself told interviewers in 1963 and in 1965 that Kumkum had recognized him, but in 1969 he denied this, having perhaps forgotten the details himself in the meantime. The most important part of this meeting was, I think, not Kumkum's recognition of Gouri Shankar by name (if this occurred, as I am inclined to believe it did), but her friendly and at the same time maternal attitude toward the young man who was a complete stranger. At the time, she was about seven and he was twenty-two years old. I shall describe this behavior below.

On the occasion (in 1961) of Dr. B. K. Verma's single visit to Misri Lal and his family at Urdu Bazar, he took some photographs of a lota (metal water vessel) and a chair used by Sundari, and also of her daughters-in-law. He then mixed these photographs with others that Kumkum had not seen and asked her if she recognized anything or anyone in any of them. Kumkum correctly identified the lota, the chair, and one of Sundari's daughters-in-law in the photographs. Although Dr. Verma assured me that Kumkum had received no guiding hints in connection with these interesting tests, I have not listed them in Table 10 because of some uncertainty about

TABLE 10. *Summary of Statements made by Kumkum*

Item	Informants	Verification	Comments
1. Her name was Sundari.	B. K. Verma, Kumkum's father	Misri Lal, Sundari's son	Kumkum pronounced the word *sunnary*, which is more the typical pronunciation in Maithili, the language of her family.
2. She lived in Urdu Bazar.*	B. K. Verma Swarna Probha Verma, Kumkum's paternal aunt Gangawati Devi Verma, Kumkum's paternal grandmother Subhadra Verma, Kumkum's mother Kumkum (1965) **	Misri Lal	According to Gangawati Devi Verma, Kumkum would say: "My house is in Urdu Bazar." At the time of my visit in 1969 most of the house in which Sundari had lived had been demolished or extensively remodeled. Two of the informants, B. K. Verma and his wife, said that Kumkum further located Urdu Bazar in Darbhanga.
3. The house was built of brick.	B. K. Verma Kumkum (1965)	Misri Lal	The houses of poor people in India are usually built of clay or mud.
4. The house had tiles.	Swarna Probha Verma Kumkum (1965)	Misri Lal	The northern portion of the house of Bikan (and Misri Lal) Mistry had a tile roof. This was the part where Sundari lived.
5. Her house was on the road.	H. C. Mishra, friend of B. K. Verma Gangawati Devi Verma	In 1969 I saw this much remodeled house on the main street in Urdu Bazar, Darbhanga.	In Indian towns many houses are directly on the street, but others are in lanes and small alleys and still others are set back from the street in independent grounds.
6. There was a guava tree on one side of the house.	B. K. Verma Kumkum (1963)	Misri Lal	This guava tree was still standing at the time of my visit in 1969.
7. Other trees around the house were plum, jilapi, and date.	Kumkum (1963)	Misri Lal	This statement was made in 1963 to Professor Pal during his visit to the Verma home in Bahera. There was a plum and a date tree at the home of Misri Lal. He did not mention a jilapi tree to me, but Professor Pal said that in 1963 Misri Lal had verified the existence of this tree near the house.

Item	Informants	Verification	Comments
8. There was a pond at the house.*	B. K. Verma Swarna Probha Verma Kumkum (1965)	Misri Lal	There was a pond behind the house of Misri Lal (where Sundari lived at one time) and also one behind the house of Jhapu Mistry, Sundari's second husband. I saw both these ponds. Ponds are very numerous in and around Darbhanga. This is not at all a specific item.
9. She paid the workers who dug out the pond with spades and carried the earth in bamboo baskets.*	Swarna Probha Verma B. K. Verma Gangawati Devi Verma Subhadra Verma	Saro Devi, Misri Lal's wife Misri Lal	B. K. Verma did not give the details of the spades and bamboo baskets. Gangawati Devi Verma stated that Kumkum said she (in the previous life) watched the pond being dug from the window of the house. Misri Lal recalled that about 1944 (he was quite unsure of the date) clay was dug from the pond for bricks. In the course of this, the pond was enlarged. The pond belonged to a Moslem landlord, but the digging of the clay was undertaken by Jhapu Mistry. Misri Lal did not recall that his mother had anything to do with this, but he was away in the armed services at the time. His wife recalled that her mother-in-law, Sundari, had sometimes paid the laborers who were digging out the pond.
10. There was a temple of Shiva near her house.	B. K. Verma	I saw this temple of Shiva quite close to the house occupied by Misri Lal in Darbhanga.	Kumkum told Swarna Probha Verma that she (in the previous life) had worshiped Shiva.
11. There was a moving picture theater to the east of her house.	B. K. Verma J. K. D. Verma, Kumkum's paternal grandfather	Misri Lal	J. K. D. Verma said that Kumkum only placed the theater "near my house." The moving picture theater is about 400 meters

* Recorded in the notebook of Swarna Probha Verma before any verifications were made.

** Statements made by Kumkum directly to investigators were made after the two families had met. They have been included here for completeness and to indicate that some memories were persisting in Kumkum up to the ages of eight and ten years.

TABLE 10 (cont.)

Item	Informants	Verification	Comments
11. (cont.)			from the house. This is considered "near" in Darbhanga. I did not learn if the theater is east of the house.
12. She went to the moving picture theater with her daughters-in-law.	B. K. Verma	Saro Devi	Sundari seems only to have gone to the theater to see religious dramas, not the usual moving pictures.
13. There was an iron safe at her home. *	Swarna Probha Verma Kumkum (1965)	Misri Lal	
14. The safe was at the northern side of the house. *	Swarna Probha Verma	Misri Lal	Sundari slept in a room on the northern side of the house overlooking the pond at the rear. The safe was located in this room.
15. Money and ornaments were kept in the safe.	Swarna Probha Verma B. K. Verma Kumkum (1965)	Misri Lal	Swarna Probha Verma mentioned money, but not ornaments, kept in the safe. So did Kumkum in 1965.
16. Her daughter-in-law had a gold chain.	Subhadra Verma	Misri Lal	Misri Lal said that his mother (not one of her daughters-in-law) had had a gold chain. But this was almost certainly one of the ornaments Sundari owned and used to lend to her daughters-in-law. (See item 43 below.) Kumkum compared her mother's gold chain with the one she said her daughter-in-law (of the previous life) had had. In doing this she said the one she was remembering was "redder" than her mother's chain. Apparently she meant to say the chain was brighter, but at the young age when she made this remark she did not know the word for bright. She also said the chain she remembered was better than her mother's chain.

17. She had a wooden chest.	B. K. Verma	Misri Lal	
18. The wooden chest contained saris and ornaments.	B. K. Verma	Saro Devi	Misri Lal said this wooden chest (or at any rate one used by his family) contained utensils only. He said that his mother had kept her saris in a suitcase and in tin boxes. His wife, however, said that her mother-in-law had kept her saris in a wooden box. From a discussion of this item with Professor Pal it seems possible that an error occurred here in the translations of the words for box and chest.
19. She had a sword hanging near her cot.*	Swarna Probha Verma B. K. Verma Kumkum (1965)	Misri Lal	Kumkum did not say in 1965 where the sword was kept. B. K. Verma remembered Kumkum saying the sword was kept near the door. Possibly the cot was also near the door. It is unusual for Indians to have swords in their homes, but most blacksmiths have them since they (usually) make them. Swarna Probha Verma said that Kumkum had never seen or heard of a sword at the time she spoke of one.
20. She had saris that she brought from her father's home.	B. K. Verma	Saro Devi	Saro Devi said her mother-in-law's father had brought her saris from Bajitpur, where he lived. She did not say that her mother-in-law had brought them from there herself.
21. A snake with a hood stayed near the iron safe.*	B. K. Verma Swarna Probha Verma Gangawati Devi Verma	Misri Lal	G. D. Verma stated only that Kumkum had said: "There is a snake in the house." There were discrepancies about what color Kumkum had attributed to the snake. Sundari had kept a black cobra as a pet in the house. The snake was still living as late as 1959.

* Recorded in the notebook of Swarna Probha Verma before any verifications were made.

TABLE 10 (*cont.*)

Item	Informants	Verification	Comments
22. She fed the snake milk and "zalli." *	B. K. Verma Swarna Probha Verma	Misri Lal	Swarna Probha Verma wrote that Kumkum had said she (in the previous life) fed milk and "zalli" to the cobra. The meaning of "zalli" has not been identified. Since the Hindi word for water is *jal*, it is just possible that Kumkum was trying to say that in the previous life she gave water to the snake, but could not pronounce the word correctly. Misri Lal did not recognize the word *zalli*. He said his mother had fed the cobra milk and also a preparation called lava. This is a type of roasted and puffed rice.
23. The snake had the end of its tail missing.	Swarna Probha Verma	Misri Lal	
24. The snake was rather fat.	Swarna Probha Verma	Unverified	After the interview, my two interpreters disagreed about whether Misri Lal had or had not verified this item.
25. There was a door with red leaves.	B. K. Verma	Saro Devi	The doors were dark red.
26. She had a red bed.	B. K. Verma Swarna Probha Verma Subhadra Verma	Misri Lal Saro Devi	The English translation of the notes of Swarna Probha Verma gives the word *cot* as used by Kumkum. However, Subhadra Verma was sure Kumkum had used the word *palang* (bedstead) and not *charpoy* (cot). Misri Lal said his mother had had a large bed, but that it was not colored. His wife, however, said it was red. A bed is to be distinguished from the simple cots, or charpoys, used by poorer persons in India. Ownership of a bed is a sign of prosperity.

Item	Informants	Verification	Comments
27. The legs of a bed were like tiger's paws.	B. K. Verma Subhadra Verma	Unverified	Subhadra Verma said Kumkum had referred to this bed with the "tiger's paws" legs as being black. Swarna Probha Verma (in 1964) remembered Kumkum as having said the legs of the bed had "carved lion faces." Misri Lal could not remember a carving like tiger's paws on the bed. Neither could his wife, Saro Devi, but she did remember that the legs were carved—in the form of flowers, she thought.
28. The bed had a drawer.	Subhadra Verma	Unverified	
29. A window of her house had iron bars.	B. K. Verma	Misri Lal	This window was in the room overlooking the pond, the room in which Sundari slept and in which were also located the iron safe, sword, snake, and a box for storing things.
30. A door had an iron bolt.	B. K. Verma	Unverified	In any case, the detail is not at all specific.
31. There were big elephants in Darbhanga.	B. K. Verma	P. Pal	Elephants can be seen both in Bahera and in Darbhanga. The Darbhanga Raj Estate owned elephants that were seen in the town of Darbhanga from time to time.
32. Her father lived at Bajitpur.*	Swarna Probha Verma B. K. Verma	Misri Lal	B. K. Verma in his testimony of 1965 said Kumkum had given the name "Wazidpur" for the place of her parents (in the previous life). I believe this error arose from his faulty memory, since his sister-in-law in her notes wrote "Bajitpur." Possibly also Kumkum mispronounced the name at times.
33. To reach her father's place, you had to cross water.*	Swarna Probha Verma	Misri Lal	Bajitpur is on the other side of the Bagmati River from Darbhanga.

* Recorded in the notebook of Swarna Probha Verma before any verifications were made.

TABLE 10 (cont.)

Item	Informants	Verification	Comments
34. She went there in a tonga.	B. K. Verma	Unverified	This is quite plausible. Tongas (two-wheeled horse-drawn vehicles) are commonly used in India for travel over intermediate distances.
35. There were mango orchards near her father's place.*	Swarna Probha Verma B. K. Verma	Misri Lal	
36. Her father had a bullock cart, but her husband did not have one.	B. K. Verma	Misri Lal	Bikan Mistry, Sundari's first husband, did not have a bullock cart; but according to Ram Chandra, the son of Jhapu Mistry, Sundari's second husband, his father had a bullock cart. So this statement is only accurate as a comparison of Sundari's father and her first husband.
37. Her father was richer than her husband.	B. K. Verma	Unverified	I did not put a direct question about this to any informant. From the other verified information I am inclined to think that Sundari's father was richer than her first husband.
38. Her father's house was larger than her husband's house.	B. K. Verma	Misri Lal	
39. There was a spotted black-and-white cow.	B. K. Verma	Misri Lal Ram Chandra	A cow remembered by Misri Lal was white, and not spotted. But Ram Chandra said in his family (Jhapu Mistry's) there was a spotted black-and-white cow.
40. Her son was called Misri Lal.*	Swarna Probha Verma B. K. Verma Gangawati Devi Verma	Misri Lal	Misri Lal was the older of two sons of Sundari and her first husband, Bikan Mistry.
41. Her son Misri Lal worked with a hammer.*	B. K. Verma Swarna Probha Verma	Misri Lal	Kumkum did not know the word for blacksmith and said her son (of the previous

222

Item	Informants	Verification	Comments
42. She had two daughters-in-law.*	Gangawati Devi Verma Kumkum (1965) Swarna Probha Verma	Misri Lal	The notes of Swarna Probha Verma did not say how many daughters-in-law Kumkum had mentioned. Sundari had two legal daughters-in-law, the wives of her sons, Misri Lal and Shiv Nandan. In addition Misri Lal had a mistress, and sometimes Kumkum seemed to refer to her as a daughter-in-law. On still another occasion Kumkum's use of the expression *daughter-in-law* must have been in reference to the wife of Sundari's stepson Laxmi Mistry, son of her second husband, Jhapu Mistry, by his first wife. (See item 56.)
43. She would lend her ornaments to her daughters-in-law.	B. K. Verma	Saro Devi	
44. One daughter-in-law was fond of her, the other antagonistic.	Swarna Probha Verma B. K. Verma	Misri Lal Saro Devi	This statement probably refers to the legal daughters-in-law of Sundari, the wives of Misri Lal and Shiv Nandan. Of these, Saro Devi, Misri Lal's wife, was her favorite, but I did not verify that she had bad relations with the other daughter-in-law. Possibly Kumkum was referring here to a mistress Misri Lal had for a time and whom she incorrectly remembered as another daughter-in-law. B. K. Verma heard a rumor in Urdu Bazar according to which this mistress had poisoned Sundari. (See p. 212.)

* Recorded in the notebook of Swarna Probha Verma before any verifications were made.

TABLE 10 (*cont.*)

Item	Informants	Verification	Comments
45. Her grandson was called Gouri Shankar.*	Swarna Probha Verma B. K. Verma Gangawati Devi Verma	Gouri Shankar, Sundari's grandson	H. C. Mishra said that Kumkum had said her *son* (of the previous life) was called Gouri Shankar and her *grandson* Misri Lal. But the three informants I have listed here all said Kumkum's statements corresponded to the later verified actual relationships of these men to Sundari. Later, as Kumkum's memories were fading, she did give the relationships incorrectly to, for example, Professor Pal in 1963.
46. She used to feed her grandson.	Gangawati Devi Verma	Gouri Shankar	This statement was apparently stimulated by Kumkum's grandmother giving her breakfast.
47. The house was jointly owned.	Kumkum (1965)	Misri Lal	Misri Lal and his brother, Shiv Nandan, lived together for a time. I cannot say definitely that they owned the house jointly, although this would be customary in Indian families.
48. She gave the red bed to her older son when he married.*	B. K. Verma Swarna Probha Verma	Misri Lal Saro Devi	Swarna Probha Verma wrote that Kumkum had said she had given a cot (color not mentioned) to her daughter-in-law (of the previous life), which is nearly the same thing as giving it to the son. From the answer of Misri Lal to a question about this bed, it seems that Sundari gave the bed to him and his wife jointly. Since they married in 1938, the statement refers to an event about twelve years before Sundari's death. I believe, but am not positive, that this was the same bed as that referred to in item 26. Variant use of the words *cot* and *bed* to mean (almost certainly) the same object is probably due to imprecise translation into English.

49. The older daughter-in-law cooked pakauri.	Gangawati Devi Verma	Unverified	Pakauri consists of fried balls of graham flour with or without vegetables added.
50. Her daughters-in-law cooked parval and tilkar for her.*	Swarna Probha Verma B. K. Verma	Misri Lal	Parval and tilkar are vegetables. B. K. Verma reported Kumkum as saying the older daughter-in-law cooked and served these vegetables. My notes do not record if both daughters-in-law cooked these vegetables, but Saro Devi said that she had cooked them for her mother-in-law. This item is not specific, since these vegetables were eaten in both families.
51. She went to fairs with her daughters-in-law and purchased things for them there.	B. K. Verma	Misri Lal Saro Devi	
52. She used to watch through the window her daughters-in-law bathing in the pond.	Subhadra Verma	Unverified	
53. She observed Ekadasis and Sundays.*	Swarna Probha Verma	Misri Lal	Ekadasis are Hindu days of fasting, falling on the eleventh day of each fortnight of the lunar month.
54. Every year she went to Gausaghat at the time of a fair to bathe.	B. K. Verma	Misri Lal	This item and item 51 probably refer to the same events. Sundari sometimes went with her daughters-in-law to the Gausaghat Fair.
55. She lost her life in an altercation.	Swarna Probha Verma	Misri Lal	Sundari died *during* an altercation, but not necessarily *because* of it. However, the notes of Dr. Jamuna Prasad, who was present when this item was reported (1964), stated that Kumkum had said, according to the informant, that "she had to lose her life

* Recorded in the notebook of Swarna Probha Verma before any verifications were made.

TABLE 10 (*cont.*)

Item	Informants	Verification	Comments
55. (cont.)			because of an altercation in the family." (See text for further details and discussion.)
56. Her older daughter-in-law poisoned her.	Gangawati Devi Verma Kumkum (1965)	Unverified	The daughter-in-law referred to here was the wife of Sundari's older stepson, Laxmi Mistry. (See item 42.) In 1965 Kumkum told Dr. Jamuna Prasad's team that her husband (of the previous life) had poisoned her. If poison was put in Sundari's food, it must have been mixed by one of Jhapu Mistry's daughters-in-law. (See text for full discussion of this item.)

the conditions in which they occurred. I also have not included Kumkum's (probable) recognition of Gouri Shankar at Bahera in Table 10.

Dialect Expressions Used by Kumkum

Kumkum's family noticed a peculiarity in the way she spoke. Maithili is the dialect of Bihari spoken in the area of Darbhanga. All the people of the area speak it, but the lower class people have a more vulgar style than educated persons. Darbhanga contains a considerable population of Urdu-speaking Moslems, and they have influenced the accent and (to some extent) the vocabulary of the Maithili spoken by Hindus in the city. Their language has thus come to differ from the Maithili spoken in the villages outside Darbhanga. Kumkum, when young, spoke with a different accent from that of her family, one that they related to the lower class argot of Darbhanga. Although the difference they noted was mostly one of accent only, her father mentioned to me a few expressions in which her choice of phrasing differed from the customary one in her family. I noted down the following examples: [6]

English	Maithili	Darbhanga argot
Have you taken your food?	Khelaun O?	Khe'lahi re? *or* Khe'lahi ge?
Did you bring it?	Anai chhe?	Le lihi re?
I have forgotten this.	I bat visar gailaunh.	I bat utar gelae.
Where have you been?	Kahan gel chalaunh?	Kahan gel rahli rahai?
It has been done.	Bhain geleh.	Ho gele.

Experiences of Kumkum's Mother during Pregnancy before Kumkum's Birth

During her pregnancy with Kumkum, Subhadra Verma developed some unusual food cravings. She liked milk, fruit, and salty food more than at other times and more than during pregnancies with her other five children. Dr. B. K. Verma confirmed that his wife had shown these unusual cravings for particular foods during the pregnancy with Kumkum and during no other. According to Subhadra Verma, these cravings on her part for milk, fruit, and salted foods during the pregnancy with Kumkum accorded with Kumkum's preferences for food as compared with those of the other five children of the family. When I talked with Kumkum in 1969, she was

[6] Dr. B. K. Verma checked my romanized rendition of the dialect expressions used by Kumkum.

fourteen. She said then that salty foods were her favorite food and she still liked milk. She said that she did not like fruit and that she could not then remember the special fondness for fruits which her mother had said she showed when she had been younger.

Sundari also was specially fond of salted foods. She was not, however, noted for an interest in fruit or milk. Fish was her favorite food, according to her son, and Kumkum did not eat fish at all.

During her pregnancy with Kumkum, Subhadra Verma dreamed of a girl child surrounded by snakes. Dreams of snakes are by no means rare in India. Subhadra Verma, however, said that she had not dreamed of them during her other pregnancies. Sundari had a rapport with snakes that enabled her to enjoy a cobra as a pet; and, as I shall describe later, Kumkum also had a special interest in snakes. In view of this unusual philia shared by the two personalities concerned in the case, Subhadra Verma's dream perhaps qualifies as a type of announcing dream.[7]

Birthmarks and Other Physical Features of Kumkum

Kumkum's father told me that at (or soon after) her birth, marks were found on the lobes of her ears at the places where earrings would be attached.[8] Misri Lal told me that his mother's ears had been pierced for earrings.

Kumkum has, for her family, a very fair complexion, one often described in India as "wheatish." She was definitely fairer than the several other members of the Verma family I saw. I was told that one older brother of Kumkum is also fair, but that all other members of the family are darker than she is. Kumkum was (in 1969) also slim and taller for her age than other children. Misri Lal said that his mother had been tall, slim, and fair in complexion.

Kumkum's Behavior Related to the Previous Life

Circumstances and Manner of Kumkum's Speaking about the Previous Life. In many cases of the reincarnation type, informants have remarked that the

---

[7] In most "announcing dreams" the central figure appearing in the dream is a human and in many instances a person already known to the dreamer and her family. The interpretation of the meaning of animals or other symbolic representations in such dreams is highly conjectural, especially if it is only made after the subject has started talking about the previous life. For other examples of abnormal cravings during pregnancy corresponding to appetites of the subject, see the cases of Gamini Jayasena and Bongkuch Promsin in later volumes of this series.

[8] For another example of birthmarks in the ears apparently related to holes pierced for earrings in the previous personality, see, in this volume, the case of Jagdish Chandra.

subject's statements are apparently stimulated by an object or event that corresponds to something similar in the previous life.[9] The case of Kumkum is particularly abundant in examples of this feature.

Kumkum's father first heard her utter a statement on the subject of the previous life when he happened to be helping with some archaeological excavations near Bahera. Kumkum saw these and commented that she had once got a pond dug out and had paid the laborers. Kumkum's mother, it seems, first heard her mention the previous life when she (the mother) was wearing a gold chain. Kumkum remarked that it was rather dull and that she had a better gold necklace. On another occasion Kumkum said to her grandmother: "Just as you give us breakfast, so I used to give breakfast to my grandson." (I do not know that this remark was made at breakfast, but it seems obviously to have been stimulated by a comparison in Kumkum's mind.) Once when Swarna Probha Verma, Kumkum's aunt, was cooking something in the kitchen, Kumkum said that something similar was cooked by "her" daughter-in-law. On another occasion, when Swarna Probha Verma was combing the hair of her mother-in-law, Gangawati Devi Verma, Kumkum said: "My daughter-in-law used to comb my hair in a similar way."

Kumkum's father said she was particularly inclined to talk of the previous life when someone was going to Darbhanga and also when she was sitting by the south window of the house. Sundari used to watch the pond being dug and her daughters-in-law bathing by looking through the window of her house facing the pond in Darbhanga.

Kumkum also talked of the previous life when she wanted something such as money. Her remarks included complaints about having more money in the previous life than she had in the Verma home. She would ask for money, saying she would buy something for "her" son. Here the memory may have stimulated the demand rather than the reverse.

Kumkum also tended to talk more about the previous life in the evenings or at night when she was with only one person.[10] She said that "she" used to look out of "her" window at the excavation of the pond and that she paid the

[9] In cases with what I call weak penetration of the memories, all or nearly all the statements occur under such circumstances and few or none occur without such stimulation. The case of Mallika (I. Stevenson. 1974. *Twenty cases*) provides an example of this; I have also investigated a number of American cases of this type.

[10] I have been impressed by the occasional reports of informants that the subject of a case talks more about the previous life in the evening and in the early morning than at other times. I believe this may have something to do with changing states of consciousness at these times. Also, in the evening at least, and in some homes in the early morning, there is less commotion in the house than at other times of day, and this may favor withdrawal of attention from the present situation and easier emergence of memories. At such times also another person, such as a mother, aunt, or grandmother, may have more time to listen to the child talk about the previous life. For further examples and comments on this feature of some cases, see the reports of those of Shamlinie Prema and Gamini Jayasena in the next volume of this series.

workers in the evening. Since it is known that Sundari at least sometimes paid the workers digging out clay for bricks from the pond, and since she would presumably pay them in the evening, at the end of the day's work, the evening may have become particularly significant for her.

Kumkum's mother discouraged her from talking of the previous life; the child found a more sympathetic listener in her paternal grandmother, to whom she talked quite spontaneously. She also talked with Swarna Probha Verma, her aunt, but more in response to questions and less spontaneously than with her grandmother. Swarna Probha Verma remarked that Kumkum talked more freely with children than with adults about the previous life.

Kumkum talked of the previous life under such pressure that she seemed to Swarna Probha Verna, her aunt, almost to be in a trance. She spoke in the present tense and was so fully absorbed by the memories that she appeared oblivious of her present surroundings. Her grandmother said that if there was no one around (to listen to her) Kumkum would speak to herself about the previous life.[11]

Kumkum began talking about the previous life at an age (three and a half) when her vocabulary was still small; and, like many other children of these cases, she supplemented her words with gestures. This was particularly true when, in order to describe the occupation of her son (of the previous life) she gestured to imitate the movements of the hammer and the bellows of a blacksmith (item 41, Table 10). On another occasion, also when Kumkum was still quite young, she wanted to compare invidiously a gold chain she remembered as that of the daughter-in-law of the previous life with her mother's gold chain (item 16, Table 10). But at that age she did not know the word for bright, and so she said that the chain she remembered was "redder" than her mother's. She also said that the other chain was better than her mother's chain.

Sometimes Kumkum became tearful when narrating events of the previous life. This happened at least once, when she was asked how she had died in the previous life. Her father said she merely wept and said nothing in response to this question. But her grandmother said that Kumkum had mentioned (presumably at another time) being poisoned by her daughter-in-law. (See item 56, Table 10). On another occasion Kumkum was with her family in a building of Darbhanga. She went up to the third floor of the building; there, her grandmother noticed that she was looking out of the window and weeping. Kumkum said nothing; but because she was gaz-

---

[11] For other examples of subjects speaking to themselves about the previous life, see the cases of Wijeratne and Sukla (I. Stevenson. 1974. *Twenty cases*). These children resemble somewhat persons in deliria, who talk (without regard to the audience) of recent or remote events of their lives that have been important to them. For examples of this, see H. G. Wolff and D. Curran. 1935. Nature of delirium and allied states. *Archives of Neurology and Psychiatry* 33:1175–1215.

ing in the direction of Urdu Bazar, the family concluded that the sight of some building there had probably activated her memories of the previous life and brought on the weeping. Kumkum was about seven years old when this happened.

Kumkum's family observed her weeping silently on other occasions, and they inferred that at such times she was probably thinking of the previous life. While attending some fair or ceremony, she would shed tears without any apparent reason. (Sundari had gone to fairs and religious ceremonies regularly.)

Some of Kumkum's memories of the previous life were of pleasant occasions. For example, she told Harish Chandra Mishra how happy her daughters-in-law (of the previous life) were when she loaned them her ornaments from the iron safe and how their joy made her happy.

Kumkum showed a strong desire to go to Urdu Bazar in Darbhanga. When she heard that someone else was going there, she asked to go also and wept when refused. Once when her family was in Darbhanga, she walked away from the rest of the group for some time before her absence was noted. When traced, she was found walking along the road toward Urdu Bazar. As she would not stop, she had to be picked up and brought back to the rest of the family.

Kumkum would tell her brothers and sisters that if they would accompany her to her previous home, she would give them plenty of coins. Concern about her son, daughters-in-law, and grandson (of the previous life) also increased Kumkum's wish to go to Urdu Bazar. She worried about the clothing and feeding of Gouri Shankar. On a holiday when gifts are customarily exchanged, she asked who would give new saris to her daughters-in-law and clothes to her grandsons. She petitioned her grandfather for the money with which to purchase these gifts. On another occasion, when Kumkum announced that she would go to Darbhanga to see her grandson, her grandfather asked her if she would take him (the grandson) a gift. To this she replied that she would take him a pair of short pants and other gifts.

Although Kumkum sometimes compared her situation with that of the previous life in terms disparaging to her family, and although she expressed a great longing to see some members of the previous family, she never expressed any wish to live again in Urdu Bazar. Moreover, she did not seem otherwise unhappy in the Verma family, whose members obviously regarded her with affection and respect.

Kumkum's Attitude toward Gouri Shankar. I have already mentioned the first visit (in 1962) of Gouri Shankar, Sundari's grandson, to Bahera, where he met Kumkum and was (probably) recognized by her in a street of the village. Kumkum brought Gouri Shankar home with her, which was definitely remarkable and not altogether a delight to her family. She announced him as "my grandson." Her family treated him hospitably, and Kumkum assisted in obtaining food for his meal. She expressed surprise that he had grown so big. (He was then in his early twenties.) He spent the night in the Verma house and left the next day.

Several months later Gouri Shankar returned. This time he was smoking a bidi, a type of cheap cigarette used by poorer persons in India. According to her father, who seems not to have been an eyewitness of this episode, Kumkum remarked to her mother: "Mother! See how ill behaved my grandson is. He smokes bidis." Gouri Shankar again spent one night with the family. The Vermas did not encourage him to return and he has not done so.

Kumkum's Sense of the Passage of Time. Although Kumkum often talked about the previous life in the present tense as if it was still "going on" for her, at other times she discriminated between the previous life and her actual situation. In talking about taking short pants to Gouri Shankar, it obviously did not occur to her that he had grown up in the time since Sundari's death.[12] This remark contrasts with another one Kumkum made as she was talking with her mother. She said that when her father (of the previous life) used to pay a visit, he brought clothes for her daughters-in-law. Kumkum's mother carelessly asked her: "When did your father go there?" To this Kumkum replied: "When did this father go? I am talking about my previous father."

Other Behavior of Kumkum Related to the Previous Life. When Kumkum was about four years old, she drew with her finger the design of a house on the earth. She subdivided the house into rooms, put in some rice and pulse, and added a snake. She forbade other children to enter the "house" without her permission.

Kumkum had an unusual interest in snakes when she was young. This by itself was not exceptional in her family, since two of her siblings were also especially interested in snakes, although her parents seem not to have been. Kumkum's mother explicitly denied any such interest in herself. I did not put the question to her father, but he certainly did not radiate enthusiasm as we were talking about cobras.

An incident that occurred when Kumkum was six left a strong impression on her family. At her school one day a cobra fell from a tree. Other children were horrified and panicked, but Kumkum went up to the snake in a friendly way and patted it on the hood and below it. The snake then

---

[12] From my observations of Indian boys I would say that most of them who wear short pants stop doing so between the ages of twelve and fourteen. Gouri Shankar was at least twenty, and possibly older, when he visited Kumkum in Bahera, but she may have made her remark about short pants when he was younger.

crawled away. Since the snake was stunned by the fall, its harmlessness may have been due to this, but the incident nevertheless confirms Kumkum's fearlessness of snakes. And this is relevant to the fact that Sundari domesticated and kept a cobra as a pet in her house, a fact that Kumkum spoke about. (See items 21–24, Table 10.)

According to her parents, Kumkum was notably more religious than the other children of the family. At a very early age she seemed to know the proper procedures for various religious ceremonies. She showed familiarity with different styles of worship at the age of five. Kumkum's father told me that she stayed in the family shrine room longer than the other children. She recited slokas (verses) from the Ramayana and the Bhagavad Gita. I should add that although her parents agreed that Kumkum was unusually religious for their family, her paternal grandmother did not. She acknowledged that Kumkum was religious but did not think her exceptionally so compared with the other children. She also thought that Kumkum had simply imitated the older children of the family when she showed what appeared to be a precocious knowledge of religious rituals. If, however, we accept the judgment of Kumkum's parents, we find in her religiousness another parallel with the behavior of Sundari.

Kumkum was said to have been more mature for her age than other children. She enjoyed housework and did it voluntarily and eagerly. She liked to feed smaller children and to look after sick persons. For example, she would (at age eight, in 1963) carry and look after her youngest brother almost the whole day; her older sisters would tend to avoid such a task. Kumkum would also pick up and carry a small child of a scheduled caste [13] whom other members of the family would not touch. Kumkum preferred the company of adults, and her talks with them sometimes assumed an adult and even a tutorial manner. She showed little interest in play and had few friends among girls of her age. This latter deficiency may have been due not so much to Kumkum's preference for adult society as to a tendency noticed in her to dominate other children. She was inclined to tell them what to do. But Kumkum was speaking with the authority that she felt she still had from the previous life. (Sundari's stepson described her as a dominant personality; she was the mistress of the house, he said.) Sundari was also much interested in young children. Her interest focused on her favorite grandson but extended to other children as well.

Kumkum showed unusual concern for beggars. She devoted the whole of Sundays to them and to sadhus.[14] She may have copied this charitableness

---

[13] Members of the scheduled castes are persons who were formerly in the untouchable castes and who, since Indian independence, have been "scheduled" for special efforts at their improvement.

[14] Sadhus are sages or holy men, frequently living an itinerant life and therefore dependent on the generosity of devout persons who, respecting their quest for religious enlightenment, give them food and other necessities.

from her mother, who also was unusually kind to beggars, but Kumkum nevertheless showed it more than the other children. Here again we find a correspondence with the character of Sundari, who was generous to beggars.

Kumkum was noted in her family as an unusually clean person, and informants about Sundari said she also was particular about cleanliness.[15]

The informants differed in their reports of Kumkum and Sundari with regard to their management of money. Kumkum's family noted that she was extremely frugal, and the word *miserly* was applied to her by Swarna Probha Verma, her aunt, and B. K. Verma, her father. Her mother described her only as "careful" with money. She would lend money to other children and expect it back with interest. (Sundari also engaged in money-lending, but, at least some of the time, without charging any interest.) Kumkum's father noted that she liked to keep coins in tattered pieces of cloth, holes, or small tin boxes. Her family regarded these habits as characteristic of low caste people but inappropriate for them.[16]

Kumkum's parsimony did not, however, accord with informants' judgments about the attitude of Sundari toward money. Her stepson said (in 1969) that she spent everything she had, and he characterized her as a "spendthrift." Dr. Jamuna Prasad's team, who studied this case (in 1966) with regard to correspondences in behavioral traits between the two personalities, also learned from their informants that Sundari was "somewhat careless with regard to money." [17]

Kumkum engaged when young in finger painting, preferring it to paint-

[15] "Cleanliness is next to godliness," said John Wesley. "And next to impossible," added Josiah Wedgwood when he heard the remark. Cleanliness was difficult to achieve in eighteenth-century England and is still so in parts of twentieth-century India; a person who is unusually attentive to cleanliness is more noteworthy in India than he or she would be in modern Europe or North America.

[16] The case of Disna Samarasinghe (reported in the next volume of this series) provides another example of the hoarding of money by the subject that related to a previous life as an elderly woman of a lower class.

[17] I am glad that occasionally our informants testify to differences in the behaviors of the present and previous personalities. If they agreed in *every* instance, one might expect important contamination of the data from one family by that of the other, if not actual collusion between the two. At the same time we should be just as interested in the differences between the reported characters of the two personalities of a case as we are in their similarities. We ask the informants to judge the subject (or previous personality) in comparison with other members of the same family or peers. Sundari, in her later years, may have seemed a spendthrift to other members of her own family, and, by their standards, she may have been one. But in her days of financial hardship (after the death of her first husband) she had to sell her ornaments to support her children. She must have learned and practiced habits of frugality then which she later relaxed but did not altogether forget when she became prosperous. Now Kumkum's family are by no means impoverished, but it is possible that Kumkum, cut down to almost nothing in the way of pocket money and remembering the later prosperity and the earlier adversity of the previous life, felt that she should practice economies. These were then perceived by her family as miserliness. By this conjecture, then, I am suggesting that an old habit from a previous life may come into prominence when a child subject becomes aware of major differences in the circumstances of the two lives.

ing with a brush. Her family regarded this habit as characteristic of gold-smiths. (It does not appear to have any connection with blacksmiths.) I did not, however, learn that Sundari had engaged in finger painting. She had done some painting, but her son said he recalled that she had used a brush and not her fingers.

Kumkum was also fond of playing a game with glass beads which closely resembles one called andi, which is played with castor seeds. Sundari had enjoyed andi and had played it often with children.

Kumkum liked gold ornaments and, as I have mentioned, rather boasted of her gold ornaments of the previous life. Her father, however, did not think her interest in gold ornaments unusual. Sundari had had many gold ornaments, at least during her prosperous years.

No description of Kumkum would be complete without reference to her intelligence, which impressed me as being distinctly superior. At the age of fourteen she was very near the top of her class (the eighth class) of about forty-five students. To me, she seemed a person of charm and poise, more mature than her years suggested. I am not alone in making this observation. When she was only five she was taken to a conference of philosophers where some of those present (to their shame) put trick questions to her about the previous life. She answered these with unruffled dignity. Someone suggested that the bars of the window of the home of the previous life were made of gold. Kumkum replied: "No. They were iron bars. I had some gold orna-ments." Another person suggested that she owned an elephant, but Kum-kum replied: "No, a cow, but I saw elephants pass by [in Darbhanga]."

According to her father, Kumkum never gave any evidence of paranormal powers apart from her memories of a previous life.

The Attitude of Kumkum's Family toward Her Memories of the Previous Life

As I mentioned earlier, Kumkum's family was afraid that she might become emotionally troubled and perhaps even die if she met the previous family. This opinion, at least of the possibility of her becoming ill, was not base-less; Kumkum had shown much emotion in narrating memories of the previous life, as I have described above. In addition, the Vermas, who are educated persons, were unenthusiastic about adding a blacksmith to the background of their family. The visit of Gouri Shankar to Bahera con-firmed their suspicions of a deep social cleavage between the families when he betrayed somewhat uncouth manners, although no one questioned the sincerity of his attachment to his grandmother. Dr. B. K. Verma told Professor Pal frankly that he did not follow through himself with verifica-tions and further study of the case because he did not want it generally known that his child was claiming to have been a blacksmith's wife in a previous life.

Comments on the Evidence of Paranormal Processes in the Case

I feel confident that the two families in this case had no contact of which they were aware before Kumkum began talking of the previous life in Urdu Bazar. I cannot exclude the possibility that on some visit to Darbhanga the Vermas had met persons who knew or had met Sundari's family. It seems most unlikely, however, that any such mutual acquaintances they may have had were more than just that. The Vermas' social circle lay quite outside that of blacksmiths. They had no occasion to go to Urdu Bazar, and Sundari's family had little reason to leave it.

Harish Chandra Misra was even vague about the existence of Urdu Bazar before he made inquiries. When I asked if he had ever heard of Misri Lal, Gouri Shankar, or Jhapu Mistry, he rejected the question firmly. "If I had known them why would I need to trace them out by Mohammed Jan?" (Mohammed Jan was his Moslem employee who knew the Urdu Bazar area of Darbhanga; he had since died.) If Harish Chandra Mishra, living in Darbhanga, did not know Sundari's family or know of them, it is extremely unlikely that the Vermas of Bahera would have known them.

Sundari led a relatively obscure life, and her death was not even recorded, so far as I know, in the Municipal Register of Darbhanga. It is difficult to understand how events of her life could have become known normally to a small girl in a village 40 kilometers away. Furthermore, the interval between the death of Sundari, around 1950, and the birth of Kumkum, in 1955, meant that when Kumkum began talking of the previous life (at about three) at least eight years had elapsed since the events she was referring to; in many instances, many more had gone by. For example, Sundari's son had married in 1938, at which time she had given him and his wife a bed. This fact, mentioned by Kumkum twenty years later, was not something that would be discussed publicly over the years in such a way as to come to the attention of a little girl like Kumkum without her parents also knowing about it.

The difference in social class between the two families would have separated them as much as geographical distance or more. It formed an important barrier to their meeting socially. It also makes it improbable that the Vermas would embellish, much less invent, this particular previous life, that of an illiterate blacksmith's wife, so as to add luster to their family name.

In short, in order to believe that Kumkum acquired her knowledge of the previous family normally, one would have to suppose contacts between the two families for which there is no evidence and very little likelihood. In addition, one would have to add some explanation of how Kumkum, according to the informants of her family, showed over many years a number of behavioral traits which were unusual in her family and which corresponded quite closely with traits reported by the informants for Sundari. In this connection, it is also noteworthy that the two families had extremely little contact, even after the first verifications of Kumkum's statements. Gouri Shankar made two visits to Bahera in 1962, and Dr. B. K. Verma made one visit only, in 1961, to Urdu Bazar. It is certain that he exchanged some information with persons who remembered Sundari, but there was much less opportunity for exchange of information than one finds in many of these cases. Such exchanges can obviously contaminate the responses of each family when the members are asked to describe the character of the person about whom they are furnishing information.

This case has three other features which I believe strengthen its authenticity beyond that of the usual one. First, the notes written down by Kumkum's aunt provide a written record, made six months before any verifications of her statements, of a major portion of what Kumkum was saying about the previous life. Second, the first verifications were made by a person outside the immediate families concerned. This was Harish Chandra Mishra, who, although a friend of Kumkum's father, was certainly not his employee or otherwise in a position of subservience that might have obliged him to confirm Kumkum's statements if they had not been true; and Harish Chandra Mishra had absolutely no acquaintance with Sundari's family, of whose existence he had not even heard prior to his inquiries. Third, the case was studied independently of me by Indian investigators (Professor Pal in 1963 and Dr. Jamuna Prasad and his team in 1965–66) who reached its scene before I did. (I had had one interview for the case in 1964 in Delhi.) The informants in Bihar could not possibly have known in 1963–66 that I might some day be able to come to the site of the case and interrogate them all over again. (I did not know this myself then.) And yet, the information I elicited later from the informants was substantively the same as that obtained in the earlier interviews by the Indian investigators.

Kumkum's Later Development

Fading of Memories in Kumkum. Kumkum's memories and behavior related to the previous life were prominent from the age of three to about the age of seven. After this, her imaged memories diminished. Nevertheless, at the age of eight (with Professor Pal) and at the age of ten (with Dr. Jamuna Prasad's team) she still preserved some memories of the previous

TABLE 11. *Correspondences in Behavior between Kumkum and Sundari*

Kumkum	Sundari	Fading or Persisting in Kumkum	Comments
1. Preferred salted foods to sweet ones	Preferred salted foods to sweet ones	Persisted to the age of fourteen	
2. Did not eat fish	Favorite food was fish		
3. Fond of fruit	Not particularly fond of fruit	Ceased before the age of fourteen	
4. Unusually religious	Unusually religious	Persisted strongly to the age of fourteen	
5. Frugal	Careless with money		
6. Generous to others, especially beggars	Generous to others, including beggars	Persisted strongly to the age fourteen	
7. Much interested in young children	Enjoyed taking care of young children	Persisted to the age of fourteen	
8. Somewhat interested in ornaments	Much interested in ornaments	Persisted to the age of fourteen	Kumkum was less interested in ornaments than Sundari had been.
9. Interested in a game played with glass beads which resembles andi	Enjoyed andi, a game played with castor beans	No information	
10. Noted for cleanliness	Noted for cleanliness	Persisted to the age of fourteen	
11. Interested in snakes	Kept a snake as a pet	Had faded by the age of fourteen	
12. Tendency to dominate others	Tendency to dominate others	No information	
13. Strong desire to go to Urdu Bazar, Darbhanga	Lived in Urdu Bazar, Darbhanga	Ceased after the age of seven	This seems to have been one of the first behavioral traits to diminish and fade.

life and was quite ready to talk about them. But by the age of fourteen, when I saw her in 1969, all the imaged memories had apparently sunk out of consciousness. She did not seem to recognize the names of Gouri Shankar or Misri Lal and said she no longer remembered the previous life at all.[18]

Many of the behavioral traits related to the previous life persisted in Kumkum at least into her teens, when I met her. She then still showed the tendency to frugality and the strong interest in religion that I have already described. She liked gold ornaments at least up until 1965 (age ten) when this was last asked about explicitly. She continued also to the age of fourteen in her fondness for salty foods and milk, but no longer claimed to like fruit specially. Her interest in small children, in doing housework, and in caring for sick persons and beggars had also persisted strongly.

Kumkum listed snakes as her favorite animal as late as 1966 (age eleven) when queried by Dr. Jamuna Prasad's team. But three years later, when I was in Bahera, she told us her favorite animal was a cat. She had a cat as a pet. There was thus some recession of her attachment to snakes, although her father said she was still interested in them.

Kumkum's strong desire to go to Urdu Bazar lasted until the age of seven, when it diminished and ceased. This coincided with the period when her imaged memories began to fade.

In Table 11 I have listed all the important personality traits of Kumkum that seem to relate to the previous life together with the corresponding traits reported by informants for Sundari and some notes on the fading of these traits in Kumkum.

Comments on the Fading and Persistence of Traits in Kumkum. In considering the fading or persistence of traits related to the previous life, we must take account, where we have reliable information, of the attitudes of the subject's parents and siblings to the traits, and also of other experiences that may strengthen or weaken a particular trait. In Kumkum's family some of her behavior related to the previous life, such as her hoarding of money and her lower class accent, aroused interest but, so far as I could tell, no antagonism. Unlike some of the other subjects of these cases, Kumkum was

[18] Kumkum may nevertheless have retained more memories of the previous life than she cared to admit in 1969. It naturally becomes increasingly difficult for a young girl, as she grows older, to continue saying that she has a son and a grandson. If the teasing of siblings does not inhibit such statements, the development of puberty almost certainly will. My surmise receives some support from a remark by her mother that Kumkum was still (in 1969) complaining that she had more money in the previous life than then. This suggests preservation of some memories in consciousness. Dr. B. K. Verma also said he thought she might still (in 1969) have memories but not wish to talk of them because she felt embarrassed. For a fuller discussion of the difficulties encountered in evaluating reports of the fading (and preservation) of memories of previous lives, see the chapter on the results of follow-up interviews in I. Stevenson. 1974. *Twenty cases.*

no hostile rebel in her family. And consequently, neither was she an out-cast. No special effort was made to discourage the habits that seemed related to the previous life and indeed her religiosity and generosity to beggars were congenial to her mother and perhaps at least partly modeled on her mother's behavior in these matters. Her mother must also have found agreeable Kumkum's interest in helping with housework and looking after the smaller children of the family. In short, a good many of the traits in Kumkum which seem related to the previous life were not exceptional in her environment except in the degree to which she showed them as compared with other children of her age. Consequently, she has not been the object of any campaign to eradicate them. This may explain perhaps why these traits persisted so long after the fading of the associated imaged memories.

Except for the preference expressed by both Sundari and Kumkum for salted foods, their tastes in food were not very similar. Sundari enjoyed fish; Kumkum did not eat fish. Sundari was not particularly fond of fruit; Kumkum, at least when younger, liked fruit to the point where her mother noticed this.

Kumkum's Marriage. A letter from Dr. B. K. Verma informed me that Kumkum was married on July 13, 1972. She remained in her parents' house for a period and then moved to her husband's village, elsewhere in Bihar. A subsequent letter from Dr. Verma told me that Kumkum had given birth to her first child, a boy, on July 7, 1973.

6. The Case of Rajul Shah

Summary of the Case and Its Investigation

Rajul Shah was born in Vinchhiya (District Rajkot), Gujarat, on August 14, 1960. She was the second child and second daughter of Pravinchandra Shah and his wife, Prabhaben. Her parents were living at that time in Rajkot, another city of Gujarat, but Rajul was actually born at the home of her maternal grandfather. In December 1960, Rajul's parents moved to another town, Keshod, where they were living in 1969 when I met them.

Rajul has spent a number of years with her paternal grandparents, V. J. Shah and his wife. This was explained to me as a kindness to her grandparents, since they had no small children in their home and Pravinchandra Shah and his wife had four other children. V. J. Shah, who was an engineer by profession, lived at Wankaner (a town in central Gujarat north of Rajkot) from 1960 to 1969, when he moved to Songad, another town near the city of Bhavnagar, close to the eastern coast of Gujarat.

Rajul was staying with her paternal grandparents, V. J. Shah and his wife, when, at the age of approximately two and a half, she began to speak of a previous life. (She had begun to speak at the age of twelve months, rather younger at this development than her older sister Vandana had been.) Rajul came running into the house one day saying she was hungry. When asked by her great-aunt where she had been, she said she had been playing with "Junagadh Jyotsna." At about this time also Rajul was observed walking round and round in a circle and murmuring to herself. When questioned about what she was doing, she said she was doing "Junagadh Girbhi." (One informant said Rajul replied: "Girbhi of Girnar.") [1] Rajul's family knew of no playmate called Jyotsna, and they conjectured that perhaps she was talking of a previous life in Junagadh. When she was asked directly if she was "from Junagadh," she replied that she was and gave her name (of the previous life) as Gita. Soon after this, Rajul left her grandparents and returned to her parents' home, where she remained for about two years. When with her parents she spoke of the previous life, but they seem to have paid little attention to her remarks.

---

[1] Mt. Girnar is a sacred mountain near Junagadh in Gujarat. Ten thousand stone steps lead to its top, where there are many temples. It is frequently visited by pilgrims and is a site for religious exercises. During the Girbhi Festival some persons make models of Mt. Girnar (usually of clay) in the streets of Junagadh. The models, conical in shape, are about two meters at the base and one and a half meters high. Children and adult women walk, sing, and dance around the model. Rajul was imitating this activity in her play.

She told her mother, however, that she had a friend called Jyotsna with whom she sang songs and played at the Junagadh Girbhi. In May 1965, when Rajul was about four and a half years old, she came to live once again with her grandparents in Wankaner. She remained with them for another year, returned again to her parents at the age of about five and a half, and then once more, at the age of about nine, came to live with her grandparents. She was living with her grandparents in Songad when I met her in 1969.

During her second stay with her grandparents, when she was between four and a half and five and a half years old, Rajul talked much more about the previous life. Many of her remarks were stimulated by her seeming to notice some differences between the circumstances and customs of her family and what she remembered of those of the previous life. (Table 12 lists a number of items illustrating these comparisons.) Rajul said much about the previous life spontaneously; she also gave some information in response to questions put to her by members of her grandfather's household, especially by one of his then unmarried daughters, Sudhaben Desai.

Rajul's family are Jains (of the Digambara branch). Some of her remarks (see items 27, 28, and 30, Table 12) about religious customs led her family to think that the previous family were not Jains, but Hindus. Rajul described the house of the previous life in some detail. Unfortunately, she could not give the previous father's name, was a bit uncertain about the previous mother's name, and quite unable to give a family name.

According to the Jain belief the soul cannot exist without a physical body until it has become purified and achieved complete salvation.[2] Her family therefore decided that since Rajul was born on August 14, 1960, Gita, if she existed, must have died at the moment of Rajul's conception, and that this event must have occurred in the latter half of October or the first half of November 1959. One of Rajul's paternal uncles by marriage, Premchand Shah, occasionally visited Junagadh on business. In the late summer or autumn of 1965 he was in Junagadh and went to the Municipal Registrar's office. (His inquiry there was remembered four years later by one of the clerks, Babulal, with whom I talked in 1969.) Premchand Shah asked to see the register of deaths in Junagadh for the period October–November 1959; he found that a child called Gita had died on October 28, 1959, thus exactly in the middle of the range of dates previously selected. The name of Gita's father was given as Gokaldas K. Thacker, and his address for 1959 was also recorded.

The Shahs then decided to visit Gokaldas K. Thacker, with a view to verifying, if they could, Rajul's statements about the previous life. Before going to Junagadh they made a written list of twenty-two statements made

2 See the brief exposition of the Jain belief and the references cited on pp. 60–62.

by Rajul about the previous life. Unfortunately, they later loaned this list to someone and it was lost.

In November 1965, V. J. Shah and his wife, accompanied by his brother Himatlal J. Shah and Premchand Shah, took Rajul to Junagadh. Since Gokaldas K. Thacker had moved after Gita's death to another house, they had some difficulty in tracing him out. They eventually found him, however, and quickly verified some of Rajul's statements. They remained in Junagadh several days, during which time Rajul met and recognized various members of the Thacker family, and the Shahs continued their verifications of her statements. As the data of Table 12 indicate, Rajul's statements showed great accuracy with reference to the life of Gita Thacker, who had died as a small child of only about two and a half years. The Thacker family were Hindus of the Lohana caste and the Vaishnava sect. Gita's father was a retail grain merchant who had his own shop.

Rajul has since paid several other visits to Junagadh. Unlike many children subjects of these cases, she never showed any longing to go to Junagadh, although she was happy (for the most part) when there and was always received affectionately by the Thacker family.

A report of the case appeared in Indian newspapers in November and December 1965, and in this way it came to my attention. At that time, Dr. Jamuna Prasad wrote to V. J. Shah with a view to beginning an investigation of the case. He received in reply a long and informative letter dated December 22, 1965. This letter summarized the development of the case that I have already described. It also gave some examples of the statements Rajul had made before the family learned that a girl called Gita had actually died in Junagadh at about the time they had expected. Later, V. J. Shah wrote an even longer and more detailed letter (dated February 1, 1966) about the case. He addressed this letter to R. C. Parikh. The latter, having learned about the case, had visited Rajul and her family and also Gita's family. (I do not know when these visits took place.) He had asked V. J. Shah to write out for him a detailed report of the case, which led to the mentioned letter of February 1, 1966. This letter (of which I have an English translation made by R. C. Parikh) and the earlier one (written in English) to Dr. Jamuna Prasad are valuable documents of the case because they were written so soon after its development.

In November 1969, I investigated the case, over a period of several days, with the assistance of Swami Krishnanand, Dr. Jamuna Prasad, and Dr. L. P. Mehrotra. We interviewed Rajul's parents and members of her paternal grandfather's household, as well as members of the Thacker family in Junagadh.

Since my visit to Rajul's family, her paternal grandfather, V. J. Shah, has furnished information about a few additional details in correspondence with me.

Persons Interviewed during the Investigation

In Songad I interviewed:

Rajul Shah
V. J. Shah, Rajul's paternal grandfather
Himatlal J. Shah, V. J. Shah's brother and Rajul's paternal great-uncle
Sushilaben Shah, Himatlal J. Shah's wife and Rajul's paternal great-aunt
Sudhaben Desai, V. J. Shah's daughter and Rajul's paternal aunt
Premchand Shah, V. J. Shah's son-in-law

In Junagadh I interviewed:

Gokaldas Karsandas Thacker, Gita's father
Kantaben Thacker, Gita's mother
Jadaoben Thacker, Gita's paternal grandmother
Nirmala Rajah, Gita's sister
Sureshbhai Thacker, Gokaldas K. Thacker's son by his first wife, and
    Gita's half brother
Kantibhai Thacker, Gokaldas K. Thacker's younger brother and Gita's
    uncle
Babulal, clerk in Municipal Registry of Junagadh
Kanji Karsan, merchant of Junagadh

In Keshod I interviewed:

Pravinchandra Shah, V. J. Shah's son and Rajul's father
Prabhaben Shah, Rajul's mother

In Uttumnagar, near Ahmedabad, I interviewed:

Kasturba Thacker, Gita's maternal grandmother

Relevant Facts of Geography and Possibilities for Normal Means of
Communication between the Two Families

As already mentioned, Rajul was born at the village of Vinchhiya, but her
parents lived then in Rajkot, from which they moved, in December 1960,
to Keshod. Rajul's conception occurred in Rajkot, presumably in October
1959. It is approximately 95 kilometers north and slightly east of Junagadh,
where Gita Thacker had lived and died.

Junagadh is a moderately large city with a population, I estimate, of at
least 200,000. Keshod is a smaller city about 32 kilometers southwest of
Junagadh. Wankaner is 40 kilometers north of Rajkot.

The two families concerned in the case stated very firmly that they had

had no acquaintance whatever with each other before the visit of the Shahs to Junagadh in November 1965.[3]

Pravinchandra Shah, Rajul's father, said they had not visited Junagadh before the end of 1962; his wife, Prabhaben, said she had not visited it before 1966. They both had, however, passed through Junagadh in moving from Rajkot to Keshod, in December 1960, and therefore soon after Gita's death.

Rajul's paternal grandfather, V. J. Shah, and his family had no connections with Junagadh except for those of Premchand, a businessman who occasionally went there. Since the Shahs were well-to-do Jains, it is most unlikely that they would have had any social contacts with a minor Hindu merchant like Gokaldas K. Thacker even if they had lived in Junagadh or had visited there often.

V. J. Shah stated that on one occasion in December 1963, he and his wife (and other members of their family) had gone to Keshod and then visited Junagadh with Rajul. They remained in Junagadh for about two hours. They visited the Digambara Jain temple there. In a letter to me dated April 20, 1974, V. J. Shah stated that to the best of his recollection the steps leading to the top of Mt. Girnar were not visible from the Jain temple they visited. In any case, Rajul had by this time already begun to talk about the previous life and had already been observed playing at the "Junagadh Girbhi," which relates to Mt. Girnar in Junagadh. Rajul may have been driven through Junagadh on other occasions, but the only one I learned about occurred when she stopped there in December 1963.

Gokaldas K. Thacker said that in Junagadh the Jains lived in a different part of the city from the one where he resided. He knew some Jains casually but had no social relations with them; and no customers of his shop were Jains. Since Pravinchandra Shah was a clerk in a rather large bank of the area, I thought that perhaps he and Gokaldas K. Thacker had encountered each other in the bank. But Gokaldas K. Thacker said that he, like many small merchants in India, had no bank account.

If the two families had had any contact prior to verification of Rajul's statements, it must have been of the most casual kind and not sufficient for either group to remember. If the Shahs had known where to find the family Rajul was referring to in her statements, they would certainly not have gone first to the Municipal Registry in Junagadh to learn if a girl called Gita had died there at the time they expected. However, I cannot exclude the possibility that they had had some casual contact which neither group could later remember.

---

[3] In a letter to me dated March 1, 1972, V. J. Shah reiterated this lack of contact between the two families concerned. He had studied an earlier version of this case report and gently reproached me for giving the reader insufficient reassurance on this point. He sent some other suggestions for corrections in the text of which I have made use in this report of the case.

The Life and Death of Gita Thacker

Gita Thacker was born in 1957, most probably in May, in Uttumnagar, a suburb of the large Gujarat city of Ahmedabad. She was born in the home of her maternal grandmother, Kasturba Thacker. Unfortunately, I have not been able to obtain a copy or statement of the registration of her birth with its exact date. Possibly her birth was not registered in the Municipal Registry at Ahmedabad. Kasturba Thacker said Gita's birth had not been registered. She gave the month of Gita's birth as July, but as she was elderly in 1969 and seemed a less reliable informant than her daughter, I favor the month of May 1957, given by Gita's mother, Kantaben Thacker.

Gita's death is recorded in the Municipal Registry at Junagadh as having taken place on October 28, 1959. The cause of death was given as measles. (I verified the entry in the Register of Deaths at Junagadh myself.) A neighbor of the Thackers who worked in the Municipal Office was delegated to convey the information of Gita's death, and, according to Gita's father, he did so two days after she died. This neighbor, or possibly a clerk in the Municipal Registry, wrongly recorded Gita's age at death as only one and a half years, whereas she was (almost certainly) two and a half years old.

Gita died of measles after four or five days of illness. She died in the Thacker home at about 4:00 A.M. The Jain informants attached some importance to this last detail, since they believe the soul goes instantly to another body at the very second of that body's conception.

Gita's body was buried, not cremated.[4] In 1969 we asked Rajul what happened after Gita's death, and she replied: "Gita was reduced to ashes. Her soul has come here." When we asked if Gita's body was buried or cremated, she said she did not know.

The Birthdate of Rajul

I do not have an official statement of the recording of Rajul's birth, but her father, Pravinchandra Shah, said he remembered very well receiving a letter written by his father-in-law on the day of birth, August 14, 1960, informing him of the news. (He had not kept the letter.) Rajul was born in the village of Vinchhiya, whereas her father worked and lived then in Rajkot. Rajul's birthdate was also given as August 14, 1960, in the letter to Dr. Jamuna Prasad from V. J. Shah dated December 22, 1965. The Shahs are well-educated people, and I see no reason to question their memories

---

[4] It is usual to bury, not cremate, the bodies of small children in India.

of this date. Their success in working backward by deducting the probable time of gestation and thus tracing Gita also provides a verification of a kind for Rajul's birthdate.

Statements and Recognitions Made by Rajul

In Table 12 I have listed all the statements and recognitions made by Rajul. So far as I know, she made all the statements before her family attempted verification of any of them. Since, however, I do not know the order in which most of them were made, I have grouped them according to topic to make them easier to understand together. I have listed the recognitions in approximately the order in which they occurred.

V. J. Shah was present at all my interviews in Songad in 1969. However, he himself did not go into many details about what Rajul had said. His daughter Sudhaben, his brother Himatlal J. Shah, and his sister-in-law Sushilaben were the main informants for these at those interviews. V. J. Shah, however, gave many details in his letters of December 22, 1965, and February 1, 1966, of what Rajul had said. I have drawn on the latter especially in listing him as an informant in Table 12.

I have indicated in Table 12 two statements Rajul made during my talk with her in 1969. She had already made similar statements to informants of her family.

Rajul's statements seem to me to follow closely what one might expect the interests of a small child to include. They show an emphasis on features of the house, members of the family, food, play, and religious worship. Rajul said rather little about *events* of the life of Gita, which would not have been particularly rich in unusual events anyway. The main events Rajul referred to were the Girbhi ceremony around the model of Mt. Girnar, to which Gita had been taken about a month before her death, and the cause of Gita's death. She attended the Girbhi ceremony just a month before her death, at the age of two and a half. Since the Girbhi ceremony related to Mt. Girnar seemed so prominent among Rajul's memories, it is worth asking whether any other factor contributed to this, additional to the fact that Gita saw this ceremony within about a month of her death. V. J. Shah informed me that Gita's sister, Nirmala, had taken Gita daily for more than a week to watch the ceremony. It appears that there was a model of Mt. Girnar quite close to their house. Nirmala Rajah did not mention to me how often she had taken Gita to the ceremony, and it did not occur to me to ask her.

In the few incorrect statements made by Rajul, one can rather often see connections between what she said and the correct facts. The mistakes were those that would likely occur in the mind of a small child through

TABLE 12. Summary of Statements and Recognitions Made by Rajul

Item	Informants	Verification	Comments
1. Her name was Gita.	Sudhaben Desai, Rajul's paternal aunt Sushilaben Shah, Rajul's paternal great-aunt Prabhaben Shah, Rajul's mother	Gokaldas K. Thacker, Gita's father	
2. She lived in Junagadh.	Sudhaben Desai V. J. Shah, Rajul's paternal grandfather*	G. K. Thacker	
3. The house had two rooms and a kitchen.	Sudhaben Desai V. J. Shah	G. K. Thacker Verified by me in 1969	V. J. Shah's testimony for this item was given in his letter dated February 1, 1966. I visited this house in Junagadh. The Thacker family moved to another house after Gita's death.
4. The house had a veranda.	H. J. Shah, Rajul's paternal great-uncle	G. K. Thacker	The veranda had been removed at the time of my visit.
5. The house was smaller than the house here [i.e., the house of Rajul's paternal grandfather in Wankaner].	H. J. Shah V. J. Shah	V. J. Shah	Rajul said: "We have a big house here. At Junagadh we had a small house." V. J. Shah's house in Wankaner had about twelve rooms. G. K. Thacker's house (in which Gita had lived) was small, with only two rooms and a kitchen. I visited it myself in 1969.
6. The house was green.	Sudhaben Desai Rajul (1969)	Incorrect	G. K. Thacker said the house Gita had lived in was not green at any time. It was yellow on the outside. A house facing theirs, where Gita had often played, was green.
7. The house was painted red at Diwali time.	Sushilaben Shah	Unverified	G. K. Thacker recalled that his house had been painted at Diwali, an important Hindu religious festival occurring in the

autumn, but he could not remember what color it had been painted.

Statement	Informants	Verification	Comments
8. She lived downstairs.	H. J. Shah V. J. Shah	Incorrect	The Thackers had lived on the second floor of the house. The error is a natural one for a small girl who played much of the time in the downstairs area, returning to the family apartment mainly to eat and sleep.
9. The house had a bhandikiya.	H. J. Shah	G. K. Thacker Verified by me in 1969	A bhandikiya is a small cupboard or place for storage. The one at the house of Gita's family was below the steps. It was shown to me.
10. They kept an oven there.	H. J. Shah	G. K. Thacker	This "oven" was more exactly a small stove used for boiling milk.
11. Her family were Lohanas.	Sudhaben Desai	G. K. Thacker	H. J. Shah denied that Rajul had made such a remark. Lohanas are a subcaste or clan group of merchants.
12. Her mother was Shanta or Kanta.	Sushilaben Shah	Kantaben Thacker, Gita's mother	Rajul sometimes said "Shanta" and sometimes "Kanta." She may have become confused because her paternal grandmother (V. J. Shah's wife) was called Shanta and she lived much of the time with her.
13. Her mother looked like my [Rajul's] mother.	H. J. Shah V. J. Shah	Both Rajul's mother and Gita's mother, as I observed when I met them, are tall and slender.	
14. My [Rajul's] father is as old as her father.	Sudhaben Desai	Incorrect	Pravinchandra Shah was born in 1932 and G. K. Thacker in 1927. Thus Rajul's father was five years younger than Gita's father.

* Statements for which V. J. Shah is given as an informant are taken from his letter to R. C. Parikh dated February 1, 1966 (see p. 243 above). His verifications were given in oral testimony to me in 1969.

TABLE 12 (*cont.*)

Item	Informants	Verification	Comments
15. My [Rajul's] father wears pajamas; her father wore dhotis.	Sudhaben Desai Prabhaben Shah	During my interviews, Rajul's father, Pravinchandra Shah, wore pajamas and G. K. Thacker wore a dhoti.	Pajamas in India are light cotton trousers often worn by office workers. Dhotis, a kind of long, loose loincloth, are worn by farmers, small businessmen, and many other Indians.
16. Her father ate from a steel plate, but others [in the family] ate from brass plates.	Sudhaben Desai Prabhaben Shah V. J. Shah	G. K. Thacker	G. K. Thacker had a steel plate that had been given to him as a gift. It was the only such plate in the house. The other family members ate off brass plates, but he sometimes used his steel plate. The Shah family had many steel plates.
17. Her father was a confectioner.	Sudhaben Desai V. J. Shah	Incorrect	Kantibhai Thacker, Gita's paternal uncle, had a milkshop and made confections. (See also items 22 and 24.) In the version of this item given by V. J. Shah, Rajul said: "We made peras." If Gita's uncle is included in the "we," as he should be in the usual Indian family, then the statement was correct. Rajul talked so much about peras that her family thought they would find that Gita's father was a confectioner. G. K. Thacker was actually a retail grain merchant.
18. My [Rajul's] father scolds me, but her father did not [scold her].	Sudhaben Desai	G. K. Thacker Kantaben Thacker Nirmala Rajah, Gita's sister Pravinchandra Shah Prabhaben Shah	Gita's mother and sister stated that Gita's father had never scolded her, but he himself said it might have happened. Pravinchandra Shah and his wife both said that he definitely scolded Rajul at times.
19. She had a younger brother.	Sudhaben Desai V. J. Shah	Incorrect	Gita had had a friend, a younger boy called Hasmukh, with whom she had played a lot. She might have considered him a "younger brother." He died fifteen days after Gita.

Statement	Informants	Subject	Comments
20. Jyotsna was a friend who lived nearby.	H. J. Shah V. J. Shah Rajul (1969)	Unverified	Rajul said in 1969 that Jyotsna lived 100 meters from "our house." No girl playmate of Gita called Jyotsna was known to the Thacker family, and I could find no trace of a Jyotsna in the neighborhood where the Thackers had lived during Gita's lifetime. V. J. Shah did not state that Rajul had said how far away Jyotsna had lived.
21. She had a grandmother.	Sudhaben Desai	Jadaoben Thacker, Gita's paternal grandmother	Rajul said: "I had a grandmother as I have one here." The point of this remark was that in each home one grandmother only was in the family, the other living elsewhere.
22. They had lots of milk in big vessels, whereas we buy so little in small pots.	Prabhaben Shah V. J. Shah	G. K. Thacker	Rajul's family did not buy much milk. In contrast, Jadaoben Thacker, Gita's grandmother, used to buy milk in rather large quantities. She boiled the milk, kept a little for the family, and sent most of it to the shop of her second son, Kantibhai Thacker (See also items 17 and 23.)
23. Her grandmother sent milk always to the shop.	Sushilaben Shah	Jadaoben Thacker Kantibhai Thacker, Gita's paternal uncle	Jadaoben Thacker used to buy milk and boil it. (See comment for the preceding item.)
24. They had a sweet shop.	Sudhaben Desai	Kantibhai Thacker	Rajul's remarks about sweet shops were stimulated by visits to the market; she would see a sweet shop and would comment that Gita's family had a similar one in Junagadh. She also added the rather critical remark that in Junagadh the peras were well displayed. Pera is a candy (sweet) made with sugar and milk which comes in many varieties. Gita's father was a grain merchant, but Kantibhai Thacker, her uncle, had a milk shop where he also sometimes sold peras.

TABLE 12 (cont.)

Item	Informants	Verification	Comments
25. Her mother prepared white peras.	Sudhaben Desai	Kantibhai Thacker	This remark was stimulated by Rajul seeing her grandmother prepare *yellow* peras. Kantibhai Thacker had a shop during Gita's lifetime where mostly he sold milk; but two or three times a month he made peras, usually white ones. In his letter dated February 1, 1966, V. J. Shah had the colors of the peras reversed from that of his daughter's testimony. That is, according to him, Rajul compared yellow peras made in her family with white ones made in the previous family with white peras. The fact that his brother made peras was unknown to G. K. Thacker, who perhaps paid less attention to his brother's business than his daughter Gita did. I did not learn whether Gita's mother ever prepared white peras, as stated by Rajul.
26. They kept the peras in a cupboard.	V. J. Shah	Unverified	Although unverified, this item is almost certainly correct. It is, however, quite unspecific. Most of the peras I have seen in shops in India are displayed in glass-fronted cupboards which protect them—to some extent—from the flies. The peras in the shop of Kanji Karsan (see item 43), who had often given peras to Gita, were displayed in such a cupboard. When Rajul went to this shop and was asked whose it was, she said: "Ours."
27. Her family used to take dinner after dark, but we [Rajul's family] take dinner here before dark.	Sudhaben Desai V. J. Shah	G. K. Thacker	Jains customarily eat their evening meal before sunset. Hindus usually eat later, often after dark. Gita's family regularly took their evening meal around 8:00 or 8:30 P.M.

Item			Commentary
28. While her grandmother performed evening puja, she [Gita] was eating.	Sudhaben Desai	G. K. Thacker	This item is related to the preceding one. Since the Jain family ate dinner before sunset, the evening worship, or puja, took place after the meal was over; in Gita's Hindu family the puja was performed before dinner. However, a child as young as Gita would start eating her meal before the puja had concluded. Jadaoben Thacker denied that she herself had performed the evening puja ceremony during Gita's lifetime, although Gita's father said she had. Jadaoben Thacker said she was nearby when Gita's aunt performed the ceremony.
29. They used to go to a temple.	H. J. Shah	Kantaben Thacker	
30. The god of my [Rajul's] family has no clothes; her god was clothed.	Sudhaben Desai	Sudhaben Desai G. K. Thacker	In this remark, Rajul compared the statues of gods and saints in the Jain temples (of the Digambara sect), which are naked, with those in the Hindu temples, which are clothed. The Thackers belong to the Vaishnava sect of Hindus, which emphasizes the worship of Vishnu. They also worship Lord Krishna. The idols of their gods are all clothed.
31. In the temple where she used to worship they gave peras [after the puja (worship)].	Sudhaben Desai	Unverified	This remark was made as a mild complaint on the occasion of being taken to a Jain temple. In fact, at the Hindu temples frequented by Gita's family the prasad, or gift of food offered in the worship, was usually fruit, not sweets like pera. Sometimes on the way home, Gita's mother would stop at the house of Gita's uncle, where she would be given biscuits, but not peras. This item therefore remains unverified. But Gita may well have seen other

253

TABLE 12 (*cont.*)

Item	Informants	Verification	Comments
31. (cont.)			people receiving peras during or after worshiping at the temples.
32. She watched the people going around the Girnar.	H. J. Shah Sudhaben Desai V. J. Shah	Nirmala Rajah	Girnar is a holy mountain near Junagadh. Every autumn, models of it are made, usually of clay. These then form the center for a ceremony of dancing and singing in which participants, usually children and female adults, move around the model. This occurs during the Girbhi ceremony. The models reproduce or suggest the 10,000 steps that lead from the base to the top of Mt. Girnar. According to Sudhaben Desai, Rajul said that Gita herself had gone around the Girnar model. It is very unlikely that Gita did so. But Gita's older sister, Nirmala Rajah, did take Gita to the Girbhi ceremony just about a month before she died. A child of that age would have been allowed to watch the ceremony but not to take an active part in it.
33. She ate peras while seated on the clay steps of the Girnar.	Sushilaben Shah	Unverified	Rajul was here referring to the clay steps of a model of the Girnar mountain. On the actual Girnar mountain, near Junagadh, steps of stone lead to the top. Gita might have sat near the steps of the model, but she could not have sat on the model itself. A small child would not have been permitted to do so. It is quite possible that Gita was eating something while seated near the model, but Nirmala Rajah did not remember what Gita had eaten, if anything, while at the Girbhi Festival.
34. She was small when she died.	Sudhaben Desai	G. K. Thacker	Gita Thacker was between two and a half and three years old when she died. Ac-

Item	Informants	Verification and Comments
	G. K. Thacker Verified by me in the Municipal Register at Junagadh in 1969	cording to her mother, Gita was born in May 1957, and, as she died at the end of October 1959, she would have been just over two and a half. The municipal records in Junagadh give her age at death as a year and a half, an error due to the fact that incorrect information was given by a neighbor who worked in the Municipal Office and was asked to notify the registrar about the death.
35. She died of "serious fever."	Sudhaben Desai	Gita died of measles after five days of illness with fever.
36. Recognition of Kantaben Thacker, Gita's mother	H. J. Shah Kantaben Thacker V. J. Shah	As Rajul and members of her family approached the Thacker house, they encountered Kantaben Thacker on the street buying milk. V. J. Shah asked Rajul: "Do you know this lady?" Rajul thought for a little and then said: "Mother of that birth." In a letter from V. J. Shah (dated December 22, 1965) Rajul's phrase is given as: "My mother of past birth." Kantaben Thacker said in 1969 that Rajul had recognized her as "Gita's mother." Kantaben Thacker's account of the scene accorded with that of V. J. Shah, apart from the phrase spoken by Rajul as she remembered it. V. J. Shah himself had met Kantaben Thacker that morning (in a preliminary visit to the Thacker family), and so he knew who she was when Rajul recognized her; but there is no evidence that he guided Rajul to make the recognition except by asking her who Kantaben was.
37. Recognition of Nirmala Rajah, Gita's older sister	H. J. Shah Nirmala Rajah	As Rajul and members of her family entered the courtyard of the Thacker house, they

TABLE 12 (cont.)

Item	Informants	Verification	Comments
37. (cont.)	V. J. Shah		saw Gita's sister, Nirmala, standing there. Someone asked Rajul: "Do you recognize this lady?" She replied: "Father's sister." This was incorrect, since Nirmala was Gita's older sister. There was, however, some resemblance between G. K. Thacker's sister and Nirmala, who was, at the time of Rajul's visit, just about two years younger than Gita's aunt had been at the death of Gita. Nirmala Rajah's account of this recognition accorded with that of H. J. Shah.
38. Recognition of G. K. Thacker, Gita's father	H. J. Shah G. K. Thacker		G. K. Thacker returned to his home after Rajul and members of her family were already there. Someone asked her: "Who is this?" She replied: "Gokaldas." However, Rajul had heard her family talking about Gokaldas. Therefore, although she could not (according to H. J. Shah) have heard anyone say who he was (at the time he entered the house), she might well have inferred that the adult man returning to the house was Gita's father. G. K. Thacker gave a somewhat different account of the recognition. He said V. J. Shah asked Rajul who Gokaldas was (that is, which person present was Gokaldas) and Rajul replied: "He is Gokaldas and he looks like my father."
39. Recognition of house Gita lived in	V. J. Shah Sureshbhai Thacker, G. K. Thacker's son by his first wife and Gita's half brother		Rajul and members of her family stood in the main street at the entrance to the side street where the Thackers had lived during Gita's lifetime, and Rajul pointed correctly to the house, indicating it as the one where a bicycle was standing.

256

40. Recognition of a temple where Gita's family worshiped	Rajul and members of her family were taken to the courtyard of a house, where Rajul was asked to indicate the temple where "her" family had worshiped. In the courtyard there was a small temple, easily recognizable. Rajul, however, also indicated a house in the courtyard as having a temple in it. From the courtyard this building looked just like an ordinary house and gave no sign of having any religious significance. Inside, however, as I saw myself when I went in, there was one room set aside as a temple. The temple idol was hidden behind a curtain. Inside the house, Rajul correctly indicated the room of the temple, but the curtain, although it concealed the idol, might also have suggested that it covered something of religious significance. Therefore this recognition seems much less important than Rajul's identification of the house from the courtyard outside. Although located in a private house, this temple was open to the public and was frequented by the Thackers.	H. J. Shah V. J. Shah
41. Recognition of Kantibhai Thacker, Gita's uncle	Rajul was taken to the shop of Gita's uncle. He was pointed out and she was asked if she could recognize him. At that moment she could not (or did not) say, but five minutes later she said: "He is Gita's uncle." Kantibhai Thacker confirmed the details of this recognition but said Rajul took ten minutes to say who he was.	H. J. Shah Kantibhai Thacker
42. Recognition of Jadaoben Thacker, Gita's paternal grandmother	A number of women were gathered together in the home of Gita's uncle. Rajul's grandfather then asked her if she recognized Gita's grandmother or aunt in the group. Rajul looked the women over and	Jadaoben Thacker V. J. Shah

257

TABLE 12 (*cont.*)

Item	Informants	Verification	Comments
42. (cont.)			then touched Jadaoben Thacker, saying: "This is Gita's grandmother." She failed to recognize the wife of Gita's uncle, who, in fact had not been married during Gita's lifetime. The recognition of Gita's grandmother was, unfortunately, much weakened as evidence by the suggestion given that she was in the group.
43. Recognition of sweet shop frequented by Gita	Kanji Karsan, owner of the sweet shop		Rajul passed several other sweet shops, when she came to this particular one she said that the display of peras was as she remembered it. This shop had a reputation for the elegance of its displays of peras. It is almost opposite G. K. Thacker's grain shop. When Gita had been taken to visit her father at his shop, the owner of the sweet shop often took her in his arms and gave her some peras. Kanji Karsan said that at his shop Rajul indicated the cabinet where the peras were displayed and said: "I ate peras from this cabinet."
	Sureshbhai Thacker		

failure to discriminate along adult lines of thinking. Thus she said Gita had a "younger brother" (item 19). Gita had no younger brother, but she often played much with a younger boy of the neighborhood.[5] Rajul said Gita lived downstairs. This was in a sense true; Gita played downstairs, although her family actually inhabited the second story of a house. Rajul said Gita's house was green, which was incorrect. But an adjoining house with a courtyard where Gita played was green. Rajul said Gita's father was a confectioner; this was incorrect for G. K. Thacker, but his younger brother *was* a confectioner.

Rajul also told her mother that she (in the previous life) used to sing songs and play at the Junagadh Girbhi with her friend Jyotsna. The Thacker family had never heard of Jyotsna, the playmate mentioned by Rajul. Even Gita's older sister said she had never recalled Gita referring to Jyotsna. Nor could I find any trace of her in the neighborhood of Junagadh where the Thackers had lived and where I may have made something of a nuisance of myself with my own efforts to find her in 1969. However, there were in that neighborhood many families with small children, and some certainly had moved away since the time of Gita's death (1959); moreover, there were no less than eight tenant families just in the house where the Thackers lived, each with one or more daughters. Therefore Jyotsna may actually have been a friend of Gita's even though the Thackers had never heard of her and I was unable to learn of such a girl.

Rajul had a girl friend named Jyotsna in Keshod, but when it was suggested to her that she was speaking of this Jyotsna, she firmly replied: "No, I am speaking about Jyotsna of Junagadh."

In this report of the case I have deleted one item that I published in my earlier report of it.[6] I had believed, and had recorded in my notes, that Rajul had remembered that Gita did not receive a name until the time of her vaccination. Rajul's mother, Prabhaben Shah, had been the informant to me for that item. V. J. Shah, however, when he saw my first report of the case, doubted it. There then ensued correspondence between him, his daughter-in-law (Prabhaben Shah), Swami Krishnanand (who had acted as my interpreter in Gujarat in 1969), and myself. Prabhaben Shah, after considering the matter further, withdrew the item and so have I. It is true that Gita did not receive her name until she was vaccinated, but not true that Rajul remembered this detail among her memories of the previous life. The family, including Rajul, learned about it during their visit to Junagadh in November 1965.

Several of Rajul's recognitions seem quite impressive to me as evidence

---

[5] In India the word *brother* is used much more loosely than in the West. Indians often refer to cousins and even good friends as brothers.

[6] I. Stevenson. 1972. Some new cases suggestive of reincarnation. I. The case of Rajul Shah. *Journal* A.S.P.R. 66:288–309.

of paranormal knowledge on her part, although others are much weaker. Her recognitions of Gita's mother (item 36) and of the house with a temple in a room that could not be seen from the courtyard (item 40) seem the strongest. Her recognition of Gita's father and uncle are rather weaker. She only partially recognized Gita's sister, Nirmala, getting Gita's relationship to her wrong, and she failed to recognize Gita's half brother, Sureshbhai. She was unable to find the correct street leading to Gokaldas K. Thacker's shop when taken near it. The value of her recognition of Gita's paternal grandmother, Jadaoben Thacker (item 42), was greatly reduced by the indication given to Rajul that Gita's grandmother might be in the group of assembled women.

Table 12 lists unverified and incorrect statements—for example, Rajul's unverified statement about Gita's playmate Jyotsna. It does not, however, include all the persons or objects presented for Rajul's recognition that she failed to recognize. There were obviously many places and some persons available to her that she did not recognize. Although I have mentioned two such failures above, it does not seem appropriate to try to list all of them. On the other hand, it is important to notice that Rajul did not recognize everyone or every place known to Gita that she saw in Junagadh.

Rajul's Behavior Related to the Previous Life

Circumstances and Manner of Rajul's Speaking about the Previous Life. Many of Rajul's remarks about the previous life were made when she noticed some object or custom of her family that reminded her of a related but different one of the previous life. For example, on seeing sweets in a shop that she thought were rather poorly displayed, she remarked: "In our shop we had the peras well arranged." Table 12 contains numerous illustrations of such stimulation of her remarks. Apart from such occasions there was no particular circumstance associated with her talking of the previous life. Most of her remarks were made, as might be expected from the foregoing, during the daytime.

Rajul, rather more than most children subjects of these cases, was able to answer questions put to her by her family and others about the previous life. After her first visit to Junagadh she became reluctant to answer questions, probably because so many had been put to her at that time. But in 1969, she answered ours very effectively.

Rajul's family said she began to speak when only about twelve months of age and that she spoke with unusual clarity for a child that young. She seems to have had well-developed speech by the time she began to talk much about the previous life, at the age of two and a half years. Her family recalled that she pronounced the word *Jyotsna* quite distinctly. It was a word quite unfamiliar to them. The only gesture Rajul had to make to explain what she was trying to communicate occurred when she was asked how old she had been at the time of death in the previous life. She then put her hand up to the right height to show that she had been small.

In the early phases of her references to the previous life Rajul apparently talked about it often. She made frequent references to Junagadh. On the other hand, she never asked to go there and, after going there once, never asked to return.

At Junagadh, she seemed happy most of the time except for a brief period just after entering the house of Gokaldas K. Thacker. Then she cried for a time, but no one understood just why she did this. The house was not the one Gita had lived in. Perhaps Rajul was overcome with emotion on meeting members of Gita's family. In general, she showed no particular emotion when talking of the previous life.

As I have already mentioned, Rajul made many comparisons of the circumstances and people of her life with those of the previous life. A few of these—for example, "You have very little milk around here," and "my present father scolds me more than my previous father"—had a slightly pejorative tone, but she was never heard to voice any general complaint about her family or to express a preference for the previous family. Indeed, Kantaben Thacker told me that V. J. Shah had told her that Rajul required some persuasion to visit their home and had expressed a fear that she might be left in Junagadh. I did not ask V. J. Shah about this specifically, and he did not mention it to me.

On the other hand, Rajul lodged no complaint against the previous family. She seems to have thought of them with affection. When the visit to Junagadh was proposed, Rajul said the family could stay at the house of Gita's father. She added: "He is a good man. He will give you tea and food."

Rajul played at the Girbhi ceremony. When she saw a model of Mt. Girnar that had been made for the annual festival, she began walking around it and murmuring to herself. The murmuring was thought by her family to represent the singing accompanying the perambulating of the participants who circle around the Mt. Girnar model. When asked what she was doing, Rajul said: "Junagadh Girbhi." Rajul at other times also walked around in circles (without a model of Mt. Girnar) and, when asked what she was doing, said: "Junagadh Girbhi."

I questioned my informants about whether Rajul might have seen other children circumambulating the model of Mt. Girnar and then later simply imitated them. Sudhaben Desai thought this most unlikely. At the age when Rajul showed this play she was indoors most of the time, and the chances of her having seen other children perform the Girbhi ceremony were very slight indeed. The adults in her family did not perform the Girbhi ceremony, and so she could not have seen them do it.

Rajul's playing at the Girbhi ceremony seems to have been the only play by Rajul that related to the previous life actually observed by her family. However, on at least one occasion, Rajul said that she had been playing with "Junagadh Jyotsna." This play was not observed. Since on another occasion, Rajul said that she and Jyotsna had played at the Girbhi ceremony, it is possible that Rajul's unobserved play with the "Junagadh Jyotsna" was another reenactment of the Girbhi songs and dances.

Rajul was noted to be cautious in answering questions about the previous life. If she did not know the answer, or did not think she knew it, she would say nothing. She sometimes answered a question after a considerable delay. Two of her recognitions in Junagadh were made (or communicated) at least five minutes after she had seen the person she was asked to identify. Sudhaben, Rajul's aunt, said that when she asked Rajul what her name had been in the previous life, Rajul could not give it just then. She then asked Rajul to make an effort to recall and a few days later Rajul said it was "Gita." But Sushilaben Shah, Rajul's great-aunt, said that when she had asked Rajul for this name Rajul had given it immediately. Perhaps, since the memories seemed to be just coming to the surface of Rajul's mind at that time, they were unstable in her consciousness.

Rajul's great-uncle sometimes tried to test her by asking the same question in different ways at different times. But her replies were always the same. Finally, on one occasion, she told him: "I have told you once. You are asking the same question again and again."

In 1969, when Rajul (at age nine) talked with us, she answered questions very pleasantly and assuredly, although she freely acknowledged that she did not know the answers to some.

Rajul's Sense of the Passage of Time. Rajul seems to have had in general a remarkably accurate sense of the difference between her life and that of Gita. It is true that on at least one occasion she engaged in playing with Jyotsna as if Jyotsna were still living and with her. But otherwise, she nearly always used the past tense in her remarks about the previous life. When asked if she could locate the house in Junagadh, Rajul said: "Maybe the house has fallen down." On another occasion, Rajul was asked whether, if she were taken to Junagadh, she could show Gita's father and mother. She replied: "Yes, by all means." Then she was asked if she could show Gita, and she replied at once: "How can I show Gita? Gita is dead. She has become Rajul." Her manner expressed a degree of impatience with the obtuseness of such a question.

Rajul's Behavior with the Previous Family. Although, as already mentioned, Rajul showed no desire to go to Junagadh, and perhaps some reluctance, she was at ease and affectionate with the Thacker family. She sat readily on the laps of both Gokaldas K. Thacker and Kantaben Thacker, Gita's parents, and behaved familiarly with them. The Thackers in turn were friendly and loving toward Rajul. Nirmala, Gita's sister, was especially delighted with Rajul and wanted her mother to invite the Shahs to stay longer. She wept when Rajul left. Rajul did not ask to remain in Junagadh or to return, but she had been taken back for several visits between the first one in November 1965, and my visit to her family in November 1969.

Other Behavior of Rajul Related to the Previous Life. Rajul addressed her mother as Bhabhi, which means sister-in-law in Gujarati, instead of calling her Ba, the usual Gujarati word for mother. Gita's paternal aunt (the sister of Gokaldas K. Thacker) had lived with Gita's family, and, as she had called Gita's mother (her sister-in-law) Bhabhi, Gita picked up this form of address and also called her mother Bhabhi. This habit of calling the mother Bhabhi then became expressed by Rajul.

In the reports of the cases of Jagdish Chandra and Bishen Chand (in this volume) I explained how children living in large joint households hear older children and adults addressing their parents by names of relationships, such as tau (uncle) and chachi (paternal aunt by marriage). In Gita's case, the word she adopted was that used by Gita's paternal aunt in addressing her sister-in-law, Gita's mother. (Bhabhi refers to the older brother's wife.) It happens, as I learned from V. J. Shah (in a letter to me dated March 24, 1973), that Rajul's older sister Vandana also called their mother Bhabhi, and so Rajul may have imitated her older sister in this matter. On the other hand, Rajul used to say, "I had a bhabhi there [in the previous life] as I have one here [in her present family]." So her use of the word *bhabhi* in addressing her mother could also have had a provenance in the previous life.

Apart from her playing at the Junagadh Girbhi, Rajul's family had not noticed any unusual features of her behavior such as dietary cravings, habits of dress, or mannerisms, that might have derived from the previous life. Peras figured prominently in her memories, and her mother said Rajul was specially fond of them. But according to Kantaben Thacker, not pera, but another sweet, pakwan, was Gita's favorite.

Rajul's mother thought Rajul was more religious than her other children, but Himatlal J. Shah, Rajul's great-uncle, did not agree and thought her not unusual in this respect. Rajul's mother said she had expressed reluctance to visit temples other than the Jain ones. (I infer, but was not told specifically, that since Rajul had referred to Hindu temples, her family had thought of taking her to some.)

Himatlal J. Shah told me Rajul had never shown any evidence of extrasensory perception apart from her statements and behavior related to the previous life.

Comments on the Evidence of Paranormal Processes in the Case

I have already reviewed the evidence which supports my belief that the two families concerned in this case did not have any mutual friends or even casual contacts prior to the development of the case. An additional factor makes it even less likely than in many other cases that information about the previous personality could have reached Rajul or her family by normal means. I refer to the fact that Gita was a small child in an obscure family whose life and death were hardly noticed outside her own family circle. There was nothing of the stirring events, such as murders, which have figured in many reincarnation cases and which may provide reasons for the diffusing of information about the previous personality.

The case is comparatively weak in behavioral features. Rajul, apart from her references to the previous life and the play related to the Girbhi ceremony, showed no unusually deviant behavior marking her off from other members of the family and which might have had its origin in the previous life. But this feature of the case accords very well with the fact that Gita died when not yet three years old. Her personality did not have time to develop the differentiated and fixed habits which persons almost always acquire as they grow older and which have appeared in the behavior of many of the other subjects of these cases.

Rajul's Later Development

At the time of my visit to her family, Rajul was nine years old. She was an intelligent, polite, and poised girl with excellent manners. She was then in the fifth class of school. Rajul's family considered her of more than average intelligence, and my much shorter observation of her leads me to agree with this judgment.

In 1969 Rajul conserved some memories of the previous life in Junagadh, and she told us that she sometimes thought about Junagadh. It did not, however, seem to be much on her mind, and her family said that she no longer spoke spontaneously about the previous life. This did not mean, however, that Rajul had forgotten the previous life. In a letter to me dated September 8, 1970, V. J. Shah, Rajul's grandfather, wrote that

Rajul no longer spoke spontaneously about the previous life because she had nothing new to say and her family had also stopped asking her about it. But when he asked her, at my request, if she still remembered the previous life, she replied: "Yes, by all means."

In December 1973, a letter to me from V. J. Shah included the information that Rajul was again living with her parents, who had moved to Wankaner. She had recently had typhoid fever, but she had fully recovered and was back at school. In a later letter (dated May 2, 1974) V. J. Shah wrote to me that Rajul, who was then approaching fourteen years of age, was healthy and working diligently at her school studies.

7

The Case of Puti Patra

Summary of the Case and Its Investigation

Puti Patra was born in November 1964, to Balai Patra, a day laborer (later a mason), and his wife, Binapani. Kajal is her correct name and Puti a nickname, but as it is the one by which she is commonly known, I shall use it in this report. Puti was born in the village of Kapasberya, which is about 5.5 kilometers from the town of Tamluk in the District of Midnapore, West Bengal. Puti had an older brother and three older sisters, although two of these girls had died before 1969.

When Puti was between one and a half and two years old, she began to talk about a previous life. She said that she had been married to one Bera and had a daughter and a son. One day the husband had come home drunk. He found his lunch was late and, becoming enraged, slapped his wife, who fell down in a faint. He attempted to revive her unsuccessfully. He then took her body to the cowshed, where he hanged her with a rope. Puti claimed that she was still living in the previous life when her husband did this; she implied that he panicked, became afraid he would be accused of murder, and hanged her body (thinking she was dead, although she was, in fact still living) in order to simulate a suicide.

Puti's statements seemed to refer to Lolita, the wife of Bansi Bera Maiti[1] who lived in the village of Salgachya, about 2 kilometers from Kapasberya. Bansi Bera had lost his first wife, Lolita, in (approximately) 1956. Puti's mother, Binapani Patra, recalled having heard that Bansi Bera's wife had committed suicide, but her father, Balai Patra, said he heard (later) from a neighbor of Bansi Bera that Lolita had died of cholera. She was about twenty-five years old at the time and left behind two small children, the younger an infant boy.

Reports of Puti's statements reached the family of Bansi Bera, but at that time none of them visited Kapasberya to see her. In October 1967, when Puti was about three, she was being carried by her father along the road in Salgachya on which the Bera house is located, and she recognized

[1] The family changed its name from Bera to Maiti some years back, but I shall use the name Bera, this being the one used by Puti.

it. She said to her father: "This is our house and this is our tank [pond]." About two weeks later Puti was passing along the same road (with her mother and older brother) and she again pointed out the house, saying: "This is the house of the Beras I am speaking about."

Some six months later, in the spring of 1968, Puti was again walking past the Bera house with members of her family when Bansi Bera's mother recognized them and asked to see the child who talked of living in their house. They exchanged a few remarks, and Puti's statements (which I quote below) were sufficiently convincing to induce weeping in Lolita's mother-in-law. Some time later, Bansi Bera's second wife and his sister-in-law came to visit Puti and questioned her about her memories of the previous life. Puti repeated to these and other persons her account of how she (in the previous life) had died. It later reached the Patras that the Beras were accusing them of tutoring Puti to make slanderous remarks about Bansi Bera.

A short report of this case was published in a Bengali newspaper, *Ananda Bazar Patrika,* on May 31, 1968. Prof. P. Pal read the account and, in March 1969, visited Puti Patra and her family to make a preliminary investigation of the case. In November 1969, accompanied by Professor Pal and also by Dr. Jamuna Prasad and Dr. L. P. Mehrotra, I visited the area and had interviews with members of both families. In 1971 I returned to the area (again with Professor Pal) for some additional interviews, especially with Puti's father, Balai Patra, whom neither Professor Pal nor I had been able to meet in 1969.

Persons Interviewed during the Investigation

In Kapasberya I interviewed:

Puti Patra
Binapani Patra, Puti's mother
Balai Patra, Puti's father
Laxmi Kanta Patra, Puti's older brother

In Tamluk I interviewed:

Bansi Bera, Lolita Bera's husband
Raddha Nath Bera, Bansi Bera's younger brother
Shyamapada Samanta, resident of village Sankera, near Salgachya

Professor Pal (in 1969) interviewed:

Gangamani Patra, Puti's paternal grandmother
Subrata Nayak, resident of Salgachya village and acquaintance of Bansi Bera

Unfortunately, Bansi Bera's mother, who would have been an important witness, had died in 1969. For reasons that I shall explain later, it did not seem likely that additional witnesses would resolve the discrepancies between the testimonies of the two families concerned. Unfortunately also, all the close relatives of Lolita Bera had died by the time of my inquiries. She came from another village named Darinda.

Relevant Facts of Geography and Possibilities for Normal Means of Communication between the Two Families

As already mentioned, Kapasberya and Salgachya are about 2 kilometers apart and about 4 or 5 kilometers from the town of Tamluk. According to the informants of both families, the immediate families had, with small exceptions, no direct acquaintance with each other prior to the development of the case. They knew each other to recognize, but had no social relationships. Members of Puti's family sometimes passed the Beras' house in going to and from their own house, which is farther from the market town of Tamluk than Salgachya is. And Balai Patra, for a time at least, went by the Bera house on his way to and from his work.

I learned of some minor exceptions to the lack of acquaintance between the two families. Balai Patra's mother, Gangamani Patra, sold vegetables along the roads of the area, and sometimes the women of the Bera home purchased from her. I found also that a paternal uncle of Bansi Bera, Hemanta Kumar Bera, lived in Kapasberya. But his home was 400 meters from the house of Balai Patra, Kapasberya being a very extended village. According to Bansi Bera, his uncle had seen Puti moving about in the village but had not talked with her. I infer, therefore, that he had had little or no acquaintance with her family. One of Lolita's nephews worked for a time with Balai Patra. He had heard of Puti's statements and asked her father about them. It was he who first confirmed one of Puti's statements to the effect that Lolita's parents had lived near a bridge (item 12, Table 13), but this fact suggests that he was asked about the truth of what Puti was saying, not that he was the source of it.

No barriers of caste separated the two families of this case such as has happened in some other cases; both families are members of the Maisha subcaste of the Vaishya caste. The Beras were distinctly more prosperous than Puti's family.

I may remark here that in the analysis of this case little depends on whether or not the two families did have more acquaintance with each other than I was able to learn about. Apart from what she said about how she had died in the previous life, Puti gave only sparse details about Lolita and her family. And these, such as that Lolita had had a son and daughter, and that her house had been near the market, are conceded to have been in the public domain, so to speak, and more or less known to the inhabitants of both Kapasberya and Salgachya. The main interest and value of the case lies in the irreconcilable (up to now) discordance between what Puti Patra said about how she had died in the previous life and what Lolita's husband said about this. We can be reasonably certain that Puti's account of these tragic moments was not derived from anything she picked up from the Bera family, at least not by normal communications. And perhaps it is also reasonable to add that if her details about the death of Lolita are accurate and did not come from the Beras, the other details of her statements also did not.

Statements and a Recognition Made by Puti

Puti's parents said they discouraged her from talking about the previous life and after a certain time they put an amulet around her arm to supplement the influence of their disapproval. From whatever effects, Puti stopped talking about the previous life spontaneously when less than four, an unusually young age. Her parents' rejection of her remarks and their general lack of interest in what she was saying account perhaps for the scantiness of the details of the previous life recalled, or at least recorded, as having been stated by Puti. I have listed them all in Table 13.

Puti made only one recognition related to the previous life, that of Bansi Bera's house, which she pointed out first as she was going along the road in front of it with her father. She was about three years old at the time. She did not show any signs of recognizing the members of Bansi Bera's family, whom she saw when she and members of her family stopped at the Bera house or when they came to see her in Kapasberya.

Puti's meetings with members of the Bera family deserve recording in some detail. The first occurred in May 1968, when Puti was about three and a half years old. I quote from the notes of Prof. P. Pal, who recorded (in March 1969) a statement by Puti's mother, Binapani Patra, as follows:

She and her husband with Puti . . . were going to a fair by passing Bansi Bera's home. . . . [Balai] Patra with Puti had gone a little ahead. Bansi's mother was standing in front of their house. She asked me: "Dear, which of your daughters says that she belongs to the Beras?" I pointed out Puti . . . with her father. She requested me to call him back so that she might see the girl and I did so. The old woman asked, "Why did you go away, my child?" to which the girl replied, "As I used to be scolded." The old woman said, "Does one go away, my child, merely being scolded?" Then Puti, pointing to her right cheek, said, "He slapped me." Bansi's mother then asked, "How many children had you?" Puti replied, "A girl and a boy." The old woman said, "With whom did you

TABLE 13. *Summary of Statements and a Recognition Made by Puti*

Item	Informants	Verification	Comments
1. Her name was Lolita.	Binapani Patra, Puti's mother	Bansi Bera, Lolita Bera's husband	Puti's mother said that Puti had not told her family spontaneously what her name in the previous life had been. The name came out under questioning only.
2. She was the wife of Bansi Bera.	Binapani Patra	Bansi Bera	As mentioned in the text, Puti gave the last name of the husband, Bera, spontaneously, but only gave the first name, Bansi, later, when questioned insistently by members of Bansi Bera's family.
3. She had a son and a daughter.	Binapani Patra	Bansi Bera	At the time of Lolita's death she had a daughter of about three and an infant son who was about one year old.
4. She had a small baby.	Binapani Patra	Bansi Bera	Puti repeatedly mentioned an infant, using the Bengali word *kachi*, which may refer to an infant of either sex. For a long time she also spoke of the husband she was remembering only as "kachir baba" (English: "the baby's father"). Puti never mentioned the name of the baby. Lolita's infant son, Amiol, was about a year old when she died. Lolita had referred to the infant as "kachi" and also with the word *koka* (English: "son").
5. Her husband returned to the home in a drunken state and was angry because lunch was not ready.	Balai Patra, Puti's father	Subrata Nayak, acquaintance of Bansi Bera	Subrata Nayak was not himself a witness of the quarrel, but reported (in an interview with Prof. P. Pal in 1969) what Bansi Bera had admitted to him. He did not say, however, that Bansi Bera had said he was drunk at the time, but only that he and his wife had quarreled because his lunch was late.

Item	Informants	Verification	Comments
6. Her husband slapped her on the right cheek.	Binapani Patra	Unverified	Binapani Patra said Puti always pointed to her *right* cheek saying: "He slapped me on *this* cheek."
7. She fell down.	Balai Patra / Binapani Patra	Unverified	According to Balai Patra, Puti said she (in the previous life) had fainted after being slapped on the cheek.
8. After she fell down they tried to revive her by sprinkling her face with water.	Balai Patra	Bansi Bera	Bansi Bera said he sprinkled water on his wife's face after she was found hanging in the cowshed. He tried thus to revive her. His statement therefore provides only a partial verification of Puti's statement. Puti's "they," presumably refers to Bansi Bera, his mother, and one of his sisters-in-law who was visiting at the time of Lolita's death.
9. Her husband then hanged her in the cowshed.	Binapani Patra / Balai Patra	Unverified	
10. She was hanged with a piece of rope.	Balai Patra	Raddha Nath Bera, Bansi Bera's younger brother	The rope was of the type used to lead cows.
11. Her house was near the market.	Binapani Patra	At Salgachya I found that the Bera house was about 175 meters from the market.	
12. Her parents' home was near a wooden bridge.	Binapani Patra / Gangamani Patra, Puti's paternal grandmother	Bansi Bera	A small bridge was located about 175 meters from the home of Lolita Bera's parents in Darinda. Professor Pal learned in 1969 that the bridge had been wooden, but was later converted to a concrete structure.
13. There was a date palm tree near the road at her house.	Binapani Patra	I saw several date palms by the road near the Bera house in Salgachya.	Date palm trees are very common in this part of India, and so the statement is in no way specific.

TABLE 13 (cont.)

Item	Informants	Verification	Comments
14. Recognition of the Beras' house in Salgachya	Balai Patra		This occurred spontaneously when Puti was about three years old. She was being carried along the road by the Beras' house in her father's arms; she then spontaneously said: "This is our house and this is our tank." There are in fact two large tanks (ponds) between the road and the Beras' house.

leave them?" Puti replied, "With kachi's [the baby's] father." The boy was then a little over one year old. Then the old woman began to cry saying, "Oh, dear. You left us." Then we left the place.

On the above occasion, Puti did not repeat her charge that Lolita's husband had hanged her in the cowshed while she was still alive. But she did not shrink from doing so later, when several other members of Bansi Bera's family visited her in Kapasberya. These were Bansi Bera's second wife, his brother Raddha Nath's wife, and his daughter and son by his first wife, Lolita (the previous personality). For the report of this encounter, I quote from my notes of the testimony of Balai Patra during my interview with him in February 1971.

The brother's [Raddha Nath's] wife asked her [Puti]: "How many children had you?" She replied: "One boy and one girl." Then she asked, "Why did you come away?" Puti replied, "My husband killed me and hanged me in the cowshed." Then Raddha Nath's wife asked: "Why did he assault you?" Puti said, "My husband came [home] in a drunken state and as lunch was not ready, he slapped me on my right cheek. Then I fell down. Then they sprinkled some water on my face, but as I did not come around, they hanged me in the cowshed."

Balai Patra said he could not be clear from Puti's remarks whether she was saying that Bansi Bera had hanged his wife in the cowshed alone or with the aid of someone else. Puti said she (that is, Lolita) was hanged with a rope.

Puti's Statement about the Interval after Lolita's Death and before Her Birth. Puti stated that after being hanged (in the previous life), she stayed near a date palm tree by the house where she had lived. She told her father: "When you were coming one day about midday from your work and passing by this house [meaning the Bera house] I was standing at the bottom of the date palm tree and came along with you to your house." Since Lolita died in 1956 and Puti was born in 1964, she seemingly condensed the memories of the experiences of eight years into this one sentence. She never mentioned having seen the funeral or cremation of Lolita Bera.

Puti's Behavior Related to the Previous Life

According to her mother, Puti began talking about the previous life at a very young age, about one and a half years. She was then unable actually to pronounce the *r* of *Bera* correctly, so that for some time her family could not understand what proper name she was giving. When they finally understood that she was saying "Bera," they still did not know to which

Bera she was referring since there were several Bera families in the area. Puti did not give the first name of the previous husband at first but, in the typical shy fashion of Indian women, alluded to him as "the little baby's father." She first mentioned the name Bansi at the age of between three and four, during the above-mentioned visit to Kapasberya of Bansi Bera's second wife and sister-in-law. At this time, Puti kept referring to "the little baby's father." One of the visitors expostulated: "I don't know who the little baby's father is. Who is this man? Give his name." Puti then mentioned the name Bansi for the first time.

During the period of her talking about the previous life, Puti seemed to do so rather often. I did not learn of any particular time of day or special stimuli for her remarks.

Puti never expressed any desire to visit the previous family or to see the house of the previous life. When asked if she would like to go there, she said "No, he [meaning Bansi Bera] used to scold and beat me."

Puti did not seem particularly interested in Lolita's children, and, when asked with whom she had left them, she said simply: "With the baby's father.[2]

As already mentioned, Puti stopped speaking spontaneously about the previous life when she was less than four years old. Whether we should attribute this early cessation of spontaneous talk to her parents' discouragement, the suggestive effect of the amulet they applied to her arm, a general weakness and low penetrance of the memories, or to some other unidentified factor, I cannot decide. We do know, however, that Puti's memories were not completely covered over at that time because her mother told me in 1971 that Puti would still talk about the previous life if questioned directly. She was then six and a half years old.

Other Relevant Behavior on the Part of Puti

Puti's mother furnished a few other details about her character which may have some connection with the previous life although not necessarily so. She said that Puti was quieter and yet lost her temper more readily than her other daughters. She easily became angry if beaten and seemed more sensitive to such chastisement than the other children of the family. When beaten, she would go away from the house, but never threatened

---

[2] The children subjects of these cases vary markedly in their expressions of desire to visit the previous families. Some, like Jagdish Chandra and Sunil Dutt Saxena (whose cases are reported in this volume), have a very strong wish to do so. Others, like Puti Patra and Lalitha Abeyawardena (whose case is to be reported in the next volume of this series), find the prospect of a visit to the previous home unattractive, or even repellent. The attitudes of the children with regard to visiting the other family usually accord well with what we can conjecture about the happiness of the previous personality in the last home lived in.

to leave the village. She was not noted to be more mature (or less so) than the other daughters of the family at the same age.

The Patra family had a cowshed. Puti showed no phobic behavior toward it. She had no other remarkable fears either. There is a school in the village of Kapasberya, but at the age of six and a half, Puti had not yet been sent to it.

Puti had not given any evidence of paranormal abilities apart from the memories she had of a previous life.

Bansi Bera's Statements about the Death of His Wife

Bansi Bera stated to me in 1969 that his wife Lolita had hanged herself with a rope in the cowshed of their house in 1956. His wife was then about twenty-five years old, he himself about thirty-two. His wife was "a bit mentally ill" and had a brother who was insane. She had been talking of suicide for some three months before she hanged herself. Nothing unusual about his wife was noticed immediately before her suicide except that she had been a little morose the previous day. They had had no quarrel that day. About 4:00 or 4:30 P.M. his wife had gone to the cowshed and had hanged herself with a rope. He himself was napping. His infant son was with him and awakened him by crying. He then called to his mother to ask his wife to look after the baby. His wife was not around, and he and his mother began to search for her. One of Bansi Bera's sisters-in-law, who happened to be visiting at the time, joined the search, and she discovered Lolita's body hanging from a beam in the cowshed. She had used a ladder to mount up before hanging herself. He sprinkled water on his wife's face to try to revive her, but when this failed, he informed the police. The police came and readily accepted the death as due to suicide. They knew his wife to have been a little "crackbrained." There was no inquest and no autopsy. Nobody in the village questioned the suicide or suggested that it was a case of murder.

Other Information about the Death of Lolita Bera

The younger brother of Bansi Bera, Raddha Nath Bera, supported his brother's account in all important particulars. He was not, however, at the house himself at the time of his sister-in-law's death, although he ordinarily lived with them. He was away attending a fair at the time. He returned to the house only after being sent for when Lolita's body was found. He knew his sister-in-law to be somewhat unstable, but he had not heard that she had made threats of suicide.

Puti's mother, Binapani Patra, told me that, at the time of Lolita's death, she understood she had committed suicide. But her husband, Balai Patra, said that a neighbor of the Beras, Param Maiti, told him that the Beras had given out that Lolita had died of cholera.[3] (He, however, asserted that Puti was telling the truth in saying that Lolita's husband had hanged her when she was alive; but this is his conjecture rather than firsthand evidence.)

Subrata Nayak, a friend of Bansi Bera, told Professor Pal in 1969 that Bansi Bera had admitted to him that on the day of his wife's death he had scolded her for not having his lunch ready. They had quarreled, and she had then gone to the cowshed and had hanged herself.

Comments on the Evidence of Paranormal Processes in the Case

I am seldom able to set aside a particular hypothesis firmly. In the present case, however, I feel quite certain that this case was not worked up fraudulently by Puti's parents, alone or together. They are simple, illiterate country folk living in poverty and barely able to earn the bare necessities of life. By 1971 Balai Patra had improved his position a little as compared with 1969. He had advanced from being a day laborer to working as a mason and was earning 5½ rupees (about 75 cents U.S.) a day. He and his family lived in a small clay hut. No discernible motive existed for them to have thought up false accusations of murder against Bansi Bera and imposed them on their child. Binapani Patra firmly denied the imputation that she had taught Puti to make false statements about the death of Lolita. She pointed out quite reasonably that she had had other daughters born during the eight years between the death of Lolita and the birth of Puti, so that if she had wanted to create trouble for the Beras she would surely have tutored one of the older daughters and not waited until ten years after Lolita's death, which by then had been largely forgotten. The Patras were certainly not gaining money or fame from Puti's statements. (Curious visitors who thronged into their hut for a time after the case received attention in a local newspaper annoyed them greatly.) They denied having any grudge against the Beras, and, if the informants are correct about the lack of significant acquaintance between the two families, it is difficult to see how they could have had enough to do with

---

[3] Cholera is endemic and at times epidemic in India. It carries its victims off rapidly, so that a person can be well one day and dead twenty-four hours later. It is therefore a convenient malady to assign as a cause of death when a person seems healthy and dies unexpectedly and suddenly.

An autopsy could have distinguished hanging from cholera as a cause of death. It is very doubtful, however, that an autopsy alone could have distinguished whether a living person was hanged by someone else and thus murdered, or hanged himself suicidally.

each other to generate a feud. Even Bansi Bera, while denying the genuineness of the case, did not presume to assert (to me, at any rate) that the parents had contrived it. But the Patras had heard that he was accusing them of coaching Puti.

I think it is worth adding that the Patras being such utterly simple persons, in the best sense of that expression, we can completely discount any motive on their part connected with religious doctrines. No Indian case known to me is less contaminated by enthusiasm for Hinduism.

If we can discount the hypothesis of fraud, as I believe we should, then we confront the fact that, concerning the events leading up to the death of Lolita, either Puti or Bansi Bera is right, but they cannot both be. Unfortunately, if we set aside Puti's statements, only one living person knows the truth about Lolita's death, and he, Bansi Bera, is an interested party in the case.

Bansi Bera has, however, been found in some discrepancies that weaken his credibility. He denied to me that he and his wife had quarreled on the day of her death. But as mentioned earlier, Subrata Nayak said that Bansi Bera had told him they had quarreled because his lunch was not ready and that he had scolded Lolita. After the quarrel, Bansi Bera had told him, Lolita had gone to the cowshed and had hanged herself. These details, as reported by Subrata Nayak, accord very well up to the crucial event with Puti's statements, and they may incline us to accept the rest of what she said also. Furthermore, in the passage I have quoted above, Raddha Nath's wife (Bansi Bera's sister-in-law) seemed to make a possibly damaging admission when she asked Puti: "Why did he [Bansi Bera] assault you?"

If it is correct, as Param Maiti asserted to Balai Patra, that the Beras gave out that Lolita had died of cholera and yet were also telling people that she had died of suicide by hanging, they were releasing irreconcilable versions which could not be accounted for by ignorance of medical facts, since no one could possibly confuse these two causes of death.[4]

On the other hand, there is a certain implausibility to Puti's account of what happened unless it is supplemented by other speculations. I refer to the extreme improbability that anyone who had merely fainted from being slapped on the cheek would not revive when lying supine on the floor. This position ordinarily restores circulation to the brain, which is abruptly deprived of sufficient blood during ordinary fainting in the upright posi-

[4] I mean no one would think that a person hanging from a beam in a barn had died from cholera. But when Bansi Bera's family found Lolita's body in the barn—however it got there—they must have taken it down before trying to revive Lolita by sprinkling water on her. Probably they carried the body into the house, and presumably it was there that the police found it. Thus although Lolita's family had, according to Bansi Bera, attributed her death to suicide, they might have had the option later of saying that it was due to cholera. But they could not have believed this themselves.

tion. It is even more unlikely that Lolita would not have revived (if still living) as she was being carried to the cowshed to be hanged there. (The distance, as I saw when I visited the house in 1969, was about 35 meters.) However, if Bansi Bera slapped his wife, she may have been knocked down, or have fallen down, in such a way as to concuss her brain with subsequent, more prolonged unconsciousness than that of a simple faint. But she would then still be breathing, and it is difficult to conceive how even the most panic-stricken husband could imagine that someone who was breathing had in fact died. Perhaps he thought (here I am for the moment accepting Puti's account) that she was about to die and that he would be accused of her murder if she did, and so he decided to simulate a suicide. And, to deprive him even further of the benefit of the doubt, he may have been perfectly aware that she was still living and thought of an apparent suicide as a convenient means of ridding himself of an irksome partner. The stunned Lolita might then have revived just before dying, in time to be aware of what was happening but too late to prevent it.

Bansi Bera has never been to visit Puti, and I find this a curious omission which may suggest to some that he does not wish to have guilty feelings aroused by a confrontation with a girl who may be his murdered wife reborn. This point impressed Professor Pal, and in a letter to me dated July 24, 1972, he wrote: "If Bansi Bera had not a guilty conscience and was in no way responsible for Lolita's death, he should have been the first person to run to see Puti, when he heard she claimed to be Lolita reborn —his first wife who had so tragically ended her life out of insanity." I find this reasonable; but think it is only fair to add that if Bansi Bera is innocent, we can forgive him for not wanting sad memories revived by unjust accusations.

Raddha Nath, Bansi Bera's brother, supported his account of the death of Lolita, but this adds little weight to the available evidence. For he said that he was absent from the home when Lolita died; therefore, he was not a firsthand witness of anything that happened before her death. And if he was allowed to know, or inferred by himself, that Bansi Bera had rashly hanged his wife to simulate a suicide, fraternal affection would almost certainly incline him to support his brother's account of events.

I considered making further inquiries among the police of Tamluk. But I was dissuaded by two factors. First, there was only a perfunctory police investigation and no postmortem examination of the body of Lolita Bera. This I learned from Bansi Bera and also from another, independent, informant, Shyamapada Samanta, in Tamluk. Second, if the police had been bribed in 1956 by Bansi Bera, they would not want this fact enquired into. And if they had not been corrupted but had neglected their duty in not requiring an inquest, they would not welcome being told fifteen years later that they ought to have gone into the matter more thoroughly at the time.

In 1971 Prof. P. Pal and I made some efforts to question persons in Tamluk concerning what they remembered about the death of Lolita Bera, which had occurred fifteen years earlier. One informant, Shyamapada Samanta, said he had heard some talk to the effect that Bansi Bera had killed his wife. But when I pressed him to say whether he had heard such talk before or after Puti Patra's statements were reported, he could not say precisely when he had heard this rumor. Possibly, reports of her statements had contaminated his memories. As I mentioned earlier, Balai Patra said that a neighbor of Bansi Bera, Param Maiti, had told him that Puti was telling the truth and that Bansi had in fact killed his wife. But how was he in a position really to know? It seemed improbable that a neighbor of Bansi Patra would repeat such a statement to me. The danger of reprisals from Bansi Bera would be very great. So I did not try to see this witness.

The reader will have to make up his own mind about the truth concerning the death of Lolita Bera. If he is a person who likes certainty, I hope he will succeed better than I have been able to do, for I have found myself vacillating—I could almost say oscillating—between believing Puti and believing Bansi Bera. But this being so, it seems to me both fair and wise to suspend judgment and await further evidence. Unfortunately, we are unlikely to obtain any. The death of Lolita is already far behind us. A Bengali able to spend several weeks or months in the area might uncover new information that would end the indecisiveness that we must accept for the present.

The question of the truth concerning the death of Lolita has some bearing on the interpretation of the whole case. If Puti is wrong and Bansi Bera right about the death of Lolita, the interpretation of the case as due to extrasensory perception becomes weakened. For we could not comfortably say that Puti got all her correct information about the Bera house and family by extrasensory perception from, say, Bansi Bera's mind, but somehow muddled the facts about Lolita's death. What Bansi Bera claimed to be the facts of her death were just as much in his mind as the other facts stated by Puti which are not in dispute, so why could she not lift them out correctly along with the rest?

On the other hand, if the case is best interpreted as one of reincarnation, we do not necessarily have to accept Puti's version of the death of Lolita. She might have remembered most things correctly but distorted some details of the last moments and death of Lolita. If Lolita and Bansi Bera quarreled on the day of her death, as Subrata Nayak said Bansi Bera admitted they did, then perhaps she, in a kind of paranoid anger such as often affects suicidal people, thought to herself that Bansi had "made her" commit suicide. And afterward, supposing that she survived death, she could have further reconstructed events until it seemed to her that he had actually hanged her. It is of interest that the detail of sprinkling her face with water gets into both accounts. Puti said Bansi Bera had sprinkled her (Lolita's) face with water after she fainted and before he panicked and hanged her in the cowshed. Bansi Bera said he had sprinkled Lolita's face with water (after they took the body down from the beam in the cowshed). Some of the children subjects of these cases seem to remember the details of the death of the previous personality very precisely, while others remember it only imperfectly and with somewhat blurred and confused images similar to those of a delirious person.[5]

[5] I believe that Ravi Shankar (I. Stevenson. 1974. *Twenty cases*) remembered details of the death of Munna accurately. And Ramoo and Rajoo Sharma (whose case is reported later in this volume) seemed to remember accurately the deaths of the related previous personalities in their case, although we have only secondhand verification of much of what they said about these deaths. On the other hand, Sunil Dutt Saxena seems to have mixed up some of the details of the death he remembered. And I think Warnasiri Adikari did so also (F. Story and I. Stevenson. 1967. A case of the reincarnation type in Ceylon: The case of Warnasiri Adikari. *Journal* A.S.P.R. 61:130–45; also in the second volume of this series).

8

The Case of Dolon Champa Mitra

Introduction

I<small>N</small> the present case the subject, a small girl, remembered a previous life as a young man. It thus has the feature of a difference of sex between the two personalities concerned. In my first book of reports of these cases I reported two cases of this type, those of Gnanatilleka and Paulo Lorenz (I. Stevenson. 1974. *Twenty cases*). In the next two volumes of this series I shall report two further cases of the "sex change" type, those of Ruby Kusuma Silva (Sri Lanka) and Ampan Petcherat (Thailand).[1]

Summary of the Case and Its Investigation

Dolon Champa Mitra (whom I shall hereafter refer to simply as Dolon) was born in Calcutta on August 8, 1967. Her parents were Audaryamoy Mitra and his wife, Kanika. They had one other child, a boy, Jayanta, who was four years older than Dolon. Audaryamoy Mitra was employed as a superintendent in the Poultry and Dairy Section at the Ramakrishna Mission Ashrama in Narendrapur, which is about 10 kilometers south of Calcutta.

Dolon began to speak clearly between the ages of one and two. She spoke coherently by the time she was two. She did not start to refer to a previous life until she was between three and a half and four.

Dolon's first remarks about the previous life occurred in the following circumstances. One day in 1971, when she was about three and a half, her mother saw her wearing her older brother's shirt and pants and reproached Dolon for this. Later, after lunch, she asked Dolon to come and rest by her side, but Dolon replied: "No . . . you scold me for wearing a shirt and pants. I was a little bigger boy in a house like a palace." Her mother, startled, said: "What are you saying?" To which Dolon replied: "Yes, mother, I am speaking the truth. I had a younger brother and sister. I had a fat aunt

[1] See also I. Stevenson. 1973. Some new cases suggestive of reincarnation. IV. The case of Ampan Petcherat. *Journal A.S.P.R.* 67:361–80.

and my mother was called Baudi. Take me near the Maharajah's palace and I shall lead you to the house."

After this outburst Dolon stated a considerable number of other details about the life she was remembering. She said the house she had lived in was a red two-storied one near a temple. Steps led up to the door of the house from the street. She located it in Burdwan, a city northwest of Calcutta. And she mentioned that she had died (in the previous life) after a long stay in a hospital. Dolon tended to bring out statements about the previous life in bits and pieces on different occasions rather than in a continuous narrative.

Among the items Dolon spoke about most often and insistently was a blue shirt that she said was in an almirah (cupboard). But she never mentioned any family names or proper names of any kind other than the name of the city Burdwan, where she said she had lived, and the name Ranjit, which she mentioned without clearly saying who Ranjit was. She also mentioned the general name baudi, by which she said her (previous) mother had been called.[2]

Dolon repeatedly requested to go to Burdwan and said that she could find the house by herself if she was taken near the Maharajah's palace there. Eventually her parents yielded to her demands and to their own curiosity, and they took her to Burdwan for the first time in October 1971. They put Dolon down in Burdwan near the Maharajah's palace and allowed her to try to find the house she was talking about. But after she had made a few unsuccessful attempts, it became apparent that from the location where they were she could not find the correct house. It was hot that day, and her parents decided to desist in the attempt and so returned with Dolon to Narendrapur.

Dolon was very unhappy over this outcome of the first visit to Burdwan and insisted on being taken there again. So her parents took her back there on March 30, 1972. But this time they sought the aid of some persons living in Burdwan. They were able to arrange this because some colleagues of Dolon's father at the Ramakrishna Mission Ashrama in Narendrapur were originally from Burdwan. One of these persons, Nilachal Samanta, and his wife both came from Burdwan; Nilachal Samanta's wife made some inquiries among her relatives there and learned that Dolon was perhaps referring to a family called De, whose members were wealthy and prominent persons of that city.

---

[2] *Baudi* is a Bengali word applied to the wife of an older brother by younger brothers and sisters. It had in this case little indicative value, although it was in fact the name by which some members of the joint family called the mother of the later identified previous personality, although he had not. For other examples of the use of names of relationships applied incorrectly by children, see the reports of the cases (in this volume) of Jagdish Chandra, Bishen Chand Kapoor, and Rajul Shah.

It was then arranged for the Mitras to take Dolon first to the home of Pratima Dawn, Nilachal Samanta's sister-in-law, who lived in Burdwan. From her house Dolon, her mother, and Pratima Dawn went to the home of Prithwis Chandra De, who was distantly related to the family tentatively identified as the one Dolon was talking about. (Dolon's father remained behind at the Dawns' house, apparently because he did not think Dolon would do any better on this attempt to find the right house than she had on the first one.)

Prithwis Chandra De was unable to go with the others to look with Dolon for the house she was talking about. Therefore, Dolon and her mother went to find the house with Pratima Dawn and Prithwis Chandra De's wife, Mira De. They took Dolon to a temple not far from the Maharajah's palace and let her then go ahead to see if she could find the way to the house she had been talking about. This time Dolon succeeded. She followed a somewhat deviant course that eventually led to a rather narrow street or lane. She went down this until she came to a small shrine room (open to the street) that she seemed to recognize but did not comment upon. She retraced her steps back up this same street and then pointed to the house of Anath Saran De and said it was the house. Mira De, not trying to mislead Dolon but genuinely uncertain herself to whom Dolon was referring, suggested that the correct house was on the opposite side of the street because she knew the owners of that house had had a boy who had been killed in a motor vehicle accident. Dolon denied this and insisted that the house she had first indicated was the correct one. It had steps leading up to the door just as Dolon had described earlier. She had, however, brought the group to what was at this time a side entrance of the house. The main entrance was a much more elegant place on the larger street around the corner; some boys guided the party to this front door. Upon knocking and making themselves known, the three women were admitted to the house with Dolon. The senior male member of the household, Anath Saran De, was at that time away in Calcutta for medical reasons, and the only adult male of the family who was at home was Anath Saran De's younger son. There were, however, numerous women in the house; one of them, Rita De, a daughter of Anath Saran De, came forward and, understanding what Dolon was saying, offered to take the visitors around the house to see what Dolon could recognize in it. Rita De took Pratima Dawn and Dolon around the house, and Dolon apparently recognized a number of rooms and objects in it. She also recognized several of the women present.

By the end of the tour of the house it had become clear to most of those present that Dolon was talking about the life of Nishith De, a young man of the family who had died some years earlier, in 1964. Nishith's mother, however, did not see the matter so simply. She received Dolon coldly when the child and her mother entered the living room. She pushed Dolon away when she went toward her. To Dolon's mother she said petulantly: "Let your daughter remain yours." Thereupon she left the living room huffily and locked herself in her own room. Later, some of her relatives wanted her to come out and meet the guests more cordially, but she refused to do so and asked them to leave the house, which they did. Dolon's preparation for this repulse had been quite deficient. Pratima Dawn said that, as they first approached the De house, Dolon had told them confidently: "Come along. My parents are good people and will say nothing to you." As her party retreated from the house an hour or so later, Dolon was in tears and was heard to murmur: "Mother scolded me."

During the return journey to Narendrapur, Dolon said she did not care to meet the previous mother again since she had refused to take her on her lap; but she still wished to meet the previous father, who had not been at his house on the day of the Mitras' visit. Dolon's parents invited him to visit them, but he had not done so up to 1974.

After the second visit to Burdwan, Dolon talked less of the previous life but continued nevertheless to refer to it from time to time and also to express the hope of meeting the father of the previous life.

Soon after the second visit of the Mitras to Burdwan, the Calcutta newspaper *Ananda Bazar Patrika* published on May 7, 1972, an article reporting the case. Dolon's father had notified the newspaper about the case on the advice of Swami Lokeswarananda, the secretary of the Ramakrishna Mission Ashrama. In July 1972 Prof. P. Pal began investigation of the case and took extensive testimony from Dolon's parents and a neighbor in Narendrapur, as well as from Pratima Dawn and some relatives of the De family in Burdwan. The reluctance of the parents of Nishith De to cooperate with inquiries left a gap in the testimony. Nevertheless, a sufficient number of close and distant relatives of Nishith's family cooperated with the investigation so that it became possible for Professor Pal to verify nearly all of Dolon's statements in a satisfactory manner.

In October and November 1972, I was in the area of Calcutta and, with Professor Pal's assistance, had two interviews with Dolon's parents at Narendrapur. I also interviewed in Burdwan several persons who had been firsthand witnesses of what Dolon had said and recognized in Burdwan. Some of them could verify from personal knowledge many of Dolon's statements made before her visits to Burdwan.

In March 1973 I returned to the area for further interviews. I then met Dolon and her parents again and talked also with some of their friends in Narendrapur who had connections in Burdwan. On a second trip to Burdwan I was able to meet Anath Saran De, Nishith De's father, and some other members of his family. I had another long talk with Pratima Dawn and also met (for the first time) her older sister, Swapna Dawn Samanta, who had been instrumental in arrangements for the Mitras' second visit to Burdwan, when Dolon had succeeded in finding the De house.

Persons Interviewed during the Investigation

In Narendrapur I interviewed:

Dolon Champa Mitra

Audaryamoy Mitra, Dolon's father

Kanika Mitra, Dolon's mother

T. P. Mukherjee, friend, colleague, and neighbor of A. Mitra at the Ramakrishna Mission Ashrama

K. L. Banerjee, secretary of the Ramakrishna Mission Ashrama

Nilachal Samanta, friend of A. Mitra and his colleague at the Ramakrishna Mission Ashrama

Sasanka Ghosh, friend of A. Mitra and a teacher at the Ramakrishna Ashrama Mission

In Burdwan I interviewed:

Anath Saran De, Nishith De's father

Rita De, Nishith De's younger sister

Sisil De, Nishith De's younger brother

Samir De, Nishith De's cousin

Swapan Kumar De, Nishith De's cousin

Swapna Dawn Samanta, Nilachal Samanta's wife

Pratima Dawn, Swapna Dawn Samanta's younger sister

Prithwis Chandra De, distant relative of Anath Saran De

Mira De, Prithwis Chandra De's wife

Prasanna Kumar De, Anath Saran De's cousin

Pranab Kumar De, Anath Saran De's cousin

Laxmi De, Pranab Kumar De's wife

Prasantha Anand Kundu, distant relative of Anath Saran De

Professor Pal had previously interviewed many of the informants at both Narendrapur and at Burdwan. He furnished me with a long report based on the notes of his interviews with the informants he saw during his earlier investigation in July 1972, and in compiling this report I have drawn on these notes as well as on those of the interviews we conducted together.

Dolon's father, Audaryamoy Mitra, spoke excellent English, but his wife spoke only Bengali. Of the other informants, T. P. Mukherjee and a few others spoke English, but most only Bengali.

The rejection of Dolon by Nishith De's mother led to difficulties in obtaining and evaluating the testimony from members of the family of Anath Saran De. I shall defer a discussion of these until later in the report.

Relevant Facts of Geography and Possibilities for Normal Means of Communication between the Two Families

I have already mentioned that Narendrapur lies about 10 kilometers south of Calcutta and may be regarded as just beyond the suburbs in the district known as 24 Purganas. Burdwan is a large town or small city located about 90 kilometers north and somewhat west of Calcutta, thus nearly 100 kilometers (approximately) from Dolon's home.

The De family members are wealthy proprietors of businesses in Burdwan, and their family must certainly be counted among the richest and best-known ones of that town.

According to Audaryamoy Mitra, the Mitras had never been to Burdwan before they took Dolon there, in October 1971, and had neither known nor heard about the Des before their second visit there, in March 1972. Since, however, they had friends who came from Burdwan, the important question is whether Dolon could possibly have learned enough about the family of Anath Saran De to account for her accurate statements about the life of Nishith De.

Nilachal Samanta, a colleague of Audaryamoy Mitra at the Ramakrishna Mission Ashrama, and his wife, Swapna, both came from Burdwan. Swapna Samanta, a member of the Dawn family of Burdwan, was acquainted there with Prithwis De and his family. When Dolon's statements were told to Prithwis De, he conjectured that perhaps she was referring to a relative of his, Anath Saran De. But Swapna Samanta (and her husband) had themselves insufficient knowledge about Anath Saran De's family to identify it with Dolon's statements by themselves. And indeed the correct identification of the family Dolon was talking about remained uncertain until she led the adults with her into the house of Anath Saran De in March 1972. It then transpired that Nilachal Samanta had known Charu De, Anath Saran De's father and Nishith De's grandfather. But Audaryamoy Mitra said that Nilachal Samanta had never talked about them with the Mitras prior to the development of the case. Nilachal Samanta confirmed this. He said that he had thought Dolon was talking about the De family because they are the only rich family living near the Maharajah's palace. His conclusion must have been tentative, however, in view of the persisting uncertainty as to the family to which Dolon was referring right up to the moment when the two families met.

Another person from Burdwan in the acquaintance of the Mitras at Narendrapur was K. L. Banerjee, whom I interviewed in November 1972.

He knew of the Des in Burdwan as a prominent family and seems to have known some of the family members, but he had no personal acquaintance with Nishith De or any member of his immediate family. He was unable to tell from what Dolon was saying which family in Burdwan she was talking about.

I also interviewed Sasanka Ghosh, another friend of Audaryamoy Mitra and a teacher at the school of the Ramakrishna Mission Ashrama in Narendrapur. He was from Burdwan and had some acquaintance with the De family, but he had never actually met Anath Saran De or Nishith De; nor had he ever been in their house. And he denied ever having spoken about the Des to the Mitras before the development of the case. He was by no means as close a friend of Audaryamoy Mitra as were K. L. Banerjee and Nilachal Samanta.

I learned of two other persons from Burdwan known to the Mitras. The first, Prof. Rajendra Chakravarty, was a professor at Burdwan University who occasionally visited the Mitras in Narendrapur. The other, Dr. Hemanga Chakravarty, was a homeopathic physician from Burdwan who lived in Narendrapur. His son had known Nishith De and he himself had known Anath Saran De. I did not meet either of these persons. Dr. Hemanga Chakravarty was away from Narendrapur on the last day I was there, when I first learned about his double friendship with the two families. Audaryamoy Mitra told me that neither Professor Chakravarty nor Dr. Chakravarty had talked about the Des to his family (the Mitras) prior to the development of the case.

The ignorance of the Mitras and their friends in Narendrapur about the person to whom Dolon was referring was shared even by the persons in Burdwan whose help they sought when they made their second visit there in April 1972. At that time Pratima Dawn and Prithwis De supposed that she might have been talking about a member of the De family but were not certain on this point until Dolon actually led the way to the De house and there made several convincing recognitions.

The Life and Death of Nishith De

Nishith De was born in 1940,[3] the son of Anath Saran De of Burdwan. He was the oldest son and much beloved by his parents. A brother, Sisil, and three sisters were born after him. Nishith attended local schools and colleges in Burdwan. He had been a student of Raj School in Burdwan and

[3] Different sources indicated variously that Nishith De was twenty-three, twenty-four, and twenty-five years old when he died, in the summer of 1964. His father, Anath Saran De, said he was twenty-three years old when he died, but the records of the hospital of the Calcutta School of Tropical Medicine give his age at death as twenty-five.

at the time of his death was a student at Burdwan Raj College working for the B.Comm. degree. He was active in athletics, playing football and cricket and taking part in football matches. He was fond of a girl who lived not far from his house and who could be regarded as his "girl friend," although they were not officially engaged. One informant, Mira De, said Nishith had been in love with her.

Nishith's family were, as I have mentioned, extremely wealthy, and they generally adopted an aloofness from less prosperous persons which had the effect of excluding from their society even some of their closest relatives. But Nishith had no trace of this snobbery. On the contrary, he mingled freely with all groups and seemed as content in the company of the proletariat as in that of the aristocratic members of his family, where he was thought by them to belong.

In 1964, at the age of about twenty-four, Nishith developed pain at the back of his head, nausea with occasional vomiting, and periodic attacks of fever. Local physicians proved unable to diagnose or treat his condition effectively; after six or eight months of this illness his condition became worse, and his father had him admitted to the hospital of the Calcutta School of Tropical Medicine. There he developed right-sided hemiplegia with aphasia. His condition continued to deteriorate, and he became comatose. He was suspected of having a brain abscess or brain tumor, but these putative diagnoses were not confirmed by opening the skull or otherwise. He died after fifteen days of coma, on July 25, 1964. As no autopsy was performed, the provisional diagnosis of some space-occupying lesion of the brain remained unconfirmed but highly probable. Nishith's body was cremated at Nimtola, Calcutta.

Statements and Recognitions Made by Dolon

I have listed in Table 14 the statements and recognitions attributed to Dolon by the informants. So far as I know, Dolon made all except a few of the statements about the previous life before the second visit to Burdwan, in March 1972. Two statements, items 22 and 34, were made to Professor Pal in July 1972 and should be evaluated accordingly. Dolon also made a few statements (for which Pratima Dawn was the informant) when she was at the Dawn house, but before going to find the De house. And I have included one statement Dolon's mother said she made as they were taken around the De house.

Apart from the name of the city, Burdwan, where she said she had lived in the previous life, Dolon gave out only one proper name, that of the person "Ranjit," who was not clearly identified; Nishith had both a cousin and a close friend called Ranjit. Notwithstanding this deficiency

I think readers will generally agree that the ensemble of statements and recognitions Dolon made apply correctly to Nishith De and could not refer to anyone else. The case is above the average in the number of correct details given by the subject.

Item 44 occurred during the Mitras' first visit to Burdwan, in October 1971. Items 45 to 57 occurred during their second visit, in March 1972.

Dolon's most impressive recognitions in Burdwan seem to have occurred when she led the way to the house of Anath Saran De. Although the informants differed as to the point along the road at which Dolon was allowed to "run free" and find her way, they agreed that she had in fact led the way unaided to the De house and across several crossroads. (I went over part of this area myself in 1972 and 1973, and, although I did not retrace the exact route taken by Dolon and those accompanying her, I could see easily enough that finding the house would require some knowledge of the streets.) During this walk Dolon was accompanied by her mother and also by Pratima Dawn and Mira De. Her parents had not been to the house before because, as already mentioned, on their first visit to Burdwan the preceding October, they had failed to find it. Pratima Dawn, who was with Dolon and a little ahead of the others, did not know that part of Burdwan well. Although she and Rita De, Nishith's sister, had attended the same college at the same time, she said she had never been to Anath Saran De's house and did not know its exact location or the way to it. Mira De, who did know the way, remained behind Dolon and was sure that she did not aid her. And when the party got into the lane where Dolon first went up and then turned around and came back, she pointed, according to her mother, to Anath Saran De's house and said: "This is the house and these are the steps." At this point Mira De was still uncertain to which house Dolon's statements might refer, and she tried to suggest to Dolon a neighboring house, whose family had lost a boy in an accident. Dolon stood and reflected for a moment and then gave a firm "No." The house of Anath Saran De, which she had indicated, had steps leading up to the entrance on that side as she had previously described.

Along the way to the De house from the place where she was "set free," Dolon led the party in a direction away from the most direct route to the De house and past the house of one Himansu Hazra, with whose daughter Nishith was said to have been in love before he died. Dolon stopped at this house and looked at it for two or three minutes without saying anything. Then she moved on and regained the correct route to the De house.

I found most unsatisfactory the testimony concerning the recognitions some informants said Dolon had made inside the house. Rita De, who had acted as hostess and had shown the visitors around the house, later denied to me that Dolon had recognized anything in the house. Mira De, who entered the house with Dolon and the other adult women, seems to

TABLE 14. *Summary of Statement and Recognitions Made by Dolon*

Item	Informants	Verification	Comments
1. She had a house in Burdwan.	Audaryamoy Mitra, Dolon's father	I visited the house of the identified previous family in Burdwan.	
2. She had a father in Burdwan.	Audaryamoy Mitra Nilachal Samanta, friend of the Mitras	Anath Saran De, Nishith De's father	Anath Saran De was the father of Nishith De, the identified previous personality of the case.
3. Her mother was called Baudi.	Kanika Mitra, Dolon's mother	Anath Saran De Prasanna Kumar De, Anath Saran De's cousin	Nishith De called his mother Ma, which in Bengali corresponds to English "mother." However, in the large joint household of the De family, Nishith's uncles and aunts called his mother Baudi, which means "older brother's wife."
4. She had been a boy.	Audaryamoy Mitra	Anath Saran De Prasanna Kumar De	
5. She had been bigger.	Kanika Mitra	Anath Saran De Prasanna Kumar De	Nishith De was about twenty-four years old when he died and was thus a grown man.
6. She had a younger brother and sister.	Kanika Mitra	In March 1973 I met in Burdwan, Sisil De, Nishith's younger brother, and Rita De, his younger sister.	Nishith De was the oldest child of the family. He had one younger brother and three younger sisters. But two sisters had married in Nishith's lifetime, leaving only one at home.
7. Her father was stout and fair-complexioned.	Kanika Mitra	Verified by me in March 1973.	Anath Saran De was moderately stout. Audaryamoy Mitra, Dolon's father, was quite slim. Anath Saran De was slightly fairer in complexion than Audaryamoy Mitra.
8. Her previous parents were better looking than her present parents.	Kanika Mitra K. L. Banerjee, friend of the Mitras	Partly verified by me in March 1973	K. L. Banerjee heard Dolon refer to the two mothers only in this comparison. Anath Saran De seemed to me a better looking man than Audaryamoy Mitra. I

NOTE: Readers should remember that although the subject was a girl, she was making statements about the life of a young man.

Item	Informants	Verification	Comments
9. Her [present] mother wore plain dresses; her previous mother wore better dresses and put on many ornaments.	Swapna Dawn Samanta, Nilachal Samanta's wife	Verified partly by me in 1972 and 1973	did not meet Nishith's mother but learned from Professor Pal that two informants (Pratima Dawn and Laxmi De) who had seen both the mothers confirmed Dolon's judgment on this point. I never met Nishith's mother, but, judging from the relative economic situations of the two families, I am quite sure that her clothes would be more expensive than the simple saris of Kanika Mitra.
10. Her grandmother [father's mother] was beautiful and had long hair.	Kanika Mitra	Incorrect	Prasanna Kumar De and his brother, Pranab Kumar De, Anath Saran De's cousins, said that Nishith's grandmother was fair and better-looking than average, but not beautiful. Her hair was said to be medium, not long.
11. She had an uncle and an aunt.	Kanika Mitra	Prasanna Kumar De	The Des, like most Indian families, lived in the household of an extended family. There were therefore several aunts and uncles of Nishith living in the house with him and his parents.
12. Her aunt [father's sister] was fat.	Kanika Mitra	Anath Saran De Prasanna Kumar De	Anath Saran De had two sisters described as fat, one markedly so.
13. Her grandfather was living there [at Burdwan] also.	K. L. Banerjee	Anath Saran De	Nishith's grandfather lived in the same house. He predeceased Nishith by four years.
14. Her house was near the Maharajah's palace.	Audaryamoy Mitra Swapna Dawn Samanta Nilachal Samanta	Verified by me during my visit to Burdwan in 1972	The De house was about 300 meters or less from the Maharajah's palace in Burdwan.
15. The house was two-storied.	Kanika Mitra	Verified by me during my visit to Burdwan in 1972 and 1973	Part of the house was two-storied, part three-storied.

TABLE 14 (cont.)

Item	Informants	Verification	Comments
16. The house was red.	Kanika Mitra	Incorrect	In 1973 the house was red in the front part, but its side on the lane or narrow street was white. According to Samir De, the entire house had been creamish colored until about 1967–68, when part of it was painted red. If this is correct, the house was not red in Nishith's lifetime.
17. The floor of the house had designs.	Kanika Mitra	Verified by me in March 1973	Dolon made this remark in comparing the floors of the previous house to those of her house, which, she said, were "common." The floors of the De house in Burdwan were made of either marble or mosaic.
18. The house was like a palace.	Kanika Mitra Swapna Dawn Samanta	Verified by me during my visits to Burdwan in 1972 and 1973	Perhaps "palace" exaggerates somewhat, but the De house was very large and elegant and seemed by far the largest residence in the area apart from the much larger Maharajah's palace, which was then used by a university.
19. The house had a separate thakurbari [shrine room].	Kanika Mitra	Verified by me during my visits to Burdwan in 1972 and 1973	The thakurbari is across the street from the De house in a separate building. Kanika Mitra had told Prof. P. Pal in July 1972 that Dolon had mentioned this item, but when I went over it again with her in November 1972, she could not remember that Dolon had mentioned the thakurbari *before* they went to Burdwan. When I discussed the item with her again, in March 1973, she at that time was again certain that Dolon had mentioned it before going to Burdwan.
20. There were images of gods shining like gold and silver at her house.	Kanika Mitra	Prasanna Kumar De	This remark must have referred to the images of the goddesses Laxmi and Durga that would be placed in the thakurbari during the Durga Festival. They had

ornaments sparkling like gold and silver. The De family's display of images during the Durga Festival was renowned in Burdwan.

Item	Informants	Verification	Comments
21. The door of the house was reached by steps.	Kanika Mitra Swapna Dawn Samanta	Verified by me during my visits to Burdwan in 1972 and 1973	Steps lead up to five doors of the De house on the side street. One of these was a principal entrance to the house during the early life of Nishith. In 1948 the house was remodeled and apparently enlarged. A new main entrance was made on another (broader) street. Thereafter Nishith usually used the new main entrance to enter the house. He continued sometimes, however, to use the side entrance. Since his bedroom was just above the stairs on that side of the house, the old entrance would often have been convenient for him.
22. There were deer and peacocks at the house.	Dolon (1972)	Anath Saran De	Dolon made this statement to Prof. P. Pal in July 1972, after the two families had met. The De family had peacocks in Nishith's lifetime and still had some in 1973. They did not have any deer. They also had hares, but Anath Saran De said they did not have hares during Nishith's lifetime. As the park of the Maharajah's palace in Burdwan (earlier) had both deer and peacocks, Dolon might have confused some memories of Nishith, who would have seen these animals there. Although Dolon might have seen peacocks at the De house before she made this remark, Pratima Dawn thought this quite unlikely since she had noticed none herself during the time they were at the house.
23. She had a blue striped shirt that was her favorite piece of clothing.	Audaryamoy Mitra Pratima Dawn, Swapna Dawn Samanta's younger sister Swapna Dawn Samanta	Pratima Dawn Kanika Mitra	I have given this item as reported by Dolon's father, Audaryamoy Mitra. Pratima Dawn gave a similar statement but said that Dolon had mentioned pants as

TABLE 14 (*cont.*)

Item	Informants	Verification	Comments
23. (cont.)	T. P. Mukherjee, friend of the Mitras Kanika Mitra		well as a shirt. According to her, Dolon had said when inside the De house but *before* they had reached Nishith's room: "There is an almirah in my room, where I used to keep my clothes. There is a blue striped shirt and pants in it. Give these to me!" This remark (and another about the rooms) led to the supposition that Dolon was talking about the life of Nishith. The other three informants did not mention the pants or say that Dolon had said the shirt was striped. They corroborated that she had referred to having a blue shirt. On the question of whether this shirt (and some similarly colored pants) had been Nishith's favorite articles of clothing, Kanika Mitra was a secondhand informant for confirmation given her by Rita De, Nishith's younger sister.
24. It was kept in an almirah.	Audaryamoy Mitra Pratima Dawn T. P. Mukherjee	Pratima Dawn Kanika Mitra	Both Kanika Mitra and Pratima Dawn verified that the blue shirt was in the almirah when it was opened at the time of Dolon's visit to the De house.
25. Books and playthings were also kept in the almirah.	Audaryamoy Mitra	Verified by me in March 1973. The almirah referred to was in the study that Nishith had used.	By "playthings" is meant here equipment for sports and games, such as a cricket bat or a badminton racket. When I examined the almirah in the study used by Nishith, it contained books mainly and also a badminton racket. This was a different almirah from that in Nishith's bedroom.
26. Her room was on the first floor above the stairs on the lane.	Pratima Dawn	Pratima Dawn Swapan Kumar De, Nishith's cousin	Pratima Dawn verified this from the inhabitants of the De house, notably Rita De, Nishith's sister. This item refers to the room where Nishith had slept. The area

of the room was pointed out to me, and although I did not go up to that floor (the second story) of the house, I could tell that the location corresponded to Dolon's description.

Item	Informants	Verification	Comments
27. There were very bright buckets in her house.	Pratima Dawn	Anath Saran De	This remark referred to brass buckets used in washing the shrine rooms of the house.
28. She had played football and cricket.	Kanika Mitra	Prasanna Kumar De; Sisil De, Nishith's younger brother	
29. Her father gave her many clothes.	Kanika Mitra	Laxmi De, Pranab Kumar De's wife	Nishith dressed well and had many clothes.
30. Her father had "heaps of money."	Kanika Mitra; K. L. Banerjee; Nilachal Samanta; T. P. Mukherjee	Pratima Dawn; Prasanna Kumar De	Anath Saran De is one of the wealthiest men in Burdwan. T. P. Mukherjee said Dolon used to gesture with her hands held widely apart in order to communicate better how very rich her previous father was.
31. Her school was some distance from the house.	Kanika Mitra	Prasanna Kumar De	The accuracy of this rather vague statement depends upon whether it referred to the school Nishith went to or the college he later attended. If it referred to the school, which was only 125–75 meters from the house, it was wrong. If it referred to the college where Nishith was a student at the time of his death, the statement should be considered correct, since the college was about 2 kilometers from the house.
32. Her family had a car.	Kanika Mitra; K. L. Banerjee	Anath Saran De	K. L. Banerjee remembered Dolon referring to "cars."
33. She went to school in a car.	Audaryamoy Mitra; Kanika Mitra	Incorrect	According to Prasanna Kumar De, Nishith went to school on foot or on a bicycle and to college on a bicycle. He did not go to

TABLE 14 (cont.)

Item	Informants	Verification	Comments
33. (cont.)			either in a car. Anath Saran De said that his son did not go to college in the car, at least not regularly. He could not say he had never gone in the car, but usually he went on his bicycle. He sometimes went in the car to the market.
34. She used to study at Raj College.	Dolon (1972)	Anath Saran De Prasanna Kumar De	Dolon mentioned this item to Professor Pal in July 1972, after she had been to Burdwan.
35. Her grandmother used to worship in the shrine room.	Kanika Mitra	Anath Saran De Prasanna Kumar De Pranab Kumar De, Anath Saran De's cousin	This remark referred to a smaller shrine room in the house itself, not the large thakurbari across the street from the house. The former would be used every day for worship, the latter only or mainly on special occasions.
36. Once when the car was going to a wedding, it struck another car and broke down.	Kanika Mitra	Anath Saran De Prithwis Chandra De, distant relative of Anath Saran De	This accident occurred about 1960, four years before Nishith's death. The car involved was actually that of a friend borrowed by Anath Saran De because his was out of order. The persons using it were going to a wedding reception. It smashed against a tree, not another car. Five persons died in the accident. Nishith, who was not himself in the car that crashed, went to the scene of the accident and also visited the survivors in the hospital. The killed persons included Dilip Kumar De, Nishith's paternal uncle. He was about the same age as Nishith, who wept much at his death.
37. "Ranjit" mentioned	Kanika Mitra	Prasanna Kumar De Anath Saran De	Dolon mentioned a person "Ranjit," but she did not specify, or her parents did not remember, how this Ranjit figured in her memories. The name could be correct for

the son of an older brother of Prasanna Kumar De, who would therefore have been a cousin of Nishith De. Nishith was friendly with this cousin. However, he had a friend also called Ranjit, with whom he was very close.

Item	Informants	Verification	Informants
38. She had a pain in the leg.	Kanika Mitra	This remark seems not to have had any connection with Nishith's terminal illness. He injured his knee when playing football. Thereafter he complained intermittently, and chronically, of pain in the knee.	Anath Saran De
39. She had a pain at the back of the head.	Audaryamoy Mitra Kanika Mitra	Nishith had complained of pain at the back of the head. He was admitted to the hospital suspected of having either a brain abscess or a brain tumor. Anath Saran De said Nishith had chiefly complained of pain at the top of his head.	Anath Saran De Prasanna Kumar De
40. She had been in a hospital a long time.	Audaryamoy Mitra Kanika Mitra	The hospital records showed that Nishith was admitted on July 4, 1964, and died on July 25, so he was there for three weeks.	Records of the hospital of the Calcutta School of Tropical Medicine
41. She had fallen from the bed at the hospital.	Kanika Mitra	Prasanna Kumar De heard about this episode from an attendant at the Hospital of the Calcutta School of Tropical Medicine in Calcutta, where Nishith had been a patient and had died. The attendant found Nishith lying on the floor one day, clutching his bed with one hand but unable to get up. The attendant helped him back into bed. Thereafter Nishith became unconscious and remained in a coma for fifteen days before he died. Thus the episode of falling from the bed in the hospital could have been one of the last events of which Nishith was conscious before he died.	Anath Saran De Prasanna Kumar De

TABLE 14 (*cont.*)

Item	Informants	Verification	Comments
42. She had died in the hospital.	Audaryamoy Mitra	Records of the hospital of the Calcutta School of Tropical Medicine	Nishith De's body was cremated. Prasanna Kumar De and other cousins carried Nishith's body out of the hospital to a truck which then transported it to the cremation grounds. Friends of Nishith joined the party at the cremation site but seem not to have participated in carrying the body from the hospital.
43. She had been carried from the hospital by friends and relatives for cremation.	Audaryamoy Mitra	Prasanna Kumar De	In July 1972 Dolon herself, in talking with Professor Pal, said that she "had died when being taken from the hospital by friends." This statement differed from what her father said she had said earlier and seems to have derived from a fusion of the images of this and the preceding item.
44. Recognition of the Annapurna Temple	Audaryamoy Mitra		During her first visit to Burdwan, in October 1971, Dolon and her parents, in their then unsuccessful effort to find the De house, had come to and entered the Annapurna Temple, which is about 250 meters from the De house. Nishith had gone to this temple, although also to others.
45. Recognition of the De house in Burdwan	Pratima Dawn Mira De, Prithwis Chandra De's wife Kanika Mitra		The informants disagreed about the place in Burdwan where Dolon was "released" to find her own way. However, assuming the place mentioned was nearest the De house to be the correct one, Dolon found her way through at least four turns in the road. She eventually reached the side road or lane on which one entrance of the De house opened. Here she went too

		far and, going up to the end of this lane, reached the thakurbari, which she looked at without saying anything. Then she turned back and identified the house of Anath Saran De as the one she was looking for. Up to this point the persons with her were not sure which was the correct house. Mira De suggested it was another house on the same street owned by a family whose boy had died in a car accident, but Dolon rejected this suggestion.
46. Recognition of a room where Nishith had studied	Pratima Dawn	On the supposition that Dolon was talking about the life of a deceased uncle in the De family, she was taken first to the room this person had occupied. But Dolon denied this was the room she (Nishith) had occupied. She was then taken to another room and there said: "I used to sit and study here sometimes." Rita De, Nishith's younger sister, who was showing the visitors through the house, then realized that Dolon was perhaps talking about her older brother, who had sometimes sat in the room they were then in. Rita De, in her testimony on this recognition and that of the next item, said that she had pointed out the two rooms *in advance* of Dolon's comments about them. She therefore did not think Dolon had recognized them independently. But her testimony disagreed with that of Pratima Dawn. (For evidence of her unreliability as a witness, see the discussion of my interview with her in the text, p. 309.)
47. Recognition of Nishith's bedroom	Pratima Dawn	After the incident described in the preceding item, the group went to a third room, which was vacant, and then to a fourth room, where Dolon said: "This is my

TABLE 14 (cont.)

Item	Informants	Verification	Comments
47. (cont.)			room." This was the room Nishith had occupied. (See comment for preceding item.)
48. Recognition of a photograph of Nishith	Kanika Mitra Pratima Dawn		In the room occupied by Nishith mentioned in the preceding item, Dolon pointed to a photograph of Nishith on the wall and said: "Here am I." This recognition was spontaneous.
49. Recognition of the almirah that contained Nishith's clothes	Kanika Mitra		According to Kanika Mitra there were two almirahs (one wooden and one steel) in the room, and she asked Dolon to show which she thought had been hers. This may have guided Dolon somewhat. She correctly indicated the wooden one. Although Pratima Dawn was present when Dolon was first taken around the De house, she said that Dolon had not recognized the almirah in Nishith's bedroom.
50. Her clothes were on the upper shelf of the almirah.	Kanika Mitra	Kanika Mitra	After pointing out the wooden almirah mentioned in the preceding item, Dolon said that her (Nishith's) clothes were on an upper shelf. She asked Rita De to open the almirah, and the blue striped shirt and pants (of items 23 and 24) were found on an upper shelf. Pratima Dawn said that she (not Dolon) had asked Rita De to open the almirah. She confirmed that the blue striped shirt was in a bundle of clothes in the almirah.
51. Recognition of keys to the drawers in another room used by Nishith	Pratima Dawn Kanika Mitra		There was a bunch of keys in the almirah mentioned in the preceding item. When Dolon saw them, she said: "These are the keys of the drawers of my reading room."

Item	Informant	Comment
		The keys were those of drawers in a room used by Nishith as a study. (See item 53.)
52. Recognition of Anath Saran De in a photograph	Pratima Dawn	There was a group photograph in the almirah mentioned in the three preceding items. It showed several stout and middle-aged men enjoying a meal. Rita De asked Dolon to point out "the father." Dolon correctly indicated Anath Saran De. The manner of phrasing the question reduced the value of Dolon's response.
53. Recognition of Nishith's study	Mira De	Mira De said that Dolon recognized Nishith's study by pointing to a room and saying: "That is my study. Who reads here [now]?" Mira De later learned from Rita De that the room Dolon had indicated had been Nishith's study. Rita De earlier had asked Dolon if "she" had had a study, and such a question may have been accompanied by signs that reduced the value of Dolon's recognition of the room.
54. Recognition of Nishith's grandmother (father's mother)	Pratima Dawn Kanika Mitra	At one period during Dolon's visit to the De house a swarm of its inhabitants surrounded her, each one asking her all at the same time: "Who am I?" Dolon became understandably flustered at this assault. But later, under quieter conditions, she made two distinct recognitions. Nishith's grandmother spoke to Dolon peacefully and asked her: "Who am I?" Dolon replied: "My grandmother." Pratima Dawn said that Dolon used the word that specifically distinguishes the father's mother from the mother's mother.

TABLE 14 (cont.)

Item	Informants	Verification	Comments
55. Recognition of Nishith's "aunt," Laxmi De	Laxmi De Pratima Dawn		This recognition occurred after Dolon's first tour of the house, during which the preceding items occurred. Laxmi De was able to get Dolon off to one side and made friends with her by giving her some sweets. Then she asked Dolon to say who she was, and Dolon replied: "Auntie of the other house." Laxmi De was the wife of Pranab Kumar De, a cousin of Anath Saran De, and lived across the street from the larger De house where Nishith lived. Since she was much older than Nishith, he would have regarded her as an "aunt" or a "cousin aunt." The word Dolon used, *kakima*, may be applied to the wives of the father's brothers or cousins.
56. Recognition of Nishith's mother	Pratima Dawn Mira De Kanika Mitra		Nishith's mother was sitting in the living room of the house with about a dozen women of similar age. Dolon's mother asked Dolon to point out her mother of the previous life. Dolon gazed at Nishith's mother for some time and then said, pointing at her: "This is my mother." The manner of posing the question reduced the value of Dolon's reply. This incident occurred toward the end of Dolon's visit to the De house, after Rita De and Pratima Dawn had been around the house with her.
57. Recognition of Sisil De, Nishith's younger brother	Swapna Dawn Samanta Kanika Mitra Laxmi De		Sisil De said that Dolon had not recognized him at the time of her visit to the De house. No one else claimed that she had. But Swapna Dawn Samanta said that afterward Dolon had said she had seen her brother. Kanika Mitra said that Dolon had remarked after leaving the De house: "My younger brother has grown big." Laxmi De said she had heard that Dolon remarked afterward that Sisil had been presented to her as an *older* brother, when in fact he was Nishith's *younger* brother.

have stayed most of the time in the main living room and therefore witnessed little of what Dolon did and said in the house. Pratima Dawn, however, was rather certain that Dolon had made some recognitions that she
(Pratima Dawn) had witnessed. Kanika Mitra also reported recognitions
made by Dolon inside the house which she had observed. However, Pratima Dawn said that Dolon's mother did not go around the house when
Rita De first took Dolon and Pratima Dawn around. Kanika Mitra, on the
other hand, insisted that she had gone around the house with the others,
and Rita De agreed that she had. After going around the house and visiting or seeing the various rooms related to the life of Nishith De, Dolon
was taken through the house again by Laxmi De, Nishith's "aunt," who apparently wanted to see just what Dolon had recognized. Possibly Pratima
Dawn confused the two tours of the house in saying that Kanika Mitra
did not accompany Dolon on the first one. I did not, however, find her
testimony deficient in other respects, and Kanika Mitra could have been
wrong. The discrepancy weakens the value of the recognitions but may
otherwise add some strength to the case by showing that Dolon's mother
and Pratima Dawn did not conspire to agree on all points. Be that as it
may, the recognitions of rooms and objects in the De house attributed to
Dolon certainly constitute the weakest aspects of the case.

I have long believed that the subjects of these cases would make more
recognitions of people if they could be left in peace and quietly questioned about particular persons one by one. But the habit—I might almost
say the invariable custom—is for all who have had the remotest connection
with the previous personality to push themselves forward and, in a crowd
and all at once, demand of the bewildered subject: "Who am I?" This
happened when Dolon first entered the De house. The inhabitants constituted a large joint family; when they learned the purpose of Dolon's
visit, a throng of them surrounded her and demanded that she recognize
them. Dolon became confused and silent. But later, under more tranquil
conditions, she seems to have made two definite recognitions of persons
in the house—Nishith's paternal grandmother and his "cousin aunt," Laxmi
De, from across the street.

Dolon was said to have recognized two other aunts of Nishith, but I
did not learn enough details about how she accomplished this to feel justified in including them as items in Table 14. She was also confronted with
Nishith's younger brother, Sisil De. He came and stood before her without
saying anything. Dolon gazed at him for a long time. Others present then
asked: "Do you know your older brother?" Dolon said: "No." Laxmi De,
who was one of my informants for this scene, said that she heard later that
Dolon had said afterward: "He was my *younger,* not my older, brother."
This would be correct for Nishith, since he was the older son (and oldest
child) of the family.

Because of the suggestive question put to Dolon, we cannot consider that she recognized Nishith's mother in a satisfactory way, and the rebuff Dolon received from her deprived us of knowing whether Dolon would have behaved affectionately toward her if given the chance. Dolon's later tears seemed to indicate she felt her love unrequited.

According to Laxmi De, Dolon behaved familiarly in the house and was comfortable when anyone took her on a lap. I find it difficult to evaluate such reports of familiarity, but informants for these cases frequently report that the subject behaves with surprising ease in the presence of the members of the previous family, who would normally be total strangers to the child and with whom he would be expected to show considerable shyness if not actual withdrawal.

Dolon's Behavior Related to the Previous Life

Circumstances and Manner of Dolon's Speaking about the Previous Life. I have already mentioned that Dolon's first remarks, at any rate the first of any length, occurred when her mother rebuked her for wearing her older brother's shirt and pants. There seemed to be no regular stimuli for her later references to the previous life. She would talk about it, her mother said, "when in that mood, in the course of play or at meals." Once she spoke with her mother when lying by her side on a bed. On another occasion she talked to her father about the previous life when returning with him from an evening walk. She spoke freely to two neighbors and fellow employees of Audaryamoy Mitra, T. P. Mukherjee and K. L. Banerjee.

As have other subjects of these cases, Dolon sometimes supplemented inadequate verbal means with gestures in order to communicate better what she wanted to say about the previous life. On at least one occasion she spread her hands widely to give a better indication of the enormous wealth of the previous father.

T. P. Mukherjee heard from his wife about an episode he had not himself observed. Dolon was playing cards one day with Mrs. Mukherjee when, for no apparent reason, she bent her head back to look at the ceiling and held her head in that position. Mrs. Mukherjee asked Dolon why she was doing that. Dolon replied that when "she" had been in the hospital she had had pain in the back of her head and had held her head back in the same position. This was an apparently completely spontaneous remark. (I did not determine whether Nishith De had held his head in this position during his terminal illness, but the position is one often assumed by persons suffering from brain diseases.)

Dolon's father remarked that sometimes she seemed to be thinking to herself, detached from current surroundings, for as long as forty-five minutes. Then she would start to speak about the previous father. Her mother noted a definite moodiness in Dolon and expressed concern about it. By "moodiness" she seems to have meant some withdrawal from ordinary activities as if thinking sadly to herself. This tendency and anxiety about it were continuing in March 1973, when I last met Dolon and her parents. Observations about it were not confined to them. Dolon's mother said her teacher had remarked that Dolon seemed moody and sometimes inattentive and idle. Otherwise the teacher thought her a child of good intelligence. Dolon's mother thought her moodiness related to the memories of the previous life because she sometimes talked about it after being moody. If so, she would not be the first subject of these cases to have been abstracted from the current world by obtrusive memories of a previous life.[4]

Dolon's parents had not heard her complain of being in a small body or in that of a girl, although she had said that she had been a larger person and a boy. She did, however, grumble at times about the comparative poverty of her family. Audaryamoy Mitra was an educated man who spoke English well; but he had a modest position and income if one may judge by the size of his dwelling, which was tiny compared with the mansion of Anath Saran De. It cannot have been soothing to him for Dolon to reminisce about the marble patterns in the floors of the house at Burdwan and compare them with the commonplace floors at the Mitra home in Narendrapur.

Dolon asked, insisted, almost clamored, to be taken to Burdwan. After the failure of her family's first expedition to find the house, she cried and did not eat well. Her chagrin turned illogically against the previous family, and she would say: "They have deserted me," as if it was up to them to trace her.[5] She urged her family to take her back to Burdwan. After returning from Burdwan the second time, she seemed somewhat satisfied or at any rate talked less about the previous life.

The informants for the case mentioned only one other occasion when Dolon wept in talking about the previous life. This occurred after Nishith De's mother pushed her away at Burdwan. Laxmi De said that when the group was leaving the house, Dolon had tears in her eyes and was murmuring: "Mother scolded me." After she and her parents returned to Narendrapur, Dolon said she did not want to go to the (previous) mother again since she had not taken her on her lap. But she said she still wanted to meet her (previous) father, who used to love her (Nishith) and would be good to her. The hope of meeting Anath Saran De persisted at least to the time of March 1973, the date of my last visit to the family, when she was still asking for the (previous) father to visit. She wanted to know if I (on

---

[4] For another example, see the case of Parmod Sharma (I. Stevenson. 1974. *Twenty cases*).

[5] For an equally irrational remark on the topic of who had deserted whom, see the comment made by Nishith's mother reported below (p. 307).

my visit to Burdwan) had asked him to visit her. Anath Saran De told me that he would somehow arrange to meet Dolon, but to the best of my knowledge he has not done so.

After the second visit to Burdwan, Dolon became much more accepting of her own mother. Prior to that occasion Swapna Dawn Samanta had heard Dolon say that her (real) mother was not her mother. Dolon showed a more flexible attitude by remarking sometimes: "I have two fathers and two mothers." The coldness toward her shown by Nishith's mother caused Dolon to reconsider the whole question of who her parents were, and she abandoned the idea of the illegitimacy, so to speak, of Kanika Mitra in her claim to be her mother. Dolon was now heard to remark: "The other mother is a rotten one!"

Dolon's Masculine Traits. As already mentioned, Dolon liked to dress herself in her older brother's shirt and pants which were much too large for her. I observed this myself. At the time of my first visit, in October 1972, she was dressed in a shirt and short pants. When I returned for a second visit about a month later, Dolon was again dressed in boys' shorts but changed into a frock while I was still at the house. I do not know if she did this spontaneously or under instruction from her parents. When I next visited the family, in March 1973, Dolon was once more wearing a shirt and shorts.[6] T. P. Mukherjee, a friend of the Mitras but more detached than they from the perplexity that such conduct can arouse in parents, told me that Dolon always preferred to wear boys' clothes such as a shirt and shorts, but that she wore dresses at school.

Dolon also showed an interest in boys' games; but there was nothing unusual about this because, where she lived, she had little choice of games if she wanted to play with other children. It happened that in the Ramakrishna Mission Ashrama, where her family lived, the close neighbors had mostly boys. The boys and girls played together, and boys' games dominated the group play. Some similar influence may have contributed to Dolon's wearing boys' clothes, but I think this unlikely.

In connection with Dolon's masculine tendencies, it is worth noting that informants about Nishith agreed that he had shown no trace of effeminacy.[7]

---

[6] The mother of another girl who claimed to remember a previous life as a man (an American case in this instance) asked my advice about the pressure that should be applied to influence or force her child to wear clothes appropriate for her anatomical sex. I recommend that such children not be encouraged to wear clothes of the sex of the previous life they seem to be remembering, but also that they not be forced to wear those of the anatomical sex. Most such children, some sooner, some later, and no doubt from a variety of social influences, eventually adopt the clothes of the anatomical sex. For examples of subjects who wore clothes of the opposite sex, see the cases of Paulo Lorenz (I. Stevenson. 1974. *Twenty cases*) and Ampan Petcherat (in the third volume of this series).

[7] Some subjects of "sex change" cases remember the lives of persons who either showed traits of the opposite sex or expressed a desire to change sex in another life. Gnanatilleka and Paulo

The Attitudes of the Adults in the Families Concerned

Dolon's parents seemed to me to show a mixture of enthusiasm and puzzlement over the utterances and behavior of Dolon. They felt some satisfaction in having a child who remembered a previous life, which is rare enough even in India. On the other hand, they were aware that Dolon had been troubled by the memories she claimed to have, and her mother especially expressed concern over Dolon's "moodiness," which she apparently connected with the child's memories of the previous life.

Sometime after Professor Pal's first visit to the family in July 1972, Dolon's parents declined permission for him to visit again on the grounds that both a local doctor and the Swami in charge of the Ramakrishna Mission Ashrama, where Audaryamoy Mitra worked, had advised them that the sooner Dolon forgot about her memories of the previous life the better. This showed, I think, that the Mitras were not seeking any additional publicity for the case. When I later wrote to ask permission to visit and renew the investigation, they cordially agreed and cooperated fully with my inquiries.

In contrast, the members of Nishith De's family showed varying reactions to Dolon's apparent memories of Nishith's life and her visit to Burdwan. Rita De, Nishith's younger sister, and Laxmi De, his "cousin aunt," received Dolon courteously, and the former helped her and those accompanying her to go around the house to observe what Dolon could recognize in it.

Unfortunately, Nishith's mother showed an attitude that approached the frontier of rudeness. As I have already mentioned, she rejected Dolon when Dolon tried to approach her, and would not take her on her lap. She got up from the living room, shut herself up in her own room, and would not come out. Later, when asked to say goodbye to the visitors, she opened her door just enough to emit an angry request for them to leave.

Mira De said that Nishith's mother remarked before she left the drawing room: "If she be my son Bulti [a nickname for Nishith], why has he not taken rebirth in our family and why has he changed sex?" [8]

Lorenz are examples of that group (I. Stevenson. 1974. *Twenty cases*). In other instances of presumed "sex change" the previous personality showed no obvious traits of the opposite sex or inclination to become a member of the opposite sex in the next life. The present case belongs to this second group, as does the case of Ruby Kusuma Silva (in the next volume of this series).

[8] This statement betrayed both a degree of intolerance and an ignorance of cases of the reincarnation type in India. Cases in which both subject and previous personality belong to the same family occur rarely in India, although they certainly do occur there sometimes and possibly more often than we realize from our present methods of learning about cases. Indians rarely claim they can voluntarily control the selection of their next parents or the sex of their next bodies. They believe that such matters are left to the processes subsumed under the heading of

When, on the day following the visit to the De house in Burdwan, Audaryamoy Mitra went with his wife to the house to make further inquiries, he was met at the door by an uncle of Nishith who had not been there the day before. He said that other residents of the house had told him about the recognitions Dolon had made. But he reported that Nishith's mother was still much upset by Dolon's visit and was weeping and refusing to eat. Dolon's parents were not encouraged to remain, but the uncle assured them the De family (or at least he) would cooperate if a "psychologist" wished to study the case further. As already mentioned, Anath Saran De was in Calcutta when the Mitras went to Burdwan, so they had no chance to meet him. They wrote him afterward, inviting him to visit Dolon, but received no reply.

The omission of Nishith's parents from the informants for this case seemed to me a serious one that called for further efforts to meet them. I wrote Anath Saran De twice to request that he allow me to hear what he could say about the case. He did not reply. Eventually, and largely through the intercession of persons known to me in Calcutta, he agreed to an interview. So I went to Burdwan with Professor Pal a second time in March 1973, mainly to meet him. Because he had been absent on the occasion of Dolon's visit to his house, he was not a firsthand witness of anything she had said and done then. He did, however, furnish much useful information verifying details of what Dolon had said about the previous life and giving further information about his deceased son, Nishith. Although he contributed little that we had not earlier heard from other informants, I felt reassured at having that information confirmed by someone as close as he had been to his son.

Sisil De, Nishith's brother, and two of his cousins, Swapan Kumar De and Samir De, also met us at this time. The latter two young men had been in the clubhouse (game room) of the De house when Dolon's party first approached it, and they had guided them to the main entrance. But neither they nor Sisil De had been firsthand witnesses of any recognition made by Dolon.

---

karma, which derives from the balance of one's merits and demerits; and from the case material of India there is almost no evidence to suggest that Indians can in fact influence the choice of parents or sex for the next life.

The usual attitude in India with regard to voluntary control over the next life contrasts with that among the Tlingits of Alaska. The latter believe, or many of them did, that they *could* influence the selection of family for the next incarnation. Furthermore, the case material among the Tlingits gives some support to this claim, and although the evidence for it is still weak and far from compelling as the only interpretation of the facts, it has some value. For examples of Tlingits who have expressed *premortem* a selection for their parents of the next incarnation, see the cases of William George, Jr., and Corliss Chotkin, Jr. (I. Stevenson. 1974. *Twenty cases*). The Igbo also believe that, at least to some extent, a person's wishes expressed before he dies may influence his circumstances in his next incarnation (V. C. Uchendu. 1964. The status implications of Igbo religious beliefs. *The Nigerian Field.* 29:27–37).

Rita De, Anath Saran De's daughter, should have been an important witness. She had been the principal hostess receiving Dolon and the adults with her when they came to the house. At that time she had seemed hospitable enough to the visitors. She must later have fallen under the influence of her mother's rejecting attitude toward the case. Between the time of my two visits to Burdwan (in October 1972 and March 1973) Pratima Dawn tried to obtain from her a written statement concerning what she had observed during Dolon's visit to her home. Not hearing from her, Pratima Dawn eventually succeeded in meeting her at the college where she studied. Rita De then told Pratima Dawn that her parents had forbidden her to discuss the case; she further sent word to me and Professor Pal advising us against trying to visit her family. As I have mentioned above, this decree was later rescinded, and Anath Saran De did receive us in March 1973. At that time, however, I felt that Rita De was much more under the orders of her mother than was her father. In our interview with her she volunteered little and answered questions in the briefest manner compatible with politeness. She denied that she had observed Dolon make any recognitions and said that she herself had "nervously" pointed out the various rooms to the party before Dolon had a chance to do so. The most remarkable of her actual or affected amnesias occurred in connection with her brother Nishith's blue striped shirt (items 23 and 50, Table 14). This shirt had figured prominently in the statements Dolon had made before coming to Burdwan. Two otherwise reliable witnesses, Kanika Mitra and Pratima Dawn, recalled that the blue shirt was found in the almirah where Dolon said it would be. (There is room for doubt as to whether Dolon had recognized the almirah itself.) And Pratima Dawn said that Rita De (at the time of Dolon's visit) had told her that the blue striped shirt had been her brother's favorite piece of clothing. Yet Rita De told us that she could not recall that her brother had a blue striped shirt. It did not seem profitable to detain her for many further questions. If this case depended on the testimony related to Dolon's recognitions in the De house, Rita De's real or pretended ignorance of what happened during Dolon's visit might have damaged it seriously. I have already given my opinion, however, that the testimony related to Dolon's recognitions, at least of rooms and objects in the house, constitutes by far the weakest portion of the case. Its considerable strengths derive from evidence about other details.

The animosity of Nishith's mother toward Dolon and the adults who brought her to the De house showed sufficiently that Dolon's statements deeply troubled her. She must nevertheless have been considerably impressed by what Dolon had recognized in the De house. (For me, as I have explained, Dolon's recognitions seemed the frailest part of the case, but Nishith's mother may have received more consistent and better testimony at the time of Dolon's visit than I could obtain later.) The evidence seemed sufficiently strong so that Nishith's mother (one informant in Burdwan told me) thought it necessary to combat it by distributing allegations that someone had tutored Dolon concerning the De house. I am myself quite sure this is false, and I hope it is also false that Nishith's mother said any such thing. Perhaps her remark, already quoted, that her son ought not to have been reborn elsewhere and as a girl, tells enough about her motives for rejecting the case. But if another factor influenced her, it could have been the great anxiety many wealthy persons have concerning the willingness of other persons to separate them from their money. In cases with wide gaps in the socioeconomic circumstances of the two families such as occurred in this one, the richer family sometimes fears demands for money on the part of the poorer one. The irrationality of such suspicions seems little reduced by the reflection that even if a subject's family were to make some demand for support, they would have no legal grounds whatever. In any case, such claims made by the subject's family occur with exceeding rarity. I have heard of a few secondhand reports of this kind but have never met with any in the hundreds of cases that I have investigated myself.

Comments on the Evidence of Paranormal Processes in the Case

Dolon made forty-four statements about the previous life, nearly all of which proved correct with regard to the life of Nishith De. And even though she never mentioned his name or that of any other member of his family, I think it must be agreed that collectively her statements corresponded closely to the facts in the life of Nishith and would fit no one else. Some of the recognitions informants attributed to Dolon have little value, but a few seem to me to have occurred under conditions where she could not have received helpful clues, and these add something to the strength of the case.

Although Dolon's parents had friends in Narendrapur who came from Burdwan, if these friends had as little knowledge of the De family as the informants said and had not spoken to the Mitras about what they did know, they could not have been the intermediaries for the passage by normal means to Dolon of all the correct information she showed about the life of Nishith. If so, then she obtained her knowledge in some way paranormally. Furthermore, this knowledge that existed in her mind was accompanied by appropriate emotions which seemed to tie her strongly to Nishith De's family and which included the longing to visit them that she so often expressed. Dolon's repeated wearing of boys' clothes also harmonized with her claim to have been a boy in the previous life.

Although some members of the De family may have thought that Audaryamoy Mitra and his wife aspired to put an end to the modesty of their circumstances by demanding money from the Des, I have no hesitation in saying that I consider such suspicions entirely groundless. Audaryamoy Mitra has never shown the slightest interest in exploiting Dolon's case for his (or her) gain. He notified the newspapers of it on the advice of the Swami who was secretary of the Ramakrishna Mission Ashrama where he worked. Later, again on the advice of a Swami at the Ashrama, he temporarily suspended investigation of the case. The fact that the case has been under the surveillance of Ramakrishna Swamis since its inception is itself strong testimony to its authenticity. The record of Dolon's statements, moreover, does not derive only from the memories of her parents; at least four other informants had heard Dolon speaking about the previous life. Although none of them had heard her say as much as her parents, collectively they were able to corroborate her parents' reports of her statements for many items.

Dolon's Later Development

I last saw Dolon in March 1973. She was then approaching six years of age. She was still talking as much as ever about the previous life and gave no evidence as yet of any fading of her memories of it. She had not said anything new about it since my last visit. She frequently asked whether "her father will come." Anath Saran De had not come, but Dolon persisted nevertheless in asserting that she had two fathers and two mothers. Her hopes seemed to triumph over her experience.

9

The Case of Veer Singh

Introduction

THIS case includes several features which give it interest additional to that of the average Indian case of the reincarnation type. First, there was an important difference in caste between the two families concerned, the subject's family being Jats and the previous personality's family Brahmins. (Economic differences between the families were much less.) The behavior reported for the subject accorded with what one would expect of a Brahmin for whom caste distinctions were important.[1]

Second, the subject claimed to remember some events occurring after the death of the previous personality and before his own birth. Some of his statements about events during this "intermission" period were verified.

Third, the relatively long interval (eleven years) between the death of the previous personality (1937) and the birth of the subject (1948) considerably exceeds the average such interval for cases in India.[2]

The case has the important weakness that its investigation did not begin until about twelve years after its main events. I have done my best to reduce the inevitable errors due to lapses in memory during such a long interval by interviewing an ample number of informants and by going over their testimony again with some of them.

Summary of the Case and Its Investigation

Veer Singh was born in the village of Salikheri, near Muzaffarnagar, Uttar Pradesh, in 1948.[3] His parents were Kali Ram Singh and his wife, Parsendi

---

[1] In the case of Jasbir the subject was a Jat who claimed to have been a Brahmin in his previous life, and Jasbir's conduct with regard to Brahmin habits closely resembled that of the subject of the present case, Veer Singh. (For the case of Jasbir, see I. Stevenson. 1974. *Twenty cases.*)

[2] For cases so far analyzed, the mean interval between death and presumed rebirth is forty-five months.

[3] This date and others of births and deaths in this case are only approximate. The families concerned relied on their memories and had no written records to supplement these. In assessing the value of dates and ages mentioned, I have compared the statements of different informants about different (or the same) events to work out the most probable chronology.

Devi. The family were farmers of the Jat caste. Veer Singh was the fourth of four children in the family. He had two older brothers and one older sister.

Veer Singh seemed to be late in learning to talk, but otherwise nothing remarkable was noted about him until he was about three. When he was still less than three years old, his family noticed that at times he refused to take food. At first he did not say why he refused food; but not long after he began to talk (at about the age of three), his mother was cooking bread one day when Veer Singh suddenly said: "I will not eat food prepared by you." When she asked him why not, he said: "I am not your son. I am the son of a Brahmin of Sikarpur." The following day a fair was held in the area, and his parents gave him a small amount of money to spend there. He threw this away contemptuously, saying that "his mother" used to give him more money. These comments aroused curiosity in the family and they asked him to tell some more. He then gave out a considerable number of details about a life he claimed to have lived in a place called Sikarpur in a Brahmin family. He said that his father was called Laxmi Chand. He described, or so his parents understood, how he had died from the effects of falling from a roof when he and his aunt had been up on the roof chasing a monkey away. He asked to go to Sikarpur.

Although Veer Singh communicated enough details for his parents to have attempted a verification of his claims in the village of Sikarpur (8 kilometers from Salikheri), they seem to have done nothing about this at the time, even though, after his first statements about the previous life, Veer Singh had shown a most obstinate refusal to eat the family's food. Other members of the village heard about Veer Singh's statements and behavior. Eventually, when Veer Singh was about four and a half, one of them, Munshi Dutt, himself a Brahmin, met in the nearby town of Shamli a man, Laxmi Chand Sharma, of Sikarpur. He had had a son, Som Dutt, who had died fifteen or more years earlier,[4] and Veer Singh's statements seemed to fit Som Dutt's life. Laxmi Chand was skeptical about the possibility that a Brahmin could be reborn as a Jat. He was also doubtful of the case because of the long interval between Som Dutt's death and Veer Singh's birth. Nevertheless, he agreed to come to Salikheri and meet Veer Singh. So he went unannounced to Salikheri, sat in a shop there, and enquired about the boy who said he was from Sikarpur. A message was sent to Veer Singh's family, and the boy came to the shop. Veer Singh recognized Laxmi Chand and called him Father, although this occurred under conditions that were unsatisfactory with regard to being sure he was in no way guided by surrounding persons. Of more importance was his embracing Laxmi Chand, an older total stranger in terms of normal prior acquaintance. Veer Singh sat contentedly on Laxmi Chand's lap.

[4] July 1937 seems the most probable date for the death of Som Dutt, but he may have died a year or two earlier.

Laxmi Chand persuaded Veer Singh's family to let him take the boy back to Sikarpur, and there (a few days later) Veer Singh made a number of other recognitions under better conditions. Some of these recognitions were spontaneous; in others he gave the names of persons concerned that he seemingly could not have known normally. An extremely strong attachment then developed between Veer Singh and Laxmi Chand's family. He spent only a few days with them on the first occasion but subsequently stayed for much longer periods, once remaining two years and on other occasions staying six months and a year. Veer Singh's family did not object to these prolonged absences, although some difficulties arose that I shall mention later.

I first heard of this case in 1963, at which time a preliminary report was sent to me. In 1964 I spent two days studying it, and I interviewed members of both families concerned in that year. (Francis Story accompanied me during this phase of the investigation.) At that time Veer Singh was about sixteen years old. He said he still preserved some unclear memories of the previous life. He distinguished the original imaged memories of the previous life, which had largely faded, from his better-preserved memories of what he had told others about it.

In 1964 we missed meeting an important informant, Laxmi Chand, Som Dutt's father. He and his family had moved in (about) 1953 to a quite different part of Uttar Pradesh. They were then living in the village of Khatima (District Nainital). When we went to Khatima we could interview several members of Som Dutt's family—his mother and older brother, for example—but Laxmi Chand was away.

In the autumn of 1969 I took up the investigation of the case again and had further interviews with informants of both the families. But I was still unsuccessful in meeting Laxmi Chand, Som Dutt's father, at Khatima. I returned there for a third time in the autumn of 1971 and was finally able to meet him. At the same time I could also talk again with other informants of his family. Subsequently, Laxmi Chand answered some remaining questions in correspondence.

As already mentioned, Veer Singh had recognized Laxmi Chand at a shop in Salikheri. Unfortunately, I could not interview the owner, Man Phool Singh, who had died before 1969. However, I did interview his son, Randhir Singh, who had been a witness of the recognition, and thus I had his account to compare with that of Laxmi Chand himself.

Persons Interviewed during the Investigation

In Salikheri I interviewed:

Veer Singh
Kali Ram Singh, Veer Singh's father

Parsendi Devi, Veer Singh's mother

Jai Singh, Veer Singh's older brother

Prem Singh, Veer Singh's older brother

Shital Prasad Singh, Kali Ram Singh's younger brother and Veer Singh's uncle

Randhir Singh, the son of Man Phool Singh, the village barber at whose shop Veer Singh first met Laxmi Chand Sharma

Munshi Dutt, villager of Salikheri

In Khatima I interviewed:

Laxmi Chand Sharma, Som Dutt's father

Bindra Devi, Som Dutt's mother

Vishnu Dutt, Som Dutt's older brother

Ravi Dutt, Som Dutt's younger brother

Sarla Devi, Som Dutt's younger sister

Relevant Facts of Geography and Possibilities for Normal Means of Communication between the Two Families

Salikheri and Sikarpur are villages 8 kilometers apart in the Muzaffarnagar District of Uttar Pradesh. Despite their closeness there seems to have been little travel or commerce between them. Kali Ram Singh, Veer Singh's father, said that neither he nor any member of his family had ever been to Sikarpur prior to the development of the case. This was confirmed by his wife, and they both said they had never met Laxmi Chand before he came to Salikheri to meet Veer Singh. Vishnu Dutt, Som Dutt's brother, and Bindra Devi, their mother, both said that they had never been to the village of Salikheri. Bindra Devi said that Veer Singh told her he had once seen her along the canal near Salikheri and had called out to her, but she had not responded. She remembered having been near Salikheri at the canal but did not recall being addressed by a strange boy. Laxmi Chand recalled that he and his wife had walked along the canal by Salikheri about a year before his first meeting with Veer Singh. A strange boy had called out to them, but they had taken no notice. Usually when they went into the large town of Muzaffarnagar for marketing they used another route, but on this occasion they were going to Meerut (another large city in the opposite direction) and so passed by Salikheri. Kali Ram Singh remembered that once when Veer Singh was about three he said tearfully that he had met "his father and mother on the road." They had not spoken to him, and that, he had said, was why he was weeping. From these several accounts it appears certain that Veer Singh had recognized one or both of Som Dutt's parents on one or perhaps two occasions without any of the adults concerned realizing that he had done so before they met formally some time later. This does not force us to believe that Laxmi Chand and Bindra Devi were in the village of Salikheri when Veer Singh recognized them. One can walk along the canal without going into the village; to go there, as I saw myself, requires a definite digression. The edge of the village is, however, quite close (about 100 meters) to the irrigation canal.[5]

That there should be so little communication between villages so near to each other is difficult for Western readers to understand until they realize how very poor the rural roads in India are even today (1974); and they were certainly much more inadequate during the years of the main events of this case than they are now. Residents of different villages of the area would go into the district town, Muzaffarnagar (24 kilometers from Salikheri), for their main shopping and business. Residents of one village would have no need or wish to visit another unless they happened to have relatives there.

In the present case, differences of caste between the two families would keep them more isolated from each other than the geographical separation between the villages. Although caste distinctions are now breaking down in India, the process proceeds much more slowly in some districts and in some families than in others. The members of Laxmi Chand's family seem to have been particularly orthodox Brahmins for whom caste distinctions remained important.

I have already mentioned that a villager of Salikheri, Munshi Dutt, made the first inquiries that brought the two families together. He was a Brahmin and had had a slight acquaintance only with Laxmi Chand. He did not even know that Laxmi Chand had lost a son. He happened to ask Laxmi Chand, when he met him in Shamli, about the details stated by Veer Singh

---

[5] A colleague, after reading a draft of this report, raised some questions about this episode which perhaps some further comments may answer. I have often said that small children in Asia are under the surveillance of their mothers and hence normally inaccessible to strangers who might furnish them with information about other people that could become the ingredients for alleged memories of a previous life. However, this exception—of Veer Singh wandering out of his village apparently by himself—proves no rule, because I have never claimed there was one. Instead, I contend that, in general, small children in Asia are watched rather carefully by their mothers and are very unlikely to be out of the control of the mother (or some other responsible relative or servant) for long enough to acquire much information from a stranger about other strangers without this fact being known to the child's parents. In Asia, as elsewhere in the world, mothers vary in their competence and vigilance. And village children have more freedom to move about by themselves than do town or city children.

My colleague also questioned the claimed ability of Kali Ram Singh to remember (about thirteen years later in his interview with me) the episode of Veer Singh coming home and saying that he had met "his father and mother on the road." I do not share any surprise about this. The remark by itself would be an unusual one for any child to make. And when, about a year and a half later, Laxmi Chand and his wife confirmed the episode, and also verified most of Veer Singh's other statements about the previous life, Kali Ram Singh's memories of this and other details would become reinforced. No doubt frequent discussions of the details within the family and with other villagers helped to fix the memories further.

because Laxmi Chand was the first Brahmin person from Sikarpur that he met after hearing about Veer Singh's statements. In short, he had no idea in advance that Laxmi Chand was the man he was looking for. (Although Veer Singh had told his mother the name of the previous father, Laxmi Chand, he had not told this name to Munshi Dutt.) From this evidence it seems extremely unlikely that Munshi Dutt could have been the intermediary for the normal transmission of knowledge about Som Dutt to Veer Singh or his family.

The Life and Death of Som Dutt

According to his father, Laxmi Chand, Som Dutt was born in Sikarpur in 1933. He was the second son and the third child in a family that eventually had seven children, some of whom were born after Som Dutt's death.

Som Dutt was about four years [6] of age when he died in Sikarpur, in July 1937. The only unusual events of his young life occurred a month or so before his terminal illness and death. Some monkeys had come onto the roof of the house, and Som Dutt's aunt had gone up to the roof to chase them away. Som Dutt followed her up to the roof, and she picked him up. She then became frightened by the monkeys and, in trying to avoid them, fell off the roof onto the ground below. The aunt seems to have dropped Som Dutt before she lost her balance and went over the edge of the roof herself. Some details of the account of this episode given me by Bindra Devi in 1964 differed from what she said in 1969 and 1971 and from the account given by her husband. Since she was in the house when it happened and he outside, I have supposed that his account was the more reliable and have based the foregoing version on what Laxmi Chand said. In any case, all accounts agreed on the main points: that the aunt had fallen off the roof while chasing (and being chased by) monkeys, that Som Dutt had been with her, but that he had not been seriously hurt, although she had.

A week or two after the above incident, Som Dutt's uncle (Laxmi Chand's brother-in-law), who was not on good terms with Laxmi Chand and his family, picked up Som Dutt (evidently in a fit of temper) and dashed the boy to the ground. The child suffered injuries from this mistreatment. He was ill for about eighteen or twenty days and then died. Laxmi Chand was away trying to get more medicines for his son when he died. At the moment of Som Dutt's death his mother and maternal uncle were with him. A trusted servant, Saddi, who was known familiarly as

---

[6] This was the age of Som Dutt at the time of his death according to his father. His mother, Bindra Devi, said he was three when he died, and his older brother, Vishnu Dutt, said he was about five at the time.

"Tau" (literally, Uncle) was in the house but, according to Bindra Devi, not present in the room at the moment of Som Dutt's death. He came into it when he heard the sobbing of those who were present.

Because Laxmi Chand was absent, Som Dutt's maternal uncle and "Tau" performed the funeral ceremony on the day of Som Dutt's death.[7]

Laxmi Chand described the injuries sustained by Som Dutt when thrown by his uncle as materially contributing to his death. But his mother (in 1964) remembered a much longer interval between this episode and the boy's later and, in her opinion, unrelated death from dysentery. In fact, Bindra Devi placed the injury of Som Dutt by the uncle *before* the episode when the aunt fell off the roof. She said he had had a fever before he died. Laxmi Chand said he had had no fever; but, as he was away for a day or more before Som Dutt died, perhaps he did not learn about his son's fever then or later. The informants for these various events were recalling in the middle and late 1960s and early 1970s events that had occurred in the middle or late 30s, that is, thirty or more years earlier. It is perhaps more surprising that their accounts in general agreed than that they differed in details, especially of chronological sequence.

Statements and Recognitions Made by Veer Singh

In Table 15 I have listed all the statements and recognitions attributed to Veer Singh by the informants for the case. I have omitted a few recognitions about which I obtained insufficient detail for any useful judgment of how they occurred.

Items 1–24 of Table 15 are statements that Veer Singh made, so far as I have been able to determine, before the two families met. Most were made when he was about three years old. The recognition of Laxmi Chand (item 25) occurred when he came to Salikheri, about a year and a half later. At that time Laxmi Chand interrogated Veer Singh to probe the extent and accuracy of his memories. Items 26–30 also occurred then. A few days later Veer Singh was taken to Sikarpur, and items 31–44 occurred during that visit. Item 45 (recognition of Som Dutt's maternal uncle) occurred on the occasion of a visit Veer Singh made with Som Dutt's older brother, Vishnu Dutt, to the home of Vishnu Dutt's (and Som Dutt's) maternal uncle who lived in Saharanpur, another city of Uttar Pradesh. Laxmi Chand said that Veer Singh recognized two other relatives at Saharanpur; but, as he was a secondhand witness of these recognitions and I did not obtain Vishnu Dutt's account of them, I have omitted them.

---

[7] For a child's funeral a simple ceremony performed by a male member of the family would suffice. In this instance, the members of the family at Salikheri probably did not know how long Laxmi Chand might remain away and so proceeded with the funeral themselves.

Veer Singh's Statements about Som Dutt's Death. In 1964 two of the informants who touched on this topic, Prem Singh (Veer Singh's older brother) and Parsendi Devi (his mother), said that Veer Singh had stated (before the two families had met) that he (in the previous life) had been on the roof of the house (in Sikarpur) and had fallen down. Veer Singh's mother clearly understood him to say that he had died from this fall. His brother mentioned additional details of Veer Singh's account, namely, that Som Dutt had been with his aunt at the time of the fall from the roof, that the aunt had become frightened, and that both had fallen down. But Prem Singh did not draw the conclusion that Som Dutt had died from his fall.

In 1964 Veer Singh's father, Kali Ram Singh, said that Veer Singh had not mentioned to him how he (in the previous life) had died. By 1969, however, he had either remembered or had heard from others that Veer Singh had said (well before the two families had met) that he (in the previous life) had fallen from a roof. In the further details of this version, Som Dutt had been on the roof with his aunt and had become frightened by a monkey; the aunt had then tried to stop him from falling and, in doing so, had fallen off herself. This account seems much closer to the facts of this episode as given by Som Dutt's family, and it may indeed have been influenced by what Kali Ram Singh had later learned from them. It will be noticed that in Kali Ram Singh's account of 1969, Veer Singh was not attributing Som Dutt's death to a fall from a roof.

According to Som Dutt's family, as I explained in an earlier section of this report, he had been involved, but not hurt, when his aunt fell from the roof; and his death had occurred later, from quite unrelated causes. His father connected Som Dutt's last illness with injuries received when his uncle threw him on the ground, as previously mentioned, but his mother thought that even this incident had no connection with Som Dutt's death, which she attributed to dysentery alone.

This discrepancy between the cause of Som Dutt's death as stated by Veer Singh according to his mother, and the facts as reported by Som Dutt's family, might have occurred if his mother had added inferences of her own to the first fragmentary statements Veer Singh made when a small child. Parents and other informants sometimes make their own interpretations of what a child has said about the previous life and later unconsciously pass on these inferences as part of the child's original statements.[8] This does not seem the correct explanation in the present case, however, because in 1964 Veer Singh himself (then aged sixteen) gave exactly the same account of how "he" had died that his family said he had given many years earlier. In the meantime, he had spent a great deal of time with Som Dutt's family, and I was surprised that he did not get the facts straight and tell

[8] The case of Imad Elawar provides several examples of this sort of interpretative addition by parents to what the child said (I. Stevenson. 1974. *Twenty cases*).

TABLE 15. *Summary of Statements and Recognitions Made by Veer Singh*

Item	Informants	Verification	Comments
1. His name was Som Dutt.	Kali Ram Singh, Veer Singh's father Prem Singh, Veer Singh's older brother	Laxmi Chand Sharma, Som Dutt's father	
2. His father was Laxmi Chand.	Parsendi Devi, Veer Singh's mother	Laxmi Chand	
3. He was a Brahmin.	Parsendi Devi Munshi Dutt, villager of Salikheri	Laxmi Chand	Sharma is a caste name of Brahmins.
4. He was from Sikarpur.	Parsendi Devi Munshi Dutt Prem Singh	Laxmi Chand	Laxmi Chand and his family lived in Sikarpur until about 1953, when they moved to Khatima.
5. He had a brother called Mum Chand.	Kali Ram Singh Parsendi Devi	Sarla Devi, Som Dutt's younger sister	Som Dutt's older brother, Vishnu Chand, was nicknamed "Mum Chand." In one place of my notes I have recorded the name as "Mom Chand," and this is almost certainly the correct name rather than "Mum Chand." Prem Singh, Veer Singh's older brother, said Veer Singh did not mention the names of Som Dutt's siblings until the two families had met, but I think he meant (or should have meant) that he himself had not heard Veer Singh mention these names before, because other members of the family said they had.
6. His mother was fair.	Parsendi Devi	I did not consider Bindra Devi unusually fair or unusually dark—compared with other women of northern India.	
7. He had three sisters.	Parsendi Devi Munshi Dutt	Vishnu Dutt, Som Dutt's older brother	Munshi Dutt and Shital Prasad said that Veer Singh said he had *one* sister. There

were actually four sisters in the family, two born during Som Dutt's life and two after his death.	Shital Prasad Singh, Kali Ram Singh's younger brother	Vishnu Dutt, Laxmi Chand	Parsendi Devi said that Veer Singh had named three sisters, but that she had forgotten one of the names. Kali Ram Singh also gave the names of only two sisters and said the second one Veer Singh had named was called Kayalasha. This was actually closer to the correct name, which, according to Dr. L. P. Mehrotra (who worked with me as an interpreter on the case), should be Kailasha. Another, younger sister, born after Som Dutt's death, was called Kaushilya. Veer Singh or his parents may have mixed these names together. And so may the interpreters or I in making notes. The discrepancy may also have arisen from poor enunciation of the name (or names) by Veer Singh when he was young. The spellings of these two names vary in my notes, but not that for Prakashi, which was the correct name of another sister. In 1972 Laxmi Chand said that Veer Singh had given him correctly the names of all six of Som Dutt's siblings on the occasion of their first meeting.
8. Two of the sisters were called Prakashi and Kasalayal.	Parsendi Devi, Kali Ram Singh		
9. They had a house in the fields.	Kali Ram Singh	Vishnu Dutt	The family had a house in the village and another one outside the village in the fields.
10. They had three bullocks.	Kali Ram Singh	Vishnu Dutt, Bindra Devi, Som Dutt's mother	Bindra Devi and Vishnu Dutt said the family had four bullocks.
11. One bullock was white; one was black.	Kali Ram Singh, Munshi Dutt, Shital Prasad Singh, Parsendi Devi, Bindra Devi	Bindra Devi	

TABLE 15 (*cont.*)

Item	Informants	Verification	Comments
12. They had one cow.	Munshi Dutt Shital Prasad Singh Kali Ram Singh	Vishnu Dutt	
13. They had one buffalo.	Munshi Dutt Shital Prasad Singh Parsendi Devi Kali Ram Singh	Vishnu Dutt	Kali Ram Singh said Veer Singh said his family had two buffalo. Vishnu Dutt said the family had four buffalo.
14. They had a servant.	Munshi Dutt Shital Prasad Singh	Vishnu Dutt	
15. They had a female camel.	Parsendi Devi	Vishnu Dutt	The family did not acquire the camel until after Som Dutt died.
16. They had a "pukka" house.	Kali Ram Singh	Sarla Devi	*Pukka* is a Hindi adjective meaning "sub-stantial," "well built," or "superior." As applied to houses it means one built of bricks, as opposed to a "kachcha" house, which is built of mud and clay.
17. The main door of the house faced east.	Shital Prasad Singh	Sarla Devi	
18. There was a peepal tree in front of the house.	Kali Ram Singh Shital Parsad Singh Prem Singh	Vishnu Dutt	Sarla Devi said the peepal tree was at the side of the house, not the front.
19. There was a well in front of the house.	Kali Ram Singh Shital Prasad Singh Prem Singh	Vishnu Dutt	
20. Near the house there is a river wider than the [irrigation] canal at Salikheri.	Kali Ram Singh	Vishnu Dutt	The river Hinden passes by the village of Sikarpur. It is about 40 meters wide; the irrigation canal that passes Salikheri is about 8 meters wide.

Item			Comments
21. There was a statue worshiped in the village [of Sikarpur].	Parsendi Devi	Vishnu Dutt	Veer Singh was evidently referring to the temple in Sikarpur which he later recognized there, saying it was the temple of the "Goddess of Land."
22. The fair was held near his village.	Shital Prasad Singh	Vishnu Dutt	A Ramlila was held about 5 kilometers from Sikarpur. For an account of the Ramlila, see the case report of Sunil Dutt Saxena (p. 128).
23. He fell down from a roof and died.	Prem Singh Parsendi Devi	Incorrect	Bindra Devi said Som Dutt's aunt and Som Dutt were on the roof chasing some monkeys away when the aunt fell off the roof and was injured, but that Som Dutt did not fall. On another occasion, during a family quarrel, one of Som Dutt's uncles picked him up and threw him on a stone. Possibly the memory of this episode became confused in Veer Singh's mind with the occasion when Som Dutt's aunt fell off the roof. Both incidents occurred some weeks or months before Som Dutt's death. (See text for further details.)
24. He had been with his aunt, who became frightened.	Prem Singh	Bindra Devi	
25. Recognition of Laxmi Chand	Munshi Dutt Randhir Singh, son of the owner of the shop where the recognition took place Laxmi Chand Shital Prasad Singh		A poorly planned test of recognition. Veer Singh was taken to a group of men in which only two were strangers in the village, and was asked if he could recognize Som Dutt's father in the group. However, Veer Singh embraced Laxmi Chand and sat contentedly on his lap in a manner that would certainly be unusual for a small child meeting a strange man for the first time. Shital Prasad may have been a secondhand witness for this item.
26. He had a younger brother, Ravi Dutt.	Laxmi Chand	Laxmi Chand	Ravi Dutt was born *after* the death of Som Dutt.

TABLE 15 (*cont.*)

Item	Informants	Verification	Comments
27. He had a younger sister, Sarla Devi.	Laxmi Chand	Laxmi Chand Sarla Devi	Sarla Devi was born about 1938, *after* the death of Som Dutt. She was older than Ravi Dutt.
28. Kaushilya Devi was also his younger sister.	Laxmi Chand	Laxmi Chand	Kaushilya Devi was the youngest child of the family, also born *after* Som Dutt's death. (See also item 8.)
29. He had an older sister, Kalayash Wati.	Laxmi Chand	Laxmi Chand	She is the same as Kailasha, referred to in the comment for item 8. The discrepancy between the name given by Laxmi Chand for this item and that mentioned in the comment for item 8 is almost certainly due to faulty rendition of the name by me. Dr. L. P. Mehrotra has told me that the name is best spelled as "Kailasha."
30. His mother was from the village of Bawli.	Laxmi Chand	Laxmi Chand	
31. Recognition of field that had belonged to Laxmi Chand	Kali Ram Singh Vishnu Dutt		This recognition occurred as Veer Singh and his father approached Sikarpur in a tonga. Veer Singh pointed to a field and said it was his. Kali Ram Singh verified that Veer Singh was correct, but learned that the land no longer belonged to Laxmi Chand. Vishnu Dutt had ridden out of the village to meet the group on his horse and overheard Veer Singh's remark, which he verified.
32. Recognition of the way to the house of Laxmi Chand in Sikarpur	Munshi Dutt Shital Prasad Singh Vishnu Dutt Laxmi Chand		Veer Singh led the way on foot from the bazar, where he was put down from the tonga, to the house of Laxmi Chand. The house was about 50 meters from the ba-zar, and there were several lanes branch-ing off, into which Veer Singh could have

turned. There was, however, a considerable crowd around him, and this naturally included persons who knew the way to Laxmi Chand's house. Someone in the crowd tried to mislead him. Informants agreed Veer Singh had indicated the way to the house but disagreed as to where inside the village he was put down from the cart that brought him and his father from Salikheri.

When Veer Singh reached the house the main door was closed and he went in by another door.

Item	Informants	Comments
	Vishnu Dutt	
33. The terrace of the house had been broken.	Bindra Devi Prem Singh	The terrace of the house had been damaged during rains and had not been repaired. Vishnu Dutt said the terrace had been damaged *during* Som Dutt's lifetime, but only removed afterward. Veer Singh made his comment as he was standing outside the house and before he entered it. Apparently some feature of it that would have been unfamiliar to Som Dutt drew his attention.
34. Recognition of Som Dutt's mother	Vishnu Dutt	Several women were sitting in a room together and Veer Singh was asked if he could recognize his (previous) mother. He went to Som Dutt's mother, Bindra Devi, and called her Mataji, which means "mother."
35. Recognition of Som Dutt's sister Kailasha	Vishnu Dutt Bindra Devi	This occurred just after the preceding recognition and was spontaneous. Veer Singh pointed to Kailasha and said: "She is my sister; call her here." Bindra Devi said Veer Singh also gave the names of Kailasha and Som Dutt's three other sisters, two of whom were born after Som Dutt's death.

TABLE 15 (*cont.*)

Item	Informants	Verification	Comments
36. Recognition of Sarla Devi, Som Dutt's younger sister	Bindra Devi Sarla Devi		Veer Singh gave her name, but I did not learn other details of this recognition. Sarla Devi was born after Som Dutt's death.
37. Recognition of family servant, Saddi ("Tau")	Vishnu Dutt Bindra Devi Laxmi Chand		The servant was called, and Veer Singh was asked to say who he was. Veer Singh said: "He is my 'Tau' who used to play with me." Laxmi Chand remembered Veer Singh using different words in this recognition, namely, "Here is Saddi [pointing him out]; he was . . . a servant." Possibly Veer Singh made both remarks. Saddi was the real name of the servant familiarly called "Tau." This latter word means, literally, "uncle" and is often used affectionately for older men, even if they are not related to the speaker.
38. Recognition that a mill had been changed in position in the house	Bindra Devi		The mill had been moved after Som Dutt's death. I think Bindra Devi was a second-hand informant for this item.
39. His father had gone to Muzaffarnagar for medicine when he died.	Bindra Devi	Bindra Devi Laxmi Chand	
40. The old servant "Tau" was present when he died.	Bindra Devi	Bindra Devi Laxmi Chand	Laxmi Chand was away when Som Dutt died and is therefore a secondhand verifier of this item. His wife said that the servant "Tau" was not actually in the room at the moment Som Dutt died, but that he came into the room as soon as he heard the crying of Bindra Devi and her brother, who were present.

Item	Informants	Verification	Comments
41. The funeral service was performed by his "mama" [maternal uncle].	Bindra Devi	Bindra Devi Laxmi Chand	Laxmi Chand did not return to Sikarpur until after the funeral.
42. A swing on which ladies were swinging had broken.	Laxmi Chand	Laxmi Chand	This incident occurred after the death of Som Dutt and before Veer Singh's birth. (See text for further details.)
43. Mukhtar Singh had moved to another village called Gahri Novabad.	Laxmi Chand	Laxmi Chand	
44. Recognition of Ravi Dutt, Som Dutt's brother	Ravi Dutt, Som Dutt's younger brother Vishnu Dutt		Ravi Dutt was coming from the fields into the village when Veer Singh was going out of the village to the fields, and they met. When Veer Singh saw him he said spontaneously: "He is my brother." He then gave his name as Ravi Dutt. Ravi Dutt was born between four and five years after Som Dutt's death.
45. Recognition of Som Dutt's maternal uncle, Hardwari Lal	Vishnu Dutt		Vishnu Dutt took Veer Singh to Saharanpur, where his and Som Dutt's maternal uncle was living. When they reached the uncle's house he was away. When he returned Veer Singh said: "He is my mamaji" and spoke his name, Hardwari Lal. In this instance Veer Singh must have had strong expectations of meeting Som Dutt's uncle, and the recognition could have been based entirely on inference.

us how Som Dutt had really died. Instead he still described how Som Dutt
had been carried by his aunt on the roof while she chased monkeys and
how they had both fallen down. The fact that in 1964 Veer Singh did not
give a version of Som Dutt's death edited and corrected from his own acquaintance with Som Dutt's family I take to be some evidence of his telling
then his original memories as best he could remember them.[9] I believe that
in Veer Singh's mind the events of Som Dutt's being thrown down by an
uncle, of his aunt's falling off a roof in his presence, and of his own death
became jumbled together. One can imagine how at the time of his death
the various images of recent and current experiences might have become
mixed together in his mind and afterward were never permanently sorted
out. And yet Veer Singh must have had some periods of clarity about how
Som Dutt had died, because Som Dutt's mother told me that Veer Singh
gave her a correct version of the death of Som Dutt, including the details
that his father had gone to Muzaffarnagar to get medicine, that he had
died while his father was away, and that the old servant "Tau" was present.
He also correctly named the man who had conducted the funeral ceremony,
Som Dutt's maternal uncle. Perhaps then, in the presence of Som Dutt's
mother, and maybe with some reminders from the house in which Som
Dutt had died, Veer Singh's memories became clearer, and later, away from
that scene, they became muddled again.

Veer Singh's Memories of Events Occurring after Som Dutt's Death and be-
fore Veer Singh's Birth. Veer Singh said that he (in the previous life) had
stayed around the home of Laxmi Chand after the death of Som Dutt and
before his (Veer Singh's) birth. He said that he had lived on a peepal tree.
There would have been nothing particularly remarkable about such a
claim if he had not also mentioned some events happening in the family
of Laxmi Chand, which various informants of that family verified.

The details Veer Singh mentioned varied in significance and freedom
from the criticism of inferability. For example, he said that he had (in the
discarnate state) attended the wedding of Som Dutt's brother Vishnu Dutt,
and he mentioned some details of that occasion. These included the food
served, but the food at Indian weddings has no more variety (within its
type) than the food one can eat at a Western wedding, so the remark lacked
all specificity.

Veer Singh made some other statements less easily accounted for. He

---

[9] Some older subjects say they have forgotten the "original" memories of the previous life and
remember only what others—for example, their parents—said they said when younger; some
other subjects, I believe, have also forgotten the original memories, but go on narrating what
they have been told about them without making any distinction between the original memories
and the later, secondhand ones. For a further discussion of this topic, see I. Stevenson. 1974.
Twenty cases.

said that he had accompanied any member of the family who went away from home alone. This statement accorded with a dream Som Dutt's mother had had some months after his death (in October 1937) in which Som Dutt appeared to her and said that his older brother, Vishnu Dutt, was going out at night to attend fairs and that he (supposedly the discarnate Som Dutt) was accompanying him.[10] October is a month of religious festivals and fairs, notably the Ramlila. Bindra Devi did not know that Vishnu Dutt was leaving the house to attend the fairs but after her dream, upon enquiring, found this was true. Vishnu Dutt confirmed this to me.

Veer Singh also talked with Bindra Devi about lawsuits the family had been engaged in during the years between the death of Som Dutt and the birth of Veer Singh. He mentioned the camel[11] that had been purchased four or five years after Som Dutt's death. (The camel had died after two years, that is, about three years before Veer Singh's birth and nearly eight before his first visit to Sikarpur.) Veer Singh had previously mentioned this camel to his family (item 15, Table 15).

Veer Singh also told Laxmi Chand the names of the children born after Som Dutt's death. As I have already mentioned, Veer Singh was credited with recognizing these other children, and I have included in Table 15 his recognitions of two of them, Ravi Dutt and Sarla Devi. His recognition of Ravi Dutt was spontaneous and seemed to me, from the reports of how it happened, to have been just as impressive as any other recognition he made.

Veer Singh also told Laxmi Chand that one Mukhtar Singh had moved to another village after his house had been robbed (item 43). This removal had occurred after Som Dutt's death.

He described how some women were playing on a swing suspended from the peepal tree he claimed to have occupied. He felt irritated by their intrusion and thought of breaking off the branch of the tree supporting the swing. Then he reflected that he might kill them. So instead he waited until the swing was near the ground and then broke the plank on which they were sitting. Laxmi Chand remembered that an accident of this type had happened after the death of Som Dutt.

[10] Bindra Devi's dream seemed to be well known in her family. It was first recounted to me in 1964 by Vishnu Dutt and later, in 1971, by his father, Laxmi Chand. Bindra Devi herself denied in 1964 that she remembered having such a dream. Then in 1971, when I saw her again at the time of interviewing Laxmi Chand, her husband, she spontaneously mentioned the dream with details as given by her son and husband. In 1964 she was considerably disturbed by the memories of Som Dutt's death—even after many years—and she seemed greatly puzzled and troubled by my inquiries, which she did not properly understand. I think these reactions influenced her memory and testimony. In 1969 and 1971 she was much more at ease.

[11] Camels are not common in this part of India, the climate not being suitable for them. The camel owned by Laxmi Chand's family was the only one in the village, but it does not seem to have been an object of special attention.

Veer Singh's Behavior Related to the Previous Life

Veer Singh's Brahmin Attitudes. As already mentioned, Veer Singh showed some rejection of his family's food even before the family members knew the reason for his refusing it. And it seems likely that he himself was perhaps only dimly aware at first that he should not eat food prepared in a non-Brahmin way.[12] Then, about the time he told his mother that he was a Brahmin and would not eat food prepared by her, he seems to have reached a full realization of the situation he thought he was in—a Brahmin living in a Jat household and forced to eat their food. At any rate, after this declaration he refused to eat the family food for about four or five months. During this time his family made the concession of having Veer Singh's milk prepared in the Brahmin style for him, but not other food. Veer Singh said that a Brahmin man of the village used to get meals prepared for him, but his family did not mention such collusion to me.

Vishnu Dutt, Som Dutt's older brother, said that Veer Singh liked to eat alone, and so had Som Dutt. This, however, would have been a personal trait common to both persons and would not necessarily have had anything to do with caste habits.

The accounts given to me of how Veer Singh overcame his fear of eating non-Brahmin food differed. Veer Singh himself said that he changed after he went to a non-Brahmin home to bring his sister back from a visit. She had been staying with this family, and when Veer Singh went there he was served only non-Brahmin food which he felt forced to eat. Afterward, he vomited it. Nevertheless, evidently reassured by his survival of this ordeal, he then began to eat non-Brahmin food. I did not learn how old he was when this episode occurred. His mother said that Veer Singh first began eating the family food again after some Brahmin children from Sikarpur had come to visit and had eaten their (the Singhs') Jat food. Perhaps their bravery emboldened Veer Singh. She said the period of his most extreme refusal to eat their food lasted four to five months. His father said Veer Singh showed some resistance to eating with them until he was eight years

---

[12] Brahmins particularly emphasize that their food must be prepared by other Brahmins, that metal utensils must be used, and that strict cleanliness must be practiced in its preparation. Laxmi Chand and his son Vishnu Dutt both told me their family was strict about food rules.

It may be asked how one small boy could have known and another small boy remember such distinctions of caste. But a child of, say, four, as Som Dutt was at the time of his death, would certainly know that his family cooked in metal vessels, and that some other families of his village did not. In addition, his family would have begun to drill him in the traditions of Brahmins; patrician children of his age in the West usually know already that their blood is bluer. As for Veer Singh, watching his mother cooking with earthenware utensils could have signaled to him that, from the point of view of a purist Brahmin, something had gone dreadfully wrong with his rebirth.

old. But even after that age Veer Singh continued to prefer to take food in a Brahmin family, although he also ate with his own family and other Jats. In 1964 he said he was then eating food in his family, but that earlier he had not done so for a period of four or five years. This figure did not refer to a continuous period of time, but included mainly the prolonged visits he had made to the family of Laxmi Chand. This brings me to the topic of these lengthy visits.

Veer Singh's Relationship with Som Dutt's Parents. Veer Singh was strongly attracted to the previous family. His very first encounter with Som Dutt's parents occurred when he was about three. I described earlier how he may have recognized them, probably outside Salikheri, as they were walking along the canal. He had called to them, but they had made no response. He returned home and told his father tearfully about this meeting and, as he saw it, rejection by "his" parents. He said he was weeping because "my father and mother did not speak to me." When, about a year later, Veer Singh met first Laxmi Chand and then Som Dutt's mother, Bindra Devi, he was immensely pleased. He expressed a strong desire to go to the other family. He refused to eat food, or rather intensified his prior refusal, in order to put pressure on his family to let him go to Sikarpur. Since he was not eating with them, his family did let him go to Sikarpur and stay for a time. Thus began a series of repeated and sometimes prolonged visits by Veer Singh to the other family. On three of these occasions he remained with Laxmi Chand's family six months, one year, and two years respectively. He ran away from his home on three occasions. Once he tried to get from Salikheri to Sikarpur, but got lost on the way. Villagers of Sikarpur thought he belonged to their village and showed him to it. Laxmi Chand's family later moved to Khatima in a distant district, that of Nainital. Veer Singh tried to reach them, but was picked up in Bareilly. Then when he was thirteen (in 1961, three years before my first visit) he ran away again and went to Khatima on the train. He stayed with Laxmi Chand's family about a month before being brought back by an uncle. He returned home unwillingly. Veer Singh's interest in being with the previous family seems to have had several motives. He was first of all attached to them personally. Second, they were Brahmins, and he believed himself living within his own caste in their midst. Third, they were somewhat richer than his family, and I suppose that the (slightly) increased comfort of their existence had some attraction for him, although no informant, including Veer Singh himself, mentioned this factor to me.

Veer Singh's family were ambivalent about his prolonged visits with the other family. On the one hand, he was not eating with them anyway, and they thought he might be better off with the other family. (This would have applied only to the early period of his extreme refusal to eat their food.) On the other hand, he was their child, and they felt need,[13] responsibility, and affection for him. So for one reason or another they would eventually terminate Veer Singh's visits to the other family by sending someone to bring him back. This was usually Shital Prasad, his uncle. So far as I know, he never came back to Salikheri voluntarily.

Up to 1964 the attitude of Laxmi Chand's family toward Veer Singh was one of wholehearted acceptance. They called him "Som Dutt" when he was with them, and he called Bindra Devi "Mataji," meaning "mother." With them he was not a mere visitor, but shared in the family work and took an interest in the family affairs. In Sikarpur and Khatima Veer Singh lived like a Brahmin.

Laxmi Chand seems at first to have been enthusiastic about adopting Veer Singh. He told me that (in about 1952) he had offered to settle one-third of his property on him and to give Kali Ram Singh the boy's weight in rupees. But when Kali Ram Singh suggested that he should implement this proposal, Laxmi Chand considered the matter differently. (Veer Singh himself, Vishnu Dutt told me in 1964, had never asked for any land or money up to that year.) Vishnu Dutt said he would not want any of their land to go to Jats. On the other hand, he said he would not object to Veer Singh's inheriting a third of his father's land (the other two-thirds going to himself and Ravi Dutt) if Veer Singh would remain with them, live as a Brahmin, and take a Brahmin wife. One can see in this attitude the same strictness about caste distinctions that Veer Singh expressed so strongly when he was between three and four years old.

Despite their disagreements as to the proper family for Veer Singh to live with, the two families maintained cordial relations with each other and Veer Singh's mother said that they exchanged gifts. Veer Singh was living mainly with his own family in 1964, but still going for short visits to Laxmi Chand's family.

By 1969 the picture had changed somewhat as regards the attitudes of Som Dutt's family toward Veer Singh. He had attenuated his visits and felt then that the only member of Som Dutt's family who really attracted him was Laxmi Chand. He had gone over to Khatima about six months earlier but, finding Laxmi Chand away, had turned around and come back to Salikheri. Formerly, he seemed to have been more interested in Bindra Devi, but she had begun to make him uncomfortable by expressing fears that he would begin to claim property. Bindra Devi confirmed this account of her attitude and said that Veer Singh had openly asked for one-third of the property at his last visit, two years before (that is, about 1967). She had told him that in that case he should stay with them and work. And by

---

[13] Indian villagers, who are nearly all farmers, need male children to help in the fields and with other work. The loss of a pair of helping hands can handicap a poor family.

1971, when I met Laxmi Chand, he had given up regarding Veer Singh as a son and heir.

A decline in the economic fortunes of Laxmi Chand may have entered into the shift in attitude toward Veer Singh on the part of Laxmi Chand and his family and, similarly for the shift in attitude toward them on the part of Veer Singh. Originally, Laxmi Chand had been somewhat more prosperous than Kali Ram Singh. But when he moved to the Nainital District (at village Khatima), although he had much more land, it was of poorer quality. What was worse, other persons of that area challenged his title to the land, and he was obliged to contend with them in vexatious court battles. The house I saw in Khatima was in a very dilapidated condition. The family were obviously having to struggle for survival, and these circumstances would have made the idea of sharing the property with someone of another family, even if they believed him their own dead son reborn, much less congenial than it might have been earlier, when they were more prosperous.

The Attitude of Veer Singh's Family toward His Memories of the Previous Life

In 1964 Veer Singh's family seemed to accept very tolerantly his claims to belong to another family. But their attitudes over the years must have fluctuated considerably. His older brother Jai Singh said he could remember how their parents had shut Veer Singh in a room for two days and had beaten him in an effort to get him to stop saying he was a Brahmin. But this failed; no sooner was he released than he began saying he was a Brahmin once more. He naturally made himself unpopular in his family by his hauteur in the matter of caste. Jai Singh described Veer Singh as still being disliked in the family for this reason as late as 1969. The unpleasantness of hearing Veer Singh say repeatedly that he was a Brahmin and they were Jats may have contributed to the willingness of his family to allow him to go to Laxmi Chand's family for prolonged visits. His absences freed them from the constant reminders of their inferiority which his manner, and sometimes his words, proclaimed.

Evidence of Extrasensory Perception on the Part of Veer Singh

As in many other cases of this type, I enquired about evidence of extrasensory perception on the part of Veer Singh. Veer Singh himself told me that he once had a dream in which he saw a theft being committed in a neighbor's house. He awoke and told the dream. It was then found that thieves were at that moment in the neighbor's house; when discovered, they ran away. Veer Singh's mother did not recall details of the dream, although she confirmed that she had heard of it. I learned of no other evidence of extrasensory perception on the part of Veer Singh.

Comments on the Evidence of Paranormal Processes in the Case

It seems to me particularly difficult to imagine that the subject or any of the other informants contrived this case. Veer Singh's family could get no credit from having a child refuse food and threaten to run away. And Laxmi Chand was at first incredulous about the idea that a Brahmin would reincarnate as a Jat. It gave no advantage to him or his family to admit that a Jat child had given remarkable evidence of people and events in their family during the life of one of their sons and after his death.

Apart from these considerations, the testimony in this case, even though given more than ten years after the main events, seemed to me singularly free of discrepancies even in details. The informants showed cooperativeness and complete candor so far as I could tell. The two principal female witnesses, the mothers of Veer Singh and Som Dutt, were both reluctant witnesses, at least initially; but I consider this due to the customary hesitation of many women in Indian villages to talk with strangers; such village women tend to shun all public exposure. In addition, Bindra Devi was evidently disturbed by the revival of memories of her son's death many years before, and in 1964 she became tearful as she talked about him. She was certainly not promoting the case. I was further impressed by the manner in which Kali Ram Singh, Veer Singh's father, gave his testimony in 1964. He had been out of the village when we came to Salikheri, and we thought we had missed him. But he returned to the village just as we were leaving. He then came to our car and, in the absence of his wife, gave testimony that fully supported what she had told us. If he had wished to avoid us, he could easily have done so. Both in Salikheri and the nearby village of Lolakhera, where we stopped on the way to Salikheri and where the case was well known, there was ample opportunity for anyone interested to tell us that the case was invented or exaggerated, but no one did.

The fact that Som Dutt had died about eleven years before Veer Singh was born adds to the strength of the case. If anyone in Salikheri had ever heard of Som Dutt when he died, which I doubt very much, they would long since have stopped talking about a small boy who had lived many years before in another village. This temporal gap, added to the small geographical one and the much larger caste difference between the two families, makes it most unlikely that Veer Singh could have learned anything about Som Dutt through normal means in his own village.

Even if Veer Singh had somehow heard of Som Dutt, we should still have to account in this case, as in so many others, for his strong personation of the previous personality. Veer Singh certainly gained nothing in his family by refusing their food and claiming that he belonged to a superior caste. And they, for their part, can hardly be imagined to have reinforced such behavior on his part. Later, no doubt, Veer Singh gained the pleasure of being with the other family, but that cannot have been a motive for his first refusals of food.

Veer Singh showed an unusual knowledge of events happening in Som Dutt's family after Som Dutt's death. And at least on one occasion he apparently showed evidence of extrasensory perception about a contemporary event. Although I obtained no other evidence of extrasensory perception of current events on his part, the case lends itself more than most others of the type to the interpretation that Veer Singh had acquired his correct information about Som Dutt's family through paranormal communications with their living members. This explanation would leave unanswered the question of why someone with such presumed great powers of extrasensory perception did not manifest these abundantly in connection with persons and situations other than those of the claimed memories of the life of Som Dutt.

Veer Singh's Later Development

In 1964 Veer Singh told me that he no longer remembered the previous life clearly. Although he could recall what he had told others, he seemed not to have retained details of the original imaged memories. In 1969, however, he said that he was then remembering the previous life in full detail, that is, as much of it as he had earlier remembered. He said that he did not think about the previous life spontaneously, but only if someone asked him about it.

He expressed a preference for Som Dutt's brothers over his own brothers, and he thought that Laxmi Chand liked him more than his father did, and more than he liked his own children. He still thought of himself as a Brahmin rather than as a Jat. However, by this time he had learned to take food with other Jat families besides his own, although he preferred to eat with Brahmins.

Veer Singh was working as a mechanic in 1969, as were his two older brothers. Although one of them, Jai Singh, objected to Veer Singh's residual snobbishness, Veer Singh himself was evidently not aware of any overt hostility toward him in his own family. He said his family did not tease him in relation to his memories of the previous life.

It seemed to me then that Veer Singh had reached a partial adjustment to his situation but that he had not fully adapted. I believe that his prolonged visits to the family of Laxmi Chand when he was a child had reinforced his Brahmin habits and attitudes and made his acceptance of his own family, to which in the end he had to return, more difficult. Thus at the age of twenty-one he was still somewhat attached to both families without having a sense of really belonging to either.

Veer Singh himself sensed that he had become to some extent caught between the two families. In 1969, when I saw him last, he was twenty-one years old. He then said that he thought he would not marry until both sets of parents involved had died. He said: "If I marry a Brahmin the Jats will be annoyed, and if I marry a Jat the Brahmins will be annoyed." He also remarked that at times he was disturbed and then wanted "to get away from both families."

10

The Case of Ramoo and Rajoo Sharma

Introduction

RAMOO and Rajoo Sharma are twin boys, both of whom have remembered previous lives as twins (together) in another village. Although they are twins, each is a distinct individual, and I could emphasize this fact more if I considered theirs as two cases instead of one. However, the reader, and I also, will have a much easier time if I put their cases together in a single report. This is not a matter of convenience only, since the informants often did not know which twin had said what or at least could not later remember to tell me. The twins' statements were often reported as if they had both made them, and indeed this may well have occurred in most instances because they were constantly together and thus very likely to talk together or in quick sequence. Sometimes, and naturally when describing which previous life each remembered, Ramoo and Rajoo made different statements. I shall draw attention to these and to some other differences between the twins during this report.

Summary of the Case and Its Investigation

Ram Narain Diwedi (Ramoo) and Shesh Narain Diwedi (Rajoo) were born in August 1964, in the village of Sham Nagara, Uttar Pradesh. (It has not been possible to fix their birthdate more precisely.) Ramoo was the firstborn of the twins. They were the children of Pandit Ram Swaroop Sharma and his wife, Kapuri Devi. Ram Swaroop was an Ayurvedic physician. The twins were the sixth and seventh children in the family. They had four older sisters and an older brother; later, a younger brother and a sister were born.

Before or during her pregnancy with the twins, Kapuri Devi had two dreams in each of which two children figured. These dreams of two children were thought retrospectively to have had some foreshadowing connection with the birth of the twins, as opposed to that of a single baby. But, apart from this, the dreams do not seem to have been given any special significance at the time, and they did not by themselves lead to an identification of Ramoo and Rajoo with particular deceased people. At birth the twins were found to have birthmarks that I shall describe later. Prior to their births Kapuri Devi had heard about the murder of two twins, Bhimsen and Bhism Pitamah Tripathi, who had lived in another village, Uncha Larpur. But she does not appear to have connected her twins with these men. Her husband, Ram Swaroop, did not even notice the birthmarks on the twins.

Ramoo and Rajoo were about two years old when they first began to speak connectedly. Their first indication of remembering a previous life came when (at the age of about three) they ran off in the direction of the main highway. When brought back and asked what they were doing, they said they were going home. No further clarification of this remark seems to have been asked or offered at the time.

They were still about three years old when the next relevant episode occurred. It happened when a stranger passed through their village, and the twins were observed to touch his feet, a sign of respect in India. Their uncle reproached them for this, since (he thought) they did not know the man. But they said they had recognized him; and they began to talk about the previous lives they remembered. (This particular man was from the village Uncha Larpur, where the twins said they had lived in their previous lives.) They said they had been called Bhimsen (Ramoo) and Bhism Pitamah (Rajoo).[1]

The twins gave a rather circumstantial account of how they had been murdered in the previous lives. They described how (in their previous lives) they had had a quarrel with one Jagannath who after a time had pretended to become reconciled and had invited them to his house in the village of Kurri.[2] There he had shown every sign of hospitality and indeed of affection; suddenly they were set upon by numerous men and, after a struggle, strangled. (I give below further details of what Ramoo and Rajoo said about the murders they remembered.) In addition to their recital of details of these gruesome killings, Ramoo and Rajoo made a number of other statements about events in the previous lives and about objects they said they had owned.[3] Word of what they were saying reached Uncha Larpur; members of the family of the murdered twins, as well as some

---

[1] Bhimsen and Bhism Pitamah were named after well-known heroes of Hindu mythology who played notable parts in the events narrated in the great epic of the *Mahabharata*. The original Bhimsen and Bhism Pitamah were not twins nor even brothers; although related, they belonged to different generations.

[2] Court records to which I shall refer again give the name of this village as Kundri Purwa. My informants usually referred to it, however, as Kurri (or by some close variant), and I shall retain this name.

[3] It is important in studying the remainder of this report for readers to remember that Ramoo said he had been Bhimsen and Rajoo said that he had been Bhism Pitamah in the previous lives. Adults concerned with the case, including myself, have sometimes become confused about which twin remembered which life; the twins themselves, so far as I know, never were.

other villagers and even the alleged murderers themselves, came over to Sham Nagara to see Ramoo and Rajoo. The twins recognized most of these people. A considerable lapse must have occurred between the twins' first recognition of the man from Uncha Larpur, if they did this when they were about three, in, say, 1968, and the subsequent visits of the deceased twins' older brother, Chandra Sen, and their mother, Ram Devi, which probably did not take place until the summer of 1971. Unfortunately, the first man recognized by the twins had died by the time my investigation of the case began.

I first learned of the case on November 20, 1971. I was in the police station at Gursahaiganj, Uttar Pradesh, making inquiries related to another case, when one of the police officers suggested that I take up the investigation of the present case. Since the case involved a murder not far from Gursahaiganj, there were some records of it in the police station there. I made notes of these and of enough other information to enable us to trace the subjects. I could do nothing more to study the case during that trip to India.

In July 1972 Dr. L. P. Mehrotra went, on my behalf, to the village Sham Nagara, where the subjects lived, and also to Uncha Larpur, the village where Bhimsen and Bhism Pitamah had lived. He took down statements from some of the principal informants. In October of the same year I went to the two villages and conducted further interviews. In March 1973, I returned to the area. I had an interview then with the twins' father, Ram Swaroop, who had not been available earlier. I also had some further interviews with other informants and was able to examine the court records for the trial of the persons accused of murdering Bhimsen and Bhism Pitamah.

Later, after I had left the area, Dr. Erlendur Haraldsson and Dr. Mehrotra succeeded in reaching another informant, Pandit Manna Lal, whom neither Dr. Mehrotra nor I had previously interviewed. They interviewed him on March 31, 1973, at Sham Nagara. He was the twins' teacher. During this period also Dr. Mehrotra and Dr. Haraldsson administered some psychological tests to Ramoo and one of his peers matched for age, sex, and social status. (Rajoo was judged not to offer a suitable control for Ramoo since the two had lived so closely together physically and emotionally.) This was part of a program for testing a group of subjects of these cases and their peers; the results are not yet ready for reporting, and I only mention the psychological testing program here for its relevance to the reader's understanding of the different contacts we have had with the twins and their family.

In 1974 Dr. Mehrotra engaged in helpful correspondence with Chandra Sen Tripathi, the older brother of Bhimsen and Bhism Pitamah, about some details concerning which I thought our knowledge insufficient. In

October 1974 I met another informant, Radhey Shyam, who had been a friend of Bhimsen and Bhism Pitamah. And I had a short visit with Ramoo and Rajoo on the same day.

Persons Interviewed during the Investigation

In Sham Nagara I interviewed:

> Ram Narain Diwedi (Ramoo) Sharma
> Shesh Narain Diwedi (Rajoo) Sharma
> Kapuri Devi, the twins' mother
> Gaya Prasad Sharma, the twins' paternal uncle and the older brother of
>   their father, Ram Swaroop Sharma
> Shyam Sunder, villager of Sham Nagara

At Jasoda Station I interviewed:

> Ram Swaroop Sharma, the twins' father

In Uncha Larpur I interviewed:

> Chandra Sen Tripathi, older brother of Bhimsen and Bhism Pitamah
> Ram Devi Tripathi, mother of Bhimsen and Bhism Pitamah
> Subedar Tripathi, a relative of Chandra Sen, Bhimsen, and Bhism
>   Pitamah
> Rajendra Kahar, villager of Uncha Larpur

In Gursahaiganj I interviewed:
> Radhey Shyam, friend of Bhimsen and Bhism Pitamah

In 1972 Dr. Mehrotra had interviewed all the principal informants I later talked with except for the twins' father, Ram Swaroop Sharma. In addition, Dr. Mehrotra had recorded that year a short statement from Ram Kishore, Bhimsen's son, who had earlier gone to Sham Nagara to see Ramoo and Rajoo. And, as mentioned above, he and Dr. Haraldsson interviewed (in 1973) Pandit Manna Lal, whom I did not meet myself.

Of the informants for Ramoo and Rajoo's side of the case, by far the most knowledgeable and competent was Gaya Prasad, their paternal uncle. Their father, Ram Swaroop, seems to have paid little attention to what they said and to have reacted negatively to what he did learn about their statements. Moreover, since he was out of the home much of the time, the twins were really closer to their uncle than to their father. Their mother,

Kapuri Devi, wished to cooperate with our inquiries so far as I could tell, but she was a shy Brahmin lady with purdah habits and could not mingle freely with us. Her opposite member in the case, Ram Devi, the mother of Bhimsen and Bhism Pitamah, had shed these inhibitions. Although also a Brahmin, she came forth and gave her statements with an easy manner. This seemed all the more creditable since our visits revived the most painful memories for her.

Relevant Facts of Geography and Possibilities for Normal Means of Communication between the Two Families

The villages of the two families concerned in this case are both in the Farrukhabad District. This is an area of the state of Uttar Pradesh northwest of the large industrial city of Kanpur. The two villages lie on different sides of the main road between Kanpur and Farrukhabad, beside which an important (meter gauge) railway line also runs. Sham Nagara is about 2 kilometers north of Jasoda Station (on the railway line), which is about 95 kilometers west of Kanpur. Uncha Larpur is about 3 kilometers south of Gursahaiganj, which is about 11 kilometers farther west than Jasoda Station and thus about 106 kilometers west of Kanpur. The two villages are approximately 16 kilometers apart. There was a poor road and also a footpath between Sham Nagara and the main trunk road at Jasoda Station. Gursahaiganj and Uncha Larpur also have a poor road connecting them; it is passable only during good weather.

The village of Kurri, where Bhimsen and Bhism Pitamah were murdered, is a little less than 1 kilometer from Uncha Larpur.

Ram Swaroop said that he had no connections with Uncha Larpur and that he, his older brother, and his wife had never visited it. Gaya Prasad confirmed this and also gave other details about possible acquaintance between the two families prior to the development of the case. He said the two families had not known each other before then, and that furthermore there had been no marriages whatever between other persons of the two villages. (For villages each without importance to the other and on opposite sides of the main road and market town only marriages between members of the villages would ordinarily provide a reason for visits from one to the other.) To reach their usual destinations the villagers of one village would not need to go anywhere near the other one.

Chandra Sen stated that neither he nor any member of his family had ever gone to Sham Nagara before the development of the case. They had, moreover, no relatives, friends, or other connections with that village. It was obvious from the manner with which Chandra Sen and his mother talked that they considered the case entirely genuine and did not entertain the possibility that Ramoo and Rajoo had obtained their information about Bhimsen and Bhism Pitamah by normal means.

The foregoing does not exclude an occasional visitor from Uncha Larpur passing through Sham Nagara, and we know that one such person from Uncha Larpur was recognized by Ramoo and Rajoo as he went through their village. This person was in fact a relative of Pandit Manna Lal, who was a teacher of Ramoo and Rajoo. However, Pandit Manna Lal did not himself live in Sham Nagara, but rather in another village, about 2 kilometers distant from Sham Nagara. Thus any relatives of his living in Uncha Larpur and coming to visit him might have passed through Sham Nagara but would not ordinarily have had any reason to stop there. Sham Nagara itself is an extremely small village, one of the smallest I have seen in India. Gaya Prasad said it had only a hundred inhabitants.

Shyam Sunder, a villager of Sham Nagara, told me that he had met Bhimsen and Bhism Pitamah on one occasion only. He happened to meet them in the police station at Gursahaiganj. He was not socially acquainted with them.

That members of the two families may have used the same shops in the market town of Gursahaiganj and even been there at the same time is not only possible but quite probable. Persons who believe that casual contacts of this kind suffice for establishing some link that paranormal processes can later exploit may certainly use this fact for developing their theories. But anyone who supposes that the two families had enough contact prior to the development of the case for the normal transmission of information to the twins has no evidence known to me to support his conjectures.

I should have thought that information about the murder of Bhimsen and Bhism Pitamah would have reached Sham Nagara in the normal course of exchanges of information in the market town of Gursahaiganj, if not more directly. Even in an area with many murders, another one always seems newsworthy. But the twins' paternal uncle, Gaya Prasad, denied that any news of the murder of Bhimsen and Bhism Pitamah had reached Sham Nagara before the twins spoke about it. His sister-in-law, their mother, however, did not agree and said that she had heard of the murder before her twins were born.

The Life and Death of Bhimsen and Bhism Pitamah Tripathi

My information about Bhimsen and Bhism Pitamah derives from the interviews with their mother, Ram Devi, their older brother, Chandra Sen, and another (more distant) relative, Subedar Tripathi. Court records of the persons tried for the murder of Bhimsen and Bhism Pitamah, which I examined at the courthouse in Fategahr, contributed additional details.

Bhimsen and Bhism Pitamah were born in the village of Uncha Larpur in 1935. Their parents were Pandit Kali Shanker, a farmer, and his wife, Ram Devi. In addition to Chandra Sen, the family also had an older daughter, Jamuna. Subsequently, two younger daughters, Rani and Urmula, were born. The family, like that of Ramoo and Rajoo, were Brahmins.

Bhism Pitamah was the older of the twins.[4] In childhood he was the taller of the two; but as they grew up their order of height became reversed, so that Bhimsen was the taller when they were adults. Bhism Pitamah did not go to school, but Bhimsen attended one up to the sixth class. The twins became farmers with their older brother, Chandra Sen. (Their father died in 1955.) The land was divided equally among the three sons of the family. They had a moderate portion of land, owning together about 50–60 bighas, which is the equivalent of about 35 acres. Bhimsen, who could write, also had the part-time position of assistant secretary in the village of Uncha Larpur.

Bhimsen and Bhism Pitamah were extremely close to each other and "went everywhere together." This, however, did not mean shutting out other members of the family from their affection nor feeling obliged to imitate each other in everything. They showed some independence when it came time to marry. Bhimsen married first, his wife being from the village of Atrauli. A year later Bhism Pitamah married a girl from Bahawalpur. Bhism Pitamah had one child, Dronacharya; Bhism Pitamah had three, Ram Kishore, Raj Kishore, and Netra Kishore.

The twins' mother, Ram Devi, said that Bhimsen was more intelligent than Bhism Pitamah; her older son, Chandra Sen, however, first said he considered Bhism Pitamah more intelligent, but then he made a distinction between two kinds of intelligence. In intellectual matters he thought Bhimsen superior and gifted with greater reasoning powers. But he believed Bhism Pitamah to have the better memory[5] and to be superior in "social intelligence." He considered Bhimsen the more aggressive of the two.

Bhimsen and Bhism Pitamah had the reputation of being good-natured, but also strong and brave. These virtues gave them a certain dominance in their village and area over less aggressive persons. They seem to have been persons who did not make trouble nor run from it. The distinction

[4] Ramoo, who remembered the life of Bhimsen, was born before Rajoo, who remembered that of Bhism Pitamah. If the case is considered as an instance of reincarnation, they may be said to have switched the order of their respective births on being reborn.

[5] Ramoo was said by informants for his family to have had more memories of the previous life he remembered (that of Bhimsen) than Rajoo had for the one he remembered (that of Bhism Pitamah). My collection of cases includes eight others in which the subject was a twin. In most of these cases one of the pair had fewer memories of a previous life than the other, or none at all. In two cases in which the second twin had no memories of a previous life, the first one, who had, said they had been together in the life he recalled.

between these two, sometimes difficult to discern, is certainly not made easier by the adversary contentions of a trial for murder. I therefore am unsure how to evaluate an allegation brought out at the trial (of their suspected murderers) that the twins were police informers. Bhimsen was said (in the court testimony) to have enabled the police to recover an unlicensed gun from one of the suspects;[6] and Bhism Pitamah had filed a suit against another of them. Actions of this kind maintain enmities if they do not create them. And the court transcript developed testimony concerning yet other quarrels between the murdered twins and the persons charged with the crime.

A dispute over land boundaries developed between the twins and two men called Jagannath and Raja Ram, of the neighboring village of Kurri; this appears to have been the precipitating factor in their murder. Jagannath erected a boundary dike of earth on what the twins considered their land.[7] The twins then knocked down this dike as an indication of their claim to the land it enclosed. They were also said to have destroyed a feeding trough of the neighbors and to have blocked a water course on their land. Jagannath and his associates said nothing about what Bhimsen and Bhism Pitamah had done, but plotted a later revenge. After about a month they suavely dissembled their feelings and affected to have forgotten all petty disagreements of the past. On the pretext of settling up a financial matter, they invited the twins to one of their houses in Kurri. This vulpine strategy succeeded excellently; I mean by this remark to praise the technique, not the monstrous crime that it implemented. The twins were last seen alive on April 28, 1964. Their tied-up bodies were recovered from a well on May 2. The bodies were badly decomposed, but the police examined them and concluded that the deceased men had been killed by strangulation. The medical examiner's report of his autopsies was more circumspect; it stated that he could not identify any cause of death. But it was also based on lesser information. His statement, dated May 4, 1964, was presumably written on the day of his examinations of the bodies. If so, two more days of the hottest Indian weather must have accelerated the

---

[6] Ramoo and Rajoo mentioned that they had had in their previous lives both a licensed gun and an unlicensed one (items 14 and 15, Table 16). Chandra Sen said that he and his brothers had had a licensed gun, but he denied that they had had an unlicensed one. Bhimsen's activity as an informer needs to be judged with understanding of conditions in that part of India, where simple prudence guides the villagers to retain their weapons while arranging to have those of their neighbors removed. A Sessions Court judge of this district, of whom I asked permission to study a court record relevant to another case (also involving a murder), when he learned of my research, advised me to drop all my projects elsewhere and move to this area. He thought the extremely high murder rate there provided an excellent milieu for the development of cases of the reincarnation type—as indeed it seems to do.

[7] Rural land boundaries are most often indicated in Asia, not by fences, but by narrow dikes of earth thrown up at the boundaries. These are usually somewhat higher than the dikes separating different fields of individual owners.

putrefaction of the cadavers; it is not surprising that the coroner did not find signs of strangulation that the police had noticed. No one, however, supposed that the two men had tied themselves up and jumped into the well. Suspicion naturally fell on the known enemies of the twins, and so the police rounded up a handful of these (in fact nine) and they were tried for the murders. But the murders had (almost certainly) been committed at night, and the police had probably netted all the eyewitnesses, so that no one remained to accuse them. For lack of direct evidence all the defendants were acquitted.

The absence of publicly identified eyewitnesses did not prevent fragments of information from reaching Chandra Sen and other members of the twins' family in Uncha Larpur. According to Subedar Tripathi, the murderers living at Kurri, after a time, began to talk freely about their exploit, and obliging villagers brought word of what they said back to Uncha Larpur. Some deduction from these reports has to be made for exaggeration, but there is an equal probability of loss of detail, as I have pointed out in the General Introduction to this volume. I considered going to Kurri myself in the hope of obtaining more and perhaps better information about the murders. But the prospects seemed so gloomy for meeting any person there who was not either one of the murderers or afraid of those who were, that I abandoned this expedition. I went instead once more to the police station at Gursahaiganj. I thought that I might find there a policeman who had participated in the inquiry after the murder; unfortunately, all such men had been posted elsewhere. We are left, then, with entirely secondhand evidence for the actual details of how Bhimsen and Bhism Pitamah died. Of this information the following reported details have some bearing on the case.

The assailants were said to have thrown acid or some corrosive and potentially blinding substance in the eyes of the twins as they first attempted to overpower them. In the first struggle one twin got himself free and ran out of the house. He then realized, however, that his brother was still a captive. He waited for him and then either returned to help his brother or was again seized by the murderers. (Chandra Sen said that he had heard that Bhism Pitamah was the twin who had temporarily freed himself.)

The strong twins were held pinned down to the floor by lathis. (These are stout poles that could be held across the body with one man on each end; with a few such lathis across the trunk and legs a man becomes quite powerless.) The twins were then strangled by sustained pressure on the neck from a cot post. It does not appear that any bladed weapon was used.

The murderers first carried the bodies and deposited them in a nullah (water course). But, as these are often dry, it then occurred to them that they could be hanged if the bodies were discovered easily; therefore they decided to conceal them more effectively by putting them in a well. At some point they had tied the bodies with ropes and probably had put them in sacks. But the bodies, when discovered four days later, were not in sacks, although they were tied with ropes. These last details I have from the firsthand testimony of Chandra Sen, who was present when the bodies of his brothers were pulled out of the well.

Statements and Recognitions Made by Ramoo and Rajoo

In Table 16 I have listed all the statements and recognitions concerning the previous lives attributed to Ramoo and Rajoo by the informants. As I mentioned earlier, the twins often spoke together, or one confirmed immediately what the other had said. It should be understood that both contributed to a particular item unless I include the name of one in parentheses immediately after giving the content for that item.

I have organized the statements in Table 16 according to topic. I believe that items 1–4, 12–19, and 30 were all mentioned by Ramoo and Rajoo when they first began to talk about the previous life, which was just after they had recognized the man from Uncha Larpur who passed through Sham Nagara (item 35). Items 5–10, 20, and 32–33 all occurred during the visit of Ram Devi, the mother of Bhimsen and Bhism Pitamah, to Sham Nagara. I have listed two statements (items 11 and 31) made by Ramoo to me in 1972; no other informant mentioned them to us.

All the recognitions occurred in Sham Nagara and were of persons who passed through it or who came there expressly to meet Ramoo and Rajoo. They have never gone to Uncha Larpur.

The testimony of Ram Swaroop (the twins' father) greatly reduced the value of one block of recognitions, those occurring during the visit (or visits) of Ram Devi to Sham Nagara (items 38–42). He said that he had been a witness of these recognitions and that Ram Devi had asked the twins such inept questions as, "Am I your mother?" "Are these children your sons?" and, pointing at a girl, "Is she your sister?" His memories, however, disagreed with those of Ram Devi herself and, for some of these recognitions, with those of the twins' mother, Kapuri Devi, and their schoolteacher, Pandit Manna Lal. It is possible that Ram Swaroop was a more careful observer (and rememberer) of just what happened on these occasions than were the other witnesses, although his general attitude of detachment and indifference to the whole case does not encourage me to think him so vigilant or the others so careless. As sometimes happens on these occasions, the twins may have been asked to make the recognitions by different persons in varying ways. For example, Kapuri Devi might have asked the twins, as she said she did, "Who is she?" pointing at Ram

Devi. Then, or later, Ram Devi herself, perhaps to make the recognition quite definite, might have said: *"Am* I your mother?" Ram Swaroop might have heard the second of these questions, but not the first. But I do not think we can discard his testimony, which certainly damages the credit I had assigned to these recognitions before I talked to him.

Some of the alleged murderers of Bhimsen and Bhism Pitamah came to Sham Nagara to see Ramoo and Rajoo. Gaya Prasad said that the twins recognized them, but I did not learn the details of this interesting encounter. Another informant, Shyam Sunder, said that Ramoo and Rajoo had recognized another person from Uncha Larpur not listed in Table 16. I have thought it better to set this item aside, however, because there did not appear to be anything sufficiently specific in the statement of recognition he attributed to Ramoo and Rajoo.

The Physical Appearance of Ramoo and Rajoo

Ramoo and Rajoo are as different as two peas in a pod are to anyone who takes the trouble to examine them closely. Ramoo is fully 5 centimeters taller than Rajoo. If it were possible, however, to look only at their faces, they might well pass that supposedly best test for zygosity—the inability to tell them apart. Their facial features are remarkably similar.

The Birthmarks on Ramoo and Rajoo. The twins each had birthmarks across their abdomens of a type that I have not seen on any other subject, although I have now examined altogether more than 200 birthmarks in subjects of these cases. Those on Ramoo and Rajoo were streaks of increased pigmentation running horizontally (more or less) across the abdomen and (on Ramoo) the lower chest. They were about 2 millimeters wide. Ramoo had five such linear marks, the first just above his navel, the fifth at the level of his xiphoid process. They were spaced apart somewhat irregularly. Rajoo had only two such marks that I could detect. The lower one was just above his navel (in a situation similar to the lowest one on Ramoo's abdomen), and the upper one was about 6 centimeters above it in a position a little below the location of the second lowest mark on Ramoo. The two lower marks on Ramoo and both those on Rajoo ran right across the abdomen; the superior three marks on Ramoo crossed only a portion of his trunk.

The twins' mother, Kapuri Devi, and their paternal uncle, Gaya Prasad, said the marks were present on their bodies at birth and had an appearance as if the bodies of the twins had been cut. Her husband had not noticed any birthmarks on the twins; in my opinion, however, he was a poor observer of the twins in this as in other respects.

TABLE 16. *Summary of Statements and Recognitions Made by Ramoo and Rajoo*

Item	Informants	Verification	Comments
1. One of them was called Bhimsen (Ramoo).	Gaya Prasad, paternal uncle of Ramoo and Rajoo	Chandra Sen, older brother of Bhimsen and Bhism Pitamah	
2. One of them was called Bhism Pitamah (Rajoo).	Gaya Prasad	Chandra Sen	
3. They had a brother, Chandra.	Gaya Prasad	Chandra Sen	Chandra Sen was one of my principal informants on his family's side of the case.
4. They lived in Uncha Larpur (Ramoo).	Gaya Prasad Manna Lal, teacher of Ramoo and Rajoo	Chandra Sen	I visited Uncha Larpur twice.
5. They had read up to the sixth class.	Ram Devi, mother of Bhimsen and Bhism Pitamah	Chandra Sen	This statement was only true of Bhimsen. Bhism Pitamah had not attended school.
6. They had studied under Thakur Tilak Singh in the village of Marhana.	Ram Devi	Chandra Sen	Thakur Tilak Singh had been Bhimsen's teacher. Chandra Sen said he came from the village of Marariya. (The discrepancy in the spelling of the village name may be due to variant romanization of the word.)
7. One of them had married a girl from Atrauli (Ramoo).	Kapuri Devi, mother of Ramoo and Rajoo Ram Devi	Chandra Sen	Bhimsen's wife came from Atrauli, a village in the Farrukhabad District.
8. One of them had married a girl from Bahawalpur (Rajoo).	Ram Devi	Chandra Sen	Bhism Pitamah's wife came from Bahawalpur. (A discrepancy in the spelling of the name of this village in my notes and those of Dr. L. P. Mehrotra is probably due to variant romanization of the word.)
9. One of them had a son called Drona (Rajoo).	Ram Devi	Chandra Sen	Bhism Pitamah's only child was a son, Dronacharya. "Drona" is the common short form of this name.

Item			Comments
10. One of them had a son called Netra Kishore (Ramoo).	Ram Devi	Chandra Sen	Netra died after Bhimsen's death, but I did not learn when. I had written "Nitya" in my notes, but Dr. L. P. Mehrotra assured me that I must have misheard his pronunciation of the correct name, Netra.
11. They had 60 bighas of land (Ramoo).	Ramoo (1972)	Chandra Sen	Chandra Sen, in answering a question about this, at first said they—all three brothers together—had 60 bighas and then revised his estimate down to 50.
12. One of them (Bhimsen) had a ring, watch, and clothes (Ramoo).	Kapuri Devi	Chandra Sen	
13. One of them (Bhimsen) had a box in which he kept his ring and watch and also a pistol and cash (rupees) (Ramoo).	Kapuri Devi	Unverified	The three brothers shared one box in which they kept clothes. The brothers had separate rooms, and Chandra Sen said that Bhimsen could have had property that he (Chandra Sen) did not know about. He verified that Bhimsen had a watch and a ring (see preceding item) but said he had no pistol. He might have had some rupees.
14. They had a licensed gun.	Gaya Prasad Manna Lal	Chandra Sen	
15. They also had an unlicensed gun.	Gaya Prasad	Incorrect	Chandra Sen denied that his brothers had an unlicensed gun.
16. The gun was hanging on a peg in the inner room (Rajoo)	Kapuri Devi	Chandra Sen Ram Devi	The gun had been kept in Ram Devi's room, hanging on the wall.
17. The belt of cartridges was also there (Rajoo).	Kapuri Devi	Chandra Sen Ram Devi	A belt of cartridges was kept with the gun.
18. They had beaten police constables.	Kapuri Devi	Chandra Sen	Ramoo and Rajoo were probably boasting here. About seven months before the murder of Bhimsen and Bhism Pitamah they

NOTE: Both twins contributed to items except when the name of one is placed in parentheses after an item, which indicates that it was attributed to him alone.

TABLE 16 (*cont.*)

Item	Informants	Verification	Comments
18. (cont.)			had a quarrel with some other persons. The police intervened on the side of their opponents. Harsh words flew about, but no blows were exchanged.
19. Jagannath was a village "grandfather" (Rajoo).	Gaya Prasad	Ram Devi	The Hindi word *dada* (English: "grand-father") may be applied to any important or dominant person in a village without regard to whether he is elderly in years. Jagannath was about 40 or 45 years of age at the time of the murders of Bhimsen and Bhism Pitamah.
20. Jagannath and Raja Ram were from the village of Kurri.	Ram Devi	Chandra Sen	The names of both Jagannath and Raja Ram appeared in the list of those charged with the murders of Bhimsen and Bhism Pitamah that I copied from the police records at Gursahaiganj.
21. They dismantled Jagannath's feeding trough (Rajoo).	Gaya Prasad	Court records at Fategahr of the trial of the persons accused of murdering Bhimsen and Bhism Pitamah	Chandra Sen said that Bhimsen and Bhism Pitamah had dismantled the boundary dike, but he did not mention their destroy-ing a feeding trough. Such troughs are sometimes built into the dikes. Testimony at the trial indicated that Bhimsen and Bhism Pitamah had destroyed the feeding trough of Jagannath and Raja Ram; they were said also to have blocked a water channel in Jagannath's field.
22. Jagannath was angry, but later became friendly (Rajoo).	Gaya Prasad	Unverified	This and the following seven items (22–29) are all suggested as correct by secondhand evidence. (See text, p. 345.)
23. Jagannath sent away the women of his house (Rajoo).	Gaya Prasad	Unverified	Since the women were presumably as-signed no roles in the planned murder, it would have been tiresome to have them around the house at the time.

Statement	Informant	Verification	Comments
24. One day Jagannath invited them to his residence.	Gaya Prasad	Unverified	The secondhand information of Subedar Tripathi suggests that the murders actually took place at a house in Kurri other than that of Jagannath.
25. Jagannath offered them milk and was very affectionate (Rajoo).	Gaya Prasad	Unverified	The secondhand information of Subedar Tripathi indicates that the murdered men were given milk to drink before being captured and killed.
26. When they started to drink the milk, they were surrounded by many persons who caught hold of them (Rajoo).	Gaya Prasad	Unverified	The secondhand information of Subedar Tripathi indicates that about thirteen or fourteen men were at the house where the twins were captured and murdered. No less than nine suspects were charged and tried for the murders.
27. These men threw acid in their eyes and made them blind (Rajoo).	Gaya Prasad Manna Lal	Unverified	Chandra Sen said he had heard that his brothers' assailants had thrown acid on them. The twins did not use the word *acid*, but described instead "something poisonous in a bottle which they threw at them." Gaya Prasad then inferred that the liquid was a corrosive and blinding acid.
28. Bhimsen managed to get loose and went out of the house (Rajoo).	Gaya Prasad	Unverified	Chandra Sen said that he had heard that Bhism Pitamah not Bhimsen, had freed himself.
29. When the one who had escaped saw that his brother was being killed, he returned again (Rajoo).	Gaya Prasad	Unverified	The secondhand information indicates that Bhism Pitamah did not return voluntarily but was recaptured while he was waiting to see if his twin brother would also escape.
30. After that they were both attacked (Rajoo).	Gaya Prasad	Police and court records of the trial of the persons accused of murdering Bhimsen and Bhism Pitamah	These records leave no doubt that Bhimsen and Bhism Pitamah were murdered, but by whom and just how remain unclear.
31. They were put in a sack and then thrown in a well.	Ramoo (1972)	Chandra Sen	The bodies of Bhimsen and Bhism Pitamah were found in a well, but not inside a sack or sacks.

TABLE 16 (*cont.*)

Item	Informants	Verification	Comments
31. (cont.)			They were tied up. It seems likely that the murderers put the bodies in sacks to conceal them when they were taken to be put in the well. It appears that the murderers hoped to carry the bodies some distance on a camel, but that they did not have time for this and so put them in a well. It would have been risky to transport dead bodies in an open bullock cart—hence, the (probable) wise use of sacks. It would have been equally foolish to leave behind the sacks, whose owners might have been traced. So at the well the tied-up bodies were probably thrown out of the sacks and into the water.
32. Raja Ram was one of their murderers.	Ram Devi Ram Kishore, Bhimsen's son	Police records at Gursahaiganj	Raja Ram was listed as one of the nine men tried (and acquitted) in connection with the murder of Bhimsen and Bhism Pitamah.
33. Hori was also one of their murderers.	Ram Kishore	Police records at Gursahaiganj	The police records at Gursahaiganj gave the name of Hori Lal as one of the nine men tried (and acquitted) in connection with the murder of Bhimsen and Bhism Pitamah.
34. Their uncle Bansagopal was a party to the murder.	Ram Devi	Chandra Sen	Bansagopal was a "village uncle" of Bhimsen and Bhism Pitamah, not a true uncle. He and they had been friendly until the brothers had said something against him. He then separated from them and became friendly with their enemies Jagannath and Raja Ram. Chandra Sen believed that he had collaborated in the murder of Bhimsen and Bhism Pitamah, but I do not think he had firsthand evidence of this.

Bansagopal's name did not figure in the list of men arraigned for the murders. I had recorded this name in my notes as "Gansagopal," but Dr. L. P. Mehrotra has told me this would be an almost impossible name. He had recorded the name as "Bansagopal" in his notes.

I assume that the two informants were talking about the same man, whose recognition apparently stimulated the first expression by Ramoo and Rajoo of their memories of the previous lives. Gaya Prasad was an eyewitness of the recognition but could not remember the name of the man recognized, who had, he said, since died. Manna Lal remembered the name (Shiv Narain) but was not an eyewitness of the recognition.

This is a doubtful recognition. Gaya Prasad said that when Chandra Sen came to Sham Nagara, he (Gaya Prasad) asked Ramoo and Rajoo: "Who is he?" To this Rajoo replied: "He is my older brother." However, Chandra Sen had not heard either of the boys make a statement about recognizing him; and Rajendra Kahar gave conflicting testimony on two occasions. In October 1972 he was an auditor and, I thought, a tacit endorser of Chandra Sen's statement that he (Rajendra Kahar) had heard the twins tell someone inside the house (where he had followed them) that their brother had come. He then supposedly later told this to Chandra Sen, who told it to me. In March 1973, however, when we went over this incident again, Rajendra Kahar said Ramoo and Rajoo had not recognized Chandra Sen.

35. Recognition of a man from Uncha Larpur

Gaya Prasad
Manna Lal

36. Recognition of Chandra Sen, older brother of Bhimsen and Bhism Pitamah

Gaya Prasad
Chandra Sen
Rajendra Kahar, villager of
    Uncha Larpur

TABLE 16 (cont.)

Item	Informants	Verification	Comments
37. Recognition of Radhey Shyam of Nanga Purwa, a friend of Bhimsen and Bhism Pitamah (Rajoo)	Gaya Prasad Radhey Shyam, friend of Bhimsen and Bhism Pitamah		Radhey Shyam said that when he went to Sham Nagara someone asked the twins: "Who is he?" Ramoo and Rajoo replied: "He is our dada." This word, meaning literally the paternal grandfather, may be applied to any elderly villager. Bhimsen and Bhism Pitamah had called Radhey Shyam "Dada."
38. Recognition of Ram Devi, the mother of Bhimsen and Bhism Pitamah	Kapuri Devi Ram Devi Manna Lal Ram Swaroop, father of Ramoo and Rajoo		Manna Lal happened to be teaching Ramoo and Rajoo at their house when Ram Devi came to Sham Nagara, and so he was a firsthand witness of the recognition. The first three listed informants gave concordant testimony indicating that the twins had recognized Ram Devi either spontaneously or in response to a nonleading question: "Who is she?" Ram Swaroop, however, gave a discrepant version, saying that Ram Devi had asked the twins: "Am I your mother?" to which they replied: "Yes." Variations of this kind in the testimony of recognitions may be due to the subject's being asked more than once and in different ways to recognize the person presented to him.
39. Recognition of the older sister of Bhimsen and Bhism Pitamah	Kapuri Devi Ram Devi Ram Swaroop		For this item also (and the next) Ram Swaroop said that Ram Devi had put a leading question to the twins: "Is this your sister?" He did not distinguish in his testimony the younger from the older sister. Kapuri Devi and Ram Devi agreed that Ramoo and Rajoo had recognized the sisters of Bhimsen and Bhism Pitamah. Neither said that the twins had given the

354

names of the sisters. Ram Devi said they had stated (correctly) that the sisters were younger than Bhimsen and Bhism Pitamah, but Kapuri Devi remembered that they had stated which was the older and which the younger sister. According to her she had indicated the visiting women and had asked the twins who they were; in short, there had been no leading question. The comments for this item apply to the following one also.

See comment for the preceding item.

Ram Devi stated that the twins correctly gave the names of her grandsons, who had accompanied her to Sham Nagara. Ram Swaroop, however, said that she asked the twins: "Are these children your sons?" to which they replied: "Yes."

See comments for the preceding item and for item 9.

40. Recognition of the younger sister of Bhimsen and Bhism Pitamah

Kapuri Devi
Ram Devi
Ram Swaroop

41. Recognition of Ram Kishore and Raj Kishore, two of Bhimsen's sons

Ram Devi
Ram Swaroop

42. Recognition of Drona, Bhism Pitamah's son (Rajoo)

Ram Devi
Ram Swaroop

The murderers, in covering their crime by concealing the bodies of Bhimsen and Bhism Pitamah in a well, also prevented me from relating the birthmarks on Ramoo and Rajoo to recorded wounds on the bodies of Bhimsen and Bhism Pitamah; I have already explained that the bodies of the murdered twins had decomposed badly by the time the police found them and even further by the time autopsies were carried out. It is known, however, that the bodies were tied with ropes when they were extracted from the well. And secondhand evidence indicates that the captured twins had been held down with lathis while they were choked to death. The birthmarks on the trunks of Ramoo and Rajoo could therefore have some correspondence either with wounds made by the lathis (if these were used) or by the ropes used to tie the twins before their bodies were disposed of.

The Behavior of Ramoo and Rajoo Related to the Previous Lives

Circumstances and Manner of the Twins' Speaking about the Previous Lives. Ramoo and Rajoo seemed particularly stimulated to talk about the previous lives when visitors from Uncha Larpur came to Sham Nagara. Otherwise they did not talk much about the previous lives under a restraint imposed on them by their family which I shall describe later.

On one occasion a chamar (low caste person) from Uncha Larpur came to Sham Nagara and taunted Ramoo and Rajoo with their defeat (on an unidentified occasion of some dispute or brawl) in the previous life. This incensed the twins, and Gaya Prasad said that they rushed toward the insulter saying: "God has made us small, but we can still devour you." [8] Ram Swaroop recounted another episode, possibly part of the incident just mentioned; he was a secondhand informant for it, but I think it deserves mention as illustrating some tendency for Ramoo and Rajoo to express the bravado for which Bhimsen and Bhism Pitamah were celebrated. A villager from Uncha Larpur came to Sham Nagara, and Ramoo ran to him saying: "Why have you come here?" The visitor replied with a remark that Ramoo considered insulting, whereupon he seized a brick that he was about to let fly, but someone caught him before he did so.

Ramoo and Rajoo adopted paternal attitudes toward the sons of Bhimsen and Bhism Pitamah. When told by them that the house in which Bhimsen and Bhism Pitamah had lived had decayed, Ramoo and Rajoo

---

[8] The word *devour* translates literally what the twins said to their antagonist. It indicates an intention to destroy utterly the person threatened. Western readers should be reminded of the giant in "Jack and the Beanstalk," who expressed similar warnings of what he planned for his victims.

instructed them to rebuild it with proper care. The twins also gave advice (evidently directed at Bhimsen's sons) that they should occasionally pay a visit to Atrauli, the native village of Bhimsen's wife. The sons of Bhimsen and Bhism Pitamah had visited Sham Nagara several times and had come once between my two visits, in 1972 and 1973. Ramoo and Rajoo addressed them familiarly as "sons."

Ramoo and Rajoo have not asked to be called by the names of Bhimsen and Bhism Pitamah.

Gaya Prasad said that when the twins met Ram Devi, the mother of Bhimsen and Bhism Pitamah, she wept and so did they. Radhey Shyam also reported that when the twins recognized him (item 37, Table 16) he wept and so did they.

Other Behavior of Ramoo and Rajoo Related to the Previous Lives. Kapuri Devi said that she heard Ramoo and Rajoo talking to each other and saying that their wives (in the previous lives) used to touch their feet when they met them.[9]

The twins showed a strong desire to go to Uncha Larpur even before they had said anything about the previous life. When they were still only about three years old, they ran off from Sham Nagara in the direction of the railway station at Jasoda. (This would be on the way to Uncha Larpur.) Asked what they were doing, they said they were going to their home. At that time they had not yet spoken any names related to the previous lives. Later they lost the desire to go to Uncha Larpur and, in fact, have never visited it.

Gaya Prasad said that he considered them generally more advanced— physically, intellectually, and socially—than other children of their age.

Although twins often show much affection for each other, I think that Ramoo and Rajoo exceeded the average in this respect. Gaya Prasad said that they were constantly together. With occasional exceptions, one would not eat unless the other was present to eat also. If one happened to go off somewhere by himself, the other was apt to call him to come back. The twins' father did not think they were more attached to each other than to the other two sons of the family, but his older brother, Gaya Prasad, disagreed and expressed his conviction that Ramoo and Rajoo *did* have a special fondness for each other.

Few differences between the twins were remarked by Gaya Prasad, who seemed to be the person who knew them best and who also was their most careful observer. Ramoo, he said, was more mischievous, and he described

---

[9] In India, unusual respect is shown to another person by touching that person's foot. Children may do this to parents, younger brothers to older ones, and wives to husbands. The gesture will be made on parting and meeting.

Rajoo as "simple." Ramoo was more talkative than Rajoo. This was true during the visit I paid to Sham Nagara when we talked most with the twins. However, from a statement Gaya Prasad made to Dr. Mehrotra in 1972, it would appear that Rajoo had talked more to him (Gaya Prasad) than had Ramoo, at least in their initial narration of what they remembered about the previous lives. Ram Swaroop, the twins' father, thought that Ramoo had more memories of the previous life than Rajoo. He also considered Ramoo more intelligent than Rajoo.

The Attitude of the Twins' Family toward Their Memories
of the Previous Lives

A superstition in northern India (and in some other areas of South Asia, but not in Sri Lanka) holds that grave misfortune comes to children who remember previous lives; some victims of this mistaken belief think that such children are likely to die young. Parents, convinced that they should not allow their children to remember previous lives, have resorted to a wide variety of measures ranging from deriding or reproving the child concerned to physically beating him. The family of Ramoo and Rajoo thought physical chastisement appropriate to their case and sometimes beat them when they were heard talking about the previous lives they claimed to remember. When the family found that beating the twins did not make them forget, they adjusted to the lesser demand that the children not talk about the previous lives outside the family and told them to deny to strangers that they remembered anything about it. Gaya Prasad granted the twins an exemption when we visited, and they talked with us, although probably not as freely as they would have done without the previous beatings and scoldings.

Gaya Prasad said that, additional to the superstition mentioned above, the twins' family feared that harm might come to them from the murderers of Bhimsen and Bhism Pitamah. The persons accused of the murders of the first twins had been acquitted for lack of firsthand testimony; the claim of Ramoo and Rajoo to remedy that deficiency could not have been welcome to such persons as Jagannath and Raja Ram of Kurri. In principle, they could not be put in legal jeopardy again and the evidence of Ramoo and Rajoo could not be admitted in court; but guilty men would not find these restrictions completely reassuring.[10] An eerie blend of anxiety

---

[10] For other examples of fear that murderers of a previous personality might assault a subject remembering the details and names of persons involved in the murder of the previous personality, see the cases of Ravi Shankar (I. Stevenson. 1974. *Twenty cases*) and Bongkuch Promsin (in the third volume of this series).

and curiosity must have brought the murderers of Bhimsen and Bhism Pitamah over to Sham Nagara for a confrontation with Ramoo and Rajoo, and I wish I had more information about this meeting. It cannot have been a joyous occasion for anyone present. The twins' father, Ram Swaroop, denied that he feared reprisals from the murderers of Bhimsen and Bhism Pitamah. His attitude of felt or affected indifference to the case must, however, have added another influence that dampened the inclination of the twins to talk about the previous lives.

Gaya Prasad mentioned another motive for suppressing the memories of Ramoo and Rajoo. Their family found distasteful the twins' talk about the previous family and some preference they had shown for it over their own family.

Comments on the Evidence of Paranormal Processes in the Case

Although the villages concerned in this case are not far apart, I did not find that their inhabitants had any direct connections with each other nor any need or likelihood of meeting except through the common use of the same market town, Gursahaiganj. It lies between the two villages, so that persons from each village can go there without passing through the other village. I am myself quite satisfied that the two families had no personal acquaintance prior to the development of the case; and, although occasional travelers from one village would pass through the other, I feel sure that such persons could not have acted as normal sources of information for Ramoo and Rajoo about the lives of Bhimsen and Bhism Pitamah without their communication of the information being known to the twins' family.

The family of Ramoo and Rajoo took no initiative in verifying the twins' statements. To this day they have not taken them to Uncha Larpur or allowed them to go there with other persons. Verifications only occurred when villagers of Uncha Larpur heard about the case and came to see the twins at Sham Nagara. But we have even stronger evidence that the twins' family sought no publicity for the case. On their own admission we know that they made substantial efforts to suppress it, and these included beating the twins in order to make them forget the previous lives or at least talk about their memories only within the confines of the family. If we accept Gaya Prasad's statement about their fear of the murderers of Kurri, which I think quite plausible, we have an additional strong reason for accepting the case as authentic, since no family could conceivably have invented or exaggerated a case that would likely incite visits from wrathful criminals.

The Later Development of Ramoo and Rajoo

In March 1973 Ramoo and Rajoo were nearly nine years old and were studying in the second class of primary school. They were, therefore, somewhat behind the level of their peers in scholastic advancement.

At that time, Ram Swaroop asserted confidently that Ramoo and Rajoo had completely stopped talking about the previous lives; but Gaya Prasad, who was in a much better position to know, said they were still talking about the previous lives to each other.

Under the temporary immunity from punishment granted them by Gaya Prasad, the twins tried to recall for us in 1972 what they still remembered of the previous lives. Ramoo was the more talkative of the two. It was clear that they remembered some details of the previous lives, for example, the name of Uncha Larpur as the village where they said they had lived. And they were quite clear as to the names of the twins whose lives they were remembering. But they had forgotten other details or mixed them up. Ramoo gave Ram Kishore as the name of a previous brother, when in fact Ram Kishore was a son of Bhimsen (whose life Ramoo was remembering.) In giving an account of the way in which Bhimsen and Bhism Pitamah had been murdered, Ramoo said they had been stabbed. This is almost certainly incorrect. The decomposition of the bodies of Bhimsen and Bhism Pitamah prevented, as I have said, an adequate determination of just how they were murdered; but nothing and no one suggested that they had been stabbed.

Glossary

Words of Asian languages in this glossary are romanized without diacriticals and are listed with an initial capital letter even when they would not be capitalized in the original language and also when, as in many instances, the English equivalents would not be capitalized.

AHIMSA.   Nonviolence.

AKHARA.   A small area set aside for wrestling and/or gymnastic practice.

ALMIRAH.   A large closet or cupboard used for keeping clothes, books, or almost anything. Some are movable like Western wardrobes, and some are built into walls.

ANATTA.   *Buddhism:* "No soul." Used in the concept that human personality contains nothing permanent, but only a stream of constantly changing states or processes. There is no enduring soul that survives physical death.

ANDI.   A game played with castor seeds and somewhat resembling marbles as played by Western children.

ATMAN.   The transcendent principle in man. The atman endures from one terrestrial life to another in successive incarnations. The atman, in contrast to the jiva (which see), does not change. *Cf.* ANATTA.

AVATAR.   An incarnation or descent of God in a human (physical) body.

AYURVEDIC MEDICINE.   Hindu traditional system of medicine practiced in India. Practitioners are called vaidyas.

BABU.   An honorific. It appears to have a lengthy history. It seems to have been first applied by the British to male clerks in government service. Then its use became extended to almost every man in northern India. It is still widely used, especially by servants addressing their male employers. Frequently the honorific suffix *-ji* is added, so that it becomes *Babuji*.

BANIA.   A subcaste of the Vaishya caste; predominantly businessmen.

BAUDI.   A Bengali word for sister-in-law, used in addressing or referring to the wife of an older brother by his younger brothers and sisters. It corresponds to the Hindi word *bhabhi*.

BAZAR.   Also bazaar. Ultimately of Persian origin. A market place.

BETEL.   A leaf of *Piper betle* which Indians chew, often with areca nuts and other seasonings or therapeutic additives.

BHABHI.   Wife of the older brother. Sometimes children of Uttar Pradesh and other parts of northern India address their mothers as Bhabhi.

BHANDIKIYA.   A small cupboard or place for storage.

BHANG.   Indian hemp used as an intoxicant.

BIDI.   A type of cheap leaf-wrapped cigarette or small cigar smoked in India especially among the lower classes. It is made with tobacco leaves and is conical in shape.

BIGHA.   A unit of land measurement. A bigha may vary in size between $\frac{1}{3}$ acre and 1 acre.

BRAHMA.   The all-pervading and creator God. With Shiva and Vishnu, he is a member of the supreme Hindu triad.

BRAHMIN.   The highest of the four basic castes of Hindus. Originally the priests and scholars. Today many still pursue these vocations, but most are otherwise occupied.

BUA.   A paternal aunt; the father's sister.

CHACHA.   The father's younger brother; one type of paternal uncle.

CHACHI.   Wife of the father's younger brother; one type of paternal aunt. *Cf.* TAI.

CHAMAR.   Member of subcaste who are mostly associated with leather manufacturing. In many parts of the country, they were, until recently, considered to be outside the caste system, so-called untouchables.

CHAPATTI.   A pancake-shaped unleavened bread usually made with wheat flour. It is a staple food in northern India.

CHARPOY.   A type of simple cot consisting of four short posts from which is suspended a net of jute cord or canvas strips on which the occupant sleeps.

COLLECTOR.   In India a government official charged with collecting taxes and also with judicial powers over a district. He is the highest administrator of the district.

DADA.   The father's father. The word is, however, widely applied to somewhat older persons having a prominent position in a family or village, and without regard to a specific relationship to that person. It is also sometimes used for an older brother.

DEVA.   A discarnate personality of higher merit living in a nonterrestrial realm. *Cf.* PRETA.

DHARMASHALA.   A place where travelers may lodge for several days with little or no charge; such places exist in all major communities and especially in important places of pilgrimage for Hindus.

DIWALI.   An important festival in Hinduism. It comes in the autumn. It was originally a type of fertility rite, but now special honor is given to

Laxmi (the goddess of wealth). A special feature of the festival is the illumination of houses with candles.

DURGA. Hindu goddess generally equated with Kali, the wife of Shiva. Durga is represented as riding on a tiger or lion.

EKADASI. The eleventh day of a fortnight in the Hindu calendar. A religious fast is observed on this day. These days occur at fortnightly intervals in relationship to the lunar cycle.

EKKA. A horse-drawn cart used for carrying passengers and merchandise.

GADDI. The place where the owner or manager of a business sits, receives his customers, and accepts money for purchases. Originally the word referred to a cushion on which someone sits, but by extension it came to represent particularly the place where a businessman sits in his shop to receive money from customers and to manage his affairs.

GHAT. Platform, usually of concrete and with steps permitting bathers to reach the water of rivers and ponds (often called tanks). Ghats are specially prominent at holy places on the Ganges, such as Benares (Varanasi).

GOONDA. A type of rough, muscular person, sometimes engaged as a bodyguard, but often also used by the employer in terrorism or other criminal activities.

GOTRA. The exogamous portion of an endogamous subcaste; the group with the members of which marriage may take place.

JAT. A large caste of relatively low social level with many members who are farmers in northwestern India.

-JI. Suffixed honorific added to a name, as in Suklaji, to indicate special respect for the person referred to.

JIJA. The older sister's husband. Not to be confused with the other type of brother-in-law, the wife's brother, who is called Sala.

JIJI. Younger sisters call their older sisters Jiji. (Older sisters address their younger sisters by name.) The husband of a Jiji is called Jija.

JILAPI. A tree that grows in India.

JIVA. Personality, or the Self in association with a physical body, gross or subtle. The jiva changes within one life and from one life to another, in contrast to the atman. The idea of the jiva corresponds roughly to the Western concept of personality.

KACHCHA. Adjective meaning crude, poorly built, inferior. With regard to houses it refers to those with walls built of straw and clay or mud. *Cf.* PUKKA.

KACHCHERI. Courthouse of a district.

KAHAR.   One of the lower castes in India. Kahars work in kitchens and otherwise as servants.

KAKIMA.   The wife of the father's younger brother. It is the Bengali equivalent of the Hindi word *chachi*. It may be used in addressing or referring to the wives of cousins who are regarded as "aunts."

KARMA (Sanskrit); KAMMA (Pali).   Literally, action. The word has come to refer more narrowly to actions whose effects are experienced later, often in another incarnation. It should not be used to describe the effects of karma.

KAYASTHA.   A subcaste in India. Its origins and relationships to other castes are obscure and debated. Members have excelled as civil servants and in other executive work.

KHATTRI.   Member of subcaste of Kshatriya caste.

KOTHI.   Often translated by the word *bungalow,* which is also a loan word from Hindi. *Kothi* and *cottage* are probably cognates, but *kothi,* as used in India, generally refers to a more substantial house than is meant when *cottage* is used in English.

KRISHNA.   One of the incarnations or avatars of God. He figures prominently in the Indian epic, *Mahabharata.*

KSHATRIYA.   The second, or warrior, caste of Hindus.

KUMAR.   An honorific given to unmarried boys and young men. Feminine: Kumari.

LADDU.   A type of sweet (candy) made from sugar and milk; popular in northern India.

LATHI.   A long, rather heavy stick, often carried and used by the police and other persons as a weapon.

LAVA.   A preparation of roasted and puffed rice.

LAXMI.   Hindu goddess of fortune and abundance; the wife of Vishnu.

LOHANA.   A subcaste of merchants of the Vaishya caste.

LOTA.   A metal vessel used for holding water, milk, or other liquids.

MAISHA.   A subcaste of the Vaishya caste.

MALISH.   A type of massage.

MAMA.   The mother's brother. His wife is called Mami.

MANTRAM.   A word or phrase having special power, especially to heal or to induce serenity, when uttered.

MARDANA.   The male quarters of a house. The female quarters are called zenana.

MATAJI.   Mother. *Maa* and *Amma* are other Hindi words for mother.

MOHALLA.   A quarter or district of a city, town, or large village.

MOKSH. Release or liberation. Used with regard to the attainment of freedom from the cycle of reincarnation when Nirvana is achieved.

MUNI. A sage or holy man. An honorific commonly given to Jain monks.

MUNSHI. An accountant or skilled clerk, especially one working for a lawyer.

NAUTCH GIRLS. Girls who engage professionally in singing and dancing, often at private homes. Some mix this vocation with an older one.

NIRVANA (Sanskrit); NIBBANA (Pali). The extinction of personality in a permanent fusion with God through the realization of the identity of the personality with God. (This definition accords with the belief of Hindus, but not with that of Buddhists, who do not believe in God as understood in Hinduism.)

NULLAH. A watercourse smaller than a river; a stream.

PAKAURI. Fried balls of graham flour, sometimes with vegetables added.

PAKWAN. A sweet or candy.

PANDA. Person charged with giving assistance to pilgrims who come to bathe in the holy water of the Ganges or some other sacred river. They provide room, board, and guidance to the pilgrims.

PANDIT. Honorific given to Brahmin scholars, but often also to members of the Brahmin caste who are not learned in any way. It may also be used in reference to scholars who are not Brahmins.

PARVAL. An Indian vegetable.

PEON. An office messenger, attendant, or orderly.

PERA. A type of sweet (candy) made with sugar and milk, especially in northern India. Peras may be white, yellow, or red.

PITAJI. Father.

PRASAD. Gift. Especially used in reference to a food given (dedicated) to a god in a ceremonial worship (puja), and then distributed to friends, the poor, or other persons.

PRETA. Entity inhabiting a nonterrestrial realm but capable of interacting with living humans and manifesting to them. Pretas are said to result from strong, unfulfilled cravings, which lead to rebirth after death in this form instead of in a higher realm as a deva.

PUJA. A ceremonial (or ritualistic) religious worship.

PUKKA. Adjective meaning substantial, well built, superior. With regard to houses it refers to those with brick walls. *Cf.* KACHCHA.

PUNARJANMA. Hindi word for reincarnation; literally, rebirth.

RABRI. An Indian sweet (dessert) made from milk and sugar.

RAISAHIB. An honorary title conferred by the British on prominent Indians whom they wished to honor or cultivate. The word is still used in reference to wealthy persons, especially those who live luxurious lives.

RAJAH. A title (usually honorary only) conferred by the British on prominent Indians whom they wished to honor or cultivate. Most rajahs had no political or territorial authority.

RAMA. One of the incarnations or avatars of God. He is the hero of the Indian epic, *Ramayana*, and of the Ramlila pageant based on it.

RAMLILA. A pageant depicting the life and exploits of Rama, with songs, dances, and acting. It is presented in many communities of India each autumn.

REBIRTH. *Buddhism:* The activation of a new physical body by effects or residues of a personality that had previously been associated with another (now deceased) physical body. *Cf.* REINCARNATION.

REINCARNATION. *Hinduism:* The union of a soul with a new physical body after the death of the physical body with which it was previously associated. *Cf.* REBIRTH.

ROHU. A type of freshwater fish popular in India, particularly among Bengalis.

SADHU. A sage or holy man given up entirely to the spiritual life; sadhus frequently are itinerant and live off the generosity of others.

SAHIB. An honorific corresponding approximately to *Sir*.

SAHU. A businessman, especially a private banker.

SALA. The wife's brother.

SALI. Sister-in-law if she is the wife of the wife's brother.

SAMSARA. Literally, a stream of becoming. Applies to the continual cycle of birth, death, and rebirth that, in Hinduism and Buddhism, only the attainment of Nirvana can stop.

SARASWATI. A Hindu goddess, the wife of Brahma. She is the patroness of learning and of the arts and sciences.

SETH. An important and wealthy businessman.

SHIVA. Hindu god associated with destruction, and also with reproduction. With Brahma and Vishnu, he is a member of the supreme Hindu triad.

SLOKA. Scriptural verse.

SRI. An honorific approximately equivalent to *Mr.* Feminine: Srimati.

SUDRA. The fourth caste of Hindus, comprising (originally) artisans, servants, and laborers.

TABLAS. A type of musical instrument consisting of small drums struck with the hand.

TAI. Wife of the father's older brother.

TANK. An English word commonly used in India to refer to a large pond of water.

TAU. A paternal uncle, specifically the father's older brother. His wife is called Tai. The father's younger brother is called Chacha, and his wife Chachi. The word *tau* is also applied loosely to older male friends of the family who are not related.

THAKUR. A member of the Kshatriya caste.

THAKURDWARA. A special room set aside for worship and having a shrine of some god. It is sometimes inside a house, sometimes in a neighboring building. In Bengali the word is *thakurbari*.

TILKAR. An Indian vegetable.

TIRTHANKARA. In Jainism, a perfected, godlike man. Jainism identifies twenty-four tirthankaras, of whom the last, Mahavira (born ca. 599 B.C.), was the effective founder of Jainism as it is known today.

TONGA. A two-wheeled horse-drawn vehicle much used for transport over short distances, especially in and around medium-sized towns.

VAIDYA. A practitioner of Ayurvedic medicine.

VAISHNAVA. A sect of Hindus emphasizing the worship of Vishnu.

VAISHYA. The third caste of Hindus, comprising (originally) businessmen, traders, and clerks.

VAKIL. Lawyer; advocate.

VISHNU. Hindu god of preservation. With Brahma and Shiva, he is a member of the supreme Hindu triad.

ZAMINDAR. Formerly, large landowners and tax-collectors in India.

ZENANA. The female quarters of a house. The male quarters are called mardana.

Index

ACHILLES, E. M., 26, 50

AKOLKAR, V. V., xi

Alaska, incidence of reported reincarnation cases in, 1, 2

Alevis of Turkey, "announcing" dreams and birthmark cases among, 68

American Society for Psychical Research, xii, xiii

Ampan Petcherat, case of, 281, 306n

AMVROSY, STARETZ, 22n

Anatta ("no soul"), concept of in Theravada Buddhism, 58

"Announcing" dreams. *See under* Dreams

ARNTZEN, F., 22, 24, 37, 38, 50

Asia, incidence of reported reincarnation cases in, 1, 2, 3, 28n

ATREYA, B. L., 166

BALLARD, P. B., 37n, 50

BARTLETT, F., 25, 26, 50

BAYER, R., 18

Behavioral traits of subjects in reincarnation cases, 6–9, 11, 44, 97–100, 132–38, 140–41, 167–73, 195–99, 228–35, 260–64, 273–75, 304–6, 330–33, 356–58

fading or persistence of, 173–75, 203, 204–5, 238–40

Bera family (case of Puti Patra), 266–80

BINET, A., 14n, 16, 50

Birthmarks and deformities in reincarnation cases, 4, 6, 67–68, 96, 166–67, 228, 338, 347, 356

Bishen Chand Kapoor, case of, xii, 6, 64, 65, 144n, 176–205, 263, 282n

Bongkuch Promsin, case of, 96n, 228n, 358n

BOSE, S. C., 145, 146, 153n, 178

Brahmanism, 60

Brahmins, customs of, 99n, 168, 330

BREKSTAD, A., 51

Buddhism, 34, 60, 104n, 113n

Burma

"announcing" dreams and birthmark cases in, 67–68

incidence of reported reincarnation cases in, 1

CARSTAIRS, M., 55, 68

CARTY, C. M., 22n, 50

Cases suggestive of reincarnation

change of caste in, 99, 148, 312, 330–31

circular relationship of with belief in reincarnation, 64–65

computer analysis of characteristics of, 3–4

cross-cultural studies of, 3–4

details of recorded prior to verification, 5–6, 144n, 176

imaged memories (cognitive knowledge) vs. behavioral memories (nonverbal behavior) in, 8n

incidence of, 1–2, 3

international census of, 1, 3

medical aspects of, 4

methods used in study of, 8–18

occurrence of birthmarks and deformities in, 4, 6, 67–68, 96, 166–67, 228, 338, 347, 356

patterns of recurring features in, 1, 3–4, 5

ratio of reported cases to their actual incidence, 2–3

sex difference in previous and present personalities, 63, 281

sources of error in data of, 18–44

without an identified previous personality, 7n

Caste, changes of in reincarnation cases, 67, 99, 148, 312, 330–31

CHANDRA, J., xii. *See also* Jagdish Chandra, case of

Characteristics of reincarnation cases

in India, 62–68

in Sri Lanka, 3